States of Emergency

T0355694

Postcolonialism across the Disciplines 11

Postcolonialism across the Disciplines

Series Editors
Graham Huggan, University of Leeds
Andrew Thompson, University of Leeds

Postcolonialism across the Disciplines showcases alternative directions for postcolonial studies. It is in part an attempt to counteract the dominance in colonial and postcolonial studies of one particular discipline – English literary/cultural studies – and to make the case for a combination of disciplinary knowledges as the basis for contemporary postcolonial critique. Edited by leading scholars, the series aims to be a seminal contribution to the field, spanning the traditional range of disciplines represented in postcolonial studies but also those less acknowledged. It will also embrace new critical paradigms and examine the relationship between the transnational/cultural, the global and the postcolonial.

States of Emergency

Colonialism, Literature and Law

Stephen Morton

Liverpool University Press

First published 2013 by
Liverpool University Press
4 Cambridge Street
Liverpool L69 7ZU

This paperback version published 2014

Copyright © 2013 Stephen Morton

British Library Cataloguing-in-Publication data
A British Library CIP record is available

ISBN 978-1-84631-849-8 cased
     978-1-78138-114-4 paperback

Typeset in Amerigo by Koinonia, Manchester
Printed and bound by CPI Group (UK) Ltd, Croydon CR0 4YY

Contents

A Note on Translations

All translations are my own unless indicated in the footnotes.

Acknowledgements

I wish gratefully to acknowledge the Faculty of Humanities at the University of Southampton for granting me a period of research leave in 2011 in which to write this book. I would also like to thank the library staff at the University of Southampton Libraries and the Science 3 reading room at the British Library for their tireless support. I owe a debt of gratitude to Alison Welsby at Liverpool University Press for being a most patient and supportive editor. Thanks must also go to the anonymous readers of the book for their incisive, detailed and constructive critical feedback.

Research seminar and conference audiences have provided helpful critical feedback on early versions of the chapters that form this book. My thanks are due to the University of Oxford Postcolonial Research Seminar, 2005; the University of Leeds Postcolonial Research Seminar, 2007; the University of Newcastle Postcolonial Research Group, 2007; the Curatorial Knowledge Research Seminar, Goldsmiths College, University of London, 2010; the University of Chichester Forum on Literature, Terrorism and 9/11, 2010; the Open University Conference on Reading Conflict, 2010; the Leeds University Conference on Crime across Cultures, 2010; the University Charles de Gaulle at Lille 3 Research Seminars on 'Le Je Postcolonial' in 2010, 2011 and 2012; the Cardiff University Critical Theory Seminar, 2011; the University of Kent AHRC Workshop on Separatism and Settler Cultures, 2011; the University of Oxford Global Journeys Conference, 2011; and the University of Reading and Birkbeck College AHRC Workshops on Terrorist Transgressions, 2011–12.

I have benefitted greatly from critical conversations with a number of good colleagues. Elleke Boehmer, Claire Chambers and Alex Tickell have offered generous and constructive critical feedback at crucial stages during the preparation of this book. Colleagues and students in the English department at the University of Southampton (past and present) have provided a friendly and rigorous critical community in which to work. I am particularly grateful to Devorah Baum, Emma Clery, Stephen Bygrave, David Glover, Clare Hanson, Stephanie Jones, Claire Jowitt, Nicky Marsh, Gail McDonald, Peter Middleton, Prem Poddar, Ranka Primorac, Sujala Singh and Barry Sloan.

I would also like to thank the following friends and colleagues for conversations and helpful critical observations at different stages of the research and writing of this book: Nazneen Ahmed, Rehana Ahmed, Andreas Behnke, Simone Bignall, Rachael Corkill, Stef Craps, Jeff Derksen, Robert Duggan, Sam Durrant, Robert Eaglestone, Esther Gabara, Janna Graham, Alex Houen, Alia Hasan Khan, David Johnson, David Landy, Pedro Lasch, Gabriel Koureas, Sue Malvern, Jean-Paul Martinon, Salhia Ben Messahel, Radhika Mohanram, Peter Morey, Stuart Murray, Pathik Pathak, Gabriel Piterberg, James Procter, Mubbashir Rizvi, Irit Rogoff, Caroline Rooney, Naomi Salaman, Zuky Serper, Robert Spencer, Neelam Srivastava, Marcelo Svirsky, Veronica Thompson, Margaret Ward, Chris Weedon, Amina Yaqin and Pascal Zinck.

Thanks also to David and Mairi Morton for kind words of encouragement, and to Stuart Morton for the pleasant distractions of cycle touring. Above all, I am indebted to Susan Kelly for her good humour, close reading and critical insight. This book is for her.

A version of Chapter 2 has appeared in Elleke Boehmer and Stephen Morton (eds), *Terror and the Postcolonial* (Oxford: Wiley-Blackwell), pp. 202–25. Part of Chapter 3 has appeared in 'States of Emergency and the Apartheid Legal Order in South African Fiction', *Journal of Postcolonial Writing*, 46/5 (2010), pp. 491–503.

Royalties from the sale of this book will be paid to Amnesty International UK.

Introduction

Countries are considered to be in a 'state of emergency' when executive power is used to suspend the normal rule of law, and power is transferred to the police or military. Emergency legislation is often associated with totalitarian governments or so-called terrorist states, but liberal democracies have also made use of emergency law in times of social and political crisis. A consideration of the etymology of states of emergency can help to clarify the difference between lawful violence, or the violence that is regarded as the exclusive right of governments and states, and lawless violence, or the violence that is deemed illegitimate by governments and states, and often branded as 'terrorism' or insurgency. The earliest usage of the word 'terrorist' in modern English was attributed to the violent actions of the French revolutionary state in the 1790s, almost fifty years before the term was used to denote an act of terror carried out by an individual (*OED*). Yet many subsequent definitions of terrorism have tended to overlook state forms of terrorism – thereby implying that the state 'has a monopoly on the legitimate use of violence'[1] and the power to define what terrorism means. In one of the more persuasive accounts of the definitional problems associated with the term, Bruce Hoffman has argued that terrorism

> is a word with intrinsically negative connotations that is generally applied to one's enemies and opponents, or to those with whom one disagrees and would otherwise prefer to ignore [...] the decision to call someone or label some organization 'terrorist' becomes almost unavoidably subjective, depending largely on whether one sympathizes with or opposes the person/group/cause concerned.[2]

---

1 Charles Townshend, *Terrorism: A Very Short Introduction* (Oxford: Oxford University Press, 2002), p. 5.
2 Bruce Hoffman, *Inside Terrorism* (New York: Columbia University Press, 2006), p. 23.

Hoffman's subjectivist definition of terrorism may recall the often quoted but unattributed relativist position expressed in the phrase 'one person's terrorist is another person's freedom fighter'. Yet what such definitions overlook is the power and authority of state institutions and actors to define what or who terrorism is. For this reason, I use the term 'terrorism' in this book to denote an effect of a dominant discourse in which certain practices of political violence are framed as 'terrorism' by a particular state or government.

A consideration of the state of emergency as a juridical and political category may therefore help to illuminate the ways in which the discourse of terrorism serves to provide a state or government with a means of justifying its use of violence and repression. Yet this assumes that the meaning of a state of emergency is self-evident. This is far from the case; for a state of emergency – in a similar way to terrorism – is a profoundly elusive and ambivalent concept. The nineteenth-century legal scholar Albert Venn Dicey defined the lawful violence that emergency powers afforded to the English state by contrasting such powers with martial law. In Dicey's account, martial law is 'unknown to the law of England' – a fact which, he claims, is 'an unmistakable proof of the permanent supremacy of the law under our constitution'.[3] And yet, English law also empowers the police and the military to use necessary force to 'put down breaches of the peace, such as riots and other disturbances', provided that such force is not excessive.[4] What excessive force means, and who gets to define the distinction between the reasonable and excessive use of force remain open questions that are shaped by the specific context in which they are addressed.

Dicey's ambivalence about emergency powers has important implications for understanding the relationship between law, state violence and colonial sovereignty, as we will see.[5] Colonial governments have clearly employed emergency legislation to control the territories and populations they govern, especially during periods of anti-colonial resistance and struggle, thereby consolidating the power of the colonial state. This is not to suggest, however, that emergency legislation was deployed in exactly the same way in every colonial or postcolonial situation. The precise historical circumstances and political traditions that led to the passing of the Anarchical and Revolutionary Crimes Act in British India in 1919 are clearly very different from the French colonial government's use of emergency legislation during the Algerian war in 1955, or the Israeli government's use of emergency powers inherited from the British mandatory government to administer the Palestinian population from 1948 to the present day. What connects these multiple histories, colonial spaces and techniques of power, as I go on to explain, is an imperative to maintain sovereignty. In broad terms, the contemporary usage of colonialism denotes 'the policy or practice

3 A.V. Dicey, *Introduction to the Study of the Law of the Constitution* (London: Macmillan, 1897), p. 270.
4 Dicey, *Introduction*, p. 272.
5 For a more detailed assessment of Dicey's position, see Johan Geertsema, 'Exceptions, Bare Life, and Colonialism', in Victor V. Ramraj (ed.), *Emergencies and the Limits of Legality* (Cambridge: Cambridge University Press, 2008), p. 339.

of acquiring full or partial political control over another country, occupying it with settlers, and exploiting it economically' (*OED*). Of course, the practice of territorial colonialism in Ireland, India, Kenya, South Africa, Algeria and Palestine was far from a coherent or unified policy. As Stephen Howe puts it, 'colonial rule in general, and the British Empire in particular, was a patchwork quilt, an enormously varied set of forms of rule and domination, largely the product of improvisation and full of contradictions and strains, rather than a deliberately constructed global system'.[6] If, as Robert J.C. Young emphasises, 'colonialism involved an extraordinary range of different forms and practices carried out with respect to radically different cultures, over many different centuries',[7] one of the critical tasks of postcolonial studies is to assess how such multifarious practices of colonial rule and governance, as well as particular forms of resistance to these practices of governmentality, can shed light on specific historical and geopolitical formations of colonial power. By tracing the use of emergency law and the mobilisation of a discourse of counter-insurgency during periods of anti-colonial resistance across a range of different colonial contexts, this book considers what the law-preserving violence of colonial governmentality can tell us about the founding violence, or law-making violence, of colonial sovereignty.[8]

By focusing on states of emergency in colonial spaces, I am not suggesting that the use of emergency law is unique to the political space of the European colony. Indeed, it may seem that the use of emergency law is an inherent practice of all modern states, whether liberal or totalitarian, colonial or postcolonial. But contemporary states of emergency owe much to colonial forms of sovereignty, not only because many colonial states permitted practices such as detention without trial, torture, execution and other forms of violent state repression, but also because the practice of colonial governmentality complicated the distinction between norm and exception that underpins the rhetoric of emergency. If, as Achille Mbembe has suggested, the European colony can in some cases be understood as 'the location par excellence where the controls and guarantees of judicial order can be suspended – the zone where the violence of the state of exception is deemed to operate in the service of "civilization"',[9] it is also true that the law has provided particular colonial states with an important technique of governmentality. The apartheid state in South Africa was based on a legal order that included the Group Areas Act, the Pass Laws and the Suppression of Communism Act, and the British colonial government in Kenya used emergency laws to discipline and punish the Kikuyu population during the struggle for land and freedom in the 1950s. The normalisation of lawful state

---

6 Stephen Howe, *Ireland and Empire: Colonial Legacies in Irish History and Culture* (Oxford: Oxford University Press, 2000), p. 110.
7 Robert J.C. Young, *Postcolonialism: An Historical Introduction* (Oxford: Blackwell, 2001), p. 17.
8 The distinction between law-making violence and law-preserving violence comes from Walter Benjamin, 'Critique of Violence', in Marcus Bullock and Michael W. Jennings (eds), *Selected Writings, Volume 1: 1913–1926* (Cambridge, MA: Harvard University Press, 1996), pp. 236–52.
9 Achille Mbembe, 'Necropolitics', *Public Culture*, 15/1 (2003), p. 23.

violence as a technique of government in colonial spaces such as these can tell us much about the use of emergency powers in the colonial present. It is for this reason that contemporary states of emergency require that we 'turn back to the colonial archive of violence and repression, to records and narratives of the colonial formations of sovereignty, policing, and surveillance', which, in the felicitous words of Elleke Boehmer, 'find such prominent afterlives in forma-tions of counter-terrorism today'.[10]

The Italian philosopher Giorgio Agamben has argued that 'the state of excep-tion [*Ausnahmezustand*] tends increasingly to appear as the dominant paradigm of government in contemporary politics'.[11] For Agamben, the state of exception is not reducible to an official declaration by a state that temporarily suspends existing rights, rules and regulations, and it also involves multiple actors, insti-tutions and sites of power. Agamben's argument – that there are structural similarities between the use of emergency measures in post-revolutionary France, Britain during the First World War and Nazi Germany during the 1930s – has far reaching implications for understanding the claims of liberal democratic societies to protect the rights and freedoms of the human subject, and raises provocative questions about the differences between liberal democratic states, totalitarian governments and colonial regimes. In Agamben's account, the state of exception denotes the law which suspends the law. More precisely, Agamben claims that the juridical order withdraws from the state of excep-tion and abandons it. For Agamben, the 'exception does not subtract itself from the rule; rather, the rule, suspending itself, gives rise to the exception, and maintaining itself in relation to the exception, first constitutes itself as a rule'.[12] It is because the law first constitutes the exception even as the law is subsequently excluded from the regime of the state of exception that Agamben expresses the law's relationship to the exception in terms of the crossed-out term in the phrase 'force of ~~law~~'.[13] By placing the word 'law' under erasure, Agamben emphasises how the force of the law to suspend the normal rule of law produces and maintains the state of exception from a position of exteriority to the state of exception as soon as the law is suspended. Yet at the same time, Agamben emphasises that the state of exception is also 'interior' to the law in so far as the force of law is required to suspend the rule of law in a time of emergency.

Agamben's philosophical formulation of the state of exception bears an inter-esting conceptual resemblance to the colonial rule of law. As Johan Geertsema has argued, the juridically empty space of the state of exception in Agamben's thought corresponds in suggestive ways with the lawless state of nature that

10 Elleke Boehmer and Stephen Morton, 'Introduction', in Elleke Boehmer and Stephen Morton (eds), *Terror and the Postcolonial* (Oxford: Blackwell, 2009), p. 7.
11 Giorgio Agamben, *State of Exception*, trans. Kevin Attell (Chicago, IL and London: University of Chicago Press, 2005), p. 2.
12 Giorgio Agamben, *Homo Sacer: Sovereign Power and Bare Life*, trans. Daniel Heller-Roazen (Stanford, CA: Stanford University Press, 1998), p. 18.
13 Agamben, *State of Exception*, p. 52.

existed in the European colonies, particularly during periods of conquest.[14] Yet the conceptual power of Agamben's thought is not matched by a detailed historical analysis of the technologies of colonial power that underpin the global state of exception, or of the diverse forms of agency and resistance to colonial sovereignty. This is perhaps unsurprising when one considers that Agamben approaches questions about sovereign power, law and violence in European classical and medieval texts as a philosopher rather than a historian. As many commentators have noted, Agamben's reflections on sovereignty and the state of exception are chiefly informed by Martin Heidegger's 'history of being' and Walter Benjamin's materialist conception of history.[15] Such an approach may shed light on the violent foundations of the modern state, but it is not without problems. For some critics, Agamben's account of the state of exception runs the risk of making loose conceptual analogies between different historical formations of sovereignty;[16] as a consequence, Agamben may seem to overlook the precise connections between particular states of exception and the proliferation of new laws, regulations and agents that are involved in contemporary states of emergency – such as those associated with the 'war on terror'.[17] It might also be argued that Agamben's preoccupation with the philosophical paradox of an emergency law that suspends the rule of law elides the concatenation of civil, military and police powers specific to European colonial spaces. The wide powers that were granted to the police and to the military in European colonial spaces such as Kenya and Algeria certainly challenged the liberal rhetoric of the civilising mission, but these powers were buttressed by the founding violence of European colonial sovereignty that denied the civil and political rights to the colonised that European nation states nominally guaranteed for its own citizens as well as for European colonial settlers.[18] Agamben's analysis of the state of exception may thus seem to overlook the historical experience of violent forms of colonial sovereignty and emergency from the standpoint of the colonised, and the specific forms of agency and resistance to colonial states of exception. To account for this historical experience, Agamben's work needs to be supplemented with an account of what Walter Benjamin called the tradition of the oppressed – a term that I return to later in this chapter. Benjamin's reflections on the tradition of the oppressed also resonate importantly with

---

14 Geertsema, 'Exceptions, Bare Life, and Colonialism', p. 353.
15 See Leland de la Durantaye, *Giorgio Agamben: A Critical Introduction* (Stanford, CA: Stanford University Press, 2009); and Ernesto Laclau, 'Bare Life or Social Indeterminacy?', in Matthew Calarco and Steven DeCaroli (eds), *Giorgio Agamben: Sovereignty and Life* (Stanford, CA: Stanford University Press, 2007), pp. 11–22.
16 See Malcolm Bull 'States don't really mind their citizens dying (provided they don't all do it at once): they just don't like anyone else to kill them', *London Review of Books*, 26/24 (16 December 2004), 3–6; and Mark Neocleous, *Critique of Security* (Edinburgh: Edinburgh University Press, 2008).
17 See Nasser Hussain, 'Beyond Norm and Exception: Guantánamo', *Critical Inquiry*, 33/4 (2007), pp. 734–47.
18 See Achille Mbembe, *On the Postcolony* (Berkeley, CA: University of California Press, 2001), pp. 24–65.

the work of Frantz Fanon – a thinker who clearly understood the relationship between sovereign violence and colonial power, even though he did not use these precise terms to describe particular formations of European colonial rule. By reading Agamben's analysis of the state of exception with and against Fanon's reflections on the lived experience of colonial violence and the historically situated forms of resistance to that violence, this book attempts to track the complex relationship between law, violence and colonial sovereignty, and anti-colonial struggle in a range of literary and cultural narratives.

The use of emergency powers and lawful state violence to maintain colonial sovereignty is also significant in terms of how it shaped and defined the political values of European liberalism, for the use of repressive measures in the European colony mirrored political debates about the use of similar measures in western liberal societies.[19] The British colonial governor of Jamaica Edward Eyre's use of punitive force in response to the Morant Bay uprising in 1862, for example, prompted questions about the legal meaning of martial law and its place in the English constitution. More specifically, in the case of Williams against Eyre in 1868 – a case which facilitated civil litigation against Eyre for assault, battery and false imprisonment – the Queen's bench ruled in favour of the colonial governor on the grounds that a 'colonial legislature had exercised its plenary power to pass a statute concerning rights and obligations arising from within the jurisdiction of the colony'.[20] This ruling was significant not only because it 'exposed an unavoidable contradiction between the supremacy of the imperial Parliament and efficient colonial government', but also because it further exacerbated what the legal historian R.W. Kostal has called the 'contingent and fragmented' concept of British imperial citizenship.[21]

While a detailed consideration of the state of emergency in nineteenth-century Jamaica is beyond the scope this book, I mention it here because it helps to elucidate the legal and political implications of colonial states of emergency. Legal historians such as Lauren Benton have emphasised how some colonised groups attempted to negotiate with the colonial rule of law in order to contest and challenge the exclusionary terms of colonial sovereignty.[22] Such scholarship may certainly work to correct 'an overly simplistic view of the colonial world as a lawless zone of indistinction or space of exception',[23] but this is not to say that the colonial law afforded colonised subjects the same kinds of rights, freedoms and protections afforded to the coloniser. The 'contingent and fragmented' concept of imperial citizenship in colonial Jamaica, for example, provides an important index to the limitations of the judicial order to

19 See Uday Mehta, *Liberalism and Empire: A Study in Nineteenth-Century British Liberal Thought* (Chicago, IL: University of Chicago Press, 1999).
20 R.W. Kostal, *A Jurisprudence of Power: Victorian Empire and the Rule of Law* (Oxford: Oxford University Press, 2006), p. 442.
21 Kostal, *A Jurisprudence of Power*, p. 443.
22 Lauren Benton, *Law and Colonial Cultures: Legal Regimes in World History, 1400–1900* (Cambridge: Cambridge University Press, 2002).
23 Geertsema, 'Exceptions, Bare Life, and Colonialism', p. 355.

protect the rights of colonised subjects from the violence of European colonial sovereignty. Hannah Arendt clearly articulated this contradiction between the rights afforded by citizenship and the violence of colonial sovereignty in her argument that colonial governance was maintained in and through a series of bureaucratic decrees that were based on the whim of colonial bureaucrats rather than the rule of law.[24] In Arendt's account, the very idea of the human that underpins the declaration of human rights is 'philosophically invalid and politically impotent'[25] precisely because the declaration of human rights is 'deeply entangled' in a history of racism and imperialism.[26] In the context of the European colony, appeals to human rights where the legal category of the human was itself circumscribed by the exclusionary logic of a racist discourse can thus seem rather hollow. While Arendt suggested that the inadequacy of human rights discourse to protect the rights of the human subject was crystal-lised in the Nazi death camps, her argument that the origins of totalitarianism in Europe can be traced back to the political formations of European colonial sovereignty also helps to elucidate the persistence of human rights violations and genocide in the postcolony.[27]

The meaning and use of colonial sovereignty and the powers it seems to grant to European colonial governments has not only been the source of much debate among political theorists, historians and legal theorists, it has also preoccupied writers and filmmakers from Edmund Candler, W.B. Yeats and F.E. Penny to Gillo Pontecorvo, J.M. Coetzee, Assia Djebar, Elias Khoury and Mohsin Hamid. This book investigates the multiple ways in which states of emergency and colonial sovereignty have been mediated in literary and cultural texts, and examines the contribution that literary and cultural texts have made to our understanding of the legal and political significance of states of emergency from the late nineteenth century to the present. More specifically, the book considers how particular historical formations of violent colonial sovereignty and states of emergency help to elucidate contemporary formations of colonial sovereignty, exemplified by the wars in Iraq and Afghanistan. This attempt to track the complex and overlapping histories, underpinning what Derek Gregory has called the colonial present,[28] necessarily involves a consideration of colonial states of emergency from the standpoint of the colonised. By adopting such an approach, this book also seeks to question the claim in western critical thought that states of emergency constitute an aporia in the legal foundations of the state. How, in other words, does the distinction between norm and exception that under-pins Carl Schmitt's theory of sovereignty help to clarify the violence of colonial

24 Hannah Arendt, *The Origins of Totalitarianism* (New York: Meridian Books, 1958), pp. 185–221.
25 Peg Birmingham, *Hannah Arendt and Human Rights* (Bloomington and Indianapolis: Indiana University Press, 2006), p. 5.
26 Birmingham, *Hannah Arendt and Human Rights*, p. 5.
27 Mahmood Mamdani, *When Victims Become Killers: Colonialism, Nativism, and the Genocide in Rwanda* (Princeton: Princeton University Press, 2002), p. 34.
28 See Derek Gregory, *The Colonial Present* (Oxford: Blackwell, 2004).

sovereignty? How might a consideration of colonial states of emergency allow us to understand the historical and political processes by which the state of emergency came to be a global political condition, as Agamben has suggested?[29] What insights into the experience of colonial sovereignty and the forms of political resistance to it does Agamben's analysis of the founding aporia of the state of exception provide? And in what ways might the historical experience of those who are forced to live under conditions of colonial violence question and complicate universalising knowledge claims about democracy and the rule of law in western political thought?

As a preliminary response to some of these questions, it is worth considering what is meant by an aporia and how this applies to states of emergency in more detail. In conventional usage, the term aporia denotes a double bind that cannot be resolved according to the formal rules or logic of a given philosophical system.[30] In these terms, a state of emergency can be understood as an exemplary case of an aporia because it is a law that suspends the law, and thus cannot be understood in purely legal terms. What Jacques Derrida has called autoimmunity, or the mechanism by which an organism 'works to destroy its own protection, [and] to immunize itself against its "own" immunity', helps to clarify the aporetic basis of a state of emergency.[31] The concept of autoimmunity is perhaps most clearly articulated in Derrida's criticism of Israel's policies in the Occupied Palestinian Territories. As Derrida explained in a discussion with Hélène Cixous and Jacqueline Rose at the London Jewish Book Week in 2004, his criticism of the Israeli government's policies in the Occupied Palestinian Territories is grounded in the claim that the permanent state of emergency in the Palestinian territories is 'unjust, first of all, unfair [to] the Palestinians, and then it is suicidal'. For Derrida, Israel's policy towards Palestine and the Palestinians exemplifies the foundational violence of all '"auto-immunity", self-immunity, when a body destroys its own protections'.[32] In this example, Israel's permanent state of emergency in the Occupied Palestinian Territories highlights the aporetic ground of political sovereignty. The very measures that the State of Israel has invoked since 1948 to defend its security as a sovereign state also threaten to bring about its downfall. As Michael Naas explains in a commentary on the concept of autoimmunity in Derrida's thought,

> As soon as sovereignty tries to extend its empire in space, to maintain itself over time, to protect itself by justifying and providing reasons for itself, it opens itself up to law and language, to the counter-sovereignty of the other,

29 See Agamben, *State of Exception*, pp. 1–31.

30 See Jacques Derrida, *Aporias*, trans. Thomas Dutoit (Stanford, CA: Stanford University Press, 1993).

31 Jacques Derrida and Jürgen Habermas, *Philosophy in a Time of Terror: Dialogues with Jürgen Habermas and Jacques Derrida* (Chicago, IL and London: University of Chicago Press, 2003), p. 150.

32 Jacques Derrida and Hélène Cixous, 'The Language of Others', Jewish Book Week, 1 March 2004. Available at <http://jewishbookweek.com/archive/010304e/transcripts2.php>. Accessed 24 March, 2009.

and so begins to undo itself, to compromise or autoimmunise itself. That is the aporetic – indeed the autoimmune – essence of sovereignty.[33]

Such an argument may be compelling in its suggestion that the aporia of emergency threatens the very legal and political foundations of the state. But this is not to say that the reading of aporias in different colonial narratives of emergency is equivalent to the subversion of colonial sovereignty that anti-colonial resistance struggles seemed to promise. Indeed, from the standpoint of the colonised, the legal aporia of emergency is not an aporia at all, but a colonial fiction that barely conceals the violence of colonial sovereignty. For this reason, it is important to distinguish between the aporetic ground of colonial sovereignty, which presents the recourse to emergency powers as an exception to the rule of law, and the sanctioned violence of the European colony, 'where the controls and guarantees of judicial order can be suspended' and 'the violence of the state of exception is deemed to operate in the service of "civilization"'.[34] For this distinction is crucial to understanding the constitutive role of violence in the political formation of the colony, and its postcolonial legacies, as we will see.

To further elucidate the distinction between the aporetic ground of colonial sovereignty and the sanctioned violence of the European colony, this book traces through a series of case studies of literary and legal texts a counter history of colonial states of emergency. Building on a methodology developed by the South Asian subaltern studies historians, which examines the inscriptions of anti-colonial insurgency in the texts and archives of colonialism,[35] the following chapters consider how the rhetoric of emergency helps to illuminate different techniques of colonial sovereignty and the forms of resistance to them. Each chapter focuses on a particular body of texts, laws and archival documents, including debates about the use of emergency legislation, indefinite detention without trial, torture and summary execution in European colonial societies as well as the narrative structures, metaphors and imagery of terror, violence and barbarism in literary and cultural texts from the high period of European colonialism in the early twentieth century to the contemporary global conjuncture that Gregory has aptly named the colonial present. In so doing, this book claims that the state of emergency operated as a travelling concept that was part of a global imperial network of counter-insurgency, negotiated between the metropolitan legal institutions of particular European empires and their colonial governments, military and police forces, and re-iterated in different colonial spaces. This mobile concept, I suggest, worked primarily to assert colonial sovereignty through force and to pre-empt as well as to counter

33 Michael Naas, '"One Nation ... Indivisible": Jacques Derrida on the Autoimmunity of Democracy and the Sovereignty of God', *Research in Phenomenology*, 36/1 (2006), p. 21.
34 Mbembe, 'Necropolitics', p. 23.
35 See Ranajit Guha, *Elementary Aspects of Peasant Insurgency in Colonial India* (Delhi: Oxford University Press, 1983), pp. 1–17; and Gayatri Chakravorty Spivak, 'Deconstructing Historiography', in Ranajit Guha (ed.), *Subaltern Studies IV: Writings on South Asian History and Society* (Delhi: Oxford University Press, 1987), pp. 330–63.

opposition to colonial rule. In framing the 'recourse' to emergency measures as an exception, the rhetoric of colonial governance suggested that the colonial state of emergency was contingent upon the specific historical and political circumstances of anti-colonial resistance and struggle in a given colonial situation. By examining the narrative structures, metaphors and imagery of terror, anti-colonial resistance, violence and counter-insurgency in a range of legal, literary and cultural texts, I try to address the formal and historical singularity of each text rather than positioning the texts as a straightforward reflection of a totality of global imperial power and sovereignty. In so doing, I attempt to address some of the pitfalls of comparative work in postcolonial studies that scholars such as Anne McClintock and Natalie Melas have identified.[36]

One of the things that connects the legal and military rhetoric of emergency in these different European colonial contexts, as we will see, is a founding metalepsis that presented opposition to colonial rule as the cause of repressive emergency measures rather than as a revolutionary political response to a repressive and exploitative system of colonial sovereignty. If, as Young suggests, terror 'violates the smooth transition between causes and effects',[37] colonial states of emergency mobilise an army of tropes and narratives to mask and obfuscate the terror and violence of colonial sovereignty. In the statutes and minutes exchanged between colonial administrators and political leaders in the metropolitan centres of European empires during periods of anti-colonial resistance, for example, the use of emergency measures was often defined as both exceptional and temporary. In broad terms, the literature of empire tended to aid and abet such a rhetorical justification of repressive measures in the European colony, particularly in its representation of political opposition to colonial sovereignty, such as violent acts of anti-colonial insurgency. In the Blackwoods' anthology *Tales of the RIC* (1921), for example, the narrator depicts the violence of anti-colonial insurgents during the Irish war of independence as a 'reign of terror', and suggests that the failure of a young Irish policeman to counter the insurgency of the Irish rebels is a sign of the British Liberal government's indifference to colonial rule in Ireland.[38] In a similar vein, the American writer Robert Ruark in colonial fictions such as *Something of Value* (1955) depicted the Land and Freedom Army in British-occupied Kenya as primitive,

---

36 Anne McClintock, 'The Angel of Progress: Pitfalls of the Term Postcolonial', *Social Text*, 31/2 (1992), pp. 84–98; and Natalie Melas, *All the Difference in the World: Postcoloniality and the Ends of Comparison* (Stanford, CA: Stanford University Press, 2007).

37 Robert J.C. Young, 'Terror Effects', in Elleke Boehmer and Stephen Morton (eds), *Terror and the Postcolonial* (Oxford: Wiley Blackwell, 2009), p. 307.

38 See John Wilson Foster, *Irish Novels, 1890–1940: New Bearings in Culture and Fiction* (Oxford: Oxford University Press, 2008), p. 434; and Royal Irish Constabulary, *Tales of the R.I.C.* (Edinburgh and London: W. Blackwood & Sons, 1921). At the time of publication, the author of *Tales of the R.I.C.* is not given in the book's publication details, and the British Library catalogue lists the author as R.I.C. Yet in a recent article, Robert A. Emery has suggested that the author of this volume was Aubrey Waithman Long, a former British military officer and governor of Derry prison. Robert A. Emery, 'The Author of *Tales of the R.I.C.*', *Notes and Queries*, 57/2 (2010), pp. 226–28.

violent, amoral and insensitive to pain.[39] In so doing, Ruark contributed to the justification of emergency measures in colonial Kenya, and the detention, torture and execution of Kenyans who were suspected of supporting the Land and Freedom Army.

If the colonial rhetoric of counter-insurgency presented emergency measures as exceptional, postcolonial writing has certainly tended to challenge the truth claims of colonial narratives of emergency. This is not to suggest, however, that postcolonial writing conforms to a singular vision of Third World liberation struggles that simply celebrates violent, anti-colonial insurgency. On the contrary: writing in the aftermath of anti-colonial nationalist struggles, many postcolonial writers are profoundly ambivalent about the use of violence as a political strategy for achieving national liberation. In Zoë Wicomb's novel *David's Story* (2000), for example, the unnamed female narrator tries to recover the repressed history of torture and interrogation that African National Congress activists in South Africa used against their own freedom fighters in the Quatro Detention Camp in Angola. In a similar vein, Ngũgĩ wa Thiong'o, in his novel *A Grain of Wheat* (1967), highlights the ways in which the violence of anti-colonial struggle in Kenya during the colonial state of emergency that lasted from 1952 until 1959 permeated the psychic as well as the political life of Kenya. In doing so, Ngũgĩ raises questions about the efficacy of violence as an emancipatory tactic for the colonised after the end of colonial rule. Such questions resonate with Arendt's caution that 'the danger of violence, even if it moves consciously within a nonextremist framework of short-term goals, will always be that the means overwhelm the end', and violence will be introduced 'into the whole body politic'.[40]

The surfeit of books and articles on terrorism produced in response to the 'global war on terrorism' might suggest that terrorism has not only been constituted as an object of contemporary knowledge, but also that terrorism is one of the defining concerns of the twenty-first century western zeitgeist. Yet there are significantly fewer studies that address the historical constitution of terrorism as an object of knowledge in the social sciences and humanities, and the political function that terrorism serves for particular colonial states. *Terror and the Postcolonial* – a collection of essays I co-edited with Elleke Boehmer – considered among other things what the discourse of terrorism tells us about the political values of contemporary western culture and its histories of violence. *States of Emergency: Colonialism, Literature and Law* attempts to push this inquiry further by considering the following questions: to what extent does a focus on the terrorist as an agent of violence obfuscate the role of the state as an agent of violence, especially in the European colonial context? What connections exist between violent forms of colonial sovereignty and the postcolonial formations of state violence that emerged after the period of decolonisation? What light

39 See Robert Ruark, *Something of Value* (London: Hamish Hamilton, 1955) and idem, *Uhuru* (London: Hamish Hamilton, 1962). For a discussion of Ruark's fiction, see David Maughan-Brown, *Land, Freedom and Fiction: History and Ideology in Kenya* (London: Zed, 1985), pp. 106–56.
40 Hannah Arendt, *On Violence* (London: Allen Lane, 1970), p. 80.

can the study of histories of colonial violence and states of emergency shed on contemporary formations of counter-terrorism? What forms of agency and resistance have been mobilised in the face of violent formations of colonial sovereignty? And what light can the study of histories of colonial violence and states of emergency shed on contemporary formations of counter-terrorism? By examining the figuration of state violence and repression in narratives of colonial violence and decolonisation, this book seeks to address these urgent questions, and to propose a critical vocation for postcolonial studies during and beyond the 'war on terror'.

The work of Edward Said, as well as that of Neil Lazarus, Priyamvada Gopal, Talal Asad, Jacqueline Rose, Derek Gregory, Joseph Massad and Achille Mbembe, has certainly helped to complicate the terms of much contemporary scholarship on terrorism by focusing on the ways in which the rhetoric of so-called terrorism serves the interests of western imperialism. Yet despite a growing interest in state terrorism and torture in modern history, postcolonial studies and legal studies, there have been few sustained comparative studies of the contribution that literary and cultural texts have made to the understanding of state terrorism and emergency legislation in colonial societies.[41] Recently, however, two areas of debate in literary studies, legal studies and politics have converged in powerful and mutually reinforcing ways to effectuate this task. First, historical studies of state terrorism in colonial societies have shown how emergency legislation was used as a legal, political and military tool of colonial rule during periods of anti-colonial insurgency.[42] Second, theories of necropolitics and sovereignty have revealed how the use of emergency measures such as detention without trial, torture and military courts were the rule rather than the exception in the political space of the European colony.[43] By situating colonial

---

41 In a recent study on terrorism, insurgency and Indian-English literature, Alex Tickell has argued that a 'cultural materialist account of the strategic "inclusive exclusions" of colonial sovereignty [can] reveal how the basic principles of liberalism – equality, individual rights and liberty – repeatedly came to points of contradiction and impasses in their connection with the work of empire'. Alex Tickell, *Terrorism, Insurgency and Indian-English Literature, 1830–1947* (London: Routledge, 2012), p. 8. In broad terms, this book shares Tickell's cultural materialist approach to exclusionary forms of violent colonial sovereignty as they are manifested in literary and legal texts concerned with state of emergency. Yet by tracing the development of what Benjamin has called the 'tradition of the oppressed' in different forms of postcolonial writing, this book also considers how the traumatic effects of a violent colonial sovereignty have been negotiated and contested in a range of colonial contexts that include, but are not restricted to, colonial India.

42 See Kostal, *A Jurisprudence of Power*; David Anderson, *Histories of the Hanged: Britain's Dirty War in Kenya and the End of Empire* (London: Weidenfeld & Nicolson, 2005); Marnia Lazreg, *Torture and the Twilight of Empire: From Algiers to Baghdad* (Princeton, NJ: Princeton University Press, 2008); Jim House and Neil MacMaster, *Paris 1961: Algerians, State Terror, and Memory* (Oxford: Oxford University Press, 2006).

43 See Mbembe, 'Necropolitics'; Judith Butler, *Precarious Life: The Powers of Mourning and Violence* (London: Verso, 2004); Agamben, *State of Exception*; Nasser Hussain, *The Jurisprudence of Emergency: Colonialism and the Rule of Law* (Ann Arbor: University of Michigan Press, 2003).

fictions of counter-insurgency and postcolonial fictions of national liberation in the context of colonial states of emergency, this book aims to demonstrate the important contribution writing and literary fiction make to our understanding of the relationship between colonialism, law and political violence in the twentieth and twenty-first centuries. More specifically, the book assesses the multiple and conflicting ways in which literary and cultural texts have either contributed to and/or interrogated the necessity for emergency legislation across a range of different historical and political contexts. By doing so, this book seeks to question, complicate and historicise the rhetoric of emergency and global insecurity that has dominated public discourse during the first decade of the twenty-first century.

Walter Benjamin's Eighth Thesis on the Concept of History and the Colonial State of Emergency

Since one of the aims of this book is to consider how colonial states of emergency were understood and experienced from the standpoint of the colonised, it is instructive to return to one of the foundational critical texts on states of emergency: Benjamin's Eighth Thesis on the concept of history. In Benjamin's words,

> The tradition of the oppressed teaches us that the 'state of emergency' in which we live is not the exception, but the rule. We must attain to a conception of history that accords with this insight. Then we will clearly see that it is our task to bring about a real state of emergency, and this will improve our position in the struggle against Fascism. One reason Fascism has a chance is that, in the name of progress, its opponents treat it as a historical norm. The current amazement that the things we are experiencing are 'still' possible in the twentieth century is not philosophical. This amazement is not the beginning of knowledge – unless it is the knowledge that the view of history which gives rise to it is untenable.[44]

Benjamin's Eighth Thesis has provided a rich resource for many critical thinkers and postcolonial theorists.[45] However, in order to assess the relevance of the thesis for understanding *colonial* states of emergency and their aftermath, it is important to distinguish between the intellectual historical context of the Eighth Thesis, and its subsequent postcolonial reiterations. Written in response to 'the Germano–Soviet Pact, the outbreak of the Second World War

---

44 Walter Benjamin, 'On the Concept of History', in Howard Eiland and Michael W. Jennings (eds), *Selected Writings, Volume 4: 1938–1940* (Cambridge, MA: Harvard University Press, 2003), p. 392.

45 See for instance Homi Bhabha, *The Location of Culture* (London: Routledge, 2004), p. 41; Elleke Boehmer, 'Postcolonial Writing and Terror', *Wasafiri*, 22/2 (2007), pp. 4–7; and Keya Ganguly, *States of Exception: Everyday Life and Postcolonial Identity* (Minneapolis, MN and London: University of Minnesota Press, 2001), pp. 24–25.

and the occupation of Europe by Nazi troops',[46] the 'Thesis' may seem bound to a particular historical moment. For Benjamin's discussion of the state of emergency in his Eighth Thesis responds in part to Hindenberg's signing of an emergency decree on 28 February 1933 in accordance with Article 48 of the Weimar Constitution, following Hitler's election to the position of German Chancellor in January 1933. But the Eighth Thesis is also a more general observation that from the standpoint of the oppressed, the state of emergency is a permanent historical condition, rather than an aberration in a liberal narrative of historical progress, which is guaranteed by the rule of law. This insight has important implications for understanding colonial states of emergency from the standpoint of the colonised, as we will see.

The Eighth Thesis is often compared to Schmitt's argument in *Political Theology* (1921) that the sovereign is the figure who has executive power over the state of emergency.[47] In a letter to Schmitt of December 1930, Benjamin describes how Schmitt's writing on sovereignty had influenced his theoretical approach to German tragic drama, even though Benjamin in *The Origin of German Tragic Drama* ultimately concluded that the notion of sovereignty and the definitive decision is put into question by German tragic drama.[48] In light of this letter, Benjamin's Eighth Thesis seems to expand the thesis developed in *The Origin of German Tragic Drama* that 'the state of exception exists not because it is superfluous but because it exists permanently as a perpetual state of lawlessness, continuing to the present'.[49] But as Agamben argues, Benjamin's critique of Schmitt also rejects the possibility of rigorously distinguishing between the state of exception and the rule.[50]

It is against Schmitt's concept of history that Benjamin's concept of the tradition of the oppressed should be understood. Although Benjamin did not live to explain what he meant by the term 'tradition of the oppressed', the idea 'implies two distinct though compatible possibilities', as John McCole contends. One of these meanings would be an 'alternate tradition of those excluded from the canons of "high" culture' – an idea that is clearly compatible with the politically engaged work of the subaltern studies historians. The other definition refers to the 'critical resources' and the 'suppressed, subversive moments' *within* high culture.[51] It is worth noting, too, that Benjamin's notes for his 'Theses on the Concept of History' include a reference suggesting that the 'tradition of the oppressed' is part of what he calls a 'fundamental aporia' in which 'Tradition is the discontinuum of what has been as opposed to history [*Historie*] as the

---

46 Michael Löwy, *Fire Alarm: Reading Walter Benjamin's 'On the Concept of History'*, trans. Chris Turner (London: Verso, 2005), p. 18.
47 Löwy, *Fire Alarm*, p. 58, and Agamben, *State of Exception*, pp. 32–36 and 52–60.
48 See Samuel Weber, 'Taking Exception to Decision: Walter Benjamin and Carl Schmitt', *Diacritics*, 22/3–4 (1992), pp. 5–18.
49 Horst Bredekamp, 'Walter Benjamin to Carl Schmitt, via Thomas Hobbes', *Critical Inquiry*, 25/2 (Winter 1999), p. 264.
50 Agamben, *State of Exception*, pp. 57–59.
51 John McCole, *Walter Benjamin and the Antinomies of Tradition* (Ithaca, NY and London: Cornell University Press, 1993), pp. 304–5.

continuum of events [...] The history of the oppressed is a discontinuum'. For Benjamin, the 'task of history is to get hold of the tradition of the oppressed'.[52] Benjamin's injunction to 'get hold of the tradition of the oppressed' is significant not only because it suggests a way of countering the linear paradigm of history as a continuum of events, but also because it provides a means of questioning the aporetic foundations of sovereignty upon which that linear paradigm of history is based. Moreover, the political and aesthetic connotations of Benjamin's concept of the 'tradition of the oppressed' have important implications for reading postcolonial texts both with and against dominant legal and literary narratives of colonial states of emergency, as we will see.

If Benjamin's Eighth Thesis offers a radical challenge to Schmitt's theory of the state of exception, it also carries a particular resonance in the colonial world, as the postcolonial theorist Homi Bhabha has argued. In his introduction to Fanon's *Black Skin, White Masks*, Bhabha describes Benjamin's 'tradition of the oppressed' as a 'language of revolutionary awareness', which he identifies as a source of political inspiration for the 'distinctive force' of Fanon's 'vision'. In saying this, Bhabha clearly situates Fanon's writing within the context of struggles for decolonisation with which it is inextricably bound. What is more, Bhabha adds that 'the state of emergency' that Benjamin diagnoses 'is also always a state of emergence'.[53] What Bhabha implies by the phrase 'state of emergence' may seem to be consistent with Benjamin's aim in the struggle against Fascism: 'to produce "the *real* state of emergency', or, more literally, the real "state of exception" [*Ausnahmezustand*], that is, the abolition of domination, the classless society'.[54] But Bhabha goes further than this. By reading Benjamin's Eighth Thesis on the concept of history both with and against Fanon's account of colonialism in *Black Skin, White Masks* and *The Wretched of the Earth*, Bhabha argues that 'the struggle against colonial oppression not only changes the direction of Western history, but challenges its historicist idea of time as a progressive, ordered whole'.[55] Such an argument is significant because it acknowledges the emergence of other multiple histories, or 'entangled temporalities', which destabilise the universalising narrative of colonial modernity.[56]

Bhabha's suggestion that Benjamin's concept of history as a permanent state of emergency 'changes the direction of Western history' may not do justice to Benjamin's critique of the liberal idea of history as progress. For the concept of history that Benjamin wishes to oppose in the Eighth Thesis is one in which fascism, tyranny and the oppression of the powerless are seen as incompatible with the values of modern liberal societies in an age of industrial capitalism, an age in which values such as peace, democracy and freedom are regarded as

52 Benjamin, cited in McCole, *Walter Benjamin*, p. 295.
53 Bhabha, *The Location of Culture*, p. 41.
54 Löwy, *Fire Alarm*, p. 60.
55 Bhabha, *The Location of Culture*, p. 41.
56 For a more detailed discussion of the 'entangled temporalities' of the postcolony, see Mbembe, *On the Postcolony*, pp. 14–18.

the norm.[57] But this categorical distinction between liberal democratic societies and totalitarian societies is undermined by the fact that the security of the state occupies a central place in liberal political thought from the Scottish liberal philosopher John Locke to the American liberal legal scholar Bruce Ackerman. The use of emergency powers is clearly possible, then, in a liberal democratic state provided that the recourse to such powers is deemed necessary because the security of the liberal state is under threat, and provided that emergency powers are exercised within the normal rule of law. As Mark Neocleous explains,

> By insisting on the rule of law, liberalism seeks to distance itself from [...] fascism per se. And yet just as early liberalism sought to distance itself from some of the main planks of reason of state and the police idea but was constantly drawn back to them, so it has also found itself in constant recourse to the main planks of political dictatorship: prerogative, exception, emergency powers.[58]

Significantly, it is '"in those zones of exception" such as the colonies' as well as in those 'emergency situations' 'during which liberalism pushes at the limits of its own constitutional constraints'[59] that Neocleous claims to find instances of liberal governments invoking emergency powers. The paradox of European colonial sovereignty was that emergency powers were invoked to maintain colonial power in the name of the liberal idea of the civilising mission – an idea that was precisely undermined by repressive practices such as curfews, restrictions on movement, detention without trial and torture. Such a paradox also reinforces Benjamin's argument contra Schmitt that the state of emergency lies firmly within the rule of law in liberal societies. It is this paradox of sovereignty that Bhabha gestures towards in his reading of Benjamin after Fanon. Bhabha's assertion that 'the order of Western historicism is disturbed in the colonial state of emergency' emphasises how liberal colonial governments' use of emergency powers that are more commonly associated with totalitarian governments would appear to question the values of progress, universal freedom and justice associated with the western liberal view of history.[60]

Bhabha does not elaborate on the significance of this statement in his essay on Fanon, and proceeds instead to discuss Fanon's engagement with psychoanalysis and his critique of western humanism. But Bhabha's observation about the correspondences between Fanon's writing and Benjamin's Eighth Thesis could be developed further with reference to Fanon's writings on the specific

---

57 Löwy, *Fire Alarm*, p. 58.
58 Neocleous, *Critique of Security*, p. 38.
59 Neocleous, *Critique of Security*, p. 38.
60 Bhabha, *The Location of Culture*, p. 41. A clear example of how western liberal thought defended the use of the state of exception as a technique of colonial government can be found in Alexis de Tocqueville's defence of martial law during the French conquest of Algeria in the nineteenth century. See Margaret Kohn, 'Empire's Law: Alexis de Tocqueville on Colonialism and the State of Exception', *Canadian Journal of Political Science*, 41 (2008), pp. 255–278.

political cause of Algerian national liberation.[61] For it was in his essay 'Algeria Face to Face with the French Torturers', first printed in the FLN publication *El Moudjahid* in 1957, that Fanon challenged the representation of the French colonial military's use of violence, torture and brutality against FLN insurgents in the French liberal press as exceptional.[62] While he concedes that the 'truly monstrous practices that have appeared since 1 November 1954 are surprising, especially because of the extent to which they have become generalized', Fanon is unequivocal in his view that such practices are systematic rather than exceptional: 'In reality, the attitude of the French troops in Algeria fits into a pattern of police domination, of systematic racism, of dehumanization rationally pursued.' 'Torture', Fanon argues, 'is inherent in the whole colonialist configuration'.[63]

To the extent that Fanon's reflections on torture during the colonial state of emergency in Algeria challenge the French liberal ideal of the *mission civilisatrice*, they can certainly be seen to 'disturb' the 'order of Western historicism'. In contrast to the moral opposition to the military's use of torture in Algeria from the French liberal intelligentsia, which opposed torture on the grounds that it undermined the democratic foundations of the modern French body politic, Fanon held that torture was part of the French colonial state. Such a view is echoed by Rita Maran's observation that the French *mission civilisatrice* was invoked by the leaders of the French colonial military in Algeria to justify the use of torture during the Algerian liberation war.[64] Significantly, Maran notes that many writers on the French left criticised the use of torture in Algeria, but did not examine how the liberal idea of colonialism as a civilising mission underpinned the justification of torture.[65] Considered in this context, Fanon's observations can be seen to correspond with Bhabha's tantalising claim that the colonial state of emergency challenges the western 'historicist idea of time as a progressive, ordered whole'.[66]

In common with subaltern historians such as Dipesh Chakrabarty, Bhabha's claim here certainly challenges the spatio-temporal logic of uneven development upon which western historicism was founded: a spatio-temporal logic which also underpinned western colonial expansion. Yet it is the enlightenment myth of European colonialism as a civilising mission, and its claim to deliver concepts such as citizenship, political sovereignty, human rights and democracy to the colonial world, that is more profoundly disturbed in the colonial state of emergency. In an essay that echoes Fanon's claim that 'torture is inherent in

---

61 For a discussion of Fanon's political commitment to decolonisation, see David Macey, *Frantz Fanon* (London: Granta, 2000), pp. 1–30; and Neil Lazarus, *The Postcolonial Unconscious* (Cambridge: Cambridge University Press, 2011), pp. 161–82.

62 See Macey, *Frantz Fanon*, pp. 348–52.

63 Frantz Fanon, 'Algeria Face to Face with the French Torturers', in *Toward the African Revolution*, trans. Haakon Chevalier (Harmondsworth: Penguin Books, 1970), p. 74.

64 Rita Maran, *Torture: The Role of Ideology in the French–Algerian War* (New York: Praeger, 1989).

65 Maran, *Torture*, p. 189.

66 Bhabha, *The Location of Culture*, p. 41.

the whole colonialist configuration', the historian Frank Furedi contends that 'Emergencies were as much pre-planned attempts at the political management of anti-colonial forces as belated responses to an unexpected challenge to the imperial order'. Citing the examples of Britain's colonial emergencies in Malaya, Kenya and Cyprus, Furedi argues that the 'dramatic character' of these emergencies made them appear exceptional, rather than a consistent strategy of British colonial rule.[67] In a similar vein, the legal historian A.W. Brian Simpson suggests that martial law and emergency legislation were common legal regimes for containing acts of insurgency against European colonial rule throughout the nineteenth and twentieth centuries. While Simpson contends that 'distinctive legal regimes and techniques for the imposition of order in emergency situations' were 'evolved at home, and then exported to British dependencies',[68] it is significant that what Simpson understands by 'home' is Ireland under British colonial rule:

> In the nineteenth century legislative authorization of emergency powers was more fully developed not in the overseas empire, but in Ireland. All Ireland was, from the Act of Union of 1800 until the establishment of the Irish Free State in 1922, an integral part of the United Kingdom, but was treated in many respects as a colony.[69]

What Simpson implies but does not explicitly state here is that the 'legislative authorization of emergency powers' in Ireland under the Act of Union was part of the British regime of colonial rule – a point which further reinforces Benjamin's critique of the distinction between the state of exception and the 'normal' rule of law.

If colonial sovereignty is characterised by the exercise of power outside the law, colonial states of emergency would seem to continue and consolidate this form of political rule rather than signalling an unprecedented break with the existing form of colonial governance. And yet, as this book goes on to show, the rhetoric of the colonial statutes, reports and minutes announcing the declaration of a state of emergency very often presented the colonial state of emergency as if it were an exceptional break from the rule of law in a liberal democracy. Such colonial rhetoric raises important questions about the differences between colonial governments and liberal democracies in a state of emergency, as well as about the way in which legal narratives of emergency often seem to draw authority from particular narrative forms that can also be found in literary texts of the colonial era.

---

67 Frank Furedi, 'Creating a Breathing Space: The Political Management of Colonial Emergencies', in Robert Holland (ed.), *Emergencies and Disorder in the European Empires after 1945* (London: Frank Cass, 1994), pp. 89–106.
68 A.W. Brian Simpson, *Human Rights and the End of Empire: Britain and the Genesis of the European Convention* (Oxford: Oxford University Press, 2001), pp. 89–90.
69 Simpson, *Human Rights and the End of Empire*, p. 78.

The Prose of Counter-insurgency and the Metalepsis of Emergency

The literature of empire provides an important resource for understanding the legal and extra-legal nuances of colonial states of emergency partly because of the ways in which the narrative structure, imagery and figurative language of such writing dramatised violent acts of insurgency against the colonial state, and often justified equally violent responses to such acts of insurgency. The South Asian historian Ranajit Guha aptly describes such forms of writing that represent acts of anti-colonial insurgency as the prose of counter-insurgency.[70] In Guha's argument, historical representations of peasant insurgency in South Asia typically denied the agency of the peasant insurgent and suggested instead that acts of insurgency are spontaneous rather than the rational outcome of organised political resistance. As a consequence, the social and political cause of the insurgent's actions is often displaced onto the atavism of the insurgent or the inefficiency of the administration. As Yumna Siddiqi explains,

> In historical prose, the meaning of insurgency is driven by the rhetorical manipulation of causes: spontaneous forces, fanatic impulses, or revolutionary energies move the peasant. Fiction may make similar claims, but it has the latitude to interweave other narrative threads with accounts of insurgency so as to color its significance.[71]

In fictions of counter-insurgency, the representation of the insurgent as a terrorist exemplifies the way in which the social and political cause of insurgency – colonial occupation – is displaced onto the culture or religion of the individual freedom fighter who is rebranded as a 'terrorist'. The act of violent anti-colonial insurgency at the centre of Candler's novel *Siri Ram Revolutionist* (1912), for example, is attributed to the cultural background of the insurgent rather than to a grievance against British colonialism in India, and the violence dramatised in Alan Western's novel *Desert Hawk* (1937) is related to the 'ancient antipathy' between Jews and Arabs rather than to the British Mandatory government's support for the expropriation of Palestinian land. Furthermore, the prose of counter-insurgency often provides the colonial state with a narrative structure and figurative language to justify the suspension of the rule of civil law in times of crisis. During the Indian rebellion of 1857, for example, reports that Sepoy soldiers assaulted white women were greatly exaggerated and used to manage the crisis in colonial authority that was 'crucial to colonial self-presentation'[72] and to justify the brutality of the subsequent counter-insurgency campaign in 1858. The prose of counter-insurgency served the British empire's attempt to use the Indian rebellion of 1857 to 'vindicate a retributive view of the world

---

70 Ranajit Guha, 'The Prose of Counterinsurgency', in idem (ed.), *Subaltern Studies*, vol. 2 (Delhi: Oxford University Press, 1983), pp. 1–42.

71 Yumna Siddiqi, *Anxieties of Empire and the Fiction of Intrigue* (New York: Columbia University Press, 2008), p. 88.

72 Jenny Sharpe, *Allegories of Empire: The Figure of Woman in the Colonial Text* (Minneapolis: University of Minnesota Press, 1993), p. 67.

and to assert the primacy of retribution in the Victorian moral cosmos'.[73] This moral rhetoric of revenge and retribution is further evidenced in the 'extravagant ferocity of Brigadier General James Neill's martial law in Benares and Cawnpore', which was one of many examples of the 'merciless reprisals visited, often on the flimsiest legal pretexts, upon Indian combatants and civilians'.[74]

The contemporary discourse of terrorism would seem to serve a similar function to the prose of counter-insurgency: to efface the violence of imperial sovereignty and occupation against which acts of violent anti-colonial insurgency are often carried out. In relation to this, the 'postcolonial terrorist' is often invoked as the cause of the expansion of US and British military power in the twenty-first century, particularly in Afghanistan and Iraq. Such a causal logic conceals the fact that the 'threat of terrorism' is an instance of what Gayatri Chakravorty Spivak has called a metalepsis: where an effect of colonial discourse is presented as a cause; or where a focus on the aesthetic connotations of terror overshadows the imperialist enterprise that produced the terrorism.[75] In this rhetorical manipulation of causes and effects, the fiction of counter-insurgency often attributes the effect of terror to the 'individual terrorist' rather than the political system of terror which they oppose. Such rhetorical manipulation is exemplified in the representation of the figure of the suicide bomber. The recent focus in western scholarship and the media on the motivations of the suicide bomber often attempt to demystify the motives of individual suicide bombers through recourse to a religious vocabulary of sacrifice, a vocabulary that contributes to the western myth of Islamic culture as a culture of death. 'To take suicide bombing as sacrifice', Asad argues, 'is to load it with a significance that is derived from a Christian and post-Christian tradition'.[76] Asad's suggestion that the sacrificial logic of the Christian tradition provides western liberal political thought with a rationale for the use of violence, in which 'some humans can be treated violently in order that humanity can be redeemed',[77] also helps to clarify the way in which the discourse of terrorism distorts the cause of suicide bombing. In presenting the social and political cause of the suicide bomber as rooted in a religious belief which is deemed to be inherently and exclusively Islamic, even though a discourse of sacrifice also underpins the western Christian tradition, the western discourse of terrorism contributes to the justification of violent counter-insurgency campaigns against human populations it deems to be terrorists.

This tendency to distort the causes of terrorism within the western imagination is further evidenced in the representation of the Israel–Palestine conflict. In 'The Essential Terrorist', an article published in *Blaming the Victims: Spurious*

---

73 Christopher Herbert, *War of No Pity: The Indian Mutiny and Victorian Trauma* (Princeton, NJ: Princeton University Press, 2008), p. 101.

74 Herbert, *War of No Pity*, p. 101.

75 Gayatri Chakravorty Spivak, *In Other Worlds: Essays in Cultural Politics* (New York: Methuen, 1987), p. 204.

76 Talal Asad, *On Suicide Bombing* (New York: Columbia University Press, 2007), p. 51.

77 Asad, *On Suicide Bombing*, p. 63.

Scholarship and the Palestinian Question (1988), Said observed how terrorism had 'displaced Communism as public enemy number one' in American public discourse; and how this elevation of terrorism in American public discourse had 'deflected careful scrutiny of the government's domestic and foreign policies'.[78] More specifically, he argues that the scholarship on terrorism is 'brief, pithy, totally devoid of the scholarly armature of evidence, proof, argument'.[79] Citing a book by the then Israeli ambassador to the United Nations, Benjamin Netanyahu, Said describes how Netanyahu's definition of terrorism is flawed because it depends 'a priori on a single axiom: "we" are never terrorists; it's the Moslems, Arabs and Communists who are'.[80] In Said's argument, it is this single axiom that provides the justification for Israeli state repression: 'the spurious excuse of "fighting terrorism" serves to legitimize every case of torture, illegal detention, demolition of houses, expropriation of land, murder, collective punishment, deportation, censorship, closure of schools and universities'.[81]

In criticising the discourse of terrorism, Said is not of course denying that acts of political violence take place and that their effects are abhorrent. Rather, he is questioning the way in which the discourse of terrorism is used by powerful states such as the US and its allies to describe and condemn violent acts of resistance to imperial occupation, instead of addressing the violence of imperial occupation itself. In this respect, Said's reflections on terrorism can be seen to develop the methodological insights of his 1978 study *Orientalism*, in which Said describes orientalism as a 'distribution of geopolitical awareness into aesthetic, scholarly, economic, sociological, historical and philological texts'.[82] Such texts did not merely describe the oriental world they imagined, but also contributed to the proliferation of repressive colonial laws and/or to the justification of the suspension of the normal rule of law during conditions of emergency, or a perceived threat to the sovereignty of the colonial state. As Nasser Hussain has suggested in his study of British colonial law in India, *The Jurisprudence of Emergency*, the colony was the place where the tensions between the rule of law and the absolute sovereignty of the state were played out.[83] And it was in and through the cultural stereotypes and imaginative geographies of colonial discourse – which Said calls orientalism – that such tensions were negotiated.

The problem with what Said calls the axiom of terrorism, then, is that it effaces the imperialist interests that are served by the discourse of terrorism by focusing on the emotional and aesthetic connotation of terror instead of examining the geopolitical context of its production. Such a problem is also

---

78 Edward Said, 'The Essential Terrorist', in Edward Said and Christopher Hitchens (eds), *Blaming the Victims: Spurious Scholarship and the Palestinian Question* (London: Verso, 1988), p. 149.
79 Said, 'The Essential Terrorist', p. 150.
80 Said, 'The Essential Terrorist', p. 152.
81 Said, 'The Essential Terrorist', p. 156.
82 Edward W. Said, *Orientalism: Western Conceptions of the Orient* (London: Routledge and Kegan Paul, 1978), p. 12.
83 Hussain, *Jurisprudence of Emergency*, pp. 6–7.

identified in some of the recent studies of terrorism in literature and culture, which start by referring to the French Revolution, and the way in which the experience of terror in late eighteenth-century France was reflected in aesthetic theories of the sublime. In a discussion of Kantian and Burkean theories of the sublime, for example, Terry Eagleton asserts that 'sublime eruptions like the French Revolution could be admired as long as they were aestheticized, contemplated from a secure distance'.[84] This vicarious experience of terrorism as a spectacle, which evokes shock and fear, has also preoccupied theorists such as Jean Baudrillard and Slavoj Žižek in their commentaries on the events of 11 September 2001. For Baudrillard, the spectacle of the World Trade Center in flames after the attacks of 11 September produced a sensation of spellbound fear amongst the public. Yet although he allows for a relationship of complicity between terrified audience and horrifying spectacle, Baudrillard also frames the terroristic event as an aesthetic phenomenon analogous to the category of terror in the aesthetic theories of the sublime formulated by Burke and Kant.[85] In a similar vein, Slavoj Žižek's comparison of the Middle East to the Desert of the Real in the Wachowski brothers' film *The Matrix* (1999), in his essay 'Welcome to the Desert of the Real!', seems to reinforce the aestheticisation of terror described by Eagleton rather than examining the geopolitical determinants of terrorism as a discourse. Such responses to the terrorist attacks on America of 11 September 2001 tend to frame the event of terrorism as an aesthetic phenomenon analogous to the category of terror in aesthetic theories of the sublime in the writing of Edmund Burke and Immanuel Kant.[86] By focusing on the affect of terror, and its aesthetic mediation in literature and visual culture, such theories obfuscate the social, economic and political dimensions of violent, anti-colonial insurgency. As a consequence, theorists such as Eagleton, Baudrillard and Žižek do little to challenge the prose of counter-insurgency.

Colonial States of Emergency and the Tradition of the Oppressed

From the standpoint of the colonial subject, terror was not only an aesthetic experience or feeling, but a brutal material and corporeal experience of sovereign power and economic exploitation. The rethinking of the aesthetic category of terror in recent postcolonial theory gestures towards the violent foundation of sovereign power in the European colony. In Bhabha's re-reading of Benjamin's Eighth Thesis, we have seen how the historical experience of the colonised teaches us that the state of emergency is the exception rather than the rule. By using Benjamin's term 'the tradition of the oppressed' to denote an emergent tradition of the colonised, Bhabha suggests that it is in the writing

---

84 Terry Eagleton, *Holy Terror* (Oxford: Oxford University Press, 2005), p. 47.
85 Jean Baudrillard, 'L'esprit du terrorisme', *South Atlantic Quarterly*, 101/2 (2002), pp. 403–15.
86 Slavoj Žižek, 'Welcome to the Desert of the Real!', *South Atlantic Quarterly*, 101/2 (2002), pp. 385–89.

and thought of the colonised that the violence of colonial power and counter-insurgency which colonial states of emergency legitimated can be publicly acknowledged and interrogated. What is more, Bhabha's application of Walter Benjamin's elusive phrase 'the tradition of the oppressed' to Fanon's thought and his formulation of a new humanism raises important questions about the meaning of 'tradition' and the relationship between aesthetics and politics in postcolonial literature and thought.

We have already seen too how Benjamin defined the tradition of the oppressed as a multiple and discontinuous historical knowledge that needs to be recovered from the dominant concept of history as the time of sovereignty.[87] In this attempt to recover a fragmented and discontinuous history, argues Shoshana Felman, Benjamin 'advances a theory of history as trauma—and a correlative theory of the historical conversion of trauma into insight'.[88] Felman's emphasis on the way in which 'the traumatized—the subjects of history—are deprived of a language in which to speak of their victimization' offers a compelling rethinking of Benjamin's thesis which is germane to the materialist analysis of colonial states of emergency under consideration in this book. Yet Felman neglects the aesthetic connotations of the word tradition as the transmission of a literary method or style, and the political contribution that the literary artwork has made to an understanding of the history of the oppressed. In the spirit of Benjamin's Eighth Thesis, I use the term 'tradition of the oppressed' as a heuristic concept to denote *both* the histories of anti-colonial resistance and struggle *and* the different aesthetic forms in and through which those histories are mediated in postcolonial writing. This is not to say that the tradition of the oppressed is a fixed object of knowledge. On the contrary, the tradition of the oppressed names the emergent and often unarticulated forms of knowledge and agency of people whose lives are subjected to the forces of imperialism. As an aporia, the tradition of the oppressed brings the sovereignty of western knowledge and reason to a standstill. If, for Benjamin, German tragic drama revealed the fault lines between sovereignty, law and violence, postcolonial writing often uses the resources of the literary to contest the exclusion of colonial subjects from the tradition of western liberal humanism within a historically specific framework of colonial sovereignty. This latter reading of the 'tradition of the oppressed' as an aesthetic category as well as 'a theory of history as trauma' might appear to be synonymous with resistance literature or the literature of protest. Barbara Harlow in a related discussion has suggested that '"resistance literature" is writing within a specific historical context, a context which may be most immediately situated within the contemporary national liberation struggles and resistance movements against western imperialist domination of Africa, Central and South America, and the Middle

---

87 The term 'sovereign time' comes from David A. Fieni's presentation at 'The Global Checkpoint: "Rights" of Passage, Performances of Sovereignty', ACLA Conference, Brown University, 30 March 2012.

88 Shoshana Felman, *The Juridical Unconscious: Trials and Trauma in the Twentieth Century* (Cambridge, MA: Harvard University Press, 2004), p. 33.

and Far East'.[89] What Harlow implies but does not explicitly say in her analysis of resistance literature is that questions of aesthetic value and form are often subordinated to the critical analysis of western imperialist domination, and the rhetoric of solidarity, militancy and resistance to imperialist domination. In the case of the novel, for example, resistance literature is often regarded as synonymous with the socialist realist novel because in 'situations of revolutionary struggle, progressives usually expect the novelist to express his or her message with as much transparency as possible so that it can reach the widest possible audience'. It is for this reason that 'social realism seems to answer more directly to the exigencies of political commitment and protest writing than more experimental or modernist literary modes can do'.[90]

This is not to suggest, however, that the tradition of the oppressed is necessarily opposed to experimental or modernist forms of writing. For the Marxist critic Lazarus the critical task of the politically committed postcolonial writer is to 'hate tradition properly'. Borrowing an aphorism from Theodor Adorno's *Minima Moralia*, Lazarus argues that to hate tradition properly means to hate the modern tradition of western bourgeois humanism properly, and to do so in such a way that opposes the false universality of western bourgeois humanism in favour of 'a true universality, with the idea of a radically transformed social order'.[91] If we extend Lazarus's argument to western imperialism, to hate tradition properly means to oppose the social and political system of western imperialism by mobilizing 'its own protocols, procedures and interior logic against it'.[92] Such a critical procedure is partly exemplified by the ways in which writers such as Ngũgĩ wa Thiong'o, Alex La Guma, J.M. Coetzee, Salman Rushdie, Zoe Wicomb and Emile Habiby have developed the aesthetic, narrative and generic strategies of modernism in order to illuminate the contradictions within both the rhetoric of the civilising mission of European colonialism and the emancipatory rhetoric of the postcolonial state.

What Benjamin, Bhabha and Felman mean by the phrase 'the tradition of the oppressed' can be linked, then, to debates about the politics of different aesthetic forms, and more specifically to the political claims that are sometimes made about postcolonial literary artworks. Deepika Bahri has cautioned that

> If criticism is prone to attach too much meaning to artistic and political expression as political work, as the many critics of postcolonialism rightly charge, it is also true that a criticism uninterested in exploring its aesthetic dimension will fail to glean its possible contribution to the emancipatory project.[93]

---

89 Barbara Harlow, *Resistance Literature* (London: Methuen, 1987), p. 4.
90 Joe Cleary, *Literature, Partition and the Nation State* (Cambridge: Cambridge University Press, 2002), p. 194.
91 Neil Lazarus, *Nationalism and Cultural Practice in the Postcolonial World* (Cambridge: Cambridge University Press, 1999), p. 3.
92 Lazarus, *Nationalism and Cultural Practice*, p. 7.
93 Deepika Bahri, *Native Intelligence: Aesthetics, Politics and Postcolonial Literature* (Minneapolis, MN: University of Minnesota Press, 2003), p. 17.

My approach to the 'tradition of the oppressed' in this book takes Bahri's caution seriously, but it also attempts to assess the possible contribution that postcolonial literary texts have made to 'the emancipatory project' of national independence struggles by considering the ways in which postcolonial texts disrupt and counter the smooth, continuous history of colonial sovereignty articulated in the literature and law of empire.

Structure of This Book

The following chapters examine how national liberation struggles and the legal, military and political techniques employed by colonial governments to contain them have been figured in literature and culture of the late nineteenth century, the twentieth century and the first decade of the twenty-first century. They do so firstly by comparing the legal and bureaucratic rhetoric of colonial statutes, gazettes, reports and minutes with the narrative structure, imagery and figurative languages of the literature and culture of empire, and secondly by assessing the ethical, political and legal arguments that the literatures of decolonisation mobilised to call the necessity for violent techniques of colonial governmentality into question. By adopting a comparative approach to the representation of colonial states of emergency, this book assesses how the particular cultural and historical experiences of colonial violence and violent anti-colonial resistance in Ireland, India, Kenya, South Africa, Algeria and Israel-Palestine are negotiated in the narrative structure, generic conventions and rhetoric of literary texts, statutes and archives, while also identifying any formal similarities between these very different texts and historical contexts. This is not to suggest that the texts selected for discussion in this book mediate the experience of violent colonial sovereignty and states of emergency in exactly the same way, or that the techniques of colonial sovereignty discussed in each case study conform to a universal theory or structure. Colonial sovereignty, insurgency and emergency are codified in different ways in particular texts and contexts, and this codification requires more extensive literary close readings in some chapters, and more engagement with legal and historical sources in others. Rather than offering a continuous linear history of colonial states of emergency, I have tried to identify recurrent metaphors, archetypes, narrative strategies and events in different narratives of emergency. In so doing, I have sought to trace correspondences between specific historical experiences of colonial sovereignty and violence from the standpoint of the colonised and 'cross-border interactions' between narratives of anti-colonial struggle.[94] Such an approach aims to demonstrate how colonial states of emergency operated as a travelling concept that buttressed violent formations of colonial sovereignty, and fanned the flames of anti-colonial insurgency. Colonial rule by force

---

94 For more on cross-border interactions, see Elleke Boehmer *Empire, the National, and the Postcolonial, 1890–1920: Resistance in Interaction* (Oxford: Oxford University Press, 2002).

may have seemed to be more pronounced during violent national liberation struggles, but as Fanon has suggested, the use of violence and force was in many cases inherent to the entire legal and political edifice of European colonial states.

By examining the ways in which colonial states of emergency are mediated in and through the aesthetic structure of literary texts, this book also seeks to question and complicate the cultural and political assumptions underpinning predominant approaches to terrorism, which often focus on the violent figure of 'the terrorist' almost to the exclusion of state-sanctioned violence. It is precisely colonial states of emergency and the acts of state violence they sanction which illuminate the often complex and contradictory responses of modern colonial states to so-called acts of terrorism; responses which also have profound political implications for the liberal axiom of colonialism's civilising mission. This focus on colonial states of emergency also aims to reassess the complex historical relationship between colonial states of emergency, the emergence of anti-colonial liberation struggles, and the ways in which these struggles have been imagined, mediated and codified in literary, legal and cultural texts. Such an approach seeks to respond to the critical task defined by Gopal and Lazarus in a special issue of the journal *New Formations* on postcolonial studies after Iraq: 'to work towards the production of a new "history of the present"' which takes on both the history of imperialism and the history of resistance to imperialism in the long twentieth century.[95] Accordingly, this book also examines how theories and histories of Third World national liberation highlighted violent forms of European colonial governance in Ireland, India, South Africa, Kenya, Algeria and Israel-Palestine, and proceeds to investigate the multiple ways in which these theories and histories inform and inflect the style and form of postcolonial writing.

Colonial states of emergency do not have a single origin or starting point, but are rather imbricated in a complex global network of power relations. The correspondences between the historical experience of British colonial sovereignty in Ireland and India are an interesting case in point, and form the basis of Part I of this book. In a speech on Ireland and India delivered in 1920, the former Irish Taoiseach Eamon de Valera spoke of the parallels between the massacres carried out by British colonial forces at Croke Park stadium, Dublin and the Jallianwallah Bagh compound in Amritsar, India.[96] Implicit in de Valera's comparison is a structural connection between British colonial sovereignty and the emergency legislation which precipitated these massacres. Chapter 1 traces the language, rhetoric and imagery of emergency in Anglo-Irish literature and law in colonial Ireland. It begins by considering how the rhetoric of the Fenian threat in newspapers such as *The Illustrated London News* and novels such as Fred Burnaby's *Our Radicals* (1886) could be seen to mirror the language of emergency in the Criminal Law and Procedure (Ireland) Act 1887, and the Defence of the

95 Priyamvarda Gopal and Neil Lazarus, 'Editorial', *New Formations*, 59 (Autumn 2006), p. 9.
96 Eamon de Valera, *India and Ireland* (New York: Friends of Freedom for India, 1920).

Realm Act of 1914. The fictional depiction of Irish home rule in Burnaby's novel *Our Radicals*, for example, precipitates a state of emergency in the fictional world of the novel that leads to the subversion of the British political establishment. Similarly, the violent actions of the revolutionaries in Tom Greer's nationalist fantasy novel *A Modern Daedalus* (1885) provide the pretext for the declaration of a fictional state of emergency in the British House of Commons. These imaginative depictions of a state of emergency in colonial Ireland not only prefigure the British government's use of repressive legal measures and extensive court-martial jurisdiction in its effort to crush the Irish war of independence, but also raise questions about the exceptional character of such measures. For in the face of growing popular support for nationalist insurgency against British colonial rule, the British government granted extensive emergency powers to the military to detain and interrogate Irish prisoners, and arranged the targeted assassination of suspected terrorists by paramilitary groups such as the Black and Tans and the Auxiliary Division of the Royal Irish Constabulary. The British government's use of emergency measures to counter violent anti-colonial insurgency in Ireland certainly marked a crisis in colonial authority. Yet, as I go on to demonstrate, the literary fiction of counter-insurgency depicted in the 1921 anthology *Tales of the R.I.C.* seemed to reinforce the British use of emergency legislation by presenting the Irish war of independence as a reign of terror. If the writing of counter-insurgency in colonial Ireland served to justify the sovereign power of the colonial state over the life and death of the colonised during a state of emergency, it is significant that the nationalist writing of Padraic Pearse and Yeats frequently drew on the rhetoric and imagery of sacrifice. For, as the concluding section of the chapter suggests, the language and imagery of sacrifice offers a dangerous counterpoint to the sovereign violence of the state. Through a series of reflections on Yeats and Eavan Boland, I suggest that sacrifice does not simply affirm the agency of the colonised over their life and death in colonial Ireland; it can also run the risk of re-inscribing violence in the political foundations of the emergent postcolonial state.

For some Bengali revolutionaries and nationalists in the early twentieth century, the Irish war of independence provided a paradigmatic example of anti-colonial struggle. The historian Michael Silvestri notes how 'both Bengali nationalists and British administrators drew comparisons between Irish resistance to the British Empire and contemporary terrorist activity in Bengal'.[97] The rhetoric and tactics of the Irish Republican Army provided Indian revolutionaries such as Subhas Chandra Bose and Kalpana Dutt with a model of anti-colonial insurgency in the 1920s and 1930s, which were invoked in their writings and speeches as well as imitated in their deeds. Chapter 2 considers the ways in which such acts of sedition and revolutionary violence in British colonial India were invoked by the British colonial authorities to justify the recourse to emergency measures in Anglo-Indian fiction and the Indian Penal Code. By

---

97 Michael Silvestri, '"The Sinn Fein of India": Irish Nationalism and the Policing of Revolutionary Terrorism in Bengal', *Journal of British Studies*, 39 (October 2000), p. 455.

tracing the state of emergency that India's revolutionaries were deemed to have created in the early twentieth-century British colonial imagination, the chapter assesses the extent to which Anglo-Indian fictions of terrorism and sedition, such as Candler's *Siri Ram Revolutionist* (1912), reveal the violent foundations that underpin the liberal rhetoric of the civilising mission in British India. If the Anglo-Indian characters in British literary representations of counter-insurgency often claim to have demystified the psychological and social causes of 'revolutionary terrorism' in colonial Bengal in order to more effectively contain it, the enigmatic revolutionary figure of the Doctor in Sarat Chandra Chatterjee's novel *Pather Dabi* (1926) constantly eludes the gaze of the colonial authorities. This fictional revolutionary, as I argue in the conclusion, not only provided a literary inspiration for subsequent revolutionaries such as Dutt, but also demonstrated that sedition is a crucial rhetorical and political strategy in the struggle against colonialism and the techniques of lawful violence that preserve it.

In his posthumously published essay 'Concerning Violence', Fanon criticises the violence of European colonial rule that was accentuated during the endgame of empire, and cites the examples of the massacre at Sharpeville, South Africa, in 1960, French counter-insurgency in Algeria during the 1950s and the state of emergency in Kenya during the 1950s. Although Fanon did not explicitly address the use of emergency legislation in these different colonial contexts, the transnational focus of his essay informs and underpins Part II of this book, which traces the parallels and correspondences between the historical experiences of colonial sovereignty and violence in South Africa, Algeria and Kenya from the standpoint of the colonised. Such parallels and correspondences are certainly borne out by the reception of Fanon's essay among different Third World intellectuals, organisations and writers, including Nelson Mandela, Steve Biko, Assia Djebar, Ngũgĩ wa Thiong'o, the FLN, the PLO, the IRA and the American Black Panthers.[98] Fanon did not live to describe the postcolonial formations of state violence that emerged after the period of decolonisation, which he evoked so vividly in *The Wretched of the Earth*. Yet his writing clearly prefigures the damaging legacy of colonial violence and repression on the psychic and political life of the postcolony, a legacy which haunts much postcolonial thought and writing.[99]

Chapter 3 considers how the writing of Richard Rive, Alex La Guma, J.M. Coetzee and Zoë Wicomb highlighted the role of emergency legislation in the formation of South Africa's apartheid state, and the enforcement of the ruling apartheid ideology. Just as the British colonial authorities in India had used emergency legislation to proscribe the public expression of disaffection with colonial rule, so the Nationalist government in South Africa used its wide legal powers to silence and foreclose literature as well as political activities that were deemed 'morally repugnant, blasphemous, socially subversive, or politically

---

98 See Homi K. Bhabha, 'Foreword: Framing Fanon', in *The Wretched of the Earth*, trans. Richard Philcox (New York: Grove Press, 2004), pp. xxviii–xxxii; and Yezid Ṣayigh, *Armed Struggle and the Search for State: The Palestinian National Movement, 1949–1993* (Oxford: Oxford University Press, 1999), p. 91.

99 For more on Fanon's prescience, see Bhabha, 'Foreword: Framing Fanon', pp. vii–xli.

seditious' to the ethos of the South African apartheid state.[100] Starting with a consideration of South Africa's emergency legislation, and the socio-historical context in which it emerged, the chapter examines how literary texts contested the apartheid government's emergency legislation by exposing the sovereign power and force which underpinned the apartheid state – in particular through practices such as indefinite detention and torture. Writing in the shadow of a political regime that also proscribed the publication of literature deemed to be offensive by the apartheid state, the representation of the violence of the state may appear to reinforce the apartheid state's authority. Yet as I go on to argue through readings of Richard Rive's *Emergency* (1964), La Guma's *In the Fog of the Season's End* (1972) and J.M. Coetzee's *Waiting for the Barbarians* (1980), it is only by interrogating the legal and extra-legal foundations upon which the violence of the apartheid state was based that one can begin to question and complicate the spectacle of power and violence that Njabulo Ndebele finds in much anti-apartheid writing. By publicly articulating the conditions of writing in a state of emergency, writers such as Rive, la Guma and Coetzee question the political autonomy of art and writing, and foreground the importance of writing as a public discourse through which to express the experience of violence sanctioned by the apartheid state.

Chapter 4 considers how the state of emergency in Kenya from 1952 to 1959 has been codified in the literary and legal rhetoric of British colonialism, and criticised by postcolonial African writers and intellectuals as a sign of the inherent violence of European colonial rule. The chapter begins by tracing how the colonial government used the deaths of white settlers and Kenyan Loyalists to justify its recourse to emergency legislation and its detention of at least 150,000 Kikuyu, who were suspected by the colonial authorities of being involved with the Land and Freedom Army, more commonly known as the Mau Mau.[101] After an analysis of the representation of the Land and Freedom Army in Ruark's *Something of Value* (1955) and Elspeth Huxley's *A Thing to Love* (1954), the chapter proceeds to examine how the colonial state of emergency and its postcolonial legacies is framed and contested in the fiction of Ngũgĩ.

Chapter 5 considers how the colonial state of emergency in Algeria from 1955–62 was mediated in a range of literary and legal texts. Beginning with an analysis of Pontecorvo's 1965 film *The Battle of Algiers*, this chapter considers the way in which the declaration of a state of emergency in Algeria in 1955 made possible the increasingly military character of French colonial policy in Algeria, a policy which is epitomised in Fanon's assertion that 'torture is inherent in the whole colonialist configuration'.[102] After an analysis of the rhetoric of necessity that was used to justify the recourse to emergency powers and the transfer of legal power to the military in the French emergency decrees of 1955 and 1956, the chapter proceeds to analyse how the French colonial state of emergency

---

100 Peter D. McDonald, *The Literature Police: Apartheid Censorship and Its Cultural Consequences* (Oxford: Oxford University Press, 2009), p. 34.
101 Anderson, *Histories of the Hanged*, p. 5.
102 Fanon, 'Algeria Face to Face with the French Torturers', p. 74.

is figured in French colonial narratives of the Algerian war, specifically Pierre Leulliette's memoir *Saint Michel et le dragon* (1961) and Jean Lartéguy's novel *Les centurions* (1962). If these narratives try to create a heroic mythology around the figure of the French paratrooper that justifies the recourse to emergency powers, memoirs of the Algerian war, such as Henry Alleg's *La question* (1958) and Louisette Ighilahriz's *Algérienne* (2001), disclose the implications of emergency powers from the standpoint of the Algerian population. By reading these narratives in conjunction with Djebar's novels of the Algerian war, *Les enfants du nouveau monde* (1962), *L'amour, la fantasia* (1985) and *La femme sans sépulture* (2002), and Soleïman Adel Guémar's *État d'urgence* (2007), the chapter concludes by tracing the emergence of a subaltern history of the Algerian war and its aftermath in recent Algerian writing.

Part III considers the parallels between formations of colonial sovereignty and anti-colonial resistance in the early part of the twentieth century and the states of emergency that have characterised what Gregory aptly calls the colonial present. In contrast to India, South Africa, Kenya and Algeria, the relative exclusion of Israel-Palestine from much scholarship in postcolonial studies has until quite recently been conspicuous.[103] This exclusion may appear particularly surprising when one considers that the Palestinian intellectual Edward W. Said played such a crucial role in forming the intellectual project of postcolonial studies, a project that for Said was inseparable from his political commitment to justice and freedom for the Palestinian people. Such a lacuna in postcolonial studies also marks a failure to address the role of European and American imperialism in the constitution and perpetuation of enmity between Israelis and Palestinians, as Gil Anidjar and Bashir Abu Manneh have argued.[104] The exclusion of Israel-Palestine from postcolonial literary studies may have something to do with the Anglophone bias of much postcolonial scholarship. Yet the publication of English translations of novels by Habiby, Ghassan Kanafani, Amos Oz and S. Yizhar, for example, clearly demonstrates that there is a readership for such fiction in the Anglophone literary sphere. Rather than perpetuate this exclusion because of the limitations of my own linguistic competence in Arabic and Hebrew, I have chosen to consider how English translations of Israeli and Palestinian writing have contributed to a broader public understanding of sovereignty, law and violence in Israel-Palestine, and the emergence of a Palestinian national narrative.

103 Some of the books that have considered the relationship between postcolonial studies and Israel-Palestine include Joseph Massad, *The Persistence of the Palestinian Question: Essays on Zionism and the Palestinians* (London: Routledge, 2006); Cleary, *Literature, Partition, and the Nation State*; Adi Ophir, Michael Givoni and Sari Hanafi (eds), *The Power of Inclusive Exclusion: Anatomy of Israeli Rule in the Occupied Palestinian Territories* (New York: Zone, 2009); Ronit Lentin (ed.), *Thinking Palestine* (London: Zed Books, 2008); and Ariella Azoulay, *The Civil Contract of Photography* (New York: Zone, 2008).
104 See Gil Anidjar, *The Jew, the Arab: A History of the Enemy* (Stanford, CA: Stanford University Press: 2003); and Bashir Abu Manneh, 'Israel in US Empire', *New Formations*, 59 (2006), pp. 34–51.

Chapter 6 examines the significance of emergency law during the period between the British mandate in Palestine and the formation of the State of Israel, and considers the ways in which literary narratives can shed light on the colonial genealogy of Israel's political sovereignty. Referring again to the literary prose of counter-insurgency, I consider how Maurice Callard's novel about the end of the British colonial mandate, *The City Called Holy* (1954), frames Zionist acts of violent anti-colonial insurgency in the generic codes of late imperial romance and the political thriller. By fictionalising the armed Jewish insurgency against the British government in mandatory Palestine, Callard draws attention to the crisis in colonial authority that armed Jewish organisations worked to bring about. In doing so, the novel also anticipates the militarisation of the emergent State of Israel in the name of security. It is this militarisation that the Israeli writer Yizhar highlights in his experimental novella *Khirbet Khizeh* (1949). As I go on to show, *Khirbet Khizeh* offers a critical if fictionalised account of the Jewish military's depopulation of Palestinian villages in 1948, and a sympathetic account of the Palestinians whom the Israeli military forced into exile. By imagining the experience of the 1948 war from the standpoint of the Palestinians, Yizhar gestures towards the emergence of a Palestinian national consciousness that is framed in relation to the *nakba*, or catastrophe, of 1948, during which an estimated 750,000 Palestinians were forced into exile.[105] It is the collective memory of the *nakba* and the subsequent occupation of the West Bank and Gaza that has preoccupied much literary fiction about Palestine. By examining the figuration of the *nakba* and the traumatic experience of displacement and dispossession in Kanafani's novella, *Men in the Sun*, Habiby's *The Secret Life of Saeed, the Ill-Fated Pessoptimist* and Khoury's *Gate of the Sun*, the final section of the chapter considers how these literary texts have experimented with narrative form in such a way that is appropriate to convey the fragmented and discontinuous structure of Palestine's history of the oppressed.

Since the terrorist attacks on America of 11 September 2001, there is a strong case for arguing that the US and British governments have invoked narratives and metaphors that are very similar to the rhetoric which was mobilised during states of emergency in former European colonies in order to justify the 'wars against terrorism' in Iraq and Afghanistan. In the concluding chapter to this study, I consider how the legal and political arguments for detention camps in the US-led 'war on terror' draw on the rhetoric of emergency to reinforce the necessity for broader police and/or military powers, and to justify measures that not only contravene the principles of international human rights legislation, but which also resemble the legal, political and military techniques of European colonial powers in the late nineteenth and early twentieth centuries. Beginning with a discussion of the legal regime which enabled the detention of 'enemy combatants' at Guantánamo Bay, this chapter proceeds to consider how Muslims have been represented in the 'post-9/11' fiction of Ian McEwan and

---

105 See Benny Morris, *The Birth of the Palestinian Refugee Problem Revisited* (Cambridge: Cambridge University Press, 2004), pp. 602–4.

Martin Amis. In so doing, I try to address to what extent the 'post-9/11' novel participates in the dominant discourse of terrorism. As a counterpoint to such representations, the chapter then moves to consider how contemporary fiction by Muslim writers such as Mohsin Hamid and Kamila Shamsie questions and complicates the prevailing tropes and narratives of militant Islam that frame the justification of emergency measures in the 'war on terror'. In doing so, the book concludes by arguing that contemporary fiction by Muslim writers not only highlights the specifically imperialist provenance of emergency measures and executive powers in American foreign policy during the Bush administration and its aftermath, but also offers a space for re-imagining the historical legacies of anti-colonialism as a countervailing narrative to the violent, exclusionary and exploitative regimes that form the colonial present.

Part I

CHAPTER 1

Sovereignty, Sacrifice and States of Emergency in Colonial Ireland

In an article published in March 1870, Jenny Marx-Longuet, daughter of the author of *The Communist Manifesto*, declared that 'Theoretical fiction has it that constitutional liberty is the rule and its suspension an exception, but the whole history of English rule in Ireland shows that a state of emergency is the rule and that the application of the constitution is the exception.'[1] Writing in response to the Gladstone government's 'Peace Preservation (Ireland) Act' of 1870, Marx-Longuet highlights a contradiction in the colonial policy of British sovereignty towards a country that was legally part of the United Kingdom between 1800 and 1922. Such a contradiction is exemplified in the tension between the rhetoric and practice of liberal colonial governmentality in nineteenth-century Ireland. As the historian Charles Townshend explains, the British Prime Minister William Gladstone was uncomfortable with the recourse to coercive measures that went against the grain of the Liberal government's political principles, and 'fumed that the "resources of civilization had not yet been exhausted" in the battle against agrarian violence'. And yet the very 'resources' that Gladstone invoked 'were nothing more than military force and repressive laws denounced in England as unconstitutional'.[2]

Marx-Longuet's comments on the British colonial government's repeated use of emergency measures in Ireland identify a more general theoretical fiction in the rhetoric of emergency legislation that such laws represent an exceptional departure from the normal rule of law. In so doing, Marx-Longuet's observation can be seen to prefigure the writings of Carl Schmitt, Walter Benjamin and Giorgio Agamben on the use of emergency law as a political technique of sover-

---

1 Jenny Marx-Longuet 'Articles on the Irish Question'. Available at <www.marxists.org/archive/marx/bio/family/jenny/1870-ire.htm>. Accessed 21 May 2011.
2 Charles Townshend, *Political Violence in Ireland: Government and Resistance since 1848* (Oxford: Clarendon, 1983), p. 104.

eignty. Yet it is also important to note that Marx-Longuet's comments refer to the use of emergency measures as a specific technique of *colonial* sovereignty. The 'Peace Preservation (Ireland) Act' of 1870, which restricted secret meetings, gave special powers to justices of the peace to make summary convictions and outlawed the publication of seditious content in newspapers, 'applied to Ireland only', as the language of the act makes clear. What is more, this act was among 105 separate Coercion Acts dealing with Ireland, acts which included laws suspending the law of habeas corpus.[3]

How, though, were such repressive measures understood in the public imagination? In what ways did literary and cultural representations of Irish nationalist violence participate in the quasi-legal rhetoric of emergency and techniques of colonial governmentality in Ireland? And how were such representations contested and challenged in Irish literature and culture? To address questions such as these, this chapter begins by tracing the language, rhetoric and imagery of emergency in Anglo-Irish literature and law in colonial Ireland. Specifically, it considers how the rhetoric of 'the Fenian terrorist threat' was mediated in newspapers such as *The Illustrated London News* and in novels such as Burnaby's *Our Radicals* (1886) and Greer's *A Modern Dædalus* (1885). The way in which *Our Radicals* frames Irish acts of political violence using generic conventions that conform to what Guha has called the prose of counter-insurgency can be seen to contribute to the justification of the British government's use of repressive measures in the Peace Preservation (Ireland) Act of 1870 and the Criminal Law and Procedure (Ireland) Act of 1887, and prefigures the British government's use of emergency laws such as the 1914 Defence of the Realm Act in its effort to crush the Irish war of independence that followed the Easter Rising of 1916. But they also foreground the way in which repressive measures were justified in Ireland on the grounds that the Irish 'were considered a "different race," possessed of a different type of character', who were in a 'different [and lower] stage of civilisation, politically, socially, intellectually', and thus 'stood in need of a "different regime"'.[4] Such forms of justification not only raise questions about the exceptional character of repressive measures in Ireland; they also shed light on the role of state violence in the maintenance of British sovereignty in Ireland. In the face of growing support for nationalist insurgency against British rule that followed the Easter Rising of 1916, the British government granted extensive emergency powers to the military to detain and interrogate Irish prisoners, and arranged the targeted assassination of 'suspected terrorists' by paramilitary groups such as the Auxiliary Division of the Royal Irish Constabulary and the Black and Tans. The British government's use of emergency measures to counter violent insurgency certainly marked a crisis in British political authority in Ireland. Yet, as I go on to demonstrate, the literary

3 See Michael Farrell, *The Apparatus of Repression: Emergency Legislation* (Derry: Field Day Theatre, 1986), and Townshend, *Political Violence in Ireland*.

4 Jenkins, *The Fenian Problem: Insurgency and Terrorism in a Liberal State 1858–1874* (Montréal: McGill-Queen's University Press, 2008), p. 340.

fictions of counter-insurgency serialised in the 1921 volume of *Blackwood's Edinburgh Magazine*, and reprinted in the anthology *Tales of the R.I.C.* (1921), seemed to reinforce the British use of emergency legislation by presenting the Irish war of independence as a reign of terror. If the writing of counter-insurgency in late colonial Ireland served to justify the sovereign power of the British government over the life and death of the Irish population during a state of emergency, it is significant that the nationalist writing of Pearse and Yeats frequently drew on the imagery and rhetoric of sacrifice. As the final section of this chapter suggests, the language and imagery of sacrifice may seem to offer a powerful counterpoint to the sovereign power of the colonial state. As Richard Kearney has suggested, sacrifice provided Republican historical narratives with a mythic idiom in which Irish hunger strikers from Terence McSwiney to Bobby Sands could be framed as martyrs to the cause of national liberation.[5] Rather than simply rehearsing the terms of this Republican narrative, however, the concluding section of this chapter considers how the sacrificial logic of the hunger strike also bears a troubling resemblance to the necropolitical logic of the colonial state of exception. Though a series of reflections on the writing of W.B. Yeats and Eavan Boland, the chapter concludes by asking how we might avoid re-inscribing this sacrificial logic in the political foundations of a still-partitioned postcolonial Ireland.

Lawlessness and Emergency in Colonial Ireland

Sensational reports of Fenian violence in the nineteenth-century British press typically depict Irish revolutionaries as savage, amoral figures. In an account of the Fenian murders of the Chief Secretary and permanent Under Secretary to the Irish administration in Dublin Castle, Lord Frederick Cavendish and Mr Thomas Henry Burke in Dublin's Phoenix Park, the 20 May 1882 issue of *The Illustrated London News* condemns the people of Dublin for failing to provide the British government with information about the murderers:

> It had been supposed that the metropolis of Ireland, the head-quarters of Irish society, was in some degree, compared with the West and the South, an abode of civilisation, with a humane, honest, and orderly population. It might have seemed impossible, in Dublin, that a band of worse than savage manslayers, after perpetrating their monstrous deed in the middle of the Park, in broad daylight, and sight of many passengers, should drive away in a hired public vehicle, and with the help, in all likelihood, of neighbouring accomplices, should elude pursuit, no positive information being given, two weeks afterwards, concerning their movements before or since the murderous act.[6]

Here, a stereotype of the Irish revolutionaries as a 'band' of 'worse than savage manslayers' is extended to a space within the imagined geographical boundaries

---

5 Richard Kearney, *Myth and Motherland* (Derry: Field Day, 1984).
6 'The Fenian Murders in Dublin', *Illustrated London News* (Saturday, 20 May 1882), p. 489.

of 'civilisation'. In so doing, the article evokes the jurisdictional space of the pale that was deemed to be subject to the sovereignty of the English government. In a discussion of Schmitt's account of the way in which the *nomos* or law of sovereignty was bound up with land appropriation, Wendy Brown explains how the 'boundary designated by a pale – a wooden stake used to make a fence – originally delineated English colonial territory in Ireland'. What 'is "beyond the pale"', Brown adds, 'appears as uncivilized in two disparate, yet politically linked senses: It is where civilization ends, but it is also where the brutishness of the civilized is therefore permitted, where violence may be freely and legitimately exercised'.[7] A similar justification for state violence seems to operate in 'The Fenian Murders in Dublin'. By attributing complicity in the 'monstrous deed' of the assassination of Cavendish and his Under Secretary to the people of Dublin, the article implies that Dublin – in a similar way to the territory beyond the pale denoted by 'the West and the South' – is a space of lawlessness and violence, a space which is ripe for repressive emergency measures.

Such measures are explicitly mentioned in 'The Dynamite Conspiracy', an article published in the 14 April 1883 issue of *The Illustrated London News*, which describes an 'atrocious conspiracy to blow up our public buildings' using dynamite. In response to this conspiracy, the article asserts, the 'American-Irish Fenian association [...] cannot possibly suppose that any political object is to be furthered by such monstrous practices' and suggests that 'the vigilance and prompt action of our police, with the additional powers of legal repression and severe punishment under a fresh Act of Parliament' will prevent the Fenians from achieving their aim of creating 'a panic in England'.[8] The promise of 'legal repression and severe punishment' in the article may have been intended to alleviate the public's fear of 'Fenian terrorists' in late nineteenth-century British society. Yet such a promise also foregrounds the way in which the authority of the state is founded on the very 'monstrous' political violence that is imputed to the 'Fenian terrorists'. In a related discussion of sovereignty, Derrida has argued that 'the arbitrary suspension or rupture of right, runs the risk of making the sovereign look like the most brutal beast who respects nothing, scorns the law, immediately situates himself above the law, at a distance from the law'.[9] While the sovereign's 'mode of being-outside-the-law' may be quite different to that of a criminal or a beast, Derrida claims that the figures of sovereign, beast and criminal have a 'troubling resemblance' – a resemblance that has significant implications for understanding the way in which the British state and the media defined Irish freedom fighters as bestial figures.[10] In a state of emergency, it is precisely this 'troubling resemblance' between the sovereign and the figure that the sovereign defines as a beast, rogue or criminal that the writing of counter-insurgency seeks to disavow, as we will see.

7 Wendy Brown, *Walled States, Waning Sovereignty* (New York: Zone, 2010), pp. 45–46.

8 'The Dynamite Conspiracy', *Illustrated London News* (Saturday, 14 April 1883), p. 356.

9 Jacques Derrida, *The Beast and the Sovereign*, vol. 1, trans. Geoffrey Bennington (Chicago: University of Chicago Press, 2009), p. 39.

10 Derrida, *The Beast and the Sovereign*, pp. 39–42.

Dynamite Novels and the Prose of Counter-insurgency

Just as the Victorian press sought to demonise the Fenians for their use of political violence, so the literary prose of counter-insurgency attempted to preserve the liberal narrative of colonialism's civilising mission in Ireland by framing Irish revolutionaries as dangerous individuals. In Colonel Fred Burnaby's posthumously published novel *Our Radicals* (1886), the Fenians are depicted as political terrorists who plot to murder leading British politicians either by assassinating them or by planting home-made explosives in their houses. By detailing the Fenians' tactics of subversive political organisation as a secret society, Burnaby evokes a terrorist network that uses the technologies of late Victorian modernity against the metropolitan centre of British imperial power. In an account of the leader of the Irish revolutionary group, Moon Barry, for example, Burnaby's narrator describes how Barry infiltrates London's spaces of political power without detection by passing as a Victorian gentleman who dons a 'false grey wig and beard' and inhabits a 'semi-detached, dilapidated-looking building, used apparently for storing wood'.[11] More importantly, as the narrator explains, Barry's improvised telephone allows him to stay in touch with his political network through a mast installed on top of the building to which are attached 'fifty different telegraph wires, which extended to various parts of the metropolis':[12]

> Proceeding a few yards down the hall, he touched a spring in the wall, which opened a door the size of an ordinary brick. Taking two indiarubber tubes from his pocket, he screwed them into the sides of the aperture, and then placed the two ends to his ears. He had improvised a telephone, there being a concealed wire which reached from the door to the mast, and which was in communication with the lines that passed over the building.[13]

Here, the Fenians' improvised telephone network represents a sophisticated knowledge of late nineteenth-century technology that poses a distinct threat to the British colonial order of things. Indeed, the image of telegraph wires extending out across London could be seen to mirror wider anxieties about the maintenance of sovereignty across the entire British Empire. The anti-colonial rhetoric of the Fenian 'skirmishers' undoubtedly contributed to such fears, as the following extract from the radical newspaper *The Irish World* makes clear:

> The Irish cause requires skirmishers. It requires a little band of heroes who will initiate and keep up without intermission a guerrilla warfare – men who will fly over land and sea like invisible beings – now striking the enemy in Ireland, now in India, now in England itself, as occasion may present.[14]

---

11 Fred Burnaby, *Our Radicals: A Tale of Love and Politics*, vol. 1 (London: Richard Bentley & Son, 1886), pp. 104, 106.
12 Burnaby, *Our Radicals*, vol. 1, p. 106.
13 Burnaby, *Our Radicals*, vol. 1, p. 107.
14 Cited in Townshend, *Political Violence in Ireland*, p. 120.

The trope of the anti-colonial guerrilla fighter as an 'invisible' and global enemy that can strike the empire at any point is developed further in Tom Greer's *A Modern Dædalus* (1885), a novel that further explores British political anxieties about the threat posed to its colonial sovereignty by the Fenian dynamite campaign in Britain.

A Modern Dædalus combines the emancipatory promises of progress and freedom associated with the European Enlightenment and the generic codes of science fiction and fantasy to frame the emergence of a violent, anti-colonial resistance struggle in Ireland. The first-person narrator, Jack O'Halloran, is an idealistic graduate in science and engineering from the north coast of Donegal, who invents a flying machine capable of crossing the Irish Sea to England. During his preliminary aerial excursions across the Irish countryside, O'Halloran witnesses the eviction of impoverished Irish tenant farmers from the air – a scene of oppression and dispossession that provides a crucial explanation for the subsequent land war in Ireland. Images of 'roofless' cabins and of 'the houseless wretches who had lived under it standing like statues of despair upon the roadside among their broken and worthless furniture' unsettle Jack's faith in the benefits of British rule for Ireland and prefigure his subsequent politicisation in the armed struggle against colonial rule.[15] As an educated liberal Catholic who supports the Union, O'Halloran expresses his 'deepest abhorrence' for the 'employment of dynamite [...] as the instrument of secret war and assassination' and refuses to allow the rebels to use his flying machines in the war against British colonial rule.[16] Such a clear expression of opposition to political violence gains particular significance in light of Jack's subsequent account of how his father and brothers had become involved in the land war. The family home, he explains, 'had been the scene of secret meetings, and the storehouse for an immense armoury of modern weapons, including dynamite bombs of New York manufacture'.[17] And yet at the same time, Jack is also outraged by the political oppression and dispossession of Irish tenant farmers by British landlords. Such an expression of strong moral feelings about the injustice of the land tenancy system in nineteenth-century Ireland provides a causal explanation for Jack's subsequent conversion to the political cause of the land war. In so doing, Greer counters 'the conservative and imperialist response to the dynamite campaign with his own spectacularly violent resistance narrative' – a narrative that uses the codes and conventions of science fiction to imagine a possible alternative to colonial rule.[18] After a failed attempt to persuade the British political establishment in London to assist him in making his invention available for the common good of the world, the narrator is imprisoned in the British Home Secretary's private chambers unless he agrees to manufacture flying machines for the British government. The exceptional circumstances of O'Halloran's detention

15 Tom Greer, *A Modern Dædalus* (London: Griffith & Co., 1885), p. 14.
16 Greer, *A Modern Dædalus*, p. v.
17 Greer, *A Modern Dædalus*, pp. 9–10.
18 Deaglán Ó Donghaile, *Blasted Literature: Victorian Political Fiction and the Shock of Modernism* (Edinburgh: Edinburgh University Press, 2011), p. 86.

by the Home Secretary shed significant light on the sovereign power of the British state during the nineteenth century, occurring as they do against the backdrop of a fictionalised debate in the House of Commons about the need for 'extraordinary powers' to save 'the country from imaginary dangers',[19] and the subsequent use of such powers to arrest all the Irish members of parliament following an armed insurrection in Ireland.[20] By imprisoning O'Halloran without reference to the legal principle of habeas corpus, the Home Secretary demonstrates his sovereign power as a figure that has the authority to decide upon the exception to the normal rule of law. In this way, *A Modern Dædalus* stages the contradictions of a British liberal government that claims to defend the rights and freedoms defined by its unwritten constitution even as it suspends such legal rights and freedoms for Irish subjects of the United Kingdom. By doing so, the narrator implies that the novel's utopian ending, which imagines the military defeat of the British colonial administration in Ireland by an Irish flying brigade, is a just response to an oppressive government.

If the British politicians in *A Modern Dædalus* exploit public fears that O'Halloran's 'terrible weapon might be of some use to those who were labouring for the disintegration of the Empire and the disruption of Society' in order to justify its use of coercive measures against Irish anti-colonial insurgency,[21] the narrator of Burnaby's *Our Radicals* situates this threat to British imperial sovereignty in the transnational circulation of seditious print media. At one point in the novel, official telegraphs from India announce that the Afghan insurgency against the British Empire is a 'great deal worse' than the 'Sepoy rebellion'.[22] Significantly, the narrator suggests that the rhetoric of anti-colonial resistance in Ireland had provided anti-colonial insurgents in South Asia with the inspiration for such acts of political resistance:

> Since the Indians had been taught to read English in the native schools, the sale of newspapers published in Ireland had increased enormously in the large towns throughout Hindostan. It was known that Irishmen had obtained Home Rule by means of outrages and murders, and this knowledge had induced the natives of Hindostan to try the same argument with a like object in their own case.[23]

By appropriating the language and tactics of violent, anti-colonial insurgency in Ireland, the narrator implies that the transnational circulation of newspapers enables the dissemination of anti-colonial ideas between India and Ireland. Against the global networks of colonial counter-insurgency, the narrator foregrounds the radical potential of certain travelling texts. In a similar way to the transnational dissemination of Frantz Fanon's 'Concerning Violence' among various anti-colonial movements, including (among others) the Irish Republican

---

19 Greer, *A Modern Dædalus*, p. 107.
20 Greer, *A Modern Dædalus*, pp. 145–46.
21 Greer, *A Modern Dædalus*, p. 94.
22 Burnaby, *Our Radicals*, vol. 1, p. 200.
23 Burnaby, *Our Radicals*, vol. 1, p. 201.

Army almost a century later,[24] the circulation of newspapers such as the *United Ireland* and *The Nation* seemed to pose a threat to British colonial sovereignty, both in Ireland and India. Indeed, the censorship of newspapers such as William O'Brien's *United Ireland* (1881, 1890–91) by Dublin Castle, and the suggestion by the Viceroy of India in 1877 that the British colonial government should adopt the 'Irish press law' to suppress seditious articles in the Indian press, both point towards a wider fear or anxiety in the British political establishment about the power of the Irish national press/print media to promote and disseminate anti-colonial feelings.[25]

In Burnaby's narrative of counter-insurgency, however, the technological literacy and organisational skills of the Irish revolutionaries are not matched by the methods they use to recruit freedom fighters in the armed struggle against British colonialism. Indeed, the novel suggests that it is only through kidnapping and blackmail that the revolutionaries are able to persuade people to participate in acts of political violence against the British Empire. One of the leading Fenian skirmishers, Maggie, is presented as a fearless anti-hero who carries out a daring attack on the *City of Rome*, a British ship carrying troops and arms to Dublin, and attempts to poison Sir Richard Digby, a leading figure in the British political establishment. After deciding to abandon this assassination, however, we subsequently learn that Maggie's commitment to the political cause of Irish independence was obtained through the kidnapping of her child, and by a threatening message she received from the chief of the Fenian organisation threatening to kill her kidnapped child if she did not 'fulfil [her] contract'.[26] By equating the Irish revolutionaries' tactics of political organisation with such acts of criminality and terror, this fictional representation serves to discredit the revolutionaries' political cause.

The narrator's framing of the Irish revolutionaries as criminals is not only consistent with the broader narrative of counter-insurgency that structures *Our Radicals*, but also contributes to the argument in favour of martial law that runs throughout the novel. In response to reports of kidnappings and extortion associated with the Fenians, the police chief, Metrale, states to one of his inspectors, 'There is only one way to stamp out secret societies and that is by force; but then that, you know, the Prime Minister says is no remedy'.[27] Against the liberal policies of the government represented in the novel by Prime Minister Cumbermore, figures such as Metrale, Sir Richard Digby and Lord Cromer press for repressive measures to defeat the Irish revolutionaries. In this way, the novel participates in broader political debates about the use of repressive legislation against Irish revolutionaries during the second half of

24 See Richard English, *Armed Struggle: A History of the IRA* (London: Macmillan, 2003), pp. 197, 234, 345.
25 See Susan A. Rosenkranz, 'Breathing Disaffection: The Impact of Irish Nationalist Journalism on India's Native Press', *South East Review of Asian Studies* (2005). Available at <www.uky.edu/Centers/Asia/SECAAS/Seras/2005/Rosenkrantz.htm>.
26 Burnaby, *Our Radicals*, vol. 2, p. 171.
27 Burnaby, *Our Radicals*, vol. 1, p. 56.

the nineteenth century. The civilian deaths caused by the bombing of Clerken-
well Prison in London in 1867, for instance, had spread public fear of 'Fenian
terrorism' and exacerbated ethnic discrimination against the Irish population
in Britain.[28] It was in the context of such public fears in Britain and Ireland that
the British government moved to introduce new emergency powers. Although
the rule of law continued to be respected in England during the Fenian crisis, it
is worth noting that the Home Secretary, Benjamin Disraeli, had discussed the
suspension of habeas corpus with the Prime Minister Lord Derby, following the
news of an attempted plot on Queen Victoria's life.[29] But in Ireland the situation was quite different. The Earl of Mayo proposed a bill to renew the Habeas
Corpus Suspension (Ireland) Act in 1868 on the grounds that

> there is not a man in Ireland really anxious for the peace and wellbeing of
> the country who does not know that an absolute necessity exists for this
> measure, and who would not experience something like a feeling of dismay
> if he thought the House would not continue it for a certain time longer.[30]

The rhetoric of necessity and public safety that the Earl of Mayo invoked to
justify the suspension of habeas corpus in Ireland also underpins the narrative
of counter-insurgency in Burnaby's *Our Radicals*. At one point, Metrale suggests
that the British police should be empowered to 'Treat Ireland as Cromwell
treated her' so that they can defeat the secret societies.[31] This reference to
Oliver Cromwell's repressive policies in seventeenth-century Ireland prefigures
the *coup d'état* which Lord Cromer leads against the British liberal government
in an attempt to restore law and order in Britain and Ireland. Like Metrale,
Digby lends support to Cromer's proposed use of martial law when he argues
that 'if, before the leaders of the Irish rebellion steeped themselves to the lips
in treason, martial law had been proclaimed, the Fenian movement would have
been long ago at an end'.[32] In saying this, Digby contributes to the exceptional
rhetoric of emergency law which justifies the violent means of military measures
with reference to the specific end of repressing the 'Fenian movement'. This
means–end relationship between Irish nationalist violence and British counter-
insurgency suggests that the criminal methods of the Fenian movement are the
cause of the *coup d'état*, and effaces the longer history of British rule in Ireland.
As an example of the literary prose of counter-insurgency in late nineteenth-
century Ireland, *Our Radicals* ultimately reinforces the necessity for repressive
measures – in spite of liberal anxieties about the implications of such a political strategy for British parliamentary democracy. In so doing, the novel also
sheds light on the logic of inclusive exclusion that underpins the British Liberal
government's policies in Ireland.

28 See Jenkins, *The Fenian Problem*.
29 William Devereux Jones, 'A Plot to Kill the Queen', *New York Historical Quarterly*, 51/4
    (1967), pp. 311–25 (15).
30 *Hansard HC*, vol. 190, col. 783 (14 February 1868).
31 Burnaby, *Our Radicals*, vol. 1, p. 83.
32 Burnaby, *Our Radicals*, vol. 1, pp. 126–27.

Narratives of Law, Violence and Counter-insurgency
during the Irish War of Independence

The contribution that narratives of counter-insurgency such as *Our Radicals* make to the legitimation of the British government's repressive policies in Ireland find a parallel in later narratives of policing and detection, such as the Blackwood's anthology, *Tales of the R.I.C.* (1921). Originally serialised in *Blackwood's Magazine* in 1921,[33] these stories offer a fictionalised account of the historical experience of the Irish war of independence from the local perspective of Ballybor, a fictional town in the west of Ireland. In the terms of positivist historiography, *Tales of the R.I.C.* may seem to have limited value as a reliable historical source.[34] Yet if we trace the ways in which the techniques of policing during the Irish war of independence are narrativised in this collection, it is possible to see how the prose of counter-insurgency worked to legitimate British sovereignty in Ireland during a time of emergency.

Focalised through the consciousness of Blake, a local Inspector in the Royal Irish Constabulary, each of these linked stories outlines the techniques of counter-insurgency that the Royal Irish Constabulary mobilised against the Irish Republican Army. In so doing, the stories recall earlier narratives of British policing in colonial Ireland, such as Robert Curtis's *The Irish Police Officer* (1861), *Curiosities of Detection* (1862) and *The History of the Royal Irish Constabulary* (1871). Like *Tales of the R.I.C.*, the short stories that constitute *The Irish Police Officer* and *Curiosities of Detection* are written from the point of view of a police officer in rural Ireland, and detail scenes of poverty, informal moneylending, lawlessness and criminality. Yet if, as the title page of *The Irish Police Officer* announces, these stories are 'founded on remarkable trials in Ireland', they tell us little about the colonial rule of law in nineteenth-century Ireland. By depicting crimes such as violent robbery, cattle rustling and murder in abstraction from the socio-economic conditions of poverty and dispossession in mid-nineteenth-century Ireland, the stories reinforce cultural stereotypes of the rural Irish peasantry as violent, uncivilised and lacking a coherent political consciousness. In 'The Sea Coast Station', for example, the narrator makes reference to threatening letters sent to local landlords from Ribbon men, but offers no account of either the political aims or the political organisation of this group. Instead, much of the story focuses on the apprehension and trial of a criminal gang who are sentenced

---

33 'The Informer', 'On the Run', 'The Landing of Arms' and 'Red Cross' were first published in *Blackwoods Magazine*, 209/1266 (April 1921), pp. 407–44; 'The R.M.', 'An Outlaw', 'The Stranger within the Gates' and 'Mr Briggs' Island' first appeared in *Blackwoods Magazine*, 209/1267 (May 1921), pp. 668–93; 'The Reward of Loyalty', 'Poteen' and 'The Mayor's Conscience' appeared in *Blackwoods Magazine*, 210/1269 (July 1921), pp. 1–24; 'A Brutal Murder', 'Seal Island' and 'A Family Affair' appeared in *Blackwoods Magazine*, 209/1270 (August 1921), pp. 199–220; 'The American Nurse', 'Father John', 'The Bog Cemetery' and 'A Jew in Gaelic Clothing' were published in *Blackwoods Magazine*, 209/1271 (September 1921), pp. 289–318; and 'Mountain Warfare' and 'The Great Round Up' appeared in *Blackwoods Magazine*, 210/1273 (November 1921), pp. 610–38.

34 See Emery, 'The Author of Tales of the *R.I.C.*', pp. 226–28.

to death for murder and robbery.[35] In a similar vein, *Tales of the R.I.C.* presents the acts of political violence planned and executed by the Irish Republican Army between 1920 and 1921 as 'sporadic' acts of 'common robbery' carried out by 'hooligan shop boys and farmer[s'] sons'.[36] What is more, by questioning the violent techniques employed by the IRA, the tales seek to challenge the emancipatory claims of the Republican movement to represent the interests of the people.[37] In an account of 'terrorist outrages' committed in Clonnalla, the narrator describes how these 'revolting and apparently purposeless murders are instigated by the I.R.A., but nevertheless they are carried out by the peasants in most cases […] Under a determined leader they appear to take kindly to political murder'.[38] By distinguishing between the IRA leadership and the local peasantry, the narrator implies that the peasantry lack a coherent sense of political subjectivity, and obey the will of the Republican leadership out of fear rather than commitment to a political programme of revolutionary struggle.

Such representations of the IRA 'Reign of Terror' during the Irish war of independence serve to disavow the violent methods of counter-insurgency, which emergency regulations such as the Defence of the Realm Acts empowered the armed Royal Irish Constabulary to employ. The story 'On the Run' mentions the recruitment of ex-British army privates and tells of how 'the Government had recruited them from all the prisons and asylums in England'. Significant also is the narrator's passing reference to the government's declaration of martial law in the counties that surround the village in which the story is set: 'to crown all, the Government had had the audacity to put several counties within easy reach of Ballyfrack under martial law'.[39] These minor details may seem marginal to the narrative of counter-insurgency at the centre of 'On the Run', which focuses on the attempt to capture John O'Hara, an IRA rebel on the run from the colonial authorities. Yet it was the increasing militarisation of the police, the authorisation of internment without trial, the designation of certain counties as military areas, selective assassination and the military execution of members of the Irish population deemed to be rebels following the Easter Rising of 1916 that precipitated such acts of anti-colonial violence.[40] As Colm Campbell has argued, 'the outbreak and continuation of the First World War

---

35 Robert Curtis, 'The Sea-Coast Station', in idem, *Curiosities of Detection; or, the Seacoast Station, and Other Tales* (London: Ward & Lock, 1862), pp. 9–82.
36 *Tales of the R.I.C.*, pp. 281–82.
37 Consider, for example, Ernie O'Malley's claim that the Volunteers were fighting a 'people's war'. Ernie O'Malley, *Raids and Rallies* (Dublin: Anvil, 1982), p. 1.
38 *Tales of the R.I.C.*, p. 215.
39 *Tales of the R.I.C.*, p. 21. The narrator may be referring here to the Lord Lieutenant's imposition of martial law in Cork, Tipperary, Limerick and Kerry on 11 December 1920. See Colm Campbell, *Emergency Law in Ireland 1918–1925* (Oxford: Oxford University Press, 1994), pp. 30–36.
40 See Charles Townshend, *The British Campaign in Ireland, 1919–1921: The Development of Political and Military Policies* (London: Oxford University Press, 1975), pp. 40–46; Campbell, *Emergency Law in Ireland 1918–1925*, pp. 8–148; and Townshend, *Political Violence in Ireland*, pp. 303–13, 325.

led to the enactment of a mass of emergency legislation, much of it operative throughout Britain and Ireland'.[41] Specifically, the Defence of the Realm Acts of 1914 and 1915 granted the British military wide powers to arrest, detain, try and kill the civilian population in military courts.[42]

Many of the stories that form *Tales of the R.I.C.* sought to challenge the repressive image of the British colonial administration in Ireland that prevailed both in the Irish nationalist press and the mainstream British liberal press by focusing on the violent tactics of the IRA. Against such narratives, nationalist memoirs and literary texts drew attention to the techniques of state violence that emergency legislation granted to the British colonial state in Ireland. In *On Another Man's Wound* (1936), the Irish revolutionary Ernie O'Malley recounts how the executions of the leaders of the Easter Rising 'had caused bitter feeling, and the arrests and the strict enforcement of martial law helped to intensify it'.[43] The violent forms of state repression that martial law enabled in the months following the Easter Rising are made palpable in O'Malley's subsequent account of the brutal techniques of torture and interrogation that the British army and the Royal Irish Constabulary used to re-assert colonial sovereignty on the bodies of Irish rebels. During his own interrogation in the 'Interview Room' at Dublin Castle in 1920, O'Malley recounts how Captain Hardy of the R.I.C. attempted to burn his face with a red hot poker and how Hardy fired his pistol directly at O'Malley's head.[44] Although the pistol was loaded with a blank cartridge, the fact that Captain Hardy had led O'Malley to believe that the gun was loaded with a live round of ammunition clearly illustrates the way in which emergency laws empowered the Royal Irish Constabulary to threaten and torture suspected Irish rebels with impunity. This is not to suggest that the British legal regime in Ireland during the Irish war of independence worked to preserve British sovereignty, however. Against the lawful violence of the British state, which sought to repress the armed struggle for independence, O'Malley uses the techniques of life-writing to dramatise the ways in which the Irish volunteers subverted the authority of the police and the military. By juxtaposing quotations from the Defence of the Realm Act and the military orders associated with martial law with accounts of the organisational structure and tactics of the Irish Volunteers,[45] O'Malley evokes an image of Britain's waning political sovereignty in Ireland – an image which is exemplified in the following sentence: 'Their campaign of terror was defeating itself; it had made conservatives liberals and had treated the lukewarm as extreme; it had affected the discipline of the army and police'.[46]

If O'Malley's memoir foregrounds the ways in which emergency legislation provided a quasi-legal framework through which the British state attempted

41 Campbell, *Emergency Law in Ireland 1918–1925*, p. 9.
42 Campbell, *Emergency Law in Ireland 1918–1925*, pp. 8–27.
43 Ernie O'Malley, *On Another Man's Wound* (Dublin: Anvil, 2002 [1936]), p. 51.
44 O'Malley, *On Another Man's Wound*, pp. 277–79.
45 O'Malley, *On Another Man's Wound*, pp. 71, 318–19.
46 O'Malley, *On Another Man's Wound*, p. 362.

to consolidate its political authority in Ireland, Yeats explores the way in which violence became generalised in the historical moment of the Irish war of independence. In 'Nineteen Hundred and Nineteen' (1919), Yeats's poetic speaker raises questions about the wider historical and philosophical significance of the violence associated with the Black and Tans. As the speaker declares in the fourth verse of the first section,

> Now days are dragon-ridden, the nightmare
> Rides upon sleep: a drunken soldiery
> Can leave the mother, murdered at her door,
> To crawl in her own blood, and go scot-free [...][47]

We have already seen how Derrida calls into question the clear distinction between the beast and the sovereign. In this quoted extract, the image of a present 'ridden' by monstrous beasts inverts such a dichotomy. For if the 'soldiery' is conventionally associated with the defence of sovereignty, in this poem the repressive measures that are marshalled against 'the mother [...] murdered at her door' by 'a drunken soldiery' clearly destabilises any clear distinction between the violence of the sovereign and the subjects it designates as enemies or beasts.

Significantly, Yeats's reference to the reprehensible actions of a 'drunken soldiery' in this quoted extract is based on the random shooting of Ellen Quinn by the Black and Tans in Kiltartan, County Galway in November 1920.[48] This reference to the violent excesses of British counter-insurgency in Ireland may appear to situate the poem in the particular context of the Irish revolutionary struggle. As Michael Wood points out, the title 'Nineteen Hundred and Nineteen' evokes a year in which two members of the Royal Irish Constabulary were killed, the Dáil Eireann had its first meeting and the Black and Tans were deployed to counter the national liberation struggle in Ireland. It also evokes the year of the Spartacist Uprising in Germany and the massacre of peaceful protestors at Amritsar in India by British colonial forces.[49] Yet, in its comparison of the lost art objects of ancient Greece and the loss of confidence in modern institutions of civil society, Yeats's poem implies that particular acts of violence such as the unpunished murder of Ellen Quinn work to unsettle predominant liberal assumptions about state violence as an exception to the British rule of law in early twentieth-century Ireland. The 'ornamental bronze and stone', an 'ancient image made of olive wood', 'Phidias' famous ivories / And all the famous grasshoppers and bees' in the first verse evoke an ancient world that cannot be recovered.[50] Just as these objects are fragile artefacts rather than timeless objects of aesthetic beauty, so the speaker asserts that the normal rule of law is

---

47 W.B. Yeats, *The Variorum Edition of the Complete Poems of W.B. Yeats*, ed. Peter Allt and Russell K. Alspach (New York: Macmillan, 1957), p. 429, lines 25–28.

48 See Michael Wood, *Yeats and Violence* (Oxford: Oxford University Press, 2010), pp. 20–30.

49 Wood, *Yeats and Violence*, pp. 32–33.

50 Yeats, *Variorum Edition of the Complete Poems*, p. 428, lines 5–8.

a 'pretty toy' or an artificial construct.[51] In so doing, Yeats's speaker encourages readers to question the widespread view that the rule of law will protect the population from the violence of 'rogues and rascals' such as the Black and Tans.

In the mythological terms of Yeats's vision of history, the violent actions of 'rogues and rascals' unfettered by the rule of law can be accounted for by the cyclical movement of history in two thousand-year cycles that is codified in Yeats's reference to the Platonic year in the second section of the poem.[52] What is more, the reference to a mythic Irish past at the end of the poem evokes figures from Irish history such as 'That insolent fiend Robert Artisson / To whom the love-lorn Lady Kyteler brought / Bronzed peacock feathers, red combs of her cocks'.[53] If we read this reference to Lady Kyteler's love for Robert Artisson as a codified reference to the sacrificial devotion of women revolutionaries such as Maud Gonne and Constance Markiewicz to the nationalist cause, it is possible to trace a profound ambivalence with the politics of sacrificial violence in Yeats's use of Irish history. As Rob Doggett puts it,

> If blood sacrifice is the ultimate goal of cultural nationalism, blood sacrifice is what Yeats discovers in this journey back into Ireland's folk past, but in this poem it is a sacrifice utterly devoid of heroism: the sacrifice of animals to an evil spirit, a fitting commentary on an Ireland where human lives continue to be sacrificed for historical causes.[54]

What the return of 'the worst rogues and rascals' in 'Nineteen Hundred and Nineteen' crucially foregrounds, however, is the lawful violence of British counter-insurgency during the Irish war of independence.[55] Indeed, the rogues in 'Nineteen Hundred and Nineteen' are not the IRA gunmen of *Tales of the R.I.C.* or the heroic volunteers of *On Another Man's Wound*; on the contrary, they are the 'drunken soldiery' to whom British sovereignty has been delegated.

Sacrificial Violence and Ireland's Tradition of the Oppressed

Yeats's representation of violence in 'Nineteen Hundred and Nineteen' may recall Marx-Longuet's claim that 'the whole history of English rule in Ireland shows that a state of emergency is the rule and that the application of the constitution is the exception'.[56] In this respect, the poem implies that violence is immanent to colonial rule, and its techniques of governmentality. Yet such a reading would be to overlook Yeats's complex relationship to what Benjamin

---

51 Yeats, *Variorum Edition of the Complete Poems*, p. 428, line 9.
52 For further discussion of the Platonic year in 'Nineteen Hundred and Nineteen', see Wood, *Yeats and Violence*, pp. 48–86.
53 Yeats, *Variorum Edition of the Complete Poems*, p. 433, lines 128–29.
54 Rob Doggett, 'Writing out (of) Chaos: Constructions of History in Yeats's "Nineteen Hundred and Nineteen" and "Meditations in Time of Civil War"', *Twentieth-Century Literature*, 47/2 (2001), p. 151.
55 See Doggett, 'Writing out (of) Chaos', p. 145.
56 Jenny Marx-Longuet 'Articles on the Irish Question'.

has called the tradition of the oppressed in the context of colonial and postcolonial Ireland. We have already seen in the introduction how the tradition
of the oppressed can be taken to mean both an 'alternate tradition of those
excluded from the canons of "high" culture' and the 'critical resources' and the
'suppressed, subversive moments' *within* high culture.[57] That Yeats contributed
to the Irish literary revival through his use of Celtic mythology in nationalist plays
such as *Cathleen Ni Houlihan* (1902) and critically engaged with ancient Greek
and Roman culture to articulate the emergence of a suppressed and subversive
rupture in history in poems such as 'The Second Coming' (1920) can be taken to
exemplify both senses of the tradition of the oppressed. Yet it is important to
note that Yeats's writing is also profoundly ambivalent about the implications of
what might be called the tradition of the oppressed in Ireland during and after
decolonisation. On the one hand, Yeats, in plays such as *Cathleen ni Houlihan*
(1902) and poems such as 'The Rose Tree' (1916) can be seen to contribute to
the rhetoric of blood sacrifice that was central to the Irish Romantic tradition of
revolutionary nationalism. In the political world of *Cathleen ni Houlihan*, Ireland
is framed as an old mother who through a combination of charm and magic
persuades Michael Gillane, a young man who is about to get married, to sacrifice his individual life and private happiness for the collective national political
struggle against British colonial rule. Read as a national allegory, *Cathleen ni
Houlihan* clearly illustrates Yeats's contribution to what Conor Cruise O'Brien
has called 'the conception of history as a series of blood sacrifices enacted in
every generation'.[58] Such a trope of sacrifice is further evidenced in the dialogue
between Pearse and Connolly about the power of their 'own red blood' to
restore the life and spirit of the nation in 'The Rose Tree'.[59] On the other hand,
even Yeats's most well-known political poems such as 'Easter 1916' (1916) seem
to recoil from the violent means by which decolonisation was to be achieved.
The repetition of the oxymoronic phrase 'a terrible beauty is born' and the
image of a symbolic 'stone' in 'the midst' of a 'living stream' raises doubts about
the efficacy of anti-colonial violence and sacrifice in the foundational myths of
the emergent nation. Indeed, for David Lloyd, the 'stone' performs a double
function in 'Easter 1916': 'as [a] gravestone on which the names of the national
martyrs are inscribed' and as a 'foundation-stone' in the narrative of the nation.
In this complex scene of writing, Yeats's figuration of violence could be seen to
anticipate Hannah Arendt's concern (mentioned in the Introduction) that 'the
means' of violent anti-colonial resistance will 'overwhelm the end' of national
liberation, and violence will be introduced 'into the whole body politic'.[60]

The ambivalence about the politics of blood sacrifice in 'Easter 1916' points
to a more complex approach to decolonisation that Edward Said attempts to
trace in *Culture and Imperialism* (1994). For Said, Yeats's writing mirrors Fanon's

---

57 McCole, *Walter Benjamin*, pp. 304–5.
58 Conor Cruise O'Brien, 'An Unhealthy Intersection', *New Review*, 2/16 (1975), pp. 3–8 (5–6).
59 Yeats, *Variorum Edition of the Complete Poems*, p. 202, line 17.
60 Arendt, *On Violence*, p. 80.

account of decolonisation in *The Wretched of the Earth*: it proceeds, in other words, from a period of nativism and cultural revival, in which Yeats celebrates ancient Irish myths as a resource for promoting national consciousness and violent anti-colonial insurgency, to a period of critical reflection on 'the need to balance violent force with an exigent political and organizational process'.[61] Said's observations on the politics of Yeats's poetics have prompted critics such as Doggett to identify a poetry that responds to the chaos and violence of Ireland's decolonisation, and Robert Spencer to trace a cosmopolitan ethos in Yeats's late work.[62] Said's reading of Yeats after Fanon also raises important questions about how Yeats negotiates the nationalist politics of sacrificial violence, and what the implications of such sacrificial violence are for Ireland's postcolonial sovereignty during and after a period of decolonisation. As I go on to suggest, Yeats's dramatic writing on the hunger strike in *The King's Threshold* (1904) helps to make sense of the complex relationship between sovereignty, sacrificial violence and decolonisation – a relationship which was also replayed in the Republican hunger strikes in Northern Ireland during the 1970s and 1980s. What is more, Yeats's reflections on sacrificial violence in the context of decolonisation are profoundly shaped by gendered constructions of the nation and national liberation struggles, as we will see. Before addressing the gendered determinants of the tradition of the oppressed in colonial Ireland, however, the following section considers the necropolitical logic of sacrificial forms of resistance such as hunger strikes.

Sacrifice, Necropolitics and the Hunger Strike

In his essay 'Necropolitics', Achille Mbembe reframes European critical theories of sovereignty and biopolitics by tracing the history of biopolitics and sovereignty in the colonial context. Georges Bataille's reflections on sovereignty and sacrifice are particularly important for Mbembe because they reveal how death and violence are also constitutive of sovereign power in the European colony.[63] What is crucial for Mbembe is that the use of sovereign political violence defined the horizon for political resistance within the European colony. This is clearly different from saying that violent, anti-colonial resistance is a causal response to particular acts of colonial terror or that counter-insurgency is a response to violent, anti-colonial insurgency. The problem with Mbembe's theory, though, is that it seems to suggest that a violent struggle to the death is the only form of political resistance available to the colonised. By privileging the Palestinian suicide bomber as an exemplary figure of the necropolitical, Mbembe seems to overlook other forms of non-violent resistance to colonial sovereignty such as

61 Edward W. Said, *Culture and Imperialism* (London: Vintage, 1994), p. 284.
62 Rob Doggett, *Deep Rooted Things: Empire and Nation in the Poetry and Drama of William Butler Yeats* (Notre Dame, IN: University of Notre Dame Press, 2006); Robert Spencer, *Cosmopolitan Criticism and Postcolonial Literature* (Basingstoke: Palgrave Macmillan, 2011).
63 See Stephen Morton, 'Terrorism, Orientalism and Imperialism', *Wasafiri*, 22/2 (2007), pp. 36–42.

hunger strikes. Like suicide bombing, the practice of hunger strikes entails a sacrificial logic in which the colonised subject sought to publicly defy the colonial sovereign's power over the bodily life and death of the colonised. 'What is [...] performed in the hunger strike', Ewa Plonowska Ziarek explains, 'is the collapse of the distinctions between sovereignty and bare life, will and passivity, potentiality and actuality, the struggle for freedom and the risk of self-annihilation'.[64] Yet, unlike suicide bombing, the hunger strike does not involve the taking of other human lives. In the context of anti-colonial insurgency in Ireland and India, self-starvation performs a symbolic act of political resistance that involves the subject of colonial rule reclaiming sovereign power over their own body.

The political significance of such a performative act has been further drawn out in W.B. Yeats's play *The King's Threshold* (1904) and Steve McQueen's film *Hunger* (2008). Although produced in quite different historical contexts, these two texts shed significant light on the way in which the 'spectacle of starving flesh' worked to challenge the sovereignty of British colonial power in Ireland.[65] First performed in 1904, *The King's Threshold* can be seen to prefigure the hunger strikes of Republican prisoners, such as the Mayor of Cork, Terence McSwiney, during the Irish war of independence. Indeed, McSwiney's death on 25 October 1920 in Brixton prison after 74 days of hunger strike prompted Yeats to revise the ending of the play, as he explains in a letter to Lady Gregory: 'my new tragic ending [is ...] a great improvement & much more topical – as it suggests the Lord Mayor of Cork'.[66] In so doing, Yeats can be seen to adapt his use of the Irish cultural past to the contingencies of contemporary political struggle in Ireland. For while the 1904 edition of the play has the main protagonist survive, in the 1922 edition he starves to death. The play focuses on the struggle of an ancient Irish poet called Seanchan, who starves himself as an act of resistance to King Guaire's declaration that poets can no longer dine at the table of the king. Seanchan declares that dining at the king's table is 'the poet's right / Established at the establishment of the world'.[67] In response to Seanchan's attempt to claim the rights to which he feels entitled, the king performs his own sovereignty in the following speech act:

> I said that I was King, and that all rights
> Had their original fountain in some king,
> And that it was the men who ruled the world,
> And not the men who sang to it, who should sit
> Where there was the most honour.[68]

---

64 Ewa Plonowska Ziarek, 'Bare Life on Strike', *South Atlantic Quarterly*, 107/1 (2008), p. 100.
65 Maud Ellmann, *The Hunger Artists: Starving, Writing, and Imprisonment* (Cambridge, MA: Harvard University Press, 1993), p. 14.
66 Cited in W.B. Yeats, *The King's Threshold, Manuscript Materials*, ed. Declan Kiely (Ithaca, NY and London: Cornell University Press, 2005), p. liii.
67 W.B. Yeats, *The Variorum Edition of the Plays of W.B. Yeats*, ed. Russell K. Alspach (London: Macmillan, 1966), p. 259, lines 44–45.
68 Yeats, *The Variorum Edition of the Plays*, p. 260, lines 46–50.

The plot of *The King's Threshold* has prompted critics such as Maud Ellmann to read the play as a parable which implies that 'the artist has to starve in order to perfect the work of art'.[69] More importantly, however, Yeats's alteration to the play's ending demonstrates how the performative acts of the hunger striker stage the limits of sovereignty. For just as Seanchan's act of resistance challenges the 'threshold' of the King's sovereignty by suggesting that poetry and writing are crucial to the foundations of sovereignty, so Republican hunger strikers framed their act of self-starvation as a challenge to the order of colonial sovereignty by refusing to allow the British state to exercise its power over the life and death of its colonial subjects.

Such a struggle between the sovereign power of the colonial state and the precarious life of the colonised is powerfully conveyed in McQueen's cinematic representation of the hunger strike of the Republican prisoner Bobby Sands in *Hunger*. In one scene, a fixed, close-up shot of Sands's barely conscious, emaciated body in a prison hospital bed is juxtaposed with the recorded voice of British Prime Minister Margaret Thatcher. The recording is extracted from Thatcher's speech at Stormont Castle, Belfast on 28 May 1981, which was broadcast in a BBC radio news report the same day:

> And faced now with the failure of their discredited cause, the men of violence have chosen in recent months to play what may well be their last card. They have turned their violence against themselves through the prison hunger strike to death.[70]

The reiteration of the archival recording of Thatcher's voice in the soundtrack could be read as a commentary on the political significance of Sands's revolting body in the cinematic frame. Thatcher's framing of the hunger strike as the Irish Republican prisoners' 'last card' emphasises the political dimension of the hunger strike as a strategy in the struggle against colonial sovereignty. More than this, the juxtaposition of Thatcher's disembodied voice and the powerful image of Bobby Sands's moribund body calls the truth claims of Thatcher's speech into question. By replaying the voice that deemed the hunger strikers 'men of violence', in other words, the film encourages viewers to read Thatcher's voice as a synecdoche for British colonial sovereignty in Northern Ireland. To paraphrase the words of Derrida in *The Beast and the Sovereign*, the scene calls attention to a 'troubling resemblance' between the voice of colonial sovereignty and the body of the colonial subject that the sovereign deems to be violent, monstrous and terrifying. Indeed, as Allen Feldman explains, the Republican hunger strikes were presented as a symbolic reversal of colonial sovereignty: 'The performance of the hunger striker would stage the abuse and violence of the [sovereign] in the eviscerated flesh of the dying protester'.[71]

---

69 Ellmann, *The Hunger Artists*, p. 59.
70 Margaret Thatcher, 'Speech at Stormont Castle Lunch', 28 May 1981. Available at <www.margaretthatcher.org/document/104657>. Accessed 18 July 2011.
71 Allen Feldman, *Formations of Violence: The Narrative of the Body and Political Terror in*

Such a resemblance may be to overlook the gendered determinants of sovereignty and sacrificial violence in the context of Republican struggles for a United Ireland in the six counties of Northern Ireland. For if McQueen's reframing of Thatcher's recorded speech is read as a synecdoche for colonial sovereignty, the recording is also marked by a gendered voice which emasculates the 'men of violence' by defining their political 'cause' as a failure, and by suggesting that 'the prison hunger strike to death' is a sign of their defeat. A consideration of the gendered determinants of sacrificial violence and anti-colonial insurgency is also crucial for understanding both the meaning and the limitations of the tradition of the oppressed in the context of colonial and postcolonial Ireland, as I suggest in the conclusion. Before doing so, however, a more detailed consideration of the sacrificial logic of the Republican hunger strikes is in order.

The representation of the Republican hunger strikes of the 1970s and early 1980s as a form of Christ-like sacrifice in political pamphlets and the murals of the Catholic neighbourhoods of North and West Belfast has a history that can be traced to the writing of Irish intellectuals such as Pearse.[72] In the final address delivered to his pupils at St Enda's School, for instance, Pearse drew explicit parallels between the sacrifice of Christ and the sacrifice of Irish rebels during the Easter rising: 'It had taken the blood of the Son of God to redeem the world. It would take the blood of the sons of Ireland to redeem Ireland'.[73] In a similar vein, Sands's writing draws on biblical images of sacrifice. His comparison of his own predicament during the hunger strike in Long Kesh to that of Christ walking to Calvary,[74] for instance, clearly exemplifies the significance of religious tropes for framing 'the cause of Irish nationalism in the spectacle of starving flesh'.[75] Such analogies with Christian notions of sacrifice may have provided the Republican movement for Irish national self-determination with a powerful cultural symbol of political resistance in the specific historical contexts of Dublin in 1916 and Northern Ireland in the 1970s and 1980s. But this is not to suggest that Christian notions of sacrifice were the cause of Republican hunger strikes or violent forms of insurgency. On the contrary, as Begoña Aretxaga has argued, the 'etiology of IRA violence […] belongs more to the history of British colonization in Ireland and, in its contemporary fashion,

---

Northern Ireland (Chicago: University of Chicago Press, 1991), p. 236.

72 See Begoña Aretxaga, *States of Terror: Begoña Aretxaga's Essays* (Reno, NV: Center for Basque Studies, University of Nevada, 2005), pp. 51–52, and S.W. Gilley 'Pearse's Sacrifice: Christ and Cuchulain Crucified and Risen in the Easter Rising, 1916', in S.W. Sykes (ed.), *Sacrifice and Redemption: Durham Essays in Theology* (Cambridge: Cambridge University Press, 1991), pp. 218–34.

73 Padraic Pearse, *The Story of a Success, Being a Record of St. Enda's College September 1908 to Easter 1916*, ed. Desmond Ryan (Dublin and London: Mansuel, 1917), p. 216. See also Gilley, 'Pearse's Sacrifice', pp. 218–34.

74 Bobby Sands, *Skylark Sing Your Lonely Song: An Anthology of the Writings of Bobby Sands* (Dublin: Mercier, 1982), p. 64.

75 Ellmann, *The Hunger Artists*, p. 14.

to the peculiarly sectarian form that colonization took in the North'.[76] Indeed, it is significant that the Republican prisoners themselves regarded the 1981 hunger strike as 'a modality of insurrectionary violence in which they deployed their bodies as weapons'.[77]

Yet in this use of the starving body as a technique of resistance to colonial sovereignty, the rhetoric and imagery of the Irish Republican narrative also raises wider questions about the place of sacrifice and violence in the political foundations of postcolonial Ireland. To what extent does the Republican nationalist tradition ultimately seek to replace the violence of colonial sovereignty with the sacrificial violence of nationalist myth? And in what ways might this myth of blood sacrifice become normalised in the dominant national narrative after decolonisation? It is concerns such as these that Richard Kearney has expressed in a discussion of the national mythology of the IRA:

> By means of a mythological repetition of the 'past', the nationalist leaders, it may be argued, sought to redeem Ireland. Incarcerated in a history of colonial oppression, the evangelists of the Provisional Republic appealed to a prehistorical mythic power whereby their present paralysis might be miraculously transcended. By *repeating* the names and deeds of the ancient heroes and martyrs of Erin they sought to resolve her sacred destiny. The only way to redeem the nation seemed to be the negation of present history in favour of some Holy Beginning, some eternally recurring Past. And this recurrence of the primordial Spirit of Erin would be brought about, following the laws of myth, by blood-sacrifice.[78]

The myth of sacrifice may furnish the Republican tradition with a counterpoint to the 'history of colonial oppression', but, as Kearney suggests, it re-inscribes a founding structure of violence in which the hunger striker's life is sacrificed for the freedom of the Irish nation. The problem with Kearney's critique of Republican narratives of sacrifice, though, is that it falls back on a dichotomy between a religious notion of sacrifice and a secular notion of politics as a struggle for sovereignty that overlooks the way in which the modern notion of the political is itself predicated on a notion of sacrificial or sacred violence that has been repressed. As Agamben has argued, the sacred rituals of violence that are practised according to certain social rules and norms furnish 'society and its ungrounded legislation with the fiction of a beginning'.[79] What distinguishes the philosophical category of the human from the animal for Agamben is the sacred exclusion of a specific form of life from the political category of the human community – a move that is repeated in modern formations of polit-

---

76 Aretxaga, *States of Terror*, p. 49.
77 Feldman, *Formations of Violence*, p. 220.
78 Richard Kearney, *Transitions: Narratives in Modern Irish Culture* (Manchester: Manchester University Press, 1988), pp. 212–13.
79 Giorgio Agamben, *Language and Death: The Place of Negativity*, trans. Karen E. Pinkus and Michael Hardt (Minneapolis, MN: University of Minnesota Press, 1991), p. 64.

ical sovereignty. This is not a simple exclusion, for, as Justin Clemens points out, 'what is excluded from human political life is precisely still included by its exclusion, that is, by being included as an *exception*'.[80] In Agamben's argument,

> politics would seem to be an almost religious ritual of sorts, a continuous reenacting of the exclusive inclusion performed upon the self in order to constitute some sense of sovereign being in relation to the others (both persons and animals) surrounding this newly formed 'humanity'.[81]

In the political space of the colony this sacred foundation of the political is particularly pronounced. Fanon's claim that the settler regards the native 'in zoological terms' takes on a new significance when it is considered in relation to Agamben's account of the sacrificial relation of inclusive exclusion that underpins the foundations of the political.[82] What the 'zoological terms' of the settler's gaze reveals is not merely the racialised logic of looking in the political space of the colony; this zoological regime of vision also sheds light on the very grounds upon which the political space of the colony is formed.

In the terms of the Republican nationalist narrative of the British colonial state, it is precisely the sacrificial logic of inclusive exclusion that underpins predominant cultural representations of the Republican movement as 'men of violence' or barbarian figures that are beyond the law. And it is precisely this sacrificial logic that the hunger strikes sought to counter through an act of self-starvation that refuses the power of the sovereign over the bodily life and death of the subject. The sacrificial politics of the hunger strike also has a significant gendered dimension – as Kearney's reference to the nationalist trope of Erin implies. If the figure of the male hunger striker tries to play with the sacrificial law of sovereignty in order to subvert it, the figure of the female hunger striker as a bearer of reproductive life raises important questions about the place of women and the gendered body in Agamben's formulation of the relationship between *zoe* and *bios*, necropolitics and biopolitics. To what extent does Agamben's universalising use of the masculine form *homo sacer* to describe all human life that is subject to the violence of sovereign power ignore the significance of the gendered body in the foundation of sovereign power and in challenges to political sovereignty? And in what ways might the sovereign's inclusive exclusion of bare life in the political order also work to produce the subject of sovereignty as a gendered subject? A consideration of the representation of women hunger strikers can help us to think through and beyond questions such as these, as the following section suggests.

---

80 Justin Clemens, 'The Role of the Shifter and the Problem of Reference in the Thought of Giorgio Agamben', in Justin Clemens, Nicholas Heron and Alex Murray (eds), *The Work of Giorgio Agamben: Law, Literature, Life* (Edinburgh: Edinburgh University Press, 2008), p. 53.
81 Colby Dickinson, *Agamben and Theology* (London: T&T Clarke, 2011), p. 72; Agamben, *Homo Sacer*, p. 107.
82 Fanon, *The Wretched of the Earth*, p. 7.

'My nation displaced': The Gendered Body
and Ireland's Tradition of the Oppressed

The self-fashioning and public commemoration of Irish revolutionaries and Republican soldiers as sacrificial figures may have made a significant contribution to the formation of nationalist narratives both in the Republic of Ireland and the North, which have worked to contest the sovereign power of the British government over the life and death of the Irish population. But to focus exclusively on the sacrificial logic of anti-colonial insurgency would be to ignore the gendered determinants of Republican narratives of anti-colonial struggle. We have already seen how Yeats appropriated figures such as Cathleen ni Houlihan from Celtic mythology in order to frame the Irish nation as the poor old woman or *Shan Van Vocht*. Literary critics and cultural historians such as Marjorie Howes and C.L. Innes have demonstrated how such patriarchal constructions of the Irish nation worked to efface women's voices and agency, even as such nationalist constructions served to contest British colonial constructions of a passive and feminised Irish nation 'threatened by Fenians and other Irish radicals'.[83] As Howes has argued, Yeats's engagement with Celtic myth needs to be set against imperialist stereotypes of the Irish character, exemplified in Matthew Arnold's view of the Irish in *On the Study of Celtic Literature* (1867).[84] In a broadly sympathetic critical assessment of Yeats's love poetry, Elizabeth Cullingford describes how Yeats 'reached back into prehistory to resurrect the tradition of human sacrifice to the goddess, in which sexuality is conflated with a violent death as the blood of a young male victim sinks into the receiving earth'.[85] Such myths may have 'offered Yeats female images that [...] intersected fruitfully with the icons of the contemporary suffrage campaign and informed the self-representations of women like Gonne and Markievicz'.[86] Maud Gonne's performance of Cathleen ni Houlihan in the eponymous play that was collaboratively written by Lady Gregory and W.B. Yeats at the Abbey Theatre in Dublin in 1902 certainly contributed to her public status in Ireland as a nationalist figurehead.[87] But this is not to say that such gendered tropes of sacrificial violence necessarily worked to empower Irish women after independence or to recognise Irish women's contribution to the history of anti-colonial resistance, as contemporary Irish poets such as Eavan Boland have suggested.

In her poetry and critical writing, Boland has offered an important challenge to the patriarchal constraints of Irish cultural nationalism. In 'Mise Eire', for example, the poetic speaker refuses the romantic image of Ireland

---

83   C.L. Innes, *Woman and Nation in Irish Literature and Society 1880–1935* (Hemel Hempstead: Harvester Wheatsheaf, 1993), p. 12.

84   Marjorie Howes, *Yeats's Nations: Gender, Class, and Irishness* (Cambridge: Cambridge University Press, 1996), pp. 16–43.

85   Elizabeth Cullingford, *Gender and History in Yeats's Love Poetry* (Cambridge: Cambridge University Press, 1993), p. 57.

86   Cullingford, *Gender and History*, p. 56.

87   See Innes, *Woman and Nation*, pp. 130–38.

in the following lines: 'I won't go back to it – // my nation displaced / into old dactyls'.[88] Here, the reference to the conventional metrical form of the dactyl combined with the titular allusion to Pearse's Irish language poem 'Mise Eire' ('I Am Ireland') emphasises the way in which the romantic tropes of the gendered nation that infuse the poetry of writers such as Yeats and Pearse have 'displaced' the speaker from the nation. In doing so, the speaker encourages readers to question the foreclosure of women's voices and histories that gendered metaphors of the nation produce. As Boland has argued in her prose narrative *Object Lessons* (1995), 'In availing themselves of the old convention, in using and reusing women as icons and fragments, Irish poets were not just dealing with emblems. They were also evading the real women of an actual past, women whose silence their poetry should have broken'.[89] Against this silencing of women's voices, Boland offers an important counterpoint to the tradition of the oppressed in dominant historical narratives of Irish nationalism. In so doing, Boland not only questions and challenges the meaning of 'tradition' and 'the oppressed' in postcolonial Ireland, she also raises questions about the modes of agency and political subjectivity that women produced in Ireland's national liberation struggles. As the historian Margaret Ward has suggested, Irish women's political organisations such as the Ladies' Land League were mobilised in the context of a colonial state of emergency that excluded women from the purview of British colonial law as revolutionary subjects. During the period between 31 January 1881 and August 1882 women were in effect 'outside the terms of the Coercion Act'.[90] The Protection of Person and Property (Ireland) Act of 2 March 1881 does not specify whether or not women were excluded from the terms of that statute, but the minutes of a subsequent Cabinet Meeting from October 1881 suggest that this law was enacted primarily to outlaw the Land League, and to imprison its leaders (including Charles Parnell).[91] It also seems significant that the subsequent actions of the Ladies Land League prompted Lord Lieutenant Cowper to introduce new measures to suppress the meetings and activities of the Ladies Land League.[92] It is possible to surmise from these sources that it was by virtue of women's exclusion from the legal category of criminal (as defined by the terms of the Coercion Act of 1881) that the Ladies' Land League was strategically included in the organisation of resistance to the eviction of Irish peasants from their homes in the late nineteenth century.

Such a paradoxical relation of inclusive exclusion casts some light on the gendered dimensions of anti-colonial insurgency, and the political tactics that Irish women have used in the struggle against British land policies in nineteenth-century Ireland. We have already seen how male Irish revolutionaries such as

88 Eavan Boland, *The Journey* (Manchester: Carcanet, 1987), p. 10.
89 Eavan Boland, *Object Lessons: The Life of the Woman and the Poet in Our Time* (Manchester: Carcanet, 1995), pp. 152–53.
90 Margaret Ward, *Unmanageable Revolutionaries: Women and Irish Nationalism* (London: Pluto Press, 1983), p. 4.
91 See CAB 37/5, no. 22, 11 October 1881.
92 Ward, *Unmanageable Revolutionaries*, p. 27.

McSwiney and the Republican prisoner Sands have used the hunger strike as a means of resisting the authority of the colonial sovereign over the body of the incarcerated prisoner. Such high-profile hunger strikes may help to make the violence of colonial sovereignty intelligible, but they can also work to erase the significance of women's participation in the hunger strike as a mode of political action. As Ziarek explains,

> Although the history of hunger strikes is often obscure, they were practiced in ancient Rome, medieval Ireland, and India as a means of protest, frequently to exert moral pressure or to force a debtor to return his debt. After the Easter Rising of 1916 in Ireland, the hunger strike was adopted in the Irish struggle for independence in 1917, and it was most famously employed by Mohandas Gandhi, who fasted at least fourteen times in British-occupied India. Nonetheless, it was militant British suffragettes who in 1909 revived and redefined the hunger strike as a modern political weapon of an organized movement by linking it for the first time with human rights.[93]

In the context of the Republican movement in Northern Ireland during the 1970s and 1980s, women prisoners detained in Armagh prison foregrounded the gendered dimensions of the hunger strike and the dirty protest as forms of political resistance. The feminist anthropologist Aretxaga has noted how some women Republican prisoners daubed their menstrual blood on the walls of Armagh prison in defiance of a patriarchal colonial regime that sought to humiliate female Republican prisoners through practices such as strip-searching.[94] For Aretxaga, the dirty protest at Armagh not only functioned as a powerful means for women Republican prisoners to distinguish their own dirty protest from that of their male comrades in Long Kesh, it also negated 'dominant models of femininity embedded in the idealized Catholic mother and elaborated in nationalist discourse around the image of Mother-Ireland'.[95]

Republican women's participation in hunger strikes also raises important questions about the gender politics of self-starvation within the context of the Republican movement. Writing of a female hunger striker at Armagh who had been released, but then died within a year of anorexia nervosa, Maud Ellmann suggests that her body was 'entangled in the rival ideologies of nation, gender and religion', and so, in consequence, 'it is impossible to know exactly why the hunger striker of Armagh destroyed herself, or what her self-starvation meant for her'.[96] The illegibility of women's self-starvation as a political act is also explored in Boland's poem 'Anorexia' (1980). On a first reading, the poem appears to pathologise the anorectic body by framing the speaker as a split subject, who defines her body as a 'witch' and a 'heretic' that needs to be

---

93 Ziarek, 'Bare Life on Strike', p. 99.
94 Begoña Aretxaga, *Shattering Silence: Women, Nationalism, and Political Subjectivity in Northern Ireland* (Princeton, NJ: Princeton University Press, 1997), pp. 137–50.
95 Aretxaga, *Shattering Silence*, p. 142.
96 Ellmann, *The Hunger Artists*, p. 3.

scorched, burned and destroyed.[97] If we read 'Anorexia' within the context of the Republican hunger strikes of the 1970s and 1980s, however, it becomes possible to interpret the poem as a critique of the patriarchal discourses of religion and nationalism, which frame and constrain women's participation in public acts of political resistance against colonial sovereignty. By foregrounding the way in which the speaker 'vomited / her hungers' in order to '[...] grow / angular and holy // past pain', the speaker attributes a quasi-religious signifi-cance to her self-starvation, which is further reinforced by her desire to 'forget [...] the fall'.[98] What is more, the speaker's comparison of her body to carceral spaces such as 'a sensuous enclosure' and a cage – exemplified in the line 'caged so' – evokes the spaces of detention at Armagh prison. In this way, 'Anorexia' encourages readers to reflect on both the possibilities and risks of hunger striking as a meaningful strategy for women's empowerment and sovereignty over their own bodily lives in the context of the Republican movement.

Conclusion

As this chapter has suggested, a critical reading of the literary prose of counter-insurgency can tease out the ways in which colonial stereotypes of violent, nationalist insurgency in Ireland served to reinforce the use of emergency law as a technique of governmentality. At the same time, a critical engagement with narratives of decolonisation in literary representations of Easter 1916 and the war of independence, and in more recent Republican narratives of the 1970s and 1980s can shed significant light on the vexed and contested meanings of the tradition of the oppressed in the context of Ireland. As we have seen, writers such as Greer and Yeats have not only illuminated the ways in which colonial sovereignty was maintained in and through the suspension of the normal rule of law, they have also explored the ways in which different forms of direct political action worked to challenge the sovereign power of the British government over the life and death of the Irish population. This is not suggest, however, that the literature of decolonisation in Ireland unequivocally endorses or champions all forms of political resistance to colonial rule, for writers such as Yeats and Boland have raised important questions about hunger striking as a tactic of anti-colonial resistance, as we have seen. To appropriate the symbolic position of the sovereign over one's own bodily life may be to subvert provisionally the sovereign's power over the incarcerated body of Republican prisoners through a strategy of mimicry, but what guarantees are there that the public spectacle of self-starvation will challenge the authority of the colonial sovereign beyond the death of the political martyr? To what extent does the practice of hunger striking and political martyrdom run the risk of introducing sacrificial violence into the political foundations of the Irish body politic? And,

---

97 Eavan Boland, *In Her Own Image* (Dublin: Arlen House, 1980), p. 17.
98 Boland, *In Her Own Image*, pp. 17–18.

in the case of Republican women's hunger strikes, what guarantees are there that the act of hunger striking will be read as a sign of women's agency, as well as a sign of anti-colonial resistance? Such questions not only mark the limits of what Benjamin called the tradition of the oppressed, they also emphasise the need for a clearer and more nuanced account of the constituency of 'the oppressed' and how such a constituency might redefine the postcolonial state of emergence in a still-partitioned Ireland.

CHAPTER 2

Terrorism, Literature and Sedition in Colonial India

In a cartoon published in the *Hindi Punch* magazine entitled 'Down with the Monster' and dated May 1908, the Indian Viceroy Lord Minto is depicted as Hercules killing the twin-headed hydra of Indian anarchism and revolution with a club, on the side of which the words 'LAW & ORDER' are inscribed in capital letters. Facing this figure, on the opposite side of the cartoon, in the smoke clouds bellowing from the dying hydra's two mouths, the following words are also written in capital letters: 'TERRORISM, SEDITION, LAWLESSNESS, and MOZUFFERPURE [*sic*] OUTRAGE'. At first glance, what this cartoon exemplifies is the moral authority of the British government's counter-terrorism strategy in early twentieth-century colonial Bengal; for the authority of the British Empire was clearly predicated upon the demonisation of nationalist insurgency. It is significant also that this illustration bears a striking similarity to a cartoon entitled 'Hercules and the Hydra' from the 12 February 1870 edition of the British *Punch* magazine, in which a muscular Gladstone is depicted in a loincloth preparing to fight the serpent with multiple heads labelled 'Fenianism' and 'Irish Land Question' among other 'social problems', such as railway reform and sanitary reform. In both of these illustrations, British colonial sovereignty is presented as a strong, heroic, masculine figure taking on a monstrous and unpredictable enemy. In this respect, the myth of Hercules and the Hydra can be seen to provide the British colonial imagination with a powerful metaphor through which to justify particular techniques of colonial governmentality and counter-insurgency. In the *Hindi Punch* cartoon, the use of verbal captions also establishes a division between law and order on the one hand and 'terrorism and sedition' on the other – a division which suggests a stable moral opposition between the colonial rule of law and the violent anarchy associated with anti-colonial nationalism. The alignment of 'terrorism' and 'sedition' in the *Hindi Punch* cartoon merits further comment. For the sedition legislation in British India, like more contemporary forms of anti-terrorism legislation which seek to proscribe literature that supposedly aims to incite or glorify 'terrorism', suggests that there is a causal relationship between writing and so-called acts of terrorism that can be inferred from the seditious writing itself. Section 5B of the 2006 British Terrorism Act, for instance, defines the glorification of terrorism in terms of the reception of statements that glorify terrorism by persons 'who could reasonably be expected to infer that what is being glorified, is being glorified' in order to encourage further acts of violence.[1] Considered in relation to such contemporary examples of anti-terrorism legislation, the *Hindi Punch* cartoonist's juxtaposition of 'terrorism', 'sedition' and 'lawlessness' seems strikingly prescient.

It is with such strong historical parallels in the formulation of anti-terrorism law that this chapter is in part concerned. By considering the way in which literary and journalistic writings came under scrutiny by the British colonial government in India and by the colonial office in London for evidence of sedition, the chapter examines how the sedition legislation in colonial India served to establish a connection between writing and 'terrorism'. In early twentieth-century British India, sedition was defined as the promotion of disaffection with the existing government via speeches, newspaper articles and songs. And by documenting cases of sedition, 'terrorist outrages' and revolutionary activity in Bombay, Bengal, Punjab, Bihar, Orissa, the United Provinces, the Central Provinces, Madras and Burma between 1897 and 1917, the 1918 *Sedition Committee Report* proposed a series of punitive and preventive emergency measures, under the aegis of martial law, which allowed courts to try accused subjects without juries, and granted the police special powers to confine individuals in 'non-penal custody' for a year or more.[2] The *Sedition Committee Report* formed the basis of the Rowlatt Act of 1919, a statute that granted extraordinary powers to the colonial police and the judiciary, and which called into question the liberal rhetoric of the British Raj. While the political reforms proposed by Edwin Montagu, the Liberal secretary of state for India, suggested that the political configuration of India was moving towards a system of self-governing institutions and responsible government, the repressive measures of the Rowlatt Act seemed to many Indians to undermine such promises. As Barbara D. Metcalf and Thomas D. Metcalf explain,

> The [Montagu–Chelmsford] reforms might well have been accepted, even by the Congress, had their enactment not been accompanied by a panic-stricken recourse to coercion on the part of the British in India. The spectre of a revival of revolutionary terrorism, together with the uncertainties of postwar economic dislocation, impelled the government in early 1919 to continue many of the powers of detention and trial without jury that had been in force during the wartime emergency. Known from the name of their author as the

---

1 Terrorism Act 2006, chapter 11. Available at <www.legislation.gov.uk/ukpga/2006/11/pdfs/ukpga_20060011_en.pdf>. Accessed 4 April 2012.
2 *Sedition Committee Report 1918* (Calcutta: Superintendent Government Printing India, 1918), pp. 205–7.

Rowlatt Acts, these measures aroused an intense hostility among Indians, to whom they appeared as a bitter reward for their wartime sacrifices.[3]

It was prominently the Rowlatt Act that prompted demonstrations of civil disobedience and provided a legal framework for the subsequent massacre of at least 379 people in the Punjabi town of Amritsar in April 1919.[4] What both the Rowlatt Report and the Rowlatt Acts reveal is a profound anxiety about British colonial sovereignty in India – an anxiety that is further reinforced in a subsequent report published in 1922 by the Interdepartmental Committee on Eastern Unrest surveying the threats to the British Empire.[5] While David Arnold has suggested that the British Raj increasingly became a kind of police state in the aftermath of India's first war of independence in 1857,[6] it was Lord Curzon's partition of Bengal in 1905 and the repressive measures introduced by the Governor General of India Lord Minto and the Secretary of State for India John Morley to control the press, as well as the possession of firearms and explosives that consolidated the authoritarian powers of the British Raj. What is more, the British colonial state's recourse to emergency measures posited a causal relationship between the affect of seditious writing and the cause of 'revolutionary terrorism'. As the historian Gerald Barrier puts it in his study of proscribed literature in British India, 'Aware that publications were both a symptom and a cause of unrest, the government coupled checks on extremist literature with enlarged executive and judicial powers to combat sedition in all forms'.[7] The increase of political assassinations and bombings in Bengal, Maharashtra and Punjab after 1905 prompted Morley to suggest to Minto that martial law might be required.[8] But it was not until 1915 that the police were granted wide powers 'of censorship, search and arrest' under the Defence of India Act, which was designed to give the government of India special powers to deal with revolutionary and German-inspired threats during the First World War, especially in the Punjab. After the end of the war in 1918, this Act was subsequently replaced by the Anarchical and Revolutionary Crimes Act of 1919, better known as the Rowlatt Act, which sought to 'devise some extra-legal measure to replace the [Defence of India] Act when it lapsed, a measure

---

3 Barbara D. Metcalf and Thomas R. Metcalf, *A Concise History of Modern India* (Cambridge: Cambridge University Press, 2006), p. 168.
4 See Nigel Collett, *The Butcher of Amritsar: General Reginald Dyer* (London: Hambledon and London, 2005); Alfred Draper, *Amritsar: The Massacre That Ended the Raj* (London: Cassell, 1981); *The Amritsar Massacre: General Dyer in the Punjab 1919* (The Stationery Office, 2000); and Alex Tickell *Terrorism, Insurgency, and Indian-English Literature* (London: Routledge, 2012), pp. 184–92.
5 See Durba Ghosh, 'Terrorism in Bengal: Political Violence in the Interwar Years', in Durba Ghosh and Dane Kennedy (eds), *Decentring Empire: Britain, India, and the Transcolonial World* (London: Sangam Books, 2006), pp. 270–71.
6 David Arnold, *Police Power and Colonial Rule: Madras 1859–1947* (Delhi: Oxford University Press, 1986), pp. 203–6.
7 N. Gerald Barrier, *Banned: Controversial Literature and Political Control in British India, 1907–1947* (Columbia, MO: University of Missouri Press, 1974), p. 16.
8 Barrier, *Banned*, p. 45.

which could be brought into force in any state of emergency, not necessarily one connected with war'.[9] This Act gave the colonial state the power to issue restrictive orders against a person 'suspected of connection with revolutionary or anarchical movements'; and to provide for the 'speedy trial' of offences in connection with revolutionary or anarchical movements where it was deemed to be necessary for 'the interests of public safety'.[10] In British colonial India, a colonial state of emergency was produced in and through the legal prose of counter-insurgency, which partly attributed the causality of revolutionary outrages to seditious writing and its subversive aim to promote disaffection with the colonial government. Yet, as I go on to suggest, the protean character of the 'revolutionary terrorist' and the 'seditionist' in colonial India persistently subverts the claims of dominant colonial narratives of 'revolutionary terror' to know, understand and control the figure of the Indian revolutionary, and at the same time works to foreground the violence of the colonial state. In this respect, the representation of the Indian revolutionary in literary and legal narratives of the early twentieth century provides an illuminating lens through which to understand contemporary forms of counter-terrorism.

Such measures can be seen to exemplify the state of legal exception, upon which sovereignty was based in colonial India. For the 'establishment of law' in colonial India not only echoes 'the discourse of a civilizing mission', it also regulates and administers violence and 'the deployment of extralegal force'.[11] The tension between the liberal discourse of colonialism as a civilising mission and the deployment of extra-legal force symbolised by the Amritsar massacre is exemplified in Winston Churchill's address to the English House of Commons of 1920, in which he argued that the massacre 'is an extraordinary event, a monstrous event, an event which stands in singular and sinister isolation'.[12] In defining the Amritsar massacre as an exception, Churchill disavowed the violence and brutality of the colonial state, and the importance of lawful violence to the maintenance of colonial power and sovereignty.[13] The emergency measures introduced and implemented during the early twentieth century in colonial India were part of a very particular series of legislative discourses that were produced in response to the figures of the 'Indian seditionist' and the 'revolutionary terrorist', and the threat to British colonial sovereignty that these figures posed. By tracing the state of emergency that India's 'revolutionary terrorists' were deemed to have created in the early twentieth-century British colonial imagination, this chapter proceeds to assess the extent to which Candler's 1912

---

9   Lady F. Tegart, *Charles Tegart: Memoir of an Indian Policeman* (British Library, MSS EUR/ C235), p. 131.

10 A. P. Muddiman, 'British India', *Journal of Comparative Legislation and International Law*, 3rd series, 3/3 (1921), p. 126.

11 Hussain, *The Jurisprudence of Emergency*, p. 68.

12 Winston Churchill 'Address to the House of Commons', *Parliamentary Debates: House of Commons*, 131 (8 July 1920), p. 1725.

13 See Purnima Bose and Laura Lyons, 'Dyer Consequences: The Trope of Amritsar, Ireland, and the Lessons of the "Minimum" Force Debate', *boundary 2*, 26/2 (1999), pp. 199–229.

novel *Siri Ram Revolutionist* reveals the violent foundations that underpin the liberal rhetoric of the civilising mission in British India. Candler's novel exemplifies a broader tendency in British literary narratives of counter-insurgency that attempt to contain the political threat posed by Indian revolutionaries in the early twentieth century by depoliticising their actions, as I argue elsewhere in a discussion of F.E. Penny's *The Unlucky Mark*, Ethel Winifred Savi's *The Reproof of Chance* and Leslie Beresford's *The Second Rising*.[14] The writing of sedition and 'revolutionary terrorism' in colonial India demonstrates the importance of subversive writing in the British colonial state's narrative of counter-insurgency, and its justification for the use of emergency measures. If the Anglo-Indian characters in British literary representations of counter-insurgency such as *Siri Ram Revolutionist* often claim to have demystified the psychological and social causes of 'revolutionary terrorism' in colonial Bengal in order to more effectively contain it, the enigmatic revolutionary figure of the doctor in Sarat Chandra Chatterjee's novel *Pather Dabi* eludes the gaze of the colonial authorities and refuses to be represented as a coherent subaltern insurgent. This fictional revolutionary, as I argue in the conclusion, not only provided a literary inspiration for subsequent revolutionaries, but also demonstrated that so-called seditious writing was a crucial rhetorical and political strategy in the struggle against colonialism. As a form of separation, sedition, from the Latin *seditio*, or going apart from, evokes a challenge to the exclusionary logic of sovereignty in early twentieth-century colonial India, and it is the multiple forms that this challenge takes which this chapter will attempt to trace.

'… so admirably vague': Sedition Legislation in the Indian Penal Code

In 'The Doctrine of Passive Resistance', the Cambridge graduate and radical Bengali nationalist Aurobindo Ghose, criticised the sedition legislation in the Indian Penal Code on the grounds that it is 'so admirably vague' that there is 'nothing to prevent [the government] from using this [legal] power in any way they like, however iniquitous or tyrannical'.[15] For Ghose, the vague phrasing and unjust application of the sedition law in the case of the proscription of the *Punjabee* newspaper in 1907 exemplified the moral and political bankruptcy of British colonial rule in India in the early twentieth century, and was symptomatic of the thinly veiled oppression and violence that underpinned the liberal political rhetoric of the British colonial government in India. For this reason, the implementation of the sedition law only served to strengthen the formulation of Ghose's political doctrine, which was based on the premise that 'the circumstances of the country and the nature of the despotism from which it seeks to

14 Stephen Morton, 'Fictions of Sedition and the Framing of Indian Revolutionaries in Colonial India', *Journal of Commonwealth Literature* 47/2 (June 2012), pp. 175–89.
15 Sri Aurobindo, 'The Doctrine of Passive Resistance', in idem, *Sri Aurobindo Volume One: Bande Mataram: Early Political Writings* (Pondicherry: Sri Aurobindo Ashram, 1995), pp. 108–9.

escape must determine what form of resistance is best justified and most likely to be effective at the time or finally successful'.[16]

In Ghose's argument, the 'means' by which 'a subject nation' will vindicate its liberty 'is best determined by the circumstances of its servitude' and, the 'present circumstances in India seem to point to passive resistance as our most natural and suitable weapon'.[17] Ghose did not rule out the use of violent resistance in anti-colonial insurgency; but argued instead that 'it is the nature of the pressure which determines the nature of the resistance' and cited 'the denial of liberty' in Russia by 'legalised murder and outrage' and 'brutal coercion' in Ireland as cases where 'the answer of violence to violence is justified and inevitable'.[18] Yet in his observation that the 'penalty of sedition is at present the chief danger which the adherent or exponent of passive resistance runs under the law'[19] it is clear that the sedition legislation not only delineates the illegality of the doctrine of passive resistance, but also questions the implicit premise of Aurobindo's justification for passive resistance: the liberal democratic character of the British colonial government.[20] Such a view is echoed in a speech that Gandhi delivered during his trial for sedition in 1922, in which he criticised the Rowlatt Act and the massacre at Jallianwala Bagh, and justified the promotion of disaffection towards the government established by law in India on moral grounds. In Gandhi's argument, Section 124A of the Indian Penal Code 'is perhaps the prince among the political sections of the Indian Penal Code designed to suppress the liberty of the citizen'.[21] By comparing the Rowlatt Act to a 'prince', Gandhi suggests that there is a relationship between sovereignty and the law – a relationship that excludes Indian subjects from the rights and freedoms associated with citizenship.

In 1867, the British Indian government passed a law proscribing the publication of seditious writing, or literature that was deemed to promote disaffection with the British colonial government. In the eyes of the British government, the literature of sedition served to establish a connection between literature and 'terrorism'. The proscription of books, pamphlets and newspapers in British India on the grounds that they were seditious has a history that can be traced back to the Press and Registration of Books Act in 1867. The 'original impetus

16 Aurobindo, 'The Doctrine of Passive Resistance', p. 119.
17 Aurobindo, 'The Doctrine of Passive Resistance', p. 98.
18 Aurobindo, 'The Doctrine of Passive Resistance', p. 98.
19 Aurobindo, 'The Doctrine of Passive Resistance', p. 109.
20 For more on the relationship between liberalism and imperialism, see Mehta, *Liberalism and Empire*; Nicholas Dirks, *The Scandal of Empire: India and the Creation of Imperial Britain* (Cambridge, MA: Belknap Press of Harvard University Press, 2006); Jennifer Pitts, *A Turn to Empire: The Rise of Imperial Liberalism in Britain and France* (Princeton, NJ: Princeton University Press, 2005); Margaret Kohn, 'Empire's Law: Alexis de Tocqueville on Colonialism and the State of Exception', *Canadian Journal of Political Science*, 41 (2008), pp. 255–78; Abdeslam E. Maghraoui, *Liberalism without Democracy: Nationhood and Citizenship in Egypt, 1922–1939* (Durham, NC: Duke University Press, 2006); and Tickell, *Terrorism, Insurgency and Indian-English Literature, 1830–1947*.
21 M.K. Gandhi, *Trial of Gandhiji* (Ahmedabad: V.R. Shah, 1965), p. 185.

for the Act of 1867 came from London, where librarians in the British Museum and administrators in the India Office felt a need to keep track of the printed matter churned out by Indian presses'.[22] However, in India, the 'act belonged to a general attempt to restore order in a world still shaking from the aftershocks of the Sepoy Mutiny and peasant uprisings of 1857–58'.[23] In this context, the documentation of Indian books in print was part of a massive process of information gathering:

> Everything was surveyed, mapped, classified, and counted, including human beings, who appeared in the first Indian census in 1872, divided neatly into castes, subcastes, and a dozen other categories determined by the columns of a printed form. The catalogues of books belonged to this effort to catalogue everything. They constituted a census of Indian literature as the imperial authorities understood it.[24]

As the book historian Robert Darnton suggests, the British colonial surveillance of so-called vernacular literatures published in India drew attention to the political dimension of the literary: 'Nothing would seem to be further from political control than an obsession with literary style, but literature under the Raj was political in itself, down to its very syntax'.[25] Yet while civil servants employed to write entries for the Bengal Library Catalogue of Printed Books in the late nineteenth century noted the political content of the literary, these books were not officially proscribed: 'the government permitted the publication of books that seemed openly seditious to the men who registered them'.[26] This liberal policy of the late nineteenth century changed with the partition of Bengal in 1905 and the perception that literature was dangerous because it promoted nationalist sentiment and in some cases advocated the use of violent resistance.

The murder of two British women in a Calcutta railway car in 1908 by a bomb intended for Mr Kingsford, an unpopular magistrate, and the subsequent discovery of a bomb-making factory in the Calcutta suburb of Alipur, brought the political dimension of literature to the attention of the authorities. For in what subsequently became known as the Alipur Bombing Case, the 'terrorists' were disaffected members of the elite Hindu *bhadralok* classes and the literary

---

22 Robert Darnton, 'Literary Surveillance in the British Raj: The Contradictions of Liberal Imperialism', *Book History*, 4 (2001), p. 136.
23 Darnton, 'Literary Surveillance in the British Raj', p. 136.
24 Darnton, 'Literary Surveillance in the British Raj', p.138. Darnton's account of the surveillance of Indian print culture is part of a broader tendency on the part of British colonial administration to survey and classify Indian culture in order to govern more effectively. See C.A. Bayly, *Empire and Information: Intelligence Gathering and Social Communication in India, 1780–1870* (Cambridge: Cambridge University Press, 1996); Bernard S. Cohn, 'The Census, Social Structure, and Objectification in South Asia', in idem, *An Anthropologist among the Historians* (Delhi: Oxford University Press, 1987), pp. 224–54; and idem, *Colonialism and Its Forms of Knowledge: The British in India* (Princeton, NJ: Princeton University Press, 1996).
25 Darnton, 'Literary Surveillance in the British Raj', p. 143.
26 Darnton, 'Literary Surveillance in the British Raj', p. 147.

intelligentsia: 'The leading agitators were men of letters, who drew their inspiration from literature, both Indian and Western, and gathered around newspapers and libraries'.[27] Indeed, the writings, songs and newspaper articles of nationalist groups such as the Anushilan Samiti and Ghadr Party were felt to promote disaffection with the British colonial government.

The meaning of sedition defined in Section 124A of the Indian Penal Code of 1867 centred on the political use of language and representation, intended to bring about disaffection with the existing colonial government. The Act declared that

> Whoever by words, either spoken or written or by signs, or by visible representation, or otherwise, brings or attempts to bring into hatred or contempt, or excites, or attempts to excite disaffection towards Her Majesty or the Government established by law in British India, shall be punished with transportation for life or any shorter term, to which fine may be added, or with imprisonment which may extend to three years, to which fine may be added or with fine.[28]

In this definition, the legal ground of sedition was predicated on a transparent model of communication, in which the intention to bring about 'hatred', 'contempt' or 'disaffection' was self-evident in the 'words', 'signs' or 'visible representation' of the seditious material, be it a printed text, speech, poster or leaflet. What the government meant by disaffection was not defined until the turn of the century, with the increase of revolutionary activities in Bengal and the perception of a causal relationship between radical literature, newspaper articles, political speeches and posters on the one hand and the increase of violent acts of anti-colonial insurgency on the other.

One of the most meticulous attempts to explain and clarify the sedition legislation in the Indian Penal Code to both lawyers and laymen was that of Walter Russell Donogh, a barrister-at-law in Calcutta, in his book *The History and Law of Sedition and Cognate Offences in British India* (first published 1911). As well as explaining the history behind the formulation of the law, and distinguishing it from similar English laws, such as the treason-felony law and the seditious libel law, Donogh offers an account of particular cases and identifies some of the problems with the phrasing of the sedition law. One such problem is hinted at in Donogh's discussion of Sir James Fitzjames Stephen's introduction to this Bill to amend the Indian Penal Code on 2 August 1870. In Donogh's account, Stephen's legal definition of disaffection or seditious intention was premised on a theory of public rhetoric as a transparent reflection of a speaker's intention, in which 'Every man who was going to speak, every man who was going to write ought to know perfectly well whether he intended to produce disaffection'.[29]

27 Darnton, 'Literary Surveillance in the British Raj', p. 152.
28 Charles Swinhoe, *The Indian Penal Code* (Calcutta: Thacker, Spink and Co., 1909), p. 66, Section 124A.
29 Walter Russell Donogh, *The History and Law of Sedition and Cognate Offences in British India*, 3rd edn (Calcutta: Thacker, Spink & Co., 1917 [1911]), p. 8.

Yet in the case of the Bangobasi sedition trial of 1891[30] and the Tilak sedition trial of 1897,[31] both counsels for the defence raised questions about the clarity of the legislation, and an amendment to the phrasing of the act was proposed in 1898. While the committee appointed to review the case for an amendment acknowledged that Section 124A of the Indian Penal Code did not constitute 'a model of clear drafting',[32] what was particularly interesting about the discussion which led to the amendment was the distinction made by Lieutenant Governor of Bengal Sir Alexander Mackenzie between the conditions of political governance in England and colonial India:

> It is clear that a sedition law which is adequate for a people ruled by a government of its own nationality and faith may be inadequate, or in some respects unsuited, for a country under foreign rule and inhabited by many races, with diverse customs and conflicting creeds. It is impossible in India to accept the test of direct incitement to violence, and limit the interference of the Government to such cases.[33]

Consequently, it was decided that the Indian sedition legislation 'prohibits alike the act and the attempt to excite disaffection'. The reason for this, as Walter Donogh explains, 'may be found in the enormous difficulty of proving that disaffection has actually resulted from the effort to produce it. This is conceivable in the case of an inflammatory speech which is followed immediately by a disturbance, or other more mistakable signs of disaffection, but in the case of seditious matter disseminated through the Press it would be next to impossible to trace a connection.[34]

The revised 1909 edition of the Indian Penal Code included case notes and three explanations that were supposed to clarify the definition and appropriate circumstances in which the sedition law could be implemented. As well as asserting that 'the expression "disaffection" included disloyalty and all feelings of enmity',[35] the Section referred to cases in which a precedent had been set for the use of the sedition law. Of these, it was the sentencing of the Maratha agitator Bal Gangadhar Tilak in 1897 to 18 months 'rigorous' imprisonment by a court in Bombay for an article that he had published in the Marathi paper the *Kesari* on 15 June 1897 that set a precedent for subsequent cases of sedition,

---

30 See Donogh, *The History and Law of Sedition*, pp. 33–41. The *Bangobasi* trial refers to a trial against the *Bangobasi* newspaper in 1891, in which it was alleged that the newspaper had used the colonial government's passing of a bill raising the age of consent for marriage from ten to twelve as a pretext for inciting disaffection amongst its readers.
31 The Tilak trial, as explained below, refers to the case against Bal Ganghadar Tilak in 1897, in which it was alleged that Tilak's newspaper, the *Kesari*, had printed poems and speeches against British colonial rule in India that had led to the assassination of the plague commissioner, Mr Rand.
32 Donogh, *The History and Law of Sedition*, p. 61.
33 Cited in Donogh, *The History and Law of Sedition*, p. 65.
34 Donogh, *The History and Law of Sedition*, p. 77.
35 Donogh, *The History and Law of Sedition*, p. 66.

which were tried during the period of nationalist agitation that followed the partition of Bengal in 1905.

The *Kesari* had published an article on 4 May 1897, in which the British government's intervention in the plague epidemic in Poona was described as a deliberate attempt to oppress the people, and the plague commissioner, Mr Rand, was described as 'tyrannical'.[36] While this article does not explicitly call for political resistance to British colonial rule, the authorities certainly perceived it as encouraging people to hate the existing colonial government. But it was in two subsequent articles published 15 June 1897 that the *Kesari* was deemed by the High Court of Judicature at Bombay to promote resistance to the colonial government. These articles contained an account of the proceedings at the Shivaji coronation festival held on 12 June 1897. Shivaji was a military chief who led the Maharashtra people against the Mughal Empire in the seventeenth century. To the colonial state, however, the *Kesari* has used the celebration of Shivaji's life as a pretext for promoting disaffection with the present British colonial government.

In an account of the *Kesari*'s seditious writing, the *Sedition Committee Report* of 1918 describes how this newspaper invoked the French revolutionaries' defence of political violence on the grounds that they were 'only removing thorns from their paths' and suggested that the 'same argument could be applied in Maharashtra'. It went on to describe how Tilak invoked the actions of Shivaji in the *Srimat Baghvad Gita*, who murdered Afzal Khan for the good of others and strove to drive the foreigners away from the land of his birth.[37] In the *Report*'s account of Tilak's speech, it is ancient Hindu stories that provide a mythological framework for resistance to British colonial rule, for just as Krishna in the *Gita* argued that 'No blame attaches to any person if he is doing deeds without being actuated by a desire to reap the fruits of his deeds', so Shivaji's violent actions were justified because they served the interests of the nation.[38] In the eyes of the Sedition Committee there was a causal relationship between the publication of these two articles and the subsequent murder of two government officers, Mr Rand and Lieutenant Ayerst, on 22 June 1897 during the celebration of the sixtieth anniversary of Queen Victoria at Government House, Ganeshkhind, Poona. It is worth noting here too that the framing of Shivaji as a Maharashtrian and Indian national hero in the political imagination of Bal Gangadhar Tilak was replayed in the Maharashtra government's notifications banning the publication of James Laine's book *Shivaji: Hindu King in Islamic India* in 2004 and 2006. Here, Shivaji was framed as a trope for communal identification and violence by Hindu fundamentalist groups such as the Sambhaji Brigade and the Shiv Sena in an effort to defend the myth of Shivaji against Laine's historical account of Shivaji – an account

36 *Sedition Committee Report 1918*, pp. 2–3.
37 *Sedition Committee Report 1918*, pp. 2–3.
38 *Sedition Committee Report 1918*, pp. 2–3.

which the Sambhaji Brigade and the Shiv Sena regard as less than favourable.[39]

The trial of Tilak for sedition in the High Court of Judicature in Bombay in September 1897 reveals a fault line both in the legal language and interpretation of this section of the penal code, which the *Sedition Committee Report* elides. In his concluding remarks on the case, the presiding judge, Mr Justice Strachey, advised the jury on how best to evaluate the case for sedition against Tilak. After explaining the language of the sedition law, and the meaning of disaffection, Strachey proceeded to advise the members of the jury to read the articles using a series of phrases that recall the language of literary interpretation:

> [...] in judging of the intention of the accused, you must be guided not only by your estimate of the effect of the articles upon the minds of the readers, but also by your common sense, your knowledge of the world, and your understanding of the meaning of words. Read the articles, and ask yourselves as men of the world whether they impress you on the whole as a mere poem and an historical discussion without mere purpose, or as attacks on the British Government under the disguise of a poem and historical discussion. It may not be easy to express the difference in words; but the difference in tone and general drift between a writer who is trying to stir up ill will and one who is not is generally unmistakeable, whether the writing is a private letter, or a leading article, or a poem, or the report of a discussion. If the object of a publication is really seditious, it does not matter what form it takes. Disaffection may be excited in a thousand different ways. A poem, an allegory, a drama, a philosophical or historical discussion, may be used for the purpose of exciting disaffection, just as much as a direct attack upon the Government. You have to look through the form and look to the real object: you have to consider whether the form of the poem or discussion is genuine, or whether it has been adopted merely to disguise the real seditious intention of the writer.[40]

Here, the judge highlights the connection between legal and literary judgement: in his reading, the seditious intention of the writer is inferred from the tone or style of the poem. In order to assess the intention of the accused, the judge further directed the jury to consider both the implied readership of the *Kesari* and the context in which the newspaper was written and disseminated:

> You have not only to consider the class of persons who subscribe to the *Kesari*, but you have also got to consider the condition and the time, not in the year 1890, or 1891, or 1892, or 1893, or even 1896, but in June 1897 and also the particular state of things at the time when the articles were disseminated among them.[41]

---

39 See James Laine, *Shivaji: Hindu King in Islamic India* (Delhi: Oxford University Press, 2001), and 'The James Laine Affair: Terrorising Scholarship', *Economic and Political Weekly*, 19 May 2007, p. 1796.

40 'Imperatrix versus Bal Gangadhar Tilak and Keshav Mahadev Bal', IOR/L/PJ/6/462/2291, p. 98.

41 'Imperatrix versus Bal Gangadhar Tilak and Keshav Mahadev Bal', p. 100.

In this statement, the judge alludes to the British colonial government's intervention in the plague epidemic at Poona, its segregation of individuals infected with the plague and those who were not infected with the plague, and its use of soldiers to conduct house-to-house visitations.[42] Such contextual details were also mediated in British colonial fictions of sedition, as we will see.

Sedition and Colonial Intelligence Gathering in Edmund Candler's *Siri Ram Revolutionist*

One of the most sustained fictional treatments of the relationship between 'seditious literature' and 'revolutionary terrorism' in colonial India can be found in *Siri Ram Revolutionist: A Transcript from Life 1907–1910*, a novel that was written by the Anglo-Indian writer, college principal and newspaper journalist Edmund Candler.[43] In his letters to his brother Henry, Candler describes the book as his 'sedition novel'.[44] *Siri Ram Revolutionist* is certainly concerned with sedition, secret societies and Bengali revolutionaries. Yet this is not to suggest that *Siri Ram* is a seditious novel, or a novel that actually promotes anti-colonial disaffection or advocates violent action against the colonial state. For like many other Anglo-Indian fictions of 'terrorism' and 'sedition', *Siri Ram Revolutionist* is precisely concerned with the threat of sedition and revolutionary acts of violent anti-colonial insurgency from the standpoint of the colonial state. The novel opens with an account of a seditious lecture delivered at a town hall in Punjab by Narasimha Swami, 'a dangerous agitator' who 'was too clever to be run down'.[45] The third-person omniscient narrator compares Narasimha's influence in the North of India to that of 'Arabindo [*sic*] Ghose in Bengal', and argues that the Swami's influence was 'more dangerous as the material he had to work with was hardier and more robust'.[46] A similar historical comparison is drawn in the same chapter between Narasimha Swami and Tilak: 'The Swami identified with the spiritual side of the revolutionary movement in the same way as Tilak was with the political'.[47]

Such comparisons with historical figures serve to locate the novel in early twentieth-century British India during a period of increasingly violent nationalist insurgency; yet they also reveal how Candler's omniscient narrator is situated

---

42 'Imperatrix versus Bal Gangadhar Tilak and Keshav Mahadev Bal', p. 104.
43 Edmund Candler, 'Siri Ram Revolutionist: A Transcript from Life', in Saros Cowasjee (ed.), *A Raj Collection: On the Face of the Waters, Flora Annie Steel; Siri Ram-Revolutionist, Edmund Candler; Indigo, Christine Weston; The Wild Sweet Witch, Philip Mason* (Delhi: Oxford University Press, 2005).
44 Rachel Corkill, 'Preface to Siri Ram Revolutionist: A Transcript from Life' in Saros Cowasjee (ed.), *A Raj collection: On the face of the waters, Flora Annie Steel; Siri Ram-Revolutionist, Edmund Candler; Indigo, Christine Weston; The wild sweet witch, Philip Mason* (Delhi: Oxford University Press, 2005), pp. 397–8.
45 Candler, 'Siri Ram Revolutionist: A Transcript from Life', p. 404.
46 Candler, 'Siri Ram Revolutionist: A Transcript from Life', p. 404.
47 Candler, 'Siri Ram Revolutionist: A Transcript from Life', p. 404.

at the centre of colonial intelligence gathering about 'sedition-mongers' and nationalist insurgents or 'terrorists'. While the narrator often appears to claim total knowledge about the Swami's 'terrorist organisation' and its methods, this claim is undermined by the novel's status as a post-hoc response to the circulation of 'seditious literature' and 'terrorist attacks' in colonial Bengal. Such a response is reconstructed through a forensic approach to the detail of Siri Ram's family background and an anthropological account of the social composition, organisation and activities of secret societies in Punjab. Indeed, it was Candler's fictional construction of the profile of a young, Punjabi extremist that prompted the novelist Joseph Conrad, in a letter addressed to Candler in 1918, to compliment the 'lofty impartiality of [Candler's] insight and the sincere sympathy of [his] treatment'. What *Siri Ram Revolutionist* gave Conrad was a 'distinct sense of enlightenment in the intricate matter of racial psychology' and 'a firmer conviction of the difficulty of the problem which politicians at home are so ready to handle on mere party lines'.[48]

One of the ways in which Candler traces the psychological motivations of Siri Ram's involvement in anti-colonial insurgency is by offering a detailed account of his social background in an Indian village. At first the narrator seems to offer an ethnographic representation of Siri Ram's family home:

> You went through the gate into the *haveli*, a cramped courtyard strewn with cow fodder, save where a little mud wall divides off a square for cooking. The mud floor here is scrupulously polished; the five brass vessels, as scrupulously clean, are laid beside the chula where the pulse is being cooked for the family, or some sort of herbal concoction for the cow. The ashes of the fire under the pot are invisible for the intense glare. In the shrine-like cupboard of clay let into the wall and protruding like a peaked cowl, the boiled smoked milk is kept all day immune from the sun. From the sacred hearth you creep through a low door into a long, low, mud walled room with a roof of beams and twigs caked with clay pierced sometimes with a smoke hole to let out the smoke or let in a shaft of light.[49]

This ethnographic description of Siri Ram's family home is clearly marked by modifying adjectives such as 'cramped' and 'shrine-like'. These modifiers serve to reinforce Merivale's racist characterisation of Indian village life as an under-developed 'mud world' that resembles 'some phase of an excrescence exuded from the earth', and presents its occupants as 'ants of the same hue'.[50] In so doing, the narrator implies that Siri Ram's motivation for carrying out acts of 'sedition' and 'terror' against the British colonial government is related to his cultural background rather than the British handling of the plague epidemic. Indeed, when Merivale discovers copies of English literary classics such as

48 'Letter to Edmund Candler', 12 November 1918, in Laurence Davies, Frederick R. Karl and Owen Knowles (eds), *The Collected Letters of Joseph Conrad Volume VI* (Cambridge: Cambridge University Press, 2002), p. 303.
49 Candler, 'Siri Ram Revolutionist: A Transcript from Life', pp. 441–42.
50 Candler, 'Siri Ram Revolutionist: A Transcript from Life', p. 442.

Alexander Pope's 'The Rape of the Lock' and Robert Louis Stevenson's *An Inland Voyage*, he starts to question what benefit an aesthetic education in English literature would be to Siri Ram, as a 'child of this clay'.[51] Such questioning serves to construct a profile of Siri Ram as a dull, melancholy and unimaginative young man who is disaffected and suggestible. It also echoes the *Times* journalist Valentine Chirol's observation in *Indian Unrest* that the British colonial education system has contributed to the Indian unrest by 'producing dangerous hybrids, more or less superficially imbued with Western ideas, and at the same time more or less completely divorced from the realities of Indian life'.[52] This characterisation is extended in the narrator's account of Siri Ram's mission to find Narasimha Swami in the mountains: while the narrator describes the beauty of the landscape in great detail, we are told that Siri Ram marches 'dully on [...] wrapped solely in his broodings'.[53]

Siri Ram is not only criticised for lacking powers of observation and imagination, but is also portrayed as inept, moody and vain. At the Bridge club, Skene surmises that Siri Ram 'has never seen a firearm' and 'couldn't hit a tree'.[54] Such an intuition is later confirmed during a target practice in the mountains when Siri Ram aims a revolver at a marmot, shoots and misses.[55] Siri Ram's vanity is further exemplified by his aspiration to be a 'political deportee' and by the narrator's speculation that Siri Ram would have been flattered if he had known that the CID had a copy of his passport.[56]

Candler's representation of Siri Ram as a moody and resentful individual – who is a passive subject of political extremism rather than an active subject of historical change – also recalls the stereotype of the effeminate Babu. This stereotype can be traced back to Lord Macaulay's description of the Bengali, who is 'physically "feeble even to effeminacy" and mentally "weak, even to helplessness"'.[57] However, it was the then Viceroy Lord Curzon's plans to partition Bengal in 1905 that prompted the re-articulation of this colonial stereotype in elite nationalist discourse during the *swadeshi* movement. As Indira Chowdhury observes, Curzon's plans to partition Bengal were perceived as an affront to *bhadralok* masculinity. In response to this affront, nationalist intellectuals such as Swami Vivekanada and Ghose sought to awaken the inert revolutionary energy of the sons of mother India through a programme of self-discipline and spiritual education, as we will see.

51 Candler, 'Siri Ram Revolutionist: A Transcript from Life', p. 443.
52 Valentine Chirol, *Indian Unrest* (London: Macmillan & Co., 1910), p. 2.
53 Candler, 'Siri Ram Revolutionist: A Transcript from Life', p. 478.
54 Candler, 'Siri Ram Revolutionist: A Transcript from Life', p. 466.
55 Candler, 'Siri Ram Revolutionist: A Transcript from Life', p. 491.
56 Candler, 'Siri Ram Revolutionist: A Transcript from Life', p. 474.
57 Indira Chowdhury, *The Frail Hero and Virile History* (Delhi: Oxford University Press, 1998), p. 4.

The Emergence of Anti-Colonial Insurgency
and the Limits of Colonial Intelligence

If *Siri Ram Revolutionist* presents a post-hoc response to 'sedition' and planned 'terrorist activities' as an a priori fiction of total omniscience about extremist organisations in British India, Candler underscores this fiction of total omniscience in a letter he wrote to his brother Henry, who was based in England. In this letter Candler emphasises the timeliness of his novel following an unspecified 'bomb outrage' in 1913; and suggests that Constable, the publishers of the first edition of *Siri Ram Revolutionist*, should take advantage of this bomb outrage to market the book further.[58] Such a view of the novel's timeliness and its sensational subject matter echoes the sensational headlines of British and Anglo-Indian newspaper reports on bomb outrages in Bengal and Punjab, a connection that also recalls the relationship between late Victorian popular fiction about terrorism, such as Robert Louis Stevenson's *The Dynamitards* and Conrad's *The Secret Agent*, and the sensational reports of Fenian conspiracies and Anarchist plots contained in the London dailies. Like the British newspaper reports and sensation fiction of the 1880s and 1890s, Candler's letter to his brother clearly suggests that he was concerned to capitalise on the timeliness and shock value of the violent revolutionaries depicted in *Siri Ram Revolutionist*. Yet it was Candler's attention to the detail of 'Indian revolutionary terrorism' and his apparently intimate knowledge of the revolutionaries which many of the contemporary newspaper reviews identified in *Siri Ram Revolutionist*. The Anglo-Indian newspaper *The Englishman* (Calcutta), for instance, praised Candler's insider knowledge of 'Indian terrorism' in *Siri Ram* by claiming that

> The book shows, what MR CHIROL failed to show [in his study *Indian Unrest*], the steps by which the mind of the student is debauched, the methods which are employed to make use of his simplicity and ignorance, and the subtle and ingenious arguments by which an honest idealist is deflected into the paths of Terrorism and crime.[59]

In a similar vein, the *Morning Post* reviewer describes *Siri Ram Revolutionist* as a 'psychological study of the Revolutionary Movement in the Punjab' and praises Candler's insight into that movement: the 'author, who is obviously engaged in educational work, has watched the growth of the movement in question from a position which brings him into close contact with the young "intellectuals" of Indian nationalism'.[60]

What is crucial, however, is the way that *the novel itself* attempts to efface a crisis at the centre of discourses of colonial intelligence and counter-insurgency. For if this crisis is read against the grain of Candler's narrative of colonial

---

58 Edmund Candler, 'Letter to Henry Candler', 8 January 1913 (British Library Deposit 1039, Box 5).
59 'Truth about Terrorists', *The Englishman* (Calcutta), Friday, 18 April 1913, p. 2.
60 'The Samajist', *The Morning Post* (Thursday, 5 December 1912).

intelligence and counter-insurgency, it is possible to trace the articulation of an emergent counter-narrative of insurgency in the seditious writing of Narasimha Swami and the insurgent acts of Siri Ram. That is to say, the insurgent acts of Siri Ram and Narasimha Swami contribute to a counter-narrative that eludes the colonial intelligence gathering of the Anglo-Indian authorities in *Siri Ram Revolutionist*. *Siri Ram's* concern with colonial intelligence gathering is foregrounded in the narrator's account of Skene, an Anglo-Indian school principal, who observes the Swami's lecture at a town hall in the Punjab for evidence of sedition and to 'discover if possible where [the Swami's] magnetism lay'.[61] For Skene, the town hall 'was in an atmosphere of intense excitement';[62] and yet there is no positive evidence that the Swami's lecture is seditious: 'There had not been a word about politics. The few allusions to Government, the British, and the Christians had been moderate and natural'.[63]

For both the narrator and Skene, the dissemination of seditious rhetoric in the Swami's lecture is not disseminated through the words of the lecture itself, but via the spiritual medium of the Swami: Skene 'felt that a message had been conveyed to the young men that had passed over his head, and that they had responded'.[64] Skene's perception of the Swami's conveyance of this seditious message might seem to recall the phenomenon of telepathy that was investigated by the Society for Psychical Research in the late nineteenth century and preoccupied writers such as Rudyard Kipling, Bram Stoker, Henry James and Sandor Ferenczi.[65] As Pamela Thurschwell has argued, telepathy is often associated with an erotic desire between the spiritual medium and their audience. In a critical analysis of the Society for Psychical Research, for instance, Thurschwell describes how 'the Society's early séance experiments involved upper class university-educated men locking themselves in rooms with working-class, sometimes foreign women, for hours on end'. In these early experiments with telepathy 'the séance became a site for transgressive contact between men and women of different classes'.[66]

Desire was also an important factor in the recruitment of young men for the revolutionary nationalist struggle. In *Siri Ram Revolutionist*, the narrator describes Narasimha Swami's telepathic powers as a coercive form of mind control or 'magnetism'.[67] Such a representation attributes occult powers to what Skene views as the Swami's corrupt influence over Skene's impressionable young students. In doing so, Skene denies the students' agency and desire to participate in acts of sedition and violent acts of counter-insurgency against the British. Such a view of Skene's students is echoed in Fraser Lovat's 1913 review

61 Candler, 'Siri Ram Revolutionist: A Transcript from Life', p. 404.
62 Candler, 'Siri Ram Revolutionist: A Transcript from Life', p. 404.
63 Candler, 'Siri Ram Revolutionist: A Transcript from Life', p. 405.
64 Candler, 'Siri Ram Revolutionist: A Transcript from Life', p. 405.
65 See Pamela Thurschwell, *Literature, Technology and Magical Thinking, 1880–1920* (Cambridge: Cambridge University Press, 2001).
66 Thurschwell, *Literature, Technology and Magical Thinking*, p. 32.
67 Candler, 'Siri Ram Revolutionist: A Transcript from Life', p. 404.

of the novel, published in *The Times Literary Supplement*. The reviewer notes that Siri Ram is an 'eager, discontented student', a phrase which implies Siri Ram's predisposition to commit revolutionary acts in the name of national liberation; however, Lovat qualifies this statement by adding that Siri Ram is 'moulded into a criminal by skilful hands'; and by the end of the novel, Lovat concludes that 'Siri Ram' is 'the ignorant victim of subtler and more unscrupulous brains than his own'.[68] In saying this, the *TLS* reviewer – like the fictional character Skene – overlooks the desire of the students to be cathected by their spiritual leaders and ultimately recruited as revolutionary subjects.

The Swami's 'magnetic influence' over Skene's students, especially Siri Ram, also recalls the practice of yoga asceticism by nationalist figures such as Swami Vivekananda and Ghose. Yoga asceticism was part of the Vedantic philosophy that was practised and preached in India, Europe and North America by the Bengali monastic Vivekananda. In a response to a lecture entitled 'Can Psychic Phenomena be Proved from a Scientific Basis', for instance, Vivekananda sought to challenge the dichotomy between objective science and spiritual phenomena by asserting that most

> of the psychical phenomena – not only little things like spirit-rappings or table rappings which are mere child's play, not merely things like telepathy which I have seen boys do even – most of the psychical phenomena which the last speaker calls the higher clairvoyance, but which I would rather beg to call the experiences of the super-conscious state of the mind, are the very stepping stones to real psychological investigation.[69]

Vivekananda's dismissal of table rappings and telepathy as 'mere child's play' in favour of a 'real psychological investigation' of 'the super-conscious state of the mind' may sound like a proto-Freudian theory of the human psyche. Yet, as Peter Heehs has argued, the Vedantic philosophy and asceticism of Swami Vivekananda was also understood in broader, nationalist terms. Although Swami Vivekananda regarded his mission as purely spiritual, his masculine rhetoric and pride in the greatness of India's religion provided spiritual inspiration to many Bengali revolutionaries.[70] Like Vivekananda, the revolutionary leader Aurobindo Ghose also developed a form of spiritualism informed by Vedantic thought. In 1904 or 1905 Ghose 'began that form of yogic practice known as *pranayama* or breath control' and, with his brother Barin, he 'began to experiment with what spiritualists call automatic writing'.[71]

The rather tenuous connection between spiritualism, nationalism and revolutionary politics evident in the writings of Aurobindo Ghose and Swami Vivekananda is causally connected in *Siri Ram Revolutionist*. In its aetiology of Siri Ram's anti-colonial violence, the narrative attributes Siri Ram's political agency

68 'Siri Ram: Revolutionist', *The Times Literary Supplement* (Thursday, 10 April 1913), p. 154.
69 Swami Vivekananda, *The Collected Works of Swami Vivekananda*, vol. IV, 8th edn (Calcutta: Advaita Ashrama, 1968), pp. 194–95.
70 Peter Heehs, *The Bomb in Bengal* (Delhi: Oxford University Press, 2004), pp. 25–26.
71 Heehs, *The Bomb in Bengal*, p. 72.

77

to the mystical and spiritual nationalism of Narasimha Swami. At the start of the novel, the narrator describes how Skene's students are 'spellbound' by the performance of the 'palpable ascetic' Narasimha Swami. The Swami's 'reputation for occult power' is later confirmed in part three of the novel,[72] in which the narrator describes the Swami's meditation in great detail:

> He would sit for hours, his eyes fixed on two pebbles at his feet, restraining his breath until the material world slipped away from him and his body floated in ether, looking down indifferently upon his shrunken body and his bowl and his staff and the grey sheep beside the stream as passing phenomena detached for the moment as the atoms cohere in the dance of matter and are reflected in the glass of illusion. Soon nothing objective would remain, and he would be drawn to the centre of the light, conscious only of the rush and beat of wings as he was swept along with the eternal energy which informs all life.[73]

For Candler, the Swami 'owed much of his magnetism' to these trances and 'had a great deal of what is called in the jargon of the séance psychic force'.[74] Following his training in Vedantic philosophy, the Swami remembered that 'the Vedas and all that they stood for were embodied in his own people' and it is this realisation that prompts his devotion to the nationalist cause: 'his flame-like energy became narrowed and concentrated into a cause. Nationalism became a cause within him'. Moreover, Candler figures the Swami as both a 'revolutionist' and an 'anarchist' who 'had no scruples' about sacrificing 'a thousand Siri Rams' and fostering 'a nursery of young murderers'.[75]

Candler's characterisation of Siri Ram as a fanatic who is brainwashed by the spiritual nationalism of Narasimha Swami clearly works to mystify the causes of violent anti-colonial insurgency, and to deny political legitimacy to the nationalist movement. However, this characterisation ignores the way in which the Swami's ascetic form of spiritualism provides a theological and rhetorical structure for the revolutionary nationalist movement. Such a history of insurgency eludes the gaze of colonial intelligence gathering in *Siri Ram Revolutionist*. At the Bridge club, Hobbs suggests that the Swami's injunction to young Bengali men to 'Go back to the Vedas' is a way of codifying and disseminating seditious messages. Such a view is subsequently elaborated upon by the narrator in a discussion of the theological basis of the revolutionary movement:

> Religion in [Siri Ram's] circle had come to mean something approaching a deification of the early Hindus, and an assumption that the same stuff was latent in the modern youth of the country, and only needed a spark to kindle it into the divine fire. Against the sacred names of Rama and Arjun and Bhima were inscribed the names of such modern martyrs as Tilak, and Kanyha Lal

72 Candler, 'Siri Ram Revolutionist: A Transcript from Life', p. 471
73 Candler, 'Siri Ram Revolutionist: A Transcript from Life', p. 471.
74 Candler, 'Siri Ram Revolutionist: A Transcript from Life', p. 471.
75 Candler, 'Siri Ram Revolutionist: A Transcript from Life', p. 472.

and Kudiram Bose who murdered the English ladies at Mozzafarpur. History was going to repeat itself. The English were the Asuras again, who ravaged the Motherland, which was now in the birth pangs of a new breed of dragon slayers who were to rid her of the evil.[76]

For the narrator and the Anglo-Indian characters in the novel, the religious ethos of 'revolutionary terrorism' in early twentieth-century Bengal exemplifies the fanatical and irrational character of Narasimha Swami and the gullibility of Siri Ram. For Narasimha and Siri Ram, however, this religious ethos provides a structure for the political organisation and militancy of the revolutionary movement. The religious ethos that underpins Siri Ram's revolutionary activities as a sedition monger, who willingly goes to prison for editing a seditious newspaper, and subsequently as an assassin of Merivale, a local Anglo-Indian magistrate, is not simply a sign of Siri Ram's fanaticism or irrationality. Rather, this religious ethos is a sign of anti-colonial insurgency that cannot be interpreted within the rational and secular framework of Candler's British colonial worldview.

Pather Dabi and the Bengali Revolutionaries of Burma

As if by way of riposte to Candler's so-called 'sedition novel' *Siri Ram Revolutionist*, Sarat Chandra Chatterjee's novel *Pather Dabi* offers a sympathetic portrayal of a secret organisation of Bengali revolutionaries who sought to renew the ethos of revolutionary nationalism in the later 1920s.[77] *Pather Dabi* presents such anti-colonial sentiment through its evocation of the injustice committed against the protagonist Apurba and the misery of the working class; as well as through the heroic rhetoric of the enigmatic character Sabyasachi (also known as the doctor), who advocates the use of revolutionary violence in anti-colonial struggle.

For the South Asian historian Tanika Sarkar, 'the model of political work celebrated in the *Pather Dabi*' closely resembles the 'cult of militant youth power' led by Subhas Chandra Bose in Bengal during the 1920s.[78] Like Bose, the character of Sabyasachi sought to recruit members of the educated, middle-class Bengali youth to mobilise support for a nationalist struggle against the British government. Yet, despite Sabyasachi's call for a social revolution in India that would overthrow the caste system and the old order that it represents,[79] he ultimately believes that it is the educated, middle classes alone who will deliver political independence to India.

---

76 Candler, 'Siri Ram Revolutionist: A Transcript from Life', p. 419.
77 Sarat Chandra Chatterjee, *Pather Dabi*, trans. Prasenjit Mukherjee (New Delhi: Rupa, 1993).
78 Tanika Sarkar, 'Bengali Middle-Class Nationalism and Literature: A Study of Saratchandra's "Pather Dabi" and Rabindranath's "Char Adhyay"', in D.N. Panigrahi (ed.), *Economy, Society and Politics in Modern India* (New Delhi: Vikas, 1985), p. 451.
79 Chatterjee, *Pather Dabi*, p. 314.

More important, however, is the fact that the majority of the novel is located in Burma. The secret organisation Pather Dabi (which has been translated into English as The Right of Way) is constituted mainly of political exiles from India, including the female characters Sumitra and Bharati, and the enigmatic figure of the doctor. This is not to suggest that the novel is explicitly aligned with Burmese nationalism. As Sarkar observes, '*Pather Dabi* expressed no affinities with the powerful anti-imperialist struggle of the Burmese people, but portrayed a debate exclusively among Indians in Burma about alternative forms of nationalist movement'.[80] The location of the novel is significant because it provides a clue to the historical and political context of the novel. Following the so-called 'terrorist outrages' committed in Bengal during the first two decades of the twentieth century, the Indian government's law enforcement officials had claimed that the detention of alleged Bengali terrorists was a success, a claim that served to justify the Rowlatt Report's recommendation of emergency measures in 1918. In response to this, many leaders of the revolutionary movement went underground in the 1920s and fled Bengal to other British territories, particularly Burma. In so doing, 'Bengali revolutionaries were able to rely on imperial networks of trading and unemployment, while evading police detection'.[81] After the release of hundreds of Bengalis who had been detained in Indian prisons in 1919 for their revolutionary activities, many of these revolutionaries fled to Burma to avoid further detention. From Burma, these individuals sought to establish new secret societies and to support the violent anti-colonial insurgency movement from outside of Bengal. This moment in the history of anti-colonial insurgency in Bengal is paralleled in *Pather Dabi* by the arrival of Sabyasachi in Rangoon after his imprisonment for three months at Poona and for three years at Singapore,[82] and by the suggestion that Apurba was involved in the *swadeshi* movement during his youth.[83]

The transnational movements and strategies of masquerade adopted by the doctor in *Pather Dabi* to avoid detention by the police and government officials in Burma certainly resemble those strategies adopted by revolutionaries to smuggle arms from Singapore, Japan and China. In her reminiscences on the Chittagong Armoury Raid of April 1930, Kalpana Dutt compares Surjiya Sen, the leader of the Chittagong Armoury Raid, to the doctor in Sarat Chandra's *Pather Dabi*.[84] In particular, Dutt describes the rumours that used to circulate about Sen or *Masterda*, as she described him:

> All sorts of things used to go around about Masterda. How he slipped through a police cordon, dressed like an old mali (gardener). How he walked through village after village, in broad daylight, talking carelessly to a police officer

80 Sarkar 'Bengali Middle-Class Nationalism and Literature', p. 453.
81 Ghosh, 'Terrorism in Bengal, pp. 271–72.
82 Chatterjee, *Pather Dabi*, p. 67.
83 Chatterjee, *Pather Dabi*, pp. 21, 65–66.
84 Kalpana Dutt, *Chittagong Armoury Raiders Reminiscences* (New Delhi: People's Publishing House, 1979 [1945]), p. 12.

companion – who did not know who he was talking to. There were scores of stories about Masterda.[85]

Such rumours of Sen's use of masquerade to evade police detection recall the use of masquerade by the revolutionary character Sabyasachi in *Pather Dabi*. In chapter 6, for example, Nimaibabu, a senior police officer of the Bengal government, attempts to apprehend the doctor at the port in Rangoon. In contrast to the government's claims that the 'revolutionary terrorists' were legible to the gaze of the police, Nimaibabu asserts that 'such a dangerous person has the most inconspicuous appearance, just like any common man. Hence it's difficult to recognise or catch him. There is special mention of this in our reports'.[86] Yet, it is the doctor's very conspicuous appearance that enables him to pass as a hashish-smoking oil mill worker with a rather unusual taste in clothes. As Apurba observes,

> The man sported long hair in the front, but so closely was it cropped in the back and sides as to make him look practically bald. It was parted in the middle, and a liberal use of lemon oil filled the room with [an] offensive smell. He wore a colourful Japanese shirt, but had no shawl. A printed handkerchief having the imprint of a tiger's face hung out of his breast pocket. Around his waist he had wrapped a fine English mill made *sari* with a black border; a pair of green stockings were tied above his knees with red laces, and on his feet he wore shoes of shining leather, the soles studded with nails to make them durable. In his hand he carried a cane with a bundle of horn. Everything on him was dirty after the long voyage.[87]

This rather comic account of the doctor's disguise is reinforced by Apurba's outburst of laughter. Apurba assures the police chief that 'he's not the man you're looking for'.[88] The veracity of this statement is, however, undermined by the fact that the narrator had earlier described Apurba's reverie on the political commitment of this elusive revolutionary figure. As a consequence, readers are also encouraged to recognise the ingenuity of the revolutionary hero and to laugh at the ineptness of the police.

The superhuman status of the doctor is further registered by a comparison with the character of Sabyasachi in the *Mahabharata*, a figure who could wield both hands with equal dexterity: 'the intelligence reports of the government reveal that in the case of this man, each of his organs is equally dextrous. He never misses a target with gun or pistol. He can swim across the mighty river Padma; nothing can stop him'.[89] This description of the doctor has prompted Sarkar to comment on the superhuman status of the doctor:

85 Dutt, *Chittagong Armoury Raiders Reminiscences*, p. 10.
86 Chatterjee, *Pather Dabi*, p. 68.
87 Chatterjee, *Pather Dabi*, p. 73.
88 Chatterjee, *Pather Dabi*, p. 73.
89 Chatterjee, *Pather Dabi*, pp. 66–67.

[...] the hero [of *Pather Dabi*], Sabyasachi, is a revolutionary who moves all over South Asia but his plans and activities are never definitely spelt out. The mystery somehow enhances his personality. Capable, literally of everything, he is the first superman in serious Bengali fiction, always a million times larger than life.[90]

It is Sabyasachi's ability to elude the gaze of colonial intelligence that reinforces his superhuman reputation. The doctor's precise movements and activities are never revealed to the other members of the secret society or to the reader.

By contrast to Anglo-Indian fictions of counter-insurgency, there are no specific acts of revolutionary violence carried out in the narrative of *Pather Dabi*. It is rather in the doctor's nationalist rhetoric that he attempts to justify the recourse to violence. The doctor freely admits to Bharati that he is 'a dangerous man [...] who goes around killing people with bombs and guns',[91] and declares that violence is necessary for the 'true emancipation' of the working class.[92] He also vehemently rejects the strategy of non-violence as an effective means to counter the violence of colonial oppression in his dialogue with Bharati:

> Peace! Peace! Peace! I'm fed up with this constant talk of peace! Do you know who are the people who've been preaching this falsehood for so long? They are the same people who have robbed the peace of others, who've usurped what was rightfully theirs. They are the preachers of the cult of peace! They have dinned this into the ears of the deprived, diseased and oppressed populace so that they now shudder at the very thought of unrest.[93]

In this speech, the doctor's rejection of peace as an effective form of resistance could be read as a rejection of the philosophy of non-violent non-cooperation advocated by Gandhi on the grounds that it hampers popular desire for political unrest. While the growing political support for Gandhi's non-cooperation movement in the 1920s would seem to contradict the doctor's argument against peace, the crucial point for the doctor is that peaceful protest does not go far enough to bring about the desired end to colonial rule. In this respect, Sabyasachi's defence of violent resistance to British colonial rule mirrors Sarat Chandra Chatterjee's own opposition to Gandhi's non-cooperation movement.[94] To support his argument against the reformist agenda of the advocates of peace, the doctor invokes the revolutionary ideas of Europe, especially of the French and Russian revolutions:

> Look at Europe [...] It has taken place in Russia, not once but several times. The French Revolution of June 1848 is still a landmark in the history of

---

90 Tanika Sarkar, *Bengal 1928–1934: The Politics of Protest* (New Delhi: Oxford University Press, 1987), p. 24.
91 Chatterjee, *Pather Dabi*, p. 225.
92 Chatterjee, *Pather Dabi*, p. 270.
93 Chatterjee, *Pather Dabi*, p. 271.
94 See Sarkar, *Bengal 1928–1934*, and Aruna Chakravarti, *Sarat Chandra: Rebel and Humanist* (New Delhi: National Book Trust, 1985).

revolutionary movements. That day the streets of Paris were drenched with the blood of peasants and workers![95]

In this passage, the doctor suggests that there is a historical precedent for the use of violence in the service of India's freedom, and in so doing appropriates the proletarian revolutions of nineteenth- and early twentieth-century Europe and applies them to the specific political circumstances of colonial India.

Significantly, the British colonial authorities noted the invocation of revolutionary ideas and events in modern Europe by 'revolutionary organisations' in Bengal to support 'revolutionary activities'. In the Rowlatt Report of 1918, the nationalist leader Tilak was quoted as saying the following to justify his use of violence: 'the people who took part in the French revolution denied that they had committed murder and asserted that they were only removing thorns from their side'.[96] Similarly the writings and actions of Russian anarchists were sometimes invoked to justify the cause of political opposition to the colonial state.[97] This is not to suggest, however, that the political beliefs of Russian anarchists and Indian revolutionaries were identical, even if some of their tactics appeared similar. Indeed, the differences between Russian anarchists and Indian revolutionaries was made clear in the following paragraph from an article supporting the bomb attack on two English ladies in Muzzafurpur in the Marathi journal, the *Kal*, which was also translated and quoted in the Rowlatt Report:

> People are prepared to do anything for the sake of [independence] and they no longer sing the glories of British rule. They have no dread of British power. It is simply a question of sheer brute force. Bomb throwing in India is different from bomb throwing in Russia. Many of the Russians side with their government against these bomb throwers, but it is doubtful such sympathy will be found in India. […] It is quite unjustifiable to call the bomb throwers in India anarchists. Setting aside the question whether bomb-throwing is justifiable or not, Indians are not trying to promote disorder, but to obtain freedom.[98]

It is precisely this attempt to set aside the ethical question of whether violence is justifiable or not that informs the doctor's rhetoric in the latter part of Chatterjee's novel. For the doctor, 'the independence of India is his sole aim in life, its

---

95 Chatterjee, *Pather Dabi*, p. 271.
96 *Sedition Committee Report 1918*, p. 2.
97 One of the intellectual figures associated with the Indian revolutionaries in Bengal, Sister Nivedeta, exchanged letters with Peter Kropotkin, and there is compelling evidence to suggest that Kropotkin's political writings informed the thinking of both Nivedeta and Aurobindo Ghose. See Heehs, *The Bomb in Bengal*, p. 27, and Boehmer, *Empire, the National, and the Postcolonial*, pp. 45–46. Yet it is also important to clarify that Kropotkin was ambivalent about the use of violence: he did not identify with the phrase 'propaganda by deed' that was attributed to anarchists in the late nineteenth century, and yet he was sympathetic to the assassination of Alexander II by Narodnya Volya. See Caroline Cahm, *Kropotkin and the Rise of Revolutionary Anarchism* (Cambridge: Cambridge University Press, 1989), pp. 92–115, 140–41.
98 *Sedition Committee Report 1918*, p. 7.

achievements [his] only dream'.[99] By his own admission, the doctor has 'no love, no affection, no compassion; good and bad are both meaningless to him'.[100] While the doctor may not share the philosophy of non-violence associated with Gandhi's political thought, his call for violent resistance is clearly articulated to the same political outcome: India's national independence and the end of British colonial rule. Just as Gandhi argued that the sedition law 'is perhaps the prince among the political sections of the Indian Penal Code designed to suppress the liberty of the citizen',[101] so the doctor argues that 'Freedom is the greatest glory of mankind. But according to the laws framed by the British, it is seditious even to wish for it, leave aside striving to achieve it'.[102]

After the partition of Bengal in 1905 and in response to the increase of 'terrorist outrages' in Bengal and Punjab, British fictions of counter-insurgency both rehearsed and contributed to a public anxiety around the figures of the Indian revolutionary and the Indian seditionist, which ultimately served to justify the introduction of emergency legislation in colonial India, as defined by the Rowlatt Report. Yet, as I have suggested in this chapter, the instability of the stereotypical figure of the Indian revolutionary as a 'dangerous hybrid' called into question the ethnocentric assumptions and knowledge upon which colonial intelligence was based. Moreover, the sedition legislation provided nationalist intellectuals and writers with a powerful rhetorical tool to criticise and contest the legitimacy of the British colonial government, and the violence upon which that government was based. During his trial for sedition in 1922, Gandhi asserted that he considered it a privilege to be tried under Section 124A of India's Penal Code because 'some of the most loved of India's patriots have been convicted under it'.[103] For Gandhi, the trial provided a political platform for questioning the legitimacy of the British colonial state on moral grounds: 'I hold it be a virtue to be disaffected towards a government which in its totality has done more harm to India than any previous system'.[104] In this respect, Gandhi's speech, like that of the doctor in *Pather Dabi*, suggests that sedition is a crucial rhetorical and political strategy in the struggle against the exclusionary techniques of British colonial governmentality in India.

By reading the literary prose of counter-insurgency against the grain, I have suggested that the framing of the seditionist and the revolutionary as dangerous individuals is an example of metalepsis, in which opposition to colonial rule is presented as the cause of repressive emergency measures rather than a revolutionary political response to a repressive and exploitative system of colonial sovereignty. This is not to say, however, that such legal and literary narratives of sedition are totalising or that emergency law and the state of violence it enables are confined to the colonial past. As Gandhi's reflections

---

99 Chatterjee, *Pather Dabi*, p. 274.
100 Chatterjee, *Pather Dabi*, p. 274.
101 Gandhi, *Trial of Gandhiji*, p. 185.
102 Chatterjee, *Pather Dabi*, p. 280.
103 Gandhi, *Trial of Gandhiji*, p. 187.
104 Gandhi, *Trial of Gandhiji*, pp. 187–88.

on Section 124A demonstrate, the authority of legal narratives are as open to political challenge and contestation as literary narratives are – an insight which should give us pause for reflection in the wake of the lawful violence associated with the techniques of governmentality employed by the postcolonial Indian state in Kashmir and Manipur.[105]

---

105 For further discussion of the ways in which the postcolonial Indian state marshalls colonial legacies in order to 'consolidate the nation as a new form of empire', see Agnana P. Chatterji, 'The Militarized Zone', in Tariq Ali et al. (eds), *Kashmir: The Case for Freedom* (London: Verso, 2011), p. 96.

Part II

CHAPTER 3

States of Emergency, the Apartheid Legal Order and the Tradition of the Oppressed in South African Fiction

In an article published in the South African Communist party newspaper *New Age* in September 1960, the left-wing writer Alex La Guma declares, 'What a calamity the Emergency has been – for Afrikaner Nationalism'.[1] While La Guma concedes that the people detained under the emergency suffered in various ways – either through bankruptcy, redundancy, imprisonment without trial or a 'sickening uncertainty' about the duration of their detention – he repeats the claim that the 'Emergency was a calamity for Afrikaner nationalism'.[2] In a rhetorical move that recalls Benjamin's Eighth Thesis on the Concept of History, La Guma suggests that the emergency highlights the fact that the suspension of civil liberties for the South African population is the *raison d'état* of the nationalist government and its apartheid policies rather than the exception. 'When the state is forced to throw aside its cloak of legality, and to surrender every claim to moral action', La Guma adds, 'it is doomed no matter how much physical force it may command'.[3] Such a prescient declaration identifies the autoimmunity of South Africa's apartheid state: the emergency measures introduced by the apartheid government would bring about its own destruction. If the emergency highlighted a 'connection [...] between the Police State and the Afrikaner people', it also prefigures the emergence of the very thing that the state is trying to control and repress: the 'multi-racial and multi-national' composition of the South African population.[4] By refusing the discriminatory policies of the government and its racist policy of separate development, and distinguishing between an 'Afrikaner people' that supported the apartheid

---

1 Alex La Guma, 'State of Emergency', in Andre Odendaal and Roger Field (eds), *Liberation Chabalala: The World of Alex La Guma* (Belville, South Africa: Mayibuye Books, 1993), p. 146.
2 La Guma, 'State of Emergency', p. 146.
3 La Guma, 'State of Emergency', p. 148.
4 La Guma, 'State of Emergency', p. 147.

policies of the 'police state' and the 'multi-racial and multi-national' population that opposed it, La Guma not only calls into question the legal foundations of apartheid, but also contributes to the invention of a South African tradition of the oppressed.

It is with the formulation of this tradition in the context of South Africa's state of emergency that this chapter is in part concerned. We have already seen in the introduction how the tradition of the oppressed in Benjamin's thought refers not only to an 'alternate tradition of those excluded from the canons of "high" culture', but also to the 'suppressed, subversive moments' within high culture.[5] Such a distinction is interesting in the South African context, when one considers that Nelson Mandela's engagement with literature during his imprisonment on Robben Island included texts such as Sophocles' *Antigone* and Shakespeare's *Julius Caesar*, as well as Nadine Gordimer's *Burger's Daughter*.[6] In this respect, Mandela's engagement with literary texts during his imprisonment can be seen to exemplify both senses of the tradition of the oppressed in Benjamin's thought. While a detailed consideration of Mandela's engagement with literature is beyond the scope of this chapter, I mention it here because it provides a useful starting point from which to investigate critical debates about politics and aesthetics in South African writing before and after the apartheid era.

For South African writers and literary critics such as Lewis Nkosi, Ndebele and Coetzee, the emergence of South African writing that was opposed to the apartheid regime, such as that of La Guma, Rive and Peter Abrahams in apartheid South Africa, was limited by its tendency to document the violence and oppression of the apartheid regime rather than imagining alternatives to such forms of state repression. In a discussion of 'Fiction by Black South Africans', for instance, Nkosi bemoans the absence of a South African novel that would compare to the 'inventive genius' of Amos Tutuola's *The Palm Wine Drinkard* or the 'imaginative power' of Chinua Achebe's *Things Fall Apart*, and proceeds to criticise 'the type of fiction' predominant in South Africa during the apartheid period that 'exploits the ready-made plots of racial violence, social apartheid, [and] interracial love affairs which are doomed from the beginning, without any attempt to transcend or transmute these given "social facts" into artistically persuasive works of fiction'.[7] In a similar vein, Ndebele argues that the treatment of apartheid South Africa has been rather superficial because it tends to rely on symbols or 'mere ideas to be marshalled this way or that in a moral debate'.[8] Instead of 'clarifying the tragic human experience of oppression', Ndebele argues that 'such fiction becomes grounded in the very negation it seeks to transcend'.[9] More specifically, Ndebele argues that the problem with

5 McCole, *Walter Benjamin*, pp. 304–5.
6 See Elleke Boehmer, *Nelson Mandela: A Very Short Introduction* (Oxford: Oxford University Press, 2008), pp. 84–86.
7 Lewis Nkosi, *Home and Exile* (London: Longmans, 1965), p. 126.
8 Njabulo Ndebele, *South African Literature and Culture: Rediscovery of the Ordinary* (Manchester: Manchester University Press, 1994), p. 28.
9 Ndebele, *South African Literature and Culture*, p. 28.

much anti-apartheid writing is its tendency to rely on spectacle.[10] It is perhaps the kind of criticism levelled against anti-apartheid writing by critics such as Nkosi and Ndebele that subsequently prompted Albie Sachs to argue in a controversial paper presented at an ANC in-house seminar entitled 'Preparing Ourselves for Freedom' that 'our members should be banned from saying that culture is a weapon of struggle' because 'it results in an impoverishment of our art'.[11] Writing as a lawyer and as a former member of the ANC during South Africa's transition from apartheid state to democracy, Sachs's proposal can be understood as an attempt to question and complicate what he regards as the caricatured cultural representations of the division between the apartheid state and the anti-apartheid movement in much anti-apartheid literature and art – cultural representations that could be damaging to the plural vision of South Africa's democratic future. In the terms of Sachs's argument, the reduction of art and literature to a transparent expression of political struggle is equivalent to imposing an 'internal state of emergency' on the arts and culture in South Africa.[12] By drawing this connection between political writing and emergency law, Sachs implies that there is a correspondence between the politics of literary and cultural representation and the authority of emergency law, and that the law-making violence of the apartheid state had somehow contaminated the codes and conventions of art and literature. By framing literature and culture as a weapon of political struggle, in other words, Sachs suggests that the ANC had placed limits on artistic expression in ways that mirrored the censorship laws of the apartheid state.[13] Yet in prescribing a new role for literature and the arts in the new South Africa, Sachs seems to subordinate the analysis of the economic, political and social divisions in South African society to questions of artistic merit.[14] Like Nkosi and Ndebele, Sachs proposes a radical humanist approach to writing in South Africa, in which the tolerant, rational and enfranchised subject of humanism can work to bring about a democratic civil society in post-apartheid South Africa. Yet, as Kelwyn Sole observes, this argument has 'enabled an unfortunate corollary to emerge', which is that 'writers should downplay the political side and urgency of their art, both in relation to how they write and what they should write about'.[15] Against such an approach, Sole has argued that 'there is still a political dimension of expression necessary in this fraught, divided country' and that 'politically-motivated writers need to

---

10 Ndebele, *South African Literature and Culture*, p. 41.
11 Albie Sachs, 'Preparing Ourselves for Freedom', in Ingrid de Kok and Karen Press (eds), *Spring Is Rebellious: Arguments about Cultural Freedom* (Cape Town: Buchu Books, 1990), pp. 19–20.
12 Sachs, 'Preparing Ourselves for Freedom', p. 28.
13 For more on the censorship laws in South Africa, see Peter D. McDonald, *The Literature Police: Apartheid Censorship and Its Cultural Consequences* (Oxford: Oxford University Press, 2009).
14 See Kelwyn Sole, 'Democratising Culture in a "New South Africa": Organisation and Theory', *Current Writing*, 6/2, (1994), pp. 1–37.
15 Kelwyn Sole, 'The Role of the Writer in a Time of Transition', *Staffrider*, 11/1–4 (1993), p. 93.

start not only refining their artistic skill, but also refining and increasing their understanding of the nuances and subtleties of politics and power'.[16]

In response to these debates, this chapter considers how literary representations of the state of emergency in apartheid South Africa foreground the ways in which a state of emergency functioned as a technique of governmentality in the apartheid state. Starting with a consideration of South Africa's emergency legislation, and the socio-historical context in which it emerged, the chapter examines how literary texts contested the apartheid government's emergency legislation by exposing the sovereign power and force underpinning the apartheid state. Writing in the shadow of a political regime that also proscribed the publication of literature deemed to be offensive by the apartheid state, the representation of state violence may appear to reinforce the apartheid state's authority. Yet, as I suggest through readings of Rive's *Emergency*, Alex La Guma's *In the Fog of the Season's End*, Coetzee's *Waiting for the Barbarians* and Rive's *Emergency Continued*, it is only by interrogating the legal and extra-legal foundations upon which the violence of the apartheid state was based that one can begin to understand 'the nuances and subtleties of politics and power'.[17] If novels such as Rive's *Emergency* and La Guma's *In the Fog of the Season's End* spell out the relationship between South Africa's emergency legislation and the apartheid regime's sovereign power over the life and death of the South African population by constructing a fictional narrative in which the violent techniques of the state are made intelligible, they also offer important insights into the forms of political organisation and collective resistance which ultimately led to the collapse of the apartheid regime. By contrast, Coetzee's *Waiting for the Barbarians*, Rive's *Emergency Continued* and Wicomb's *David's Story* raise important questions about the difficulties and challenges of representing torture, police violence and political struggles in literary narratives. This is not to suggest, however, that these texts are merely concerned with the politics of representation. For what these three novels share in common is a critique of the legal distinction between the normal rule of law and the state of exception; and a commitment to invent a literary form that can do justice to the traumatic and fragmentary history of the oppressed both during and after the apartheid era.

Racism, Biopolitics and the Apartheid Legal Order

From the standpoint of the oppressed, the state of emergency in apartheid South Africa did not begin with the election of the Nationalist party in 1948, but can rather be traced to the formation of British colonial institutions such as the Department of Native Affairs, which regulated the exclusion of Africans from citizenship and the establishment of a racially repressive labour market in the 1920s and 1930s. Indeed, it was the transformation of the Department of

---

16 Sole, 'The Role of the Writer in a Time of Transition', pp. 93–94.
17 Sole, 'The Role of the Writer in a Time of Transition', pp. 93–94.

Native Affairs from an obscure and ineffective administrative department into an efficient and centralised state bureaucracy that gave apartheid its institutional form.[18] And it was the legal powers granted to such state bureaucracies over the lives and bodies of the colonised which provide an important frame of reference through which to understand the state of emergency in apartheid South Africa, as we will see.

In the narrow terms of South African law, the state of emergency has its provenance in the South African Public Safety Act. In some respects, the language and principles of the Public Safety Act of 1953 may appear to mirror the emergency legislation of other governments. 'The notion of public safety', as A.S. Mathews explains, 'is generally associated with the maxim [attributed to Cicero] *salus populi suprema lex* – the safety of the people is the highest law'.[19] Moreover, the Public Safety Act empowered 'the state president to declare by proclamation in the *Gazette* that a state of emergency exists within the Republic or South West Africa or any of their areas'.[20] The president's powers under this act included 'the prohibition of gatherings and processions, the dispersal by force of illegal gatherings, the detention of persons without trial or access, broad and sweeping crimes and the suppression of publications and organizations'.[21] Yet in the South African statute, there is a slippage between the protection of the public and the protection of the state, and one consequence of this slippage is that there is 'no clear-cut differentiation between the various concepts of state security, public safety and government security'.[22] This slippage was particularly pronounced in the declaration of a state of emergency in 1960, which allowed the Government to issue regulations that 'permitted arrest without warrant and detention without trial'.[23] As John Dugard explains, the Public Safety Act of 1953 gave the South African government 'a completely free hand':

> The writ of *habeas corpus* is ousted and the courts are rendered powerless. There is no commission to which an aggrieved detainee can appeal, such as one finds in the emergency laws of other countries, nor is there any body empowered with the task of objectively determining whether the emergency is in fact justified by the prevailing conditions.[24]

While it was the Public Safety Act of 1953 that made possible the South African government's declaration of a state of emergency in March 1960 following the police massacre of 67 black demonstrators at Sharpeville and the subsequent protests that ensued, the force and significance of this statute only becomes clear when considered in the context of a broader series of discrimi-

18 See Ivan Thomas Evans, *Bureaucracy and Race: Native Administration in South Africa* (Berkeley: University of California Press, 1997).
19 *The Law of South Africa*, 21, ed. W.A. Joubert (Durban Pretoria: Butterworths, 1984), p. 297.
20 *The Law of South Africa*, 21, p. 299.
21 *The Law of South Africa*, 21, p. 300.
22 *The Law of South Africa*, 21, p. 297.
23 John Dugard, *Human Rights and the South African Legal Order* (Princeton, NJ: Princeton University Press, 1978), p. 110.
24 Dugard, *Human Rights and the South African Legal Order*, p. 111.

natory laws and policies introduced after the election of the Nationalist Party in 1948, which Brian Bunting has called South Africa's Nuremberg laws. These laws included the Group Areas Act, the Suppression of Communism Act and the Immorality Amendment Act, among many others.[25] Bunting's comparison of the South African Nationalist Party's apartheid legislation with the Nuremberg laws of 1935 is apposite in that the apartheid legislation sought to privilege the rights and freedoms of South Africans deemed by the state to be white over those South Africans deemed to be coloured, Indian or black and to proscribe sexual relations between South Africans deemed to be white and non-white in the same way that the 1935 Nuremberg laws of the Third Reich had outlawed marital and extra-marital sexual relations between people the state deemed to be German and those it deemed to be Jewish. For Deborah Posel in *The Making of Apartheid*, however, Bunting's claim that apartheid was part of an all-embracing grand plan imposed by the Afrikaner Nationalist party overlooks the complex ways in which the growth of an urban African proletariat and patterns of migrant labour from the countryside to Johannesburg and Cape Town also shaped the direction of the Nationalist government's influx control policies in the 1950s.[26] Such a focus on the history of migrant labour is certainly important, but it can work to overstate the determining power of class division in the formation of apartheid to the exclusion of other important social factors, as Aletta J. Norval has argued.[27] Rather than assuming that an a priori form of social division constitutes the apartheid political order, Norval posits a genealogy of apartheid that traces 'the ignoble history of the contingent processes and [the] struggles through which it became hegemonic'.[28] Norval's genealogical approach to the history of apartheid is certainly preferable to the aprioristic mode of thinking that she criticises. Yet it is also important to note that the processes through which apartheid became hegemonic were made possible by the introduction of political techniques and laws that foreclosed the contingency of political resistance and struggle.

If the government's influx control policies in the 1950s were partly a response to the contradictory demands of white South African capital for cheap African labour on the one hand and to those of the Nationalist party for a total segregation of the white and black South African populations on the other, these policies can also be understood as a particularly pernicious form of biopolitical control. In Michel Foucault's argument, biopolitics refers to the development of political techniques for controlling the life of the population. Racism, according to Foucault, has a particular biopolitical function; a function which is, he says, 'primarily a way of introducing a break between the domain of life that is under power's control: the break between what must live and

25 Brian Bunting, *The Rise of the South African Reich* (Harmondsworth: Penguin, 1969), pp. 142–60.
26 Deborah Posel, *The Making of Apartheid, 1948–1961: Conflict and Compromise* (Cape Town: Oxford University Press South Africa, 1997).
27 Aletta J. Norval, *Deconstructing Apartheid Discourse* (London: Verso, 1996), p. 59.
28 Norval, *Deconstructing Apartheid Discourse*, p. 61.

what must die'.[29] Racism, in other words, has a biological rationale, which is to eliminate the 'inferior race' that is perceived as a threat to the species in general.[30] In South Africa during the apartheid era, however, since the ruling white minority was economically dependent on the living labour of the races it deemed to be inferior, the elimination of such races was not compatible with the economic demand for cheap African labour in urban areas,[31] and so the state introduced policies to control and regulate the segregation of the population; the movement, residence and employment of Africans; and the political organisation and mobilisation of African labour. Yet even these policies were far from perfect. As the historian Keith Breckenridge has argued, the attempt by the Verwoerd government in the 1950s to centralise the administration and regulation of the African population through the establishment of a new, supposedly cost effective Central Identity Bureau was ultimately a panoptic fantasy that masked the fact that the apartheid state was 'much less able to produce meaningful intelligence about its subjects than the older chaotic, paper-based and decentralized state that it replaced'.[32] Such historical insights not only call into question the effectiveness of the influx control policies as a form of biopolitical control, they also help to account for the shift to an even more draconian form of government in the 1960s.

For many South African writers, intellectuals and activists, it was the massacre of 67 demonstrators by the police at Sharpeville on 18 March 1960 that symbolised the violence of the apartheid state, and marked a shift in the tactics of the African resistance movement from a form of resistance loosely associated with M.K. Gandhi's idea of peaceful non-cooperation to the formation of the armed resistance wing of the ANC known as the Spear of the Nation, or Umkhonto weSizwe (MK).[33] The Sharpeville massacre 'crystallised the sheer oppressive horror of apartheid in the form of a tangible body count' and undermined 'any future moral authority for the political system of white minority South Africa'.[34] The massacre at Sharpeville followed a series of peaceful protests against the pass laws organised by the leader of the Pan-African Congress, Robert Sobukwe, in the Johannesburg residential areas of Vanderbijl Park and Sharpeville and the

---

29 Michel Foucault, *Society Must Be Defended: Lectures at the Collège de France, 1975–76*, trans. David Macey (London: Allen Lane, 2003), p. 254.

30 Foucault, *Society Must Be Defended*, pp. 255–56.

31 Deborah Posel argues that the 'architects of Apartheid [...] grappled with ways of curtailing the growth of the urban African population, without thereby undermining the economic benefits of African labour'. One resolution to this tension was proposed by the '"practical" notion of Apartheid', which held that 'the problems generated by African proletarianisation could be solved by improved state control, rather than by fundamental restructuring of the country's labour markets'. Posel, *The Making of Apartheid*, pp. 8, 55.

32 Keith Breckenridge, 'Verwoerd's Bureau of Proof: Total Information in the Making of Apartheid', *History Workshop Journal*, 59 (2005), pp. 85–108 (104).

33 See Mbulelo Vizikhungo Mzamane, 'Sharpeville and Its Aftermath: The Novels of Richard Rive, Peter Abrahams, Alex La Guma, and Lauretta Ngcobo', *Ariel*, 16/2 (1985), pp. 31–44.

34 Philip Frankel, *An Ordinary Atrocity: Sharpeville and Its Massacre* (New Haven: Yale University Press, 2001), p. 6.

Cape Town area of Langa. Moreover, the widespread political unrest sparked by the Sharpeville massacre provided the minister of justice with a pretext to declare a state of emergency in South Africa under the Public Safety Act of 1953. This law gave the state the power to 'detain indefinitely without trial any person suspected of engaging in subversive activities against the state', and to impose heavy penalties for 'distributing any publications or pamphlets critical of the state'.[35] Just as the colonial authorities in India had used acts of 'revolutionary terrorism' as a pretext to proscribe criticism of the British colonial state (as we saw in Chapter 2), so the apartheid state in South Africa used Sharpeville and the political unrest that it provoked as a pretext to proscribe all black political activity.

'Legislation and More Legislation': Spaces of Resistance and the Apartheid Rule of Law in Richard Rive's *Emergency*

Richard Rive's novel *Emergency* (first published 1964) traces the political educa-tion of its central protagonist, high school teacher Andrew Dreyer, to the imposi-tion of the pass laws, the Immorality Act and the Public Safety Act. The novel takes place in Cape Town over a period of three days between the aftermath of the Sharpeville massacre and the declaration of a state of emergency, and includes a series of flashbacks to the protagonist's childhood. As Rive explains in his autobiography, *Writing Black*,

> 1960 had been the year of Sharpeville and Langa. I watched Philip Kgosana's historic march from Langa to Cape Town with 30 000 Blacks, and attended protest meetings all over the Peninsula until these were summarily banned. The following year I decided to write a novel spread over the three most crucial days of the Sharpeville unrest, 28 to 30 March. I called the novel *Emergency*, since I saw it as being concerned with both the state of emergency which had been declared and the social and political emergence of the main character, Andrew Dreyer, whose life had in some ways ran parallel to mine.[36]

By defining the novel as rooted in experience, Rive distinguishes *Emergency* from the liberal writing of Olive Schreiner and Alan Paton which 'may be loosely defined as writing mostly by Whites about Blacks to move Whites out of their socio-political complacency' and aligns his novel instead with the protest writing of Sol Plaatje and Abrahams.[37] Part *Bildungsroman*, part political thriller, *Emergency* follows Dreyer's various attempts to elude the security police, who suspect his involvement with the Pan-African Congress, as well as his illicit relationship with a white South African student called Ruth Talbot. In so doing, Rive combines the generic codes of nineteenth-century European fiction with the conven-tions of urban protest writing associated with *Drum* magazine to articulate the

35 Mzamane, 'Sharpeville and Its Aftermath', p. 33.
36 Richard Rive, *Writing Black* (Cape Town: David Phillip, 1981), p. 19.
37 Rive, *Writing Black*, p. 21.

competing political positions and anxieties facing many black South Africans in the immediate aftermath of the Sharpeville massacre. The fact that *Emergency* was the first novel to be banned under the Suppression of Communism Act also lends further credence to the novel as a work of protest literature.

The novel begins with an account of the anti-pass law demonstration in Cape Town, and a police warning that 'the Meetings Ban is being violated'.[38] In this passage, the narrator describes a 'tense and hostile atmosphere',[39] in which the protagonist, Andrew Dreyer, had run away from a 'baton charge' and the police stand with 'hands resting on their revolver holsters'.[40] Dreyer's involvement in the anti-pass law demonstration prompts a subsequent interrogation by the police, who repeatedly ask him if he's a member of the Pan African Congress, a question that he flatly refuses to answer. In doing so, the police tacitly invoke the Suppression of Communism Act of 1950, a statute which defined 'communist' as anyone who is 'deemed by the Governor General […] to be a communist' and 'aims at the encouragement of feelings of hostility between the European and non-European races of the Union'.[41] The Suppression of Communism Act thus expanded the definition of communist to include anyone 'demanding equal economic, social and political rights for all South Africans'.[42] When the police press Dreyer on the question of whether he is a member of any 'left-wing organizations', Dreyer dryly replies that he is a member of the 'Ottery Road Table Tennis Club and Steenberg High School Cultural Society'.[43]

In the fictional world of Rive's South Africa, the apartheid rule of law is framed in part as a regime of biopolitical control, a regime that not only attempts to control and separate the white and black populations according to a principle of racial purity, but does so by trying to regulate and police the sexual conduct of the population.[44] During Ruth Talbot's interrogation by the security police about the nature of her involvement with Andrew Dreyer, for example, the police insinuate that she and Dreyer are 'more than intimate friends'.[45] Such an allegation is significant because it clearly highlights the way in which the security police resort to a particular lexicon of sexual metaphors and innuendo that can be traced back to nineteenth-century discourses of sexuality. As Foucault puts it in *The Will to Knowledge*, 'a policing of sex' did not mean 'the rigor of a taboo, but the necessity of regulating sex through useful and public discourses'.[46] In

---

38 Richard Rive, *Emergency* (London: Faber & Faber, 1964), p. 19.
39 Rive, *Emergency*, p. 21.
40 Rive, *Emergency*, pp. 22–23.
41 'Suppression of Communism Act', Act no. 44 of 1950, *Statutes of the Union of South Africa*, p. 551.
42 Norval, *Deconstructing Apartheid Discourse*, p. 137.
43 Rive, *Emergency*, p. 26.
44 For more on Dutch colonial discourses of race and sexuality, see Ann Laura Stoler, *Race and the Education of Desire: Foucault's History of Sexuality and the Colonial Order of Things* (Durham, NC.: Duke University Press, 1995).
45 Rive, *Emergency*, p. 81.
46 Michel Foucault, *The Will to Knowledge: The History of Sexuality, Volume One*, trans. Robert Hurley (Harmondsworth: Penguin, 1998), p. 25.

Emergency, such a mode of policing sexuality through sexual metaphors may seem to further highlight the tensions within the apartheid state between a biopolitical power that seeks to 'let live' in order to maintain the capitalist economy and a necropolitical power that seeks to eliminate a form of life that is deemed to threaten the racial purity of the apartheid state. Such a combination of necropolitical and biopolitical power is further complicated by the ways in which the legal discourses of race and sexuality appear to regulate the lives of the individual subject in *Emergency*. Foucault distinguishes between a biopower that focuses on the life of the population and a sovereign power that appears to focus on the individual subject.[47] This distinction becomes blurred in Rive's representation of the apartheid state's policing of race and sexuality. If the apartheid state attempted to control the population through a centralised bureaucracy that approached the population as anonymous, in *Emergency* this policing of the population is experienced as a form of power that addresses individual subjects. The discursive address of the apartheid legal order may be addressed to the population, but it is interpreted and internalised by the individual subject as a manifestation of sovereign power. A significant example of the way in which the security police maintain control over the life and sexuality of the population is evidenced in a heated argument between Ruth Talbot and Mrs Carollisen, Dreyer's landlady. Following a visit by the security police, Mrs Carollisen admonishes Ruth for having a sexual relationship with Andrew on the grounds that 'He's a Coloured Man'.[48] When Ruth protests on moral grounds (she asks Mrs Carollisen whether Andrew's race should 'make a difference'), Mrs Carollisen defends her criticism of Ruth and Andrew's relationship, arguing that 'she didn't make the law',[49] and that she has to protect the public reputation of her home and family. Furthermore, by emphasising that she 'will not expose [her] self to scandal',[50] Mrs Carollisen does not only publicly articulate her complicity with the apartheid regime over her solidarity with the plight of racialised South Africans such as Andrew, but also demonstrates the way in which the law of apartheid became hegemonic by claiming to protect the interests and values of the white community. As Aletta J. Norval explains, 'The legislation on mixed marriages, immorality and population registration formed the basis of a philosophy that saw "racial purity" as a virtue. On this view, the maintenance of racial purity required legislation for it could be preserved only if there existed a generalized "heightened racial consciousness"'.[51] In her dialogue with Ruth Talbot, however, Mrs Carollisen's 'heightened racial consciousness' is prompted by a fear of the law and the security police. For in the earlier exchange between the police and Mrs Dreyer, it is clear from the police's questions that protection from

47 See Alex Houen, 'Sovereignty, Biopolitics, and the Use of Literature', in Stephen Morton and Stephen Bygrave (eds), *Foucault in an Age of Terror: Essays on Biopolitics and the Defence of Society* (Basingstoke: Palgrave Macmillan, 2008), pp. 70–71.
48 Rive, *Emergency*, p. 82.
49 Rive, *Emergency*, p. 83.
50 Rive, *Emergency*, p. 84.
51 Norval, *Deconstructing Apartheid Discourse*, p. 125.

scandal is a euphemism for a threat to the reputation and security of her family and household because of her association with Andrew Dreyer, a suspected communist. Such an encounter would seem to reinforce Norval's observation that 'in the construction of apartheid hegemony the organization of consent has tended to be aimed at "insiders", while the production of acquiescence, if not consent, with regard to "outsiders" proceeded largely, although not wholly, through brute domination'.[52]

As the novel's epigram from Kenko Hoshi suggests, *Emergency* tends to articulate the experience of the apartheid rule of law, and the declaration of a state of emergency following the Sharpeville massacre from the standpoint of the 'outsiders' or the oppressed rather than those who stand to benefit from apartheid: 'So long as people are being ill-governed, suffer from hunger, criminals will never disappear. It is extremely unkind to punish those who, being sufferers from hunger, are compelled to violate laws'.[53] What this epigram implies is that it is 'ill-government' and poor socio-economic conditions ('hunger') that define the illegality of black South Africans living under apartheid rule. But as Rive proceeds to suggest in *Emergency*, the 'ill-government' of which Kenko Hoshi speaks is more precisely the security police's maintenance of the apartheid legal order, and the de facto relegation of South Africa's black and coloured population to a position outside the law. Such a view parallels Mbembe's claim that violent forms of governmentality are normalised in many European colonial spaces. If colonial sovereignty is defined in part through military rule that is 'not subject to legal and institutional rules', it is also maintained through the territorialisation of physical and social space. Invoking Fanon's account of the spatial character of colonial occupation in *The Wretched of the Earth*, Mbembe argues that in the colonial context, 'Sovereignty meant occupation, and occupation meant relegating the colonised into a third zone between subjecthood and objecthood'.[54] For Mbembe, such a spatial form of political sovereignty is evidenced in the 'spatial institution' of the South African township, which was scientifically planned for the purposes of controlling the black population:

> The functioning of the homelands and townships entailed severe restrictions on production for the market by blacks in white areas, the terminating of land ownership by blacks except in reserved areas, the illegalisation of black residence on white farms (except as servants in the employment of whites), the control of urban influx and later, the denial of citizenship.[55]

Richard Rive's *Emergency* articulates the extra-legal position of South Africa's black and coloured population, partly through its imagination of the state's territorialisation of physical and social space, but also through the novel's account of the powers conferred onto the state by the Public Safety Act of 1953. In the following dialogue between Andrew Dreyer and Justin, two anti-

52 Norval, *Deconstructing Apartheid Discourse*, p. 4.
53 Cited in Rive, *Emergency*, n.p.
54 Mbembe, 'Necropolitics', p. 26.
55 Mbembe, 'Necropolitics', p. 26.

apartheid activists, Rive makes palpable the legal and political implications of the state of emergency:

> 'Let's not fool ourselves. This is a last ditch stand. The twilight of three hundred years of white rule.' Justin attempted a smile. 'They will throw everything they have into it. There will be more raids, arrests, baton charges, gaolings. But what I'm most afraid of,' he looked up at Andrew, 'is that they might declare a state of emergency.'
> 'And that means?' Andrew asked the question although he really knew the answer.
> 'A hell of a lot. For instance, the armed forces are called out and anyone can be detained without a warrant for as long as the Minister of Justice decides.'
> 'Yes, I realized that.'
> 'No redress to courts, and I think one can be kept in solitary confinement for thirty days. Anyone can be picked up for questioning, and God help you if you refuse to answer their questions.'
> 'So,' said Andrew breathlessly, 'these boys can get really tough.'
> 'Yes, and they certainly will. I advise you to get away while the going is good. You and Abe. Disappear. You might both end up in gaol for a long, long time.'
> 'But what about you?'
> 'I still have some work to do here trying to persuade black workers to stay out on strike and Coloured workers to come out in support. Tomorrow I have pamphlets to distribute in Langa. After that I might lie low. If you can, come along and help.'
> Andrew remained silent.
> 'You know,' he said after a time, 'there is just a chance that they might not declare a state of emergency.'
> 'True, they might not. But don't build up false hopes. Prepare for the worst. Get away before you are caught.'[56]

The tone of resignation to the authority of the state in this dialogue may seem to reinforce Nkosi's criticism that novels such as *Emergency* 'exploit the ready-made plots of racial violence, social apartheid, [and] interracial love affairs which are doomed from the beginning, without any attempt to transcend or trans-mute these given "social facts" into artistically persuasive works of fiction'.[57] Yet such a reading would not only be to overlook Rive's subsequent metafic-tional reflections on the political efficacy of writing under a state of emergency in his posthumously published novel, *Emergency Continued* (1990), it would also be to elide the ways in which *Emergency* details the effects of apartheid through the inscription of biopolitical and spatial discourses.

Much of Dreyer's narrative is haunted by memories of his childhood home in District Six, a neighbourhood in Cape Town from which the inhabitants were forcibly removed in 1966 under the apartheid government's Group Areas Act, and re-housed in the Cape Flats township. Writing in the early 1960s, Rive antic-ipates such policies by presenting his protagonist as a figure who is constantly

---

56 Rive, *Emergency*, p. 171.
57 Nkosi, *Home and Exile*, p. 126.

on the move and has no place to live. In this respect, his very life seems to be increasingly controlled and regulated by the spatial and biopolitical power of the apartheid state. While he feels nostalgia for his 'warm and vibrant [...] childhood in District Six',[58] he is also forced to move from his sister's house to Mrs Carollisen's house to his friend Abe's house. Furthermore, Dreyer's painful recollection of his physical abuse by his brother and brother-in-law because they perceive him as a coloured South African highlights the way in which the racist values of the apartheid state are internalised and articulated as a violent disavowal of racial difference. Dreyer's successful academic performance at high school and his subsequent success at university provokes rage in his brother-in-law, Kenneth, who calls him a 'lazy, black son-of-a-bitch',[59] and repeatedly assaults him. While Kenneth justifies his violent behaviour towards his brother-in-law on the grounds that Dreyer is defined as 'coloured' in the official, racial-ised terms of apartheid legislation, his behaviour can also be understood as a violent disavowal of any association with the population classified as coloured by the apartheid regime, a disavowal that reinforces his attempt to pass as white even though Kenneth is registered as 'coloured'.[60]

Dreyer's success at university is also framed in part as a dilemma about polit-ical commitment. When he realises that his involvement in a Modern Youth Association protest against train apartheid on the Cape Town suburban line 'could very well mean the end of his academic career',[61] Dreyer decides not to go on the protest and determines 'to work harder during the following years, politics or no politics'.[62] It is during Andrew's final year at university that a 'spate of apartheid legislation poured out unabated' – including the Group Areas Act, the Suppression of Communism Act, the Population Registration Act and the Immorality Amendment Act – and the narrator tells us that Andrew was only 'vaguely aware of what was happening around him. Only on rare occasions did he read newspapers'.[63] Here, Rive suggests that Dreyer's narrative of education and the narrative of his burgeoning political consciousness are mutually exclu-sive. Yet, as the narrator goes on to explain, it is precisely Andrew's experience of racial abuse by his brother-in-law, and his determination to get an education in spite of his impoverished background in the slum area of District Six, that leads to his politicisation.

Dreyer's final decision to take political action against the apartheid govern-ment in the aftermath of the Sharpeville massacre may, however, appear to be both ill-timed and impetuous. His decision to distribute political pamphlets at Langa during the State of Emergency is viewed with suspicion by the black population at Langa who question whether he supports the PAC or the ANC,

58 Rive, *Emergency*, p. 38.
59 Rive, *Emergency*, p. 115.
60 Rive, *Emergency*, p. 123.
61 Rive, *Emergency*, p. 120.
62 Rive, *Emergency*, p. 121.
63 Rive, *Emergency*, p. 125.

when the coloured population are not on strike,[64] and his friend Abe questions his sanity. Moreover, the fact that Andrew's pamphlet campaign escalates into a riot, in which a police van is transformed into a 'blazing inferno' and the police are forced to seek cover in a nearby shop,[65] suggests that legitimate acts of protest have limited political efficacy in the context of a state of emergency. Dreyer's final act of political resistance may be a failure, but what is crucial is the non-racial ethos of his political praxis. Dreyer's political position, like the ANC Freedom Charter of 1955, is 'avowedly non-racial' and affirms 'that South Africa belonged to all its inhabitants, white and black'.[66] As Abe asserts in a political debate with Dreyer, 'I have found most organizations to be riddled with racialism. For God's sake I am not a non-European or a Coloured man. I am a South African'.[67] By the end of the novel, Andrew not only rejects the apartheid state's racial classification system and what he regards as the racialism of the Pan African Congress, he also refuses to go underground, preferring instead to live his life in spite of apartheid. Such a decision can be read as a singular form of resistance to the biopolitical regime of the apartheid state, which affirms the life of the population in spite of the apartheid regime's attempt to relegate racialised South Africans to a state of exception.

'The less you know, the better': Torture, Writing and Political Organisation in Alex La Guma's *In the Fog of the Season's End*

If Andrew Dreyer's acts of resistance to the apartheid regime's lawful violence in 1960 seem to be a form of political madness,[68] Alex La Guma's novel *In The Fog of the Season's End* (1972) announces the repression of political opposition by the apartheid state in the aftermath of the Rivonia trial in 1964, a trial in which many of the leading figures of the ANC, the Pan-African Congress and the South African Communist Party were tried and imprisoned. The sovereign power of the apartheid state is demonstrated, for instance, in the prologue, where the narrator reveals the violence of the colonial state through the detectives' clipped address to the prisoner as they drive to the city limits: '"No more lawyers. Those times are past [...] We even keep the magistrates away now" [...] "We'll make you shit," the driver said viciously'.[69] In this minimal dialogue, La Guma reveals the implications of emergency legislation for any member of the population that opposes the apartheid regime. Not only does the emergency legislation enable the police to circumvent the law of habeas

---

64 Rive, *Emergency*, p. 124.
65 Rive, *Emergency*, p. 243.
66 See Rodney Davenport and Christopher Saunders, *South Africa: A Modern History* (Basingstoke: Macmillan, 2000 [1977]), p. 404; and Daryl Robert Lee, 'A Rival Protest: The Life and Work of Richard Rive, a South African Writer', doctoral dissertation (University of Oxford, 1998).
67 Rive, *Emergency*, p. 246.
68 See Lee, 'A Rival Protest'.
69 Alex La Guma, *In the Fog of the Season's End* (London: Heinemann, 1972), p. 2.

corpus, which requires the state to present the body of the prisoner to a court, and to deprive the anonymous prisoner of the right to a lawyer, but the rhetorical threat of physical violence in the detective's speech also demonstrates how the police have sovereign power over the bodily life and functions of the colonised. Indeed, this promise is subsequently enacted when the security police humiliate Elias by urinating on him, beating him with a pistol whilst he is hung from manacles,[70] and subjecting him to electric shocks, which cause his body to jerk like a 'broken puppet on badly manipulated strings'.[71] Is it through such images of the body in pain that La Guma stresses how the political foundation of the South African state during apartheid is based on terror rather than democracy and the rule of law. As Elias asserts, 'You are going to torture me, maybe kill me. But that is the only way you and your people can rule us. You shoot and kill and torture because you cannot rule in any other way a people who reject you'.[72] In this speech, the prisoner, who is later revealed to be Elias Tekwane, demystifies the violent foundations of the apartheid state at the very moment that the apartheid state threatens to enact its violence on the body of the colonised population. In this way, La Guma suggests that torture is a synecdoche for the apartheid state and its legal order. Significantly, Elias's speech also echoes the words of Nelson Mandela at the Rivonia Trial in 1964, in which he defended the armed liberation struggle against the apartheid state by arguing that 'a Government which uses force to maintain its rule teaches the oppressed to use force to oppose it'.[73] Yet in contrast to Mandela, there is no rhetorical space for Elias's speech to be heard in the context of the torture chamber. As the sportsman, one of Elias's torturers, declares, 'You're not at a bloody public meeting now. We'll make you piss blood'.[74]

La Guma's depiction of Elias's suffering may seem to reinforce Ndebele's criticism that much anti-apartheid writing makes a spectacle out of the power and repression of the apartheid state. Yet La Guma's self-conscious comparison of the struggle against apartheid to popular cinematic genres such as the gangster film and the western encourages readers to reflect on the discontinuities between aesthetic and political representation. For Beukes, the struggle against apartheid is

> like a bloody gangster picture itself. Life had become mysterious rides, messages left in obscure places, veiled telephone conversations. The torture chambers and the third degree had been transferred from celluloid strips in segregated cinemas to the real world which still hung on to its outward visible signs of peace: the shoppers innocently crowding the sidewalks, the racing results, the Saturday night parties, the act of love.[75]

70 La Guma, *In the Fog of the Season's End*, p. 7.
71 La Guma, *In the Fog of the Season's End*, p. 173.
72 La Guma, *In the Fog of the Season's End*, p. 6.
73 Nelson Mandela, *No Easy Walk to Freedom* (London: Heinemann, 1965), p. 168.
74 La Guma, *In the Fog of the Season's End*, p. 6.
75 La Guma, *In the Fog of the Season's End*, p. 25.

By contrasting the gangster picture with the 'real world', La Guma's narrator emphasises how the violence of the state is precisely not spectacular; for if the 'real world' is characterised by 'its outward visible signs of peace', such as consumerism and socialising, these visible signs of peace involve the relegation of state violence, repression and torture to a place beyond public representation. Crucially for La Guma's narrator, the cultural practices of cinema-going, shopping and gambling cannot be separated from the material reality of apartheid. For just as the 'cinemas' are 'segregated', so the practice of shopping, gambling and Saturday night parties are far from innocent. Indeed, what is implicit in the narrator's assertion that these cultural practices are 'outward visible signs of peace' is the unthinking complicity of those who participate in such cultural practices with the violence and political segregation of the apartheid legal order.

La Guma's extended metaphor of the anti-apartheid movement as a wounded boxer may also seem to figure the struggle against apartheid as a spectacle of physical violence. Yet the narrator's detailed account of the movement as a wounded body also conveys significant historical information about the organisational tactics of the ANC.[76] Specifically, the narrator's account of how the 'leaders and cadres retreated into exile'[77] corresponds with the predominant historical view that the state forced the ANC and the anti-apartheid movement into exile in the 1960s. As the ANC historian Francis Meli explains, 'After Rivonia, the underground machinery of the ANC was almost completely destroyed, with ANC and other political leaders in jail, exiled, banned or under one form of restriction or another'.[78] Indeed, it is significant that the novel ends with three ANC freedom fighters travelling 'north and across the border […] to be trained for the military wing'.[79] Although the narrator does not specify to which country these rebels are fleeing, the reference to 'the north' suggests Angola, Namibia or Mozambique. In so doing, the narrator alludes to the operational tactics of the ANC following the Rivonia trial, which involved many ANC cadres travelling outside of South Africa for military training in guerrilla warfare.[80] La Guma's comparison of the fragmentation of the resistance movement after Sharpeville, the emergency and the banning of the ANC to a wounded boxer may appear to reinforce the view of historians such as Howard Barrell that 'ruthless security force action destroyed the organisational capacity of MK, the ANC and SACP inside South Africa'.[81] Such a historical defeat is unambiguously registered in and through the physiological image of the movement's 'raw nerve fibres and

---

76 La Guma, *In the Fog of the Season's End*, pp. 48–49.

77 La Guma, *In the Fog of the Season's End*, pp. 48–49.

78 Francis Meli, *South Africa Belongs to Us: A History of the ANC* (London: James Currey, 1988), p. 161.

79 La Guma, *In the Fog of the Season's End*, p. 143.

80 Howard Barrell, 'Conscripts to Their Age: African National Congress Operational Strategy, 1976–1986', doctoral dissertation (University of Oxford, 1993). Available at <http://home.intekom.com/southafricanhistoryonline/pages/sources>. Accessed August 2011.

81 Barrell, 'Conscripts to Their Age'.

tired muscles', establishing 'shaky communication with centres abroad'.[82]

Yet, at the same time, the narrative structure and plot of *In the Fog of the Season's End* highlights the radical capacity of writing as a form of insurgency against the apartheid state. It is precisely the movement's production and distribution of radical leaflets reassuring the people of the continued operations of the ANC that prompts the violent counter-insurgency campaign of the South African security police towards the end of the novel. When Beukes inspects the leaflets in Tommy's apartment, 'Like a bladdy bank robber counting the loot […] sitting there under the pale, blue electric light in the shabby room',[83] he discloses the following message:

> We bring a message … you will wonder that men and women would risk long terms of imprisonment to bring you this message. What kind of people do these things? The answer is simple. They are ordinary people who want freedom in this country … From underground we launched the new fighting corps … sent youth abroad to train as people's soldiers, technicians, administrators … We will fight back … To men who are oppressed freedom means many things … Give us back our country to rule for ourselves as we choose … Many ways to fight for freedom …[84]

On scanning though this leaflet, Beukes 'feels the pricking in his scalp, down his back', and this physical sensation prompts the following free indirect statement: '*By the week-end they would be searching for them*'. For Beukes, however, this fear of the apartheid state is countered with a feeling of bravado: 'Then he thought angrily, the sons of bitches, we aren't dead yet, not by a bladdy long chalk'.[85] By structuring the narrative of *In the Fog of the Season's End* around the dissemination of political leaflets, La Guma also conveys significant details about the political tactics of the outlawed ANC in the latter half of the 1960s.

Such historical details parallel the ANC leader Govan Mbeki's detailed instructional essay, 'Notes on Leafleting and Pamphleteering', which was concerned with identifying the 'role of the written word in spreading ideas', and, more specifically, with 'examining the best manner in which an *outlawed* ANC can set about the task of carrying its message to the masses of the people, whom it seeks to lead, in order to achieve its goals'.[86] 'With the banning of the ANC by the South African government in 1963, the material conditions of communication, political education and mass mobilization had radically altered'.[87] And these changing material conditions required new political tactics. While Govan Mbeki states that pamphlets are effective forms of disseminating in-depth

---

82 La Guma, *In the Fog of the Season's End*, p. 49.
83 La Guma, *In the Fog of the Season's End*, p. 58.
84 La Guma, *In the Fog of the Season's End*, p. 58.
85 La Guma, *In the Fog of the Season's End*, p. 58.
86 Govan Mbeki, *Learning from Robben Island: The Prison Writings of Govan Mbeki* (London: James Currey in association with the UCW Historical & Cultural Centre Project, 1991).
87 Barbara Harlow, *After Lives: Legacies of Revolutionary Writing* (London: Verso, 1996), pp. 113–14.

policies and programmes to leading cadres in the ANC, he argues that it is 'the leaflet [that] is one of the most vital media, under conditions of illegality, to inspire [the people] with confidence that the Organisation is alive, working amongst them and as committed as ever to the struggle for liberation'.[88] It is precisely this political function that the leaflet serves in *In the Fog of The Season's End*. By informing the people that the organisation is not 'dead yet' and that the ANC will continue to fight the apartheid regime from underground, the leaflets articulate a radical message of resistance; a message which is repeated in the national press the following day:

> The headlines splashed in black, astounded letters: 'Explosions scatter pamphlets ... Leaflet bombs hit the city ... Underground movement still active'. The woman who had murdered her husband had been relegated to an inside page. 'The Minister of police made the observation that the leaflet explosions were an indication that undermining elements were still active. The public must not think that the dangers are a thing of the past ...' A picture showed two uniformed police looking down at parts of a leaflet bomb. A report from another city stated that crowds going to work that morning had suddenly been harangued by speeches broadcast from tape-recorders left with timing devices in abandoned cars. Other items said that leaflets from the illegal underground movement had been found in letterboxes, under doors and in pathways in various parts. A headline announced italically: 'Security police promise widespread investigations'.[89]

What is astounding about these headlines both to Beukes and to readers of *In the Fog of the Season's End* is the violent character and scale of the campaign. While Beukes's involvement in the dissemination of leaflets corresponds with the report that the leaflets 'had been found in letterboxes, under doors and in pathways in various parts', the account of the leaflet explosions suggests the involvement of MK, the armed wing of the ANC, who plotted a sabotage campaign against government buildings following the massacre at Sharpeville.[90] In this respect the political plot of *In the Fog of the Season's End* may seem to resemble that of other South African sabotage novels of the apartheid era, such as C.J. Driver's *Elegy for a Revolutionary* and Hilda Bernstein's *Death Is Part of the Process*.[91] Yet in contrast to these novels, which follow the planning and execution of a sabotage campaign against the government, and the subsequent apprehension of the protagonists by the security police, La Guma's narrator does not account for the circumstances that led to these explosions or to the 'speeches broadcast from tape-recorders left with timing devices in abandoned cars'. This omission connects the partial perspective of the narrator to the organisational tactics of the ANC, which involved withholding the identity and

---

88 La Guma, *In the Fog of the Season's End*, p. 99.
89 La Guma, *In the Fog of the Season's End*, pp. 144–45.
90 See Barrell, 'Conscripts to Their Age'.
91 C.J. Driver, *Elegy for a Revolutionary* (London: Faber, 1969); Hilda Bernstein, *Death Is Part of the Process* (London: Sinclair Browne, 1983).

programmes of ANC members from each other. It is for this reason that Govan Mbeki's explanation of the ANC's organisational tactics in leafleting campaigns is apposite for understanding the political significance of writing in *In the Fog of the Season's End*:

> If a distributor is caught red-handed he is immediately arrested. The police will want to obtain as much information as possible about the chain of command. This knowledge is more important to them than obtaining a conviction against one individual. In planning distribution it is important that the chain is broken at occasional intervals so that a person who is caught can give information up to a point simply because he does not know beyond this point.[92]

While Beukes 'wonders where the leaflets had been printed; who had brought them in' and how they had been transported, he also appears to internalise the strategic thinking of the ANC leadership. As the narrator puts it, 'The less you knew, the better'.[93] By telling a story about the subversive potential of writing under a state of emergency, and the risks involved in disseminating writing that called the authority of the apartheid state into question, La Guma's novel also foregrounds the subversive potential of South African literary fiction to disseminate the human rights violations of the apartheid regime to an international reading public.

'He is here under the emergency powers, that is enough': Torture, Sovereignty and the Rule of Colonial Law in J.M. Coetzee's *Waiting for the Barbarians*

If the torture of Elias Tekwane in La Guma's *In the Fog of the Season's End* is a powerful trope for the apartheid legal order and its suspension of civil law, for Coetzee the literary representation of torture raises important ethical and political questions for the South African writer. In an essay entitled 'Into the Dark Chamber', Coetzee asks, 'Why are writers in South Africa drawn to the torture room?' In Coetzee's argument, the 'dark, forbidden chamber is the origin of novelistic fantasy per se; in creating an obscenity, in enveloping it in mystery, the state creates the preconditions for the novel to set about its work of representation'.[94] For Coetzee, however, 'there is something tawdry about *following* the state in this way, making its vile mysteries the occasion of fantasy'.[95] Rather than simply representing the violence of the apartheid state, Coetzee asserts that the 'true challenge' facing the writer concerned with torture is 'how not to play the game by the rules of the state, how to establish

---

92 La Guma, *In the Fog of the Season's End*, pp. 98–99.
93 La Guma, *In the Fog of the Season's End*, p. 58.
94 J.M. Coetzee, 'Into the Dark Chamber', in David Atwell (ed.), *Doubling the Point* (Cambridge, MA: Harvard University Press, 1992), p. 364.
95 Coetzee, 'Into the Dark Chamber', p. 364.

one's own authority, how to imagine torture and death on one's own terms'.[96] Of the South African novels that Coetzee claims have aestheticised torture and violence, La Guma's *In the Fog of the Season's End* is singled out for its 'dark lyricism':

> It is as though, in avoiding the trap of ascribing an evil grandeur to the police, La Guma finds it necessary to displace that grandeur, in an equivalent but negative form, onto their surroundings, lending to the very flatness of their world hints of a metaphysical depth.[97]

Coetzee's critique of La Guma's displacement of violence in *In the Fog of the Season's End* is illuminating in its ethical caution against the aestheticisation of violence, but it overlooks the way in which La Guma's narrator both reveals the violent foundation of the colonial state in order to promote resistance to the apartheid regime in South Africa and details the organisational tactics of the ANC. As Abdul JanMohamed puts it, 'in this novel the self-as-an-individual discovers his being in his existence for others, in his existence as a social being'.[98] For JanMohamed, Elias not only achieves consciousness of 'the social conditions in South Africa, but also of the only way out of those oppressive circumstances'.[99] Indeed, it is Elias's resistance to the will of his torturers at the end of the novel that signals his commitment to his comrades, and to the struggle against the regime. In this sense, Elias gains sovereignty over his life (and death) by refusing to cooperate with the South African security forces. In doing so, Elias not only refuses the sovereign power of the torturer, but also the apartheid system that the torturer represents.

Coetzee's criticism of Alex La Guma's *In the Fog of the Season's End* may be limited by its focus on La Guma's representation of the torture chamber. Yet his approach to the violence of the colonial state in *Waiting for the Barbarians* is nevertheless of particular interest because of its exploration of the law's ambivalent relationship to torture in a colonial state of emergency. The novel is set on the frontier of an unnamed empire, and the narrative is reported from the first-person perspective of an unnamed magistrate. One effect of this refusal of geographical reference is that the novel foregrounds the role of the law in the maintenance of colonial sovereignty without tying the narrative to a specific colonial context. Significantly, the novel opens with an account of how the magistrate's legal authority in this colonial outpost is transferred to Colonel Joll of the Third Bureau, which is 'the most important division of the Civil Guard'.[100] This transfer of power from the magistrate to Colonel Joll is made possible by emergency legislation, as the magistrate explains briefly in an account of his first meeting with Colonel Joll: 'We sit in the best room of the inn with a flask

---

96 Coetzee, 'Into the Dark Chamber', p. 364.
97 Coetzee, 'Into the Dark Chamber', p. 365.
98 Abdul R. JanMohamed, *Manichean Aesthetics: The Politics of Literature in Colonial Africa* (Amherst: University of Massachusetts Press, 1983), p. 258.
99 JanMohamed, *Manichean Aesthetics*, p. 259.
100 J.M. Coetzee, *Waiting for the Barbarians* (London: Minerva, 1997 [1980]), p. 2.

between us and a bowl of nuts. We do not discuss the reason for his being here. He is here under the emergency powers, that is enough'.[101] The magistrate does not elaborate on what these 'emergency powers' are, or how they relate to the empire's legal order. But his suggestion that the emergency powers provide an adequate explanation for the colonel's presence in the frontier town not only makes it clear that the colonel's authority is greater than that of the magistrate, it also implies that to raise questions about these emergency powers is to challenge the legitimacy of the empire's sovereign power. And to challenge the legitimacy of the empire's sovereign power in the fictional world of *Waiting for the Barbarians* is tantamount to an act of treason, as the magistrate subsequently realises.

If the emergency powers are 'enough' for Joll to account for his violent counter-insurgency campaign against the barbarians, the magistrate's subsequent attempts to persuade the townspeople and the Third Bureau to recognise the humanity of the so-called barbarians clearly emphasise that the magistrate does not accept the violent practices of torture that are carried out under the emergency powers. As a figure who embodies the law, the magistrate would seem to draw a clear line between the normal rule of law and the violent methods of interrogation and punishment exercised by the Third Bureau under the emergency powers granted to them. When he publicly voices his opposition to the torture of the barbarian prisoners in the town square, for example, he does so on the legal grounds of the prisoners' human rights:

> 'Look!' I shout. 'We are the great miracle of creation! But from some blows this miraculous body cannot repair itself! How – !' Words fail me. 'Look at those men!' I recommence. '*Men!*' Those in the crowd who can crane to look at the prisoners, even at the flies that begin to settle on their bleeding welts'.[102]

If the magistrate's repetition of the word *men* here is taken to mean the humanity of the barbarian prisoners, this barely intelligible appeal could be interpreted as a defence of the rule of law, and the recognition of the prisoners' rights as legal subjects. Yet the security police's violent proscription of the magistrate's verbal protest clearly demonstrates that the magistrate's fragmentary speech acts do not have the force of law. As Joll asserts in response to the magistrate's demand for a trial, 'the administration of justice is out of the hands of civilians and in the hands of the Bureau'.[103] This statement seems to confirm the magistrate's earlier suspicions during his imprisonment that he will be detained indefinitely, rushed 'through one of the closed trials they conduct under the emergency powers, with the stiff little colonel presiding and his henchmen reading the charges and two junior officers as assessors to lend the proceedings an air of legality in an otherwise empty courtroom', and dragged from 'the courtroom to the executioner'.[104] In this respect, the magistrate's legal status formally

101 Coetzee, *Waiting for the Barbarians*, p. 1.
102 Coetzee, *Waiting for the Barbarians*, p. 117.
103 Coetzee, *Waiting for the Barbarians*, p. 124.
104 Coetzee, *Waiting for the Barbarians*, p. 103.

resembles that of the detainees who were indefinitely detained at the US war prison in Guantánamo Bay, Cuba. As Judith Butler explains, these 'prisoners are not considered "prisoners" and receive no protection from international law'. In Butler's argument, 'the humans who are imprisoned in Guantanamo do not count as human [...] they are not subjects in any legal or normative sense'.[105] Like the detainees in Guantánamo Bay, the magistrate is also stripped of his legal subjectivity. As Warrant Officer Mandel asserts to the magistrate during his confinement, he is not technically a prisoner because the Third Bureau has no record of him.[106] Such a statement may seem to contradict the legal principle of habeas corpus, but under a state of emergency it clearly highlights the extra-legal status of the detainee. For in situations where the normal rule of law is suspended, the detainee is subjected to the sovereign power of the state: 'The act by which the state annuls its own law has to be understood as an operation of sovereign power, or rather, the operation by which a lawless sovereign power comes into being'.[107] It is precisely the violence of this sovereign power that the magistrate experiences while he is in detention. He reflects at one point during his confinement that the Third Bureau 'will use the law against me, then they will turn to other methods' and concludes that for 'people who do not operate under statute', such as Joll and Mandel, 'legal process is simply one instrument among many'.[108] What both Joll and Mandel exemplify, in other words, is the 'petty sovereign' who reigns 'in the midst of bureaucratic army institutions mobilized by aims and tactics of power they do not inaugurate or fully control'. Such 'petty sovereigns' are nevertheless 'delegated with the power to render unilateral decisions, accountable to no law and without any legitimate authority'.[109] And it is this lawless sovereign power that allows Mandel to subject the magistrate to unspeakable torture:

> [...] my torturers were not interested in degrees of pain. They were interested only in demonstrating to me what it meant to live in a body, as a body, a body which can entertain notions of justice only as long as it is whole and well, which very soon forgets them when its head is gripped and a pipe is pulled down its gullet and pints of salt water are poured into it until it coughs and retches and flails and voids itself.[110]

Here, the magistrate explicitly connects the 'notions of justice' he cherishes to the rights of the human body that are supposedly guaranteed by the 'normal' rule of law. When the 'normal' rule of law is suspended, however, the magistrate realises that his body is stripped of legal rights and dehumanised; it is merely a body that can be tortured and killed.

---

105 Judith Butler, *Precarious Life: The Powers of Mourning and Violence* (London: Verso, 2004), p. xvi.
106 Coetzee, *Waiting for the Barbarians*, p. 137.
107 Butler, *Precarious Life*, p. 61.
108 Coetzee, *Waiting for the Barbarians*, p. 92.
109 Butler, *Precarious Life*, p. 61.
110 Coetzee, *Waiting for the Barbarians*, p. 126.

While the magistrate questions the human rights abuses that are carried out during the state of emergency, this is not to suggest that he simply defends the cause of the barbarians. After his failed attempt to protest against Colonel Joll's 'spectacle of cruelty', the magistrate reflects on the limitations of his position as a defender of the rule of law:

> *Justice*: once that word is uttered, where will it all end? Easier to shout *No!* Easier to be beaten and made a martyr. Easier to lay my head on the block than to defend the cause of justice for the barbarians: for where can that argument lead but to laying down our arms and opening the gates of the town to the people whose land we have raped? The old Magistrate, defender of the rule of law, enemy in his own way of the State, assaulted and imprisoned, impregnably virtuous, is not without his own twinges of doubt.[111]

What the magistrate's 'twinges of doubt' reveal here is not only the limitations of his protest, but his own complicity with the empire and the actions of the Third Bureau. The magistrate is both outraged and fascinated by the violent methods Colonel Joll employs to interrogate prisoners at the start of the novel, and speculates on the interrogation methods Joll employs. Yet he also tries to encourage a young male prisoner to confess to the colonel. In so doing, he realises that 'an interrogator can wear two masks, speak with two voices, one harsh, one seductive'.[112] The magistrate's ambivalent relationship with the barbarian girl similarly demonstrates how the magistrate, as a figure of colonial law, is regarded by the barbarians as complicit with the violent actions of the empire. When the magistrate invites the barbarian girl to his quarters under the guise of offering her shelter, he shudders at the thought of how the 'distance between myself and her torturers […] is negligible'.[113] The magistrate's relentless questioning of the girl's ordeal of being tortured and his attempt to purify his feelings of guilt for her pain by stripping her and washing her maimed feet and body each night she stays in his quarters points to a homology between Colonel Joll's desire to know the truth about the barbarian insurgency through his interrogation of prisoners and the magistrate's desire to know what happened in the space of the torture chamber. Indeed, the magistrate's question, 'Is it she I want or the traces of a history her body bears?',[114] suggests a connection between the magistrate's sexualised reading of the woman's scarred body and the torturer's use of physical pain to extract information from the body of the torturer. As Rosemary Jolly says of the magistrate's relationship with the girl, 'he treats her body as a surface, a map of a surface, a text'.[115]

The magistrate asserts at one point in *Waiting for the Barbarians* that 'there

---

111 Coetzee, *Waiting for the Barbarians*, p. 118.
112 Coetzee, *Waiting for the Barbarians*, p. 8.
113 Coetzee, *Waiting for the Barbarians*, p. 29.
114 Coetzee, *Waiting for the Barbarians*, p. 70.
115 Rosemary Jolly, 'Territorial Metaphor in Coetzee's *Waiting for the Barbarians*', *Ariel*, 20 (1989), p. 72.

is nothing to link' him 'with torturers'.[116] After his own experience of torture, however, he realises that the distinction between the normal rule of law and the violent practices of interrogation carried out under the emergency powers is untenable: 'I was not, as I liked to think, the indulgent pleasure-loving opposite of the cold rigid Colonel. I was the lie that Empire tells itself when times are easy, he the truth that Empire tells when harsh winds blow'.[117] The magistrate is a 'lie', in other words, because the rule of law that he symbolises is the condition of possibility for the emergency powers, which allow Colonel Joll to torture the barbarians, rather than a safeguard against such practices. When the magistrate says that Colonel Joll 'is here under the emergency powers, that is enough',[118] he obfuscates the relationship between the rule of law and the emergency powers because he does not go far enough in questioning the origins of the emergency powers, and his own position as the guardian of the empire's legal order. For to do so would be to acknowledge that the emergency powers are produced by the very juridical order that he represents. As Neocleous puts it, 'Far from suspending law or bracketing off the juridical, emergency powers lie firmly within the legal domain'.[119]

Waiting for the Barbarians has been variously read as an allegory of apartheid South Africa, as a novel that exceeds allegorical readings and as a prescient tale about the abuse of human rights during the 'war on terrorism'.[120] In the censor's report on *Waiting for the Barbarians*, the novel was described in terms of its intertextual allusions to canonical western literature as 'a somewhat Kafkaesque type of narrative, with the narrator an elderly somewhat Quixotic Magistrate [...] The locale is as obscure as Erewhon and any symbolism more so'. The report goes on to conclude that although 'the book has considerable literary merit, it quite lacks popular appeal'.[121] It is precisely because of what the censors regarded as the novel's universality, in other words, that the novel escaped the censors' ban. The irony of this particular history of the novel's reception has been discussed further by the critic Peter D. McDonald, who finds an affinity between 'Coetzee's formalist appeal to the literary as a discourse with its own distinct, or more strongly rivalrous mode of existence' and the 'censors' privileged aesthetic space'.[122] In McDonald's account, Coetzee's idea of the literary lies in its 'irreducible power to intervene in the public sphere on

---

116 Coetzee, *Waiting for the Barbarians*, p. 48.
117 Coetzee, *Waiting for the Barbarians*, p. 148.
118 Coetzee, *Waiting for the Barbarians*, p. 1.
119 Neocleous, *Critique of Security*, p. 73.
120 See Susan VanZanten Gallagher, *A Story of South Africa: J.M. Coetzee's Fiction in Context* (Cambridge, MA: Harvard University Press, 1990); Derek Attridge, *J.M. Coetzee and the Ethics of Reading: Literature in the Event* (Chicago: University of Chicago Press, 2004); Patrick Lenta, '"Legal Illegality": *Waiting for the Barbarians* after September 11', *Journal of Postcolonial Writing*, 42/1 (2006), pp.71–83; and Robert Spencer, 'J.M. Coetzee and Colonial Violence', *Interventions*, 10/2 (2008), pp. 173–87.
121 Cited in Peter D. McDonald, 'The Writer, the Critic, and the Censor: J.M. Coetzee and the Question of Literature', *Book History*, 7 (2004), p. 290.
122 McDonald, 'The Writer, the Critic, and the Censor', p. 294.

its own terms, since its effectiveness, including its political effectiveness and its literariness were inseparable'.[123] Yet the fact that the censors did not proscribe the novel raises important questions about the novel's 'political effectiveness'. If protest literature in apartheid South Africa is defined in part by its explicit challenge to state terrorism, a challenge that was borne out by the censorship of literary texts such as *Emergency* and *In the Fog of the Season's End*, then Coetzee's *Waiting for the Barbarians* would seem to refute the efficacy of such a mode of political writing.

To further clarify the political significance of *Waiting for the Barbarians*, it is helpful to briefly compare the novel to Richard Rive's posthumously published novel *Emergency Continued*. Like *Waiting for the Barbarians*, *Emergency Continued* wrestles with the demand for political commitment that is placed on the South African writer in apartheid South Africa. The novel dramatises the protagonist Andrew Dreyer's struggle to write about the state of emergency in South Africa during the 1980s. In various letters to his friend Abe Hanslo (who is now a lecturer in African literature at York University, Toronto) Dreyer compares the condition of writing about the political situation in his first novel of the 1960s and the situation in the 1980s. He details, for instance, how schoolteachers and their pupils are subjected to daily police surveillance, are shot at with rubber bullets, tear gassed, arrested and detained,[124] and questions whether such shocking events are appropriate subjects for fiction because they 'verge on the melodramatic'.[125] By embedding the draft of the sequel to the novel in an epistolary form, Rive raises questions about the status of *Emergency Continued* as a posthumously published novel; and whether the novel can 'be read as a novel at all'.[126] Indeed, the narrator's constant concern in *Emergency Continued*, that he is the subject of police surveillance, suggests that the novel might itself be a censored text, as Adam Sitze has argued.[127] Moreover, if *Emergency Continued* is read as a sequel to Rive's 1964 novel *Emergency*, the titular adjective 'continued' suggests that the state of emergency in apartheid South Africa is the rule rather than the exception. The emergency legislation referred to in the title of *Emergency Continued* was based on the laws that were passed in the 1960s. As Stephen Ellman explains,

> The most conventional of South Africa's unconventional security laws may be those which permit detention and interrogation without trial. Perhaps the most notorious is section 29 of the Internal Security Act, the modern formulation of a power first granted in the 1960s during the era when the government sought, seemingly with success, to crush organized black opposition to apartheid.[128]

---

123 McDonald, 'The Writer, the Critic, and the Censor', pp. 296–97.
124 Richard Rive, *Emergency Continued* (Claremont, South Africa: David Philip, 1990), p. 4.
125 Rive, *Emergency Continued*, p. 5.
126 Adam Sitze, 'Emergency Continued', *Law and Humanities*, 2/1 (2008), p. 61.
127 Sitze, 'Emergency Continued', p. 61.
128 Stephen Ellman, *In a Time of Trouble: Law and Liberty in South Africa's State of Emergency* (Oxford: Clarendon Press, 1992), p. 15.

As a sequel to *Emergency*, *Emergency Continued* thus highlights the permanent state of emergency upon which the apartheid state is based, and participates in what Benjamin calls the 'real state of emergency': in this case, the abolition of the apartheid state. In *Emergency Continued*, it is the detention without trial of his colleague Joe Ismail and 149 other anti-apartheid activists which prompts Dreyer's vocal and public criticism of the apartheid state.[129] Such opposition to the apartheid security laws echoes the anti-apartheid rhetoric of the ANC, which focused on the legal illegality of the apartheid state. Indeed, it is significant that Dreyer subsequently alludes to the opening of Nelson Mandela's speech at the Rivonia trial in April 1964 in a public speech Dreyer delivers at his friend Justin's funeral in the 1980s. In response to the judge's request for a plea of guilty or not guilty at the Rivonia trial, Mandela said that 'The government should be in the dock, not me. I plead not guilty'.[130] Like Mandela, Justin is an anti-apartheid activist who was sentenced to imprisonment on Robben Island. In his eulogy to Justin, Dreyer recounts how he had uttered the following words at a trial in 1969: 'It is not I who am here in the dock, but the illegal South African government'.[131] By alluding to Mandela's speech in *Emergency Continued*, Rive calls into question the legality of the continued state of emergency, and voices his support for the justice that Justin's life and struggle against the apartheid state represent.[132]

The literary self-consciousness of *Emergency Continued* as a protest novel that criticises the South African's government is also exemplified in Dreyer's reflections on the reception of his first novel, which received modest reviews, was banned and then unbanned.[133] Joe Ismail, one of Dreyer's teaching colleagues, argues that the novel would not have been published had Dreyer 'not been black', and accuses Dreyer of 'climbing on the protest bandwagon'.[134] Just as Coetzee's essay 'Into the Dark Chamber' tries to circumvent the narrow definition of politics dictated by the rules of the state by exploring the sovereign violence of the colonial state through a fictional narrative, so Dreyer in *Emergency Continued* asserts his individual right to break ranks with the party line of his colleagues and schoolchildren, even if it means risking being branded as a traitor who supports the apartheid regime.[135] There is also a certain similarity between the ways in which Rive and Coetzee approach the idea of literary autonomy in apartheid South Africa during a state of emergency: an idea which is exemplified in Coetzee's call for a novel which displayed a 'true rivalry, even enmity' towards history by operating according to its 'own paradigms

---

129 Rive, *Emergency Continued*, pp. 108–9.
130 Nelson Mandela, cited in Joel Joffe, *The Rivonia Story* (Bellville: Mayibuye, 1995), pp. 58–59.
131 Rive, *Emergency Continued*, p. 178.
132 It is significant also that '"Justin", in Latin, designates he who is just, upright, or righteous'. See Sitze, 'Emergency Continued', p. 65.
133 Rive, *Emergency Continued*, p. 23.
134 Rive, *Emergency Continued*, p. 13.
135 Rive, *Emergency Continued*, pp. 96–97.

and myths, perhaps going as far as to show up the mythic status of history – in other words, demythologising history'.[136] If Coetzee's *Waiting for the Barbarians* withdraws from the specific historical context of apartheid South Africa, it does so in order to demythologise the myth of colonialism as a civilising mission by exposing the violence that is sanctioned by the colonial rule of law. Rive's *Emergency Continued* does not withdraw from the history of apartheid South Africa, but rather uses historical events such as the march to Pollsmoor prison in 1985 to demand the release of Nelson Mandela, and the 'Trojan Horse' episode, in which police launched a brutal covert operation against demonstrators to foreground the techniques of the protest novel. In doing so, *Emergency Continued* questions the subordination of the literary to the exigencies of the anti-apartheid struggle during the state of emergency in the 1980s, even as the narrator is clearly committed to the political cause of the anti-apartheid struggle.

Yet such a comparison of *Waiting for the Barbarians* to *Emergency Continued* also overlooks important differences between the politics of literary form in these two novels. By suggesting that *Emergency Continued* is a text that is subject to the gaze of the apartheid state in the form of the censor's literary judgement, Dreyer's narrative not only destabilises the critical relationship between the novel and its readers, it also foregrounds the political and legal implications of aesthetic judgement under the apartheid state's emergency rule. In the words of Adam Sitze, the 'epistolary form of [the] narrative of apartheid's "normal emergency" [in *Emergency Continued*] doubles as an allegory of the institutional and disciplinary conditions under which *disinterested* aesthetic judgement has attained the directly juridical status of a *state discretionary power*'.[137] The literary self-consciousness of the magistrate's confessional narrative in *Waiting for the Barbarians*, by contrast, draws attention to his complicity as a figure of imperial law in the actions of the colonial regime. Such complicity is significant because it deconstructs the distinction between the rule of law that he represents and the acts of violence perpetrated by Colonel Joll and the Third Bureau. In doing so, the novel obliquely reinforces Nelson Mandela's argument in 1962 that it is the apartheid government's 'administration of the law, which brings the law into such contempt and disrepute', and that as a consequence 'one is no longer concerned to stay within the letter of the law'.[138]

In different ways, then, both *Waiting for the Barbarians* and *Emergency Continued* may seem to anticipate Sachs's call for the suspension of protest literature in South Africa at the end of the apartheid era. The problem with this approach, however, is that it can tend to foreclose a more complex understanding of the history – and historiography – of the oppressed in post-apartheid South Africa. The South African writer Wicomb explores this problem further in *David's*

---

136 J.M. Coetzee, 'The Novel Today', *Upstream*, 6 (1988), pp. 2–5.

137 Sitze 'Emergency Continued', p. 69.

138 Nelson Mandela, 'Posterity Will Prove That I Was Innocent', in idem, *Nelson Mandela in His Own Words: From Freedom to the Future: Tributes and Speeches* (London: Little Brown, 2003), p. 23.

Story (2000), a novel which challenges the official history of the ANC liberation movement by investigating the treatment of female freedom fighters in the ANC's military wing, Umkhonto weSizwe (MK).

Writing the History of the Oppressed in Zoë Wicomb's *David's Story*

David's Story is ostensibly a fragmentary transcript of David Dirkse's memoirs as an MK guerrilla fighter, and his genealogical research into his Griqua ancestry. Yet this reading is complicated by the unnamed female ghost writer of the memoirs, who interrupts David's narrative by asking pointed and specific questions about the life of a female MK guerrilla fighter called Dulcie, and about her plight in an ANC detention camp in Angola. This focus on the history of the ANC's detention camp not only complicates the heroic nationalist narrative of the anti-apartheid struggle, it also suggests that there are formal parallels to be drawn between the temporal suspension of the normal rule of law in apartheid South Africa and the spatial topography of the Quatro Detention Camp in Angola, which was established to detain and interrogate suspected infiltrators and informers who had infiltrated the ANC organisation.[139]

It is precisely such questions about Dulcie and the Quatro Detention Camp in Angola that David tries to evade. In a rather heated exchange between the ANC veteran David and the unnamed female narrator/amanuensis, David dismisses the narrator's interest in Dulcie's experiences as a female guerrilla as 'irrelevant' and refuses to answer questions about the details of Dulcie's life.[140] He then proceeds to mock the narrator's belief in 'the *Cry Freedom* vision of schoolkids bursting into spontaneous rebellion over the Afrikaans language',[141] and suggests that this is a sign of the narrator's liberal humanism: 'Brilliant, isn't it, how your arty lot just love these lies about irrepressible human nature and the spirit of freedom bubbling in the veins of the youth'.[142] Against this liberal humanist vision of political resistance, David stresses the important role of MK in the organisation of protests against the apartheid regime: 'Without a military movement orchestrating the whole thing there would not and could not have been a Soweto '76'.[143]

As a former ANC guerrilla fighter, David's emphasis on the important role of armed struggle and political organisation in the anti-apartheid movement may seem compelling. His insistence that Dulcie 'would make no distinction between the men and women with whom she works'[144] in the ANC also highlights the

---

139 Todd Cleveland, '"We Still Want the Truth": The ANC's Angolan Detention Camps and Post-apartheid Memory', *Comparative Studies of South Asia, Africa and the Middle East*, 25/1 (2005), p. 65.
140 Zoë Wicomb, *David's Story* (New York: Feminist Press, 2000), p. 78.
141 Wicomb, *David's Story*, p. 80.
142 Wicomb, *David's Story*, p. 80.
143 Wicomb, *David's Story*, pp. 79–80.
144 Wicomb, *David's Story*, p. 78.

narrator's inability to 'imagine a woman who takes that kind of thing seriously – protocol and hierarchy, the saluting and standing to attention, the barking of orders, the uniform'.[145] In this way, the novel reinforces the literary critic Meg Samuelson's observation that neither the masculine discourse of militarism nor the liberal discourse of the narrator's western feminism can account for the singular 'figure of the female guerrilla'.[146] Yet despite this limitation, the narrator's fictionalised account of Dulcie's torture in the ANC detention camp highlights the difficulty of recovering the story of women's involvement in the armed liberation struggle against the apartheid government that David so disparages as improper history.[147] Like the magistrate's account of his torture in *Waiting for the Barbarians*, Wicomb's narrator elides the details of Dulcie's torture: 'On the very first visit, one of them, the wiry one who seems to be in charge, spoke: Not rape, that will teach her nothing, leave nothing; rape's too good for her kind, waving the electrodes as another took off her night-clothes'.[148] The narrator's fictionalised account of Dulcie's torture may not be rape in the strict sense of the term, and is described in quasi-surgical terms as a 'shadow-play of surgeons'. But the suggestion that electrodes are forcibly applied to Dulcie's body clearly underscores the sexualised character of the torture technique to which her body was subjected.[149] David's ambivalent desire for Dulcie, and the narrator's intimation that he might also have been one of her torturers, similarly recalls the magistrate's ambivalent desire for the barbarian girl in *Waiting for the Barbarians*. At one point in the text, the narrator asserts that Dulcie associates the nightly visits of her torturers in the detention camp with the 'pretence of a relationship' with David, but she 'does not know why or how'.[150] In a similar vein, the recursive structure of David's narrative, coupled with his unreliable memory, suggest that he is also gripped by the trauma of what happened in the ANC detention camp, without being able to process or narrate that history. Consider the following extract in which David begins to remember a scene from the detention camp:

> We sit in silence; I am conscious of his shoulder tense against mine. Then, when David speaks, his voice drops to a tortured whisper, and I am glad that I cannot see his face in the dark: It's here in close-up before my eyes, the screen full-bleed with Dulcie. Who? Is it you put it in my head? The terrible things happening to Dulcie? It's here, in close-up – and he stumbles to his feet with a horrible cry, knocking me over as he charges out.[151]

145 Wicomb, *David's Story*, p. 79.
146 Meg Samuelson, 'The Disfigured Body of the Female Guerrilla: (De)Militarization, Sexual Violence and Re-domestication in Zoë Wicomb's *David's Story*', *Signs: Journal of Women in Culture and Society*, 32/4 (2007), p. 838.
147 Wicomb, *David's Story*, p. 199.
148 Wicomb, *David's Story*, p. 178.
149 Samuelson, 'The Disfigured Body of the Female Guerrilla', pp. 846–47.
150 Wicomb, *David's Story*, p. 184.
151 Wicomb, *David's Story*, p. 201.

The shock of David's screen memory here not only complicates his earlier dismissal of the narrator's attempt to reconstruct the history of women's involvement in the armed liberation struggle, it also clarifies David's earlier assertion that Dulcie is 'a kind of scream echoing through my story'.[152] In this respect, Dulcie's torture in the ANC detention camp can be seen to haunt the official history of the ANC liberation narrative. In contrast to La Guma's use of torture as a trope for the repression of the apartheid regime, the story of Dulcie's torture is a 'scream' because it draws attention to the impossibility of representing the history of the gendered subaltern in terms of the ANC's history of the anti-apartheid struggle in post-apartheid South Africa. As the critic Dorothy Driver puts it in the afterword to the Feminist Press edition of the novel, Dulcie is 'the unrepresentable body in pain, "a disturbance at the time of liberation"'.[153]

Conclusion

If Rive's *Emergency* and La Guma's *In the Fog of the Season's End* exemplify what Benjamin termed the tradition of the oppressed in apartheid South Africa – a tradition that highlights the sovereign power and lawful violence of the apartheid state – Wicomb's *David Story* raises crucial questions about the form and meaning of the tradition of the oppressed in post-apartheid South Africa. As a work of feminist historiographic metafiction, the novel draws attention to the impossibility of recovering subaltern histories from a broadly masculine narrative of anti-colonial struggle, and emphasises the political value of fiction in imagining histories that could not otherwise be represented. In this respect, the novel offers a troubling and sophisticated 'understanding of the nuances and subtleties of politics and power' in post-apartheid South Africa.[154] Such postcolonial narratives are also crucial in guarding against the transformation of the tradition of the oppressed into a fetish that effaces post-apartheid formations of state violence and inequality.

152 Wicomb, *David's Story*, p. 134.
153 Wicomb, *David's Story*, p. 218.
154 Sole, 'The Role of the Writer in a Time of Transition', pp. 93–94.

CHAPTER 4

Torture, Indefinite Detention and the Colonial State of Emergency in Kenya

In June 2009 the London lawyers Leigh Day filed a legal case against the British government on behalf of five Kenyans representing the Mau Mau Veterans' Association for atrocities and human rights violations committed during the state of emergency in Kenya between 1952 and 1960. In a letter addressed to the then British Prime Minister, Gordon Brown, the former detainees begin by invoking the Kikuyu proverb 'Muingatwo na kihoto dacokago; muingatwo na njuguma niacokaga' ('He who is defeated with unjust force will always come back, he who is dealt with justly will never come back'). By framing their demand for justice within the rhetorical structure of a Kikuyu proverb, the detainees situate their public address to the British government within the ethical and legal frame of reference of Kikuyu society. In so doing, the proverb legitimates the detainees' claim with reference to the legal values and codes of Kikuyu society and culture, and defines the authority of the former detainees as legal subjects with the right to address the figure of British parliamentary sovereignty, the prime minister. In the letter, the former detainees proceed to explain how they are Kenyans in their 70s and 80s who have travelled to London from 'our rural villages to tell the world of the torture and trauma we have lived through at the hands of the British colonial regime'. The detainees are careful to emphasise that their claim is not 'a case about colonialism or politics'. Yet their assertions that 'thousands of Kenyans were detained during the Kenyan emergency', that 'thousands were tortured and treated inhumanely' and 'that this violence was known about and authorised at the highest levels of Government in London at the time' clearly link the traumatic aftermath of Britain's state of emergency in Kenya with the violence of colonial rule.[1] Moreover, by demanding that the British government publicly acknowledge the historical

---

1 'Letter to Gordon Brown from the Mau Mau Veterans'. Available at <www.leighday. co.uk/documents>. Accessed July 27, 2009.

wrongs committed against the Kikuyu population, the five Mau Mau veterans sought redress for the British colonial government's systematic torture, brutalisation and detention without trial of thousands of Kenyans during the state of emergency.

Such a demand for truth and justice is not without precedent. After all, writing letters to leading colonial administrators and senior British government officials was a crucial part of the political campaign for many suspected 'Mau Mau terrorists' detained without trial in British concentration camps during the 1950s.[2] In one letter held in the Kenya National Archives, Albert Mbogo Njoroge, a detainee at the Gutundu Works Camp at Kiambu, poses the following two questions: 'What is the meaning of the word emergency? Is emergency inhuman deeds?'[3] By asking the question, 'What is the meaning of the word emergency?', Njoroge can be seen to address the British colonial authorities from the standpoint of a Kikuyu detainee who understands the meaning of the word 'emergency' in terms of the very 'inhuman deeds' of violence of which he had direct physical experience rather than in the terms of an abstract legal definition of a state of emergency as a law which suspends the normal rule of law. In doing so, Njoroge unmasks the very *raison d'être* of the British colonial state of emergency: to discipline and punish the anti-colonial resistance movement in Kenya and to re-assert British colonial sovereignty in Kenya. At the same time, the letters of detainees such as Gakaara wa Wanjau illuminate the ways in which detainees used the postal system to create 'trans-continental advocacy networks that could be brought to bear on colonial officers'.[4]

Such letters from Kikuyu detainees also shed significant light on the use of the state of emergency as a quasi-legal technique of sovereignty in European colonies, and, in so doing, offer an important supplement to predominant political accounts of the state of exception. We have already seen, for instance, how Agamben's theories of sovereign power and the state of exception elide the normalisation of emergency powers as a technique of European colonial sovereignty. To further elucidate the colonial genealogy of the state of exception, this chapter considers how the state of emergency in Kenya from 1952 to 1960 has been codified in the rhetoric of British colonialism, and criticised by African writers and intellectuals engaged in struggles for decolonisation as a sign of the inherent violence and injustice of British colonial rule.

Beginning with a discussion of Ngũgĩ's critique of colonial narratives of the emergency period, this chapter proceeds to consider how the colonial government used the deaths of white settlers and Kenyan Loyalists to justify its use of emergency legislation to detain an estimated 150,000 Kikuyu people who were suspected by the colonial authorities of being involved with the Land and

---

2 See Caroline Elkins, *Britain's Gulag: The Brutal End of Empire in Kenya* (London: Jonathan Cape, 2005), pp. 205–8.
3 Cited in Elkins, *Britain's Gulag*, p. 206.
4 See Derek R. Peterson, 'The Intellectual Lives of Mau Mau Detainees', *Journal of African History*, 49.1 (2008), p. 75.

Freedom movement, more commonly known as the Mau Mau.[5] If, as Ngũgĩ suggests, colonial histories of the emergency period in Kenya, such as Fred Majdalany's *State of Emergency*, tried to attribute the cause of violent, anti-colonial insurgency to racial stereotypes of Kikuyu culture, colonial fictions of the Mau Mau insurgency such as Robert Ruark's *Something of Value* (1955) and Elspeth Huxley's *A Thing to Love* (1954) foreground the ways in which such historical explanations depend on racist metaphors, images and narratives that reinforce the British colonial rhetoric of the civilising mission in Kenya. In so doing, Ruark and Huxley demonstrate the importance of narrative and rhetoric in the justification of Kenya's state of emergency and the framing of the Kikuyu as violent insurgents. As a counterpoint to such narratives, the chapter considers how novels such as Ngũgĩ's *Weep Not, Child* and *A Grain of Wheat* spell out the relationship between the formal declaration of a state of emergency and the repressive techniques of colonial governmentality that such a declaration enabled. In so doing, I suggest that the narratives of emergency in *Weep Not, Child* and *A Grain of Wheat* not only disclose the colonial genealogy of the state of exception; these narratives also highlight the forms of agency and resistance to the racial and ethnic frames of the British colonial administration that attempted to reduce the Kikuyu people to a form of bare life. Ngũgĩ's literary fiction also raises important questions about the legacy of British colonial sovereignty, and the way in which emergency powers became normalised after independence. By tracing the ways in which the memory of the Land and Freedom fighters are commemorated in Ngũgĩ's novel *Matigari*, the chapter concludes by assessing how Ngũgĩ's fiction has contributed to the invention of a tradition of the oppressed in postcolonial Kenya.

Ngũgĩ, Fanon and the Colonial State of Emergency in Kenya

We have already seen in the introduction how European colonial governments mobilised a repository of narratives and metaphors to mask and obfuscate the terror and violence of colonial sovereignty, particularly during national independence struggles. The colonial rhetoric surrounding the state of emergency in Kenya is no exception to this tendency. The case for the declaration of a state of emergency in Kenya was predicated in part on the colonial stereotype of the Land and Freedom Army resistance fighters, also known as the Mau Mau. This stereotype was based on the myth surrounding the oathing ceremonies, which were a tactic of political organisation in which resistance fighters swore an oath of unity to the political cause of *ithaka na wiyathi*, or land and freedom.[6] But it was also linked to the violent attacks carried out by some members of the Land and Freedom Army against white settlers and against Kikuyu chiefs and their followers who were loyal to the British colonial state.[7] It was the failure

5 Anderson, *Histories of the Hanged*, p. 5.
6 See Elkins, *Britain's Gulag*, p. 25; and Anderson, *Histories of the Hanged*, p. 27.
7 Anderson, *Histories of the Hanged*, p. 87.

of the European imagination to comprehend that the violent acts of the Land and Freedom Army were an expression of political opposition to the policies of the British colonial state that prompted European settlers and government officials to frame such acts of violent anti-colonial insurgency as a kind of illness or psychological disease brought on by the corrupting effects of oathing ceremonies.[8] For the oathing ceremonies were associated in the European mind with a racist stereotype of African religion and culture as atavistic and anti-western. Such stereotypes could certainly be understood to disavow the role of the oath in western societies. As Agamben has argued in *The Sacrament of Language* (2011), the oath functions as a particular kind of speech act in which a human subject puts their own life at stake before a figure of legal or religious authority.[9] By disavowing the significance of the oath in the political culture of western societies, colonial stereotypes of 'Mau Mau' oathing ceremonies also disavow the constitutive role of the oath in defining the subject's relationship to competing forms of sovereignty. Indeed, the counter-oathing ceremonies that the British colonial administration introduced in the detention camps to 'rehabilitate' Kikuyu detainees suspected of being 'Mau Mau' insurgents during the colonial state of emergency in Kenya foreground the way in which British colonial sovereignty also depended on the performance of an oath that put the subject's life at stake in a way that mirrored the violence that the rhetoric of British colonialism attributed to 'Mau Mau' oathing rituals. What is more, such colonial stereotypes of the 'savagery' of 'Mau Mau' oathing rituals served to deny the social and economic significance of the Kikuyu's grievances: the systematic expropriation of Kikuyu land by white settlers in the first half of the twentieth century, the increasing control and regulation of Kikuyu labour, and the levying of unpopular forms of taxation, such as the hut tax and the poll tax.[10] In this way the recourse to a colonial state of emergency in Kenya was justified through the use of a metalepsis, or a rhetorical manipulation of causes and effects, in which the 'evil savagery' of the Mau Mau is presented as the cause of the colonial state of emergency, rather than a political response to the violent system of colonial sovereignty, race labour and the forced dispossession of Kikuyu land.

It is precisely this rhetorical manipulation of causes and effects in the dominant colonial narrative of the Kenyan state of emergency that the Kenyan writer Ngũgĩ contests in his essay, 'Mau Mau: Violence, and Culture'. First written in 1963 (the year of Kenya's independence) and published in his 1972 essay collection *Homecoming*,[11] this essay is ostensibly a review of Majdalany's

8 Anderson, *Histories of the Hanged*, p. 88.
9 Giorgio Agamben, *The Sacrament of Language: An Archaeology of the Oath*, trans. Adam Kotsko (Cambridge: Polity, 2011).
10 See Elkins, *Britain's Gulag*, pp. 15–16.
11 In a footnote to the version of the review published in *Homecoming*, Ngũgĩ states that the review of Majdalany's book was first written in 1963. This footnote does not say whether this 1963 version of the review was published, and if so where it was published. In view of the fact that the version of the review that appears in *Homecoming* is informed

contemporary journalistic account of the colonial state of emergency in Kenya, *State of Emergency* (1963). But Majdalany's book also provides Ngũgĩ with an example of how some European journalists and historians as well as colonial administrators and white settlers distorted the significance of the colonial state of emergency in Kenya. It is for this reason that Ngũgĩ begins his essay with an account of the economic, political and cultural conditions of British colonialism in Kenya that precipitated the political revolt against colonial rule in the 1950s. In Ngũgĩ's account, the 'white settler came early in the century and he immediately controlled the heart of the economy by appropriating the best part of the land for himself. Alienation of land, after all, was then the declared British colonial policy for the region which later became Kenya'. The only way in which white settlers were able to consolidate this 'economic position', Ngũgĩ continues, was by forcing 'black men to work in labour gangs' and rationalising this 'exploitation of African land and labour by claiming he was civilizing a primitive people'. By beginning his critique of Majdalany's *State of Emergency* with an account of the colonial expropriation of land, the exploitation of African labour power and the colonial rhetoric that was mobilised to justify this expropriation, Ngũgĩ implies that the 'Mau Mau revolution of 1952' was grounded in a political struggle over land and labour.[12] Such an argument is made plain later in the review when Ngũgĩ explicitly states that the 'basic objectives of Mau Mau revolutionaries were to drive out the Europeans, seize the government, and give back to the Kenya peasants their stolen property and land'.[13]

In highlighting the rational political objectives of the Land and Freedom Army, Ngũgĩ also challenges the colonial stereotype of the Mau Mau as atavistic and primitive, and emphasises that the Mau Mau oath 'was a commitment to sabotage the colonial machine and to kill if necessary'. Significantly, his analysis of the violent acts of anti-colonial insurgency echoes Fanon's assertion in *The Wretched of the Earth* that 'At the individual level, violence is a cleansing force'.[14] In Ngũgĩ's argument, the crucial point about acts of violence – as with oaths – is 'the nature of the particular historical circumstances that make them necessary and the cause they serve'.[15] By framing the use of violence in terms of its particular historical circumstances, Ngũgĩ judges the use of violence according to a moral logic of means and ends: 'Violence in order to change an intolerable unjust social order is not savagery: it purifies man. Violence to protect and

---

by Fanon's reflection on violence and decolonisation in *The Wretched of the Earth* (a book that was first published in French in 1963), and that Ngũgĩ first came across Fanon while studying for a master's degree at the University of Leeds in 1964, it is quite possible that the version of the review that appears in *Homecoming* is a revised version of the review that was published in 1963.

12 Ngũgĩ wa Thiong'o, *Homecoming: Essays on African and Caribbean Literature, Culture and Politics* (London: Heinemann Educational, 1972), p. 26.

13 Ngũgĩ, *Homecoming*, p. 28.

14 Frantz Fanon, *The Wretched of the Earth*, trans. Richard Philcox (New York: Grove Press, 2004 [1961]), p. 51.

15 Ngũgĩ, *Homecoming*, p. 28.

preserve an unjust, oppressive social order is criminal and diminishes man'.[16] This suggestion that violence 'purifies man' borrows from Fanon's suggestion that violence is a 'cleansing force' for the psychic life of the colonised. What is more, Ngũgĩ can be seen to develop Fanon's point that the 'praxis' of violence through liberation 'enlightens the militant because it shows him the means and the ends'.[17] By linking the violent means of anti-colonial struggle to the specific political goals of the Land and Freedom movement in colonial Kenya, in other words, Ngũgĩ implies that anti-colonial violence has a political and moral as well as psychotherapeutic purpose. Just as Fanon suggested that violence is 'the perfect mediation' because the 'colonized man [*sic*] liberates himself in and through violence',[18] so for Ngũgĩ violence is a means for the colonised to assert sovereignty over both their land and their lives.

Ngũgĩ's rethinking of Fanon in the context of the Kenyan state of emergency in the 1950s is important also because it helps to clarify how the use of violence by the European colonial government was not an exceptional measure specific to the circumstances of the state of emergency, but was rather part of the repressive apparatus of the colonial state. For the state of emergency, Ngũgĩ contends, only 'intensified' the violence that the British colonial government had already 'perpetrated' on the 'African people for fifty years'.[19] It is precisely this history of violent colonial sovereignty and dispossession that colonial narratives of the state of emergency in Kenya sought to distort by framing the state of emergency as a necessary and measured response to the 'savage' attacks on European settlers and Kenyan loyalists by Mau Mau guerrillas, and by effacing the brutal methods of counter-insurgency that the British colonial administration mobilised to suppress the resistance movement. Such a gross historical distortion is exemplified for Ngũgĩ in Majdalany's reliance on the records of 'the Colonial Office, the Kenya government officials, members of the administration at the time of the Emergency, the generals and the chiefs – who were all anti-Mau Mau',[20] and by his failure 'to tell the full story of several crucial incidents'. For Ngũgĩ, this failure is exemplified in Majdalany's account of the Lari massacre:

> Majdalany recounts what is generally called the Lari massacre in colonial records, but does not add that many of the killed were collaborators with the enemy and hence traitors to the African cause: that many innocent men and women were afterwards led to the forest and summarily executed by the government forces. I know six who were taken from my village, which was miles from Lari. The relatives of the six murdered people tried to take the case to the courts, but this never came to anything. Such was the nature of colonial justice in Kenya, even before this period of war.[21]

16 Ngũgĩ, *Homecoming*, p. 28.
17 Fanon, *The Wretched of the Earth*, p. 44.
18 Fanon, *The Wretched of the Earth*, p. 44
19 Ngũgĩ, *Homecoming*, p. 29.
20 Ngũgĩ, *Homecoming*, p. 28.
21 Ngũgĩ, *Homecoming*, p. 29.

Ngũgĩ's critique of *State of Emergency* identifies a broader tendency in histories of the emergency period in Kenya to elide and distort the rational political grievances of the Land and Freedom movement, and to downplay the violent practices that the colonial government encouraged and legitimated through its range of emergency measures. It is this historical elision and distortion in dominant colonial narratives of the emergency that Ngũgĩ attempts to address in his literary fiction, as we will see later in the chapter. Before doing so, however, the following section considers the meaning of the state of emergency in Kenya, and analyses the ways in which the state of emergency was framed and justified in the literature and law of empire.

Writing the Colonial State of Exception in British Kenya

The formal declaration of a state of emergency in Kenya took place on 20 October 1952 after several exchanges between senior government officials, such as the colonial secretary in London, Oliver Lyttelton and the colonial governor of Kenya, Sir Evelyn Baring. The emergency regulations, together with Baring's proclamation, were published in an *Official Gazette Extraordinary* on 21 October 1952. These emergency powers were framed with reference to the British Emergency Powers (Defence) Act of 1939, a statute which had given the British government unrestricted power to detain individuals deemed dangerous to the state in a time of war, following the outbreak of the Second World War.[22] But the correspondence between senior colonial officials in Kenya also raised questions about the limitations of the British Emergency Powers (Defence) Act of 1939 to detain individuals deemed dangerous to the stability of the colonial government. In one exchange between colonial officials dated 11 October 1952, there is a suggestion that the Malayan Emergency Regulations ordinance of 1948, which had been used to suppress communist resistance to the colonial government in Malaya, provided a more robust legal framework for the Kenyan state of emergency. The reason for this is that the Malayan state of emergency had empowered the state to detain suspected insurgents indefinitely, and that the period of detention would not expire at the end of the colonial state of emergency. The British Emergency Powers (Defence) Act of 1939, by contrast, had 'no such provision'.[23] Despite such reservations, the published declaration of 20 October 1952 would seem to indicate that the emergency regulations were perfectly adequate for the purposes of the colonial government's counter-insurgency strategy. According to Part II, Section 6 (I) of the *Official Gazette Extraordinary*, the United Kingdom Emergency Powers Order in Council of 1939 empowered the Governor of Kenya to

---

22 See A.W.B. Simpson, *In the Highest Degree Odious: Detention without Trial in Wartime Britain* (Oxford: Clarendon Press, 1992).

23 PRO, CO 822/ 443.

make such Regulations as appear to him to be necessary or expedient for securing the public safety, the defence of the territory, the maintenance of public order and the suppression of mutiny, rebellion and riot, and for maintaining supplies and services essential to the life of the community.[24]

These regulations included making 'provision for the detention of persons and the deportation and exclusion of persons from the territory', authorising the seizure of 'any property or undertaking', 'the entering and search of any premises', providing for the amendment of 'any law, for suspending the operation of any law and for applying any law with or without modification'. The emergency regulations also provided for the 'apprehension, trial and punishment of persons offending against the Regulations', but they did not authorise 'the making of provisions for the trial of persons by Military Courts'.[25] The *Official Gazette Extraordinary* also included a separate Government Notice subtitled Emergency Regulations 1952, which defined in detail Baring's interpretation of these broad emergency powers as they appeared 'necessary or expedient' to him for maintaining political order in British Kenya. These regulations detailed the terms of detention orders and police powers to detain suspected persons, as well as outlawing acts likely to cause 'mutiny, sedition or disaffection', public meetings or processions likely to 'give rise to grave disorder', the 'publication of alarming reports', subversive publications, and the possession of firearms and explosive substances, as well as a 'sword, spear, cutlass, *panga*, *simi*, axe, hatchet, knife or other dangerous weapon'.[26] Such regulations certainly highlight the wide powers afforded to the Governor of Kenya to assert sovereignty over the British colony. And these powers are further evidenced in the amendments to the emergency regulations passed in April and May 1953, which made the unlawful possession of firearms, explosives and ammunition 'a capital offence';[27] and created 'emergency zones', or geographical areas in which 'scheduled offences' such as possession of offensive weapons, consorting with armed persons or persons 'acting prejudicially to public safety' could be tried immediately in a Court of Emergency Assize.[28] These latter amendments also included clear guidelines on the punishment and treatment of detainees in the detention camps.[29] Yet even though the regulations empowered the Governor of Kenya and various other agents and institutions of the colonial state to detain, torture, violate and execute the Kikuyu population with impunity, this violent exercise of colonial sovereignty was not self-evident from the Emergency Regulations themselves.

24 Colony and Protectorate of Kenya, *Official Gazette Extraordinary*, 21 October 1952, p. 487.
25 Colony and Protectorate of Kenya, *Official Gazette Extraordinary*, 21 October 1952, p. 487.
26 Colony and Protectorate of Kenya, *Official Gazette Extraordinary*, 21 October 1952, pp. 491–94.
27 Colony and Protectorate of Kenya *Official Gazette Supplement*, 27, 16 April 1953, p. 339.
28 Colony and Protectorate of Kenya *Official Gazette Supplement*, 45, 12 June 1953, pp. 523–8.
29 Colony and Protectorate of Kenya *Official Gazette Supplement*, 33, 5 May 1953, pp. 395–407.

At the time that the state of emergency was declared, the colonial government had determined that they would arrest, try and detain the leader of the Kenyan African Union, Jomo Kenyatta, for his role in aiding and abetting the violent acts carried out by the Land and Freedom movement. This strategy would ultimately prove to be counterproductive, for it made Kenyatta into a symbol of political resistance, even though he had more moderate political leanings and did not support the violent methods of resistance employed by the Land and Freedom movement.[30] What is crucial, however, is that the emergency regulations consolidated the sovereignty of the colonial government, and allowed it to exercise greater and greater control over the life and death of the Kikuyu population.

As with the states of emergency in South Africa, India and Ireland, the effects of the colonial state of emergency cannot be understood with reference to the letter of the law alone. For although the colonial government gazettes contain detailed information defining the specific legal powers accorded to colonial governments, they tend to occlude any discussion of the constitutive role of cultural representation and cultural stereotypes in framing the Land and Freedom Army as savage, inhuman figures who could be tortured and killed with impunity. Indeed, it was in texts such as F.D. Corfield's official history of the origins and growth of Mau Mau (1960), J.C. Carothers' report *The Psychology of Mau Mau* (1954) and Louis Leakey's analysis of the Mau Mau's political demands and tactics (1952 and 1954) that the colonial fiction of the Mau Mau was invented. These cultural stereotypes were reiterated in British newspaper reports of Mau Mau atrocities, in journalistic accounts of the state of emergency in Kenya, such as Majdalany's *State of Emergency*, and in popular novels such as Robert Ruark's *Something of Value* (1954) and Elspeth Huxley's *A Thing to Love* (1954).[31]

The Emergency Mentality in Colonial Settler Fiction

The rhetoric of terrorism plays an important role in Kenya's narrative of emergency and the justification of human rights abuses, such as detention without trial, torture and extra-judicial killings. And this rhetoric is clearly reflected in colonial settler fictions of the 1950s, such as the American writer Robert Ruark's bestseller *Something of Value* (1954) and Elspeth Huxley's *A Thing to Love*.[32] In their suggestion that the Land and Freedom movement contributed to a condition that Ruark describes as 'Kenya nerves',[33] these novels can be seen to exemplify the literary prose of counter-insurgency. For in presenting the violent methods of the 'Mau Mau' as the cause of the emergency, and suggesting that these acts of violence are symptoms of an inherently regressive tendency

---

30 See Elkins, *Britain's Gulag*, p. 36, and Anderson, *Histories of the Hanged*, p. 67.
31 See Maughan-Brown, *Land, Freedom and Fiction*.
32 Robert Chester Ruark, *Something of Value* (London: Hamish Hamilton, 1955); Elspeth Huxley *A Thing to Love* (London: Chatto & Windus, 1954).
33 Ruark, *Something of Value*, p. 484.

among the Kikuyu, these works of literary fiction efface the political demands of the Land and Freedom movement and reinforce the argument for rehabilitation in detention camps presented by 'experts' such as Carothers and Leakey. What is more, by fictionalising in grotesque detail the violent acts carried out against Kenyan loyalists and white settlers, these novels contribute to the European colonial fiction of the Mau Mau as cold-blooded savages, a stereotype which underpins the 'emergency mentality' that was prevalent among the white settler community in Kenya during the 1950s. In Caroline Elkins' argument, this emergency mentality converged with the 'draconian legislation passed by Baring' in such a way that ensured that the 'treatment of Mau Mau suspects, with rare exception, was devoid of any humanity'.[34] This convergence of emergency legislation and the unofficial appointment of the white settler community in the counter-insurgency campaign worked to produce a colonial state of exception in Kenya, in which the emergency laws that granted special powers to the colonial governor were used to empower other agents and institutions such as the Kenyan African Rifles and the Home Guard, as well as the settler community. And by framing the Land and Freedom Army in the terms of colonial stereotypes, this colonial state of exception created the conditions for the detention, torture and execution of the Kikuyu population with impunity.

The image of the Land and Freedom movement as atavistic, cold-blooded 'terrorists' is clearly exemplified in Ruark's novel *Something of Value*. At the centre of the novel's terrorist plot is the violent murder of Jeff Newton, his children and the mutilation of his wife, Elizabeth, by the Mau Mau. This violent act is reported first through a telephone call to the settler protagonist, Peter McKenzie, and his wife Holly on their wedding night, from Noel, the local police constable. In this telephone call, we learn from Peter's subsequent explanation to Holly that 'Jeff's dead. Lisa may live. Two of the kids as well. Dead. Caroline and Harry. House burnt'.[35] The telegraphic style of this report is immediately followed by an account of how the Mau Mau 'Killed Jeff and the kids and cut up Lisa pretty badly'.[36] The gory details of Jeff's murder are further evoked through the third-person narrator's account of the crime scene:

> 'You'd better see,' the P.C. said. 'That's Jeff.' [...] What was under the blanket might have been Jeff. The head was missing. Some portion of the legs were there, and some parts of the trunk. You could not really say what was there, and what wasn't there, any more than you could say what exact shape the meat that makes a hamburger patty was before it became a hamburger patty. Jeff Newton had been struck more than a hundred times with *pangas*.[37]

This lurid description of Jeff's fragmented corpse evokes the language and imagery of 'Mau Mau' attacks in newspapers such as *The Daily Mail* wherein 'Grisly photographs of alleged oathing ceremonies were displayed along-

34 Elkins, *Britain's Gulag*, pp. 55–56.
35 Ruark, *Something of Value*, p. 374.
36 Ruark, *Something of Value*, p. 374.
37 Ruark, *Something of Value*, p. 377.

side headlines decrying the movement's "terrorism" and bloody cannibalistic rituals'.[38] What is more, Ruark's use of analepsis and repetition to emphasise the violence and terror of the attack on the Newton household clearly serves to sensationalise and to exaggerate the significance of Mau Mau attacks on settler farms, and to efface the political demands of the Kikuyu for land, political representation and sovereignty.

Like the representation of the Mau Mau in government reports and European newspapers, Ruark reinforces the monstrous image of the Land and Freedom movement through his vivid and detailed descriptions of Mau Mau oathing ceremonies. In one account of an oath, a man describes how the Mau Mau oath is 'much stronger than the old *githathi*' and 'makes all the Kikuyu blood brothers'.[39] This oath, as the narrator subsequently explains, involves the oath-taker passing through an arch of leaves, drinking the stomach contents of a sacrificial sheep and repeating the following words:

> 'If I am told to bring in the head of a European, I will do so, or this oath will kill me and all my family.
> '*If I am called by my brotherhood in the middle of the night and am naked, I will go forth naked, or this oath will kill me and all my family, and if I betray my brotherhood, this oath will kill me and all my family.*
> '*If I steal anything from a European, I will say nothing, or this oath will kill me and all my family.*
> '*At all times, I will say that all land belongs only to the Kikuyu, or this oath will kill me and all my family.*
> '*If I send my children to mission schools, this oath will kill me and all my family.*
> '*If I am called on to rescue Jomo Kenyatta, I will do so, or this oath will kill me.*[40]

By disclosing in detail the words as well as the rituals associated with the Mau Mau oath, Ruark's narrator creates a fiction of total omniscience about the Land and Freedom movement: a narrative device which suggests that the intelligence of the British colonial authorities in Kenya is similarly totalising.

Moreover, by dehumanising the Land and Freedom movement in his representation of the oathing ceremonies, Ruark encourages his implied European readers to regard the Mau Mau characters in the novel as a form of bare life that can be tortured and killed with impunity. We have already seen how Agamben defines the figure of *homo sacer*, or the subject who could be killed without being sacrificed, as the hidden foundation of the political in modern European nation states.[41] In European colonies such as Kenya, however, the foundation of the political is not so much hidden as manifested in and through the subjection of the colonised to the violence of the colonial state. If the modern European nation state incorporates the figure of bare life into a political discourse of citizenship, the absence of a stable and coherent concept of citizenship in

---

38 Elkins, *Britain's Gulag*, p. 308.
39 Ruark, *Something of Value*, p. 279.
40 Ruark, *Something of Value*, p. 279.
41 Agamben, *Homo Sacer*, p. 89.

colonial Kenya has significant implications for the human rights of the Kenyan population.[42] Ruark's fictional representation of Kikuyu freedom fighters as monstrous savages serves to reinforce the stereotype of the colonised as a form of life that can be tortured and killed with impunity. Furthermore, by framing the narrative of counter-insurgency at the centre of *Something of Value* in terms of the colonial rhetoric of the civilising mission, Ruark provides a frame of reference through which he attempts to justify the violent methods used for screening and rehabilitating Kikuyu prisoners in the detention camps.

Ruark's depiction of the settlers' 'emergency mentality' is exemplified in the following sentence in the third section of *Something of Value*: 'Life in Kenya had suddenly become a thing of triggered tension, of constant irritation and irritability, of glum experience of catastrophe'.[43] Here, the adjective 'triggered' simultaneously operates as a metonym for the smooth causal relationship between terror and its effects, and implies that it is the Mau Mau attacks on the settlers which have triggered the violent acts of counter-insurgency, rather than the forced dispossession of Kikuyu land. Such a view is reinforced by a long passage of free indirect speech attributed to 'the settlers', in which we are told that 'the only way to stamp [the violence] out is to really pitch into the old Kikuyu and show him a thing or two about terror'.[44] It is in passages such as these that Ruark gives the lie to the official rhetoric of the British counter-insurgency campaign in Kenya that was promulgated by Baring and Alan Lenox-Boyd.

To understand the effect of the Emergency Regulations, Elkins contends, it is important to know that it was the settlers as well as the Kikuyu loyalists who were assigned the task of 'enforcing these harsh laws'.[45] This difference between the colonial governor's suspension of the rule of law in British-occupied Kenya that the emergency powers enabled and the transfer of power to the white settlers and to Kenyan loyalists foregrounds the uncertain zone between the rule of law and the violence of political sovereignty.[46] This distinction between the rule of law and the violence of political sovereignty is particularly pronounced in the European colony. In *Something of Value*, the state of emergency gives settlers such as Joseph Watson and Peter McKenzie a legal pretext to torture, brutalise and murder the Kikuyu with impunity. Following the report of the murder of two more white families, the narrator describes a conversation between Watson and 'a man of high authority', in which the anonymous figure of authority delivers a letter empowering Watson to torture Kikuyu detainees. Ruark's narrator does not reveal the actual content of the letter, which suggests that the letter contains the force of law even if the letter is not a formal law or emergency statute. The significance of this official letter is also alluded to in the following elliptical statement of the 'man of high authority': 'If we could

---

42 See R.W. Kostal, *A Jurisprudence of Power: Victorian Empire and the Rule of Law* (Oxford: Oxford University Press, 2006), p. 443.
43 Ruark, *Something of Value*, p. 397.
44 Ruark, *Something of Value*, pp. 396–97.
45 Elkins, *Britain's Gulag*, p. 56.
46 See Agamben, *State of Exception*.

get just one big man to talk, and if we could place a finger squarely on *one* big oath administrator'.[47] Here, the use of the conjunction 'if' with the modal verb 'could' and the first-person plural pronoun 'we' suggests that this is a polite request involving both the speaker and the addressee. But this phrasing clearly masks the rhetorical force of the colonial bureaucrat's utterance, which is intended as a command to Watson to obtain information from Kikuyu detainees about leading oath administrators. Such a reading is borne out by the colonial official's final words to Watson: 'Do it yourself. I'm off, but something's to be done. You go and do it. Not me'.[48] It is also important to note that the 'man of high authority' declares that he does not 'want to hear the details' of Watson's interrogation methods. The reason for this, as the colonial official explains in a statement that seems wilfully ambivalent, is that if he does not know 'about it' he 'can't talk about it'.[49] The senior colonial official's ambivalent use of the shifting deictic pronoun 'it' is particularly significant here because it mirrors the ambivalence of emergency law. On the one hand, the colonial bureaucrat unofficially commands the white settlers to torture and brutalise suspected Mau Mau detainees, but on the other hand he officially distances himself from the acts of violence that the official letter makes possible. In so doing, the colonial official attempts to preserve the sovereignty of the colonial government through the use of violent methods of counter-insurgency, which are deemed necessary to protect the sovereignty of the colonial government, while officially denying the use of these methods. In this respect, the rhetoric of emergency law can be seen as a form of doublespeak.

It is this indirect and ambivalent command from a colonial bureaucrat to use any means necessary to apprehend the leaders of the Land and Freedom Army that empowers the fictional settlers in *Something of Value* to torture and execute suspected Mau Mau detainees. For McKenzie and his fellow settlers, the counter-insurgency campaign against the Land and Freedom Army is frequently compared to a safari, as illustrated in the following observation: 'For many, Mau Mau had become a sport, an easy exit from the unending labour of crops and cattle'.[50] This comparison is certainly consistent with the novel's generic frame of reference, which includes frequent accounts of McKenzie's reputation as a great white hunter and his various encounters with great game in the Northern Frontier District of Kenya. Such an analogy may appear to romanticise the counter-insurgency campaign. Yet Ruark's representation of the British counter-insurgency campaign in Kenya as an extended safari or hunting trip also points towards the violence of colonial sovereignty in Kenya, which frames the landscape as a state of exception in which both animals and humans can be killed with impunity. This zoological framing of the Land and Freedom movement is borne out by the following unguarded comment of an unnamed

47 Ruark, *Something of Value*, p. 453.
48 Ruark, *Something of Value*, p. 453.
49 Ruark, *Something of Value*, p. 453.
50 Ruark, *Something of Value*, p. 477.

131

white settler during the counter-insurgency movement: 'If we have any more days like this last one they'll be shoving Mau Mau on license, and it'll cost you an extra seventy-five quid for the second one, like elephant'.[51]

Official accounts of the emergency period in Kenya tended to present the counter-insurgency campaign as a form of rehabilitation, in which 'social and economic change' was offered to 'those Kikuyu who confessed their oaths and then cooperated with colonial authorities in the detention camps, and eventually in the Emergency villages in the Kikuyu reserves'. 'Rehabilitation', Elkins explains, 'would be the inducement needed to lure the Kikuyu away from Mau Mau savagery and toward the enlightenment of Western civilization'. In the rhetoric of British colonial governmentality, rehabilitation was crucial to the civilising mission, which formed the *raison d'être* of British colonial rule in Kenya.[52] One of the techniques proposed to achieve the goal of rehabilitation was a counter-oathing ceremony in which Mau Mau adherents were encouraged to 'vomit the poison of Mau Mau'.[53] A fictionalised version of this counter-oathing ceremony is staged in *Something of Value*. In a scene that prefigures the use of mock executions by the CIA against suspected al-Qaeda operatives, Henry and Peter McKenzie torture Njogu, a suspected Mau Mau leader, by repeatedly suffocating him in a gas mask, resuscitating him and leading him to believe that he has transformed into a demon. The traumatic ordeal of this mock execution forces Njogu to confess his involvement with the Land and Freedom movement, to inform on his comrades and to 'vomit out' the Mau Mau oaths he had taken in a *githathi* ceremony administered by a Kikuyu *mundumugu*. By focalising this scene of cruelty through the consciousness of Peter McKenzie, the narrator encourages readers to view the settlers' violent treatment of Njogu as effective because it leads to a confession and produces valuable information about the leaders of the Land and Freedom Army. In a similar vein, the narrator appears to condone the settlers' summary execution of Mau Mau prisoners because it persuades a young boy who is forced to witness the killing to disclose the identity and whereabouts of Njogu to the settlers. Elsewhere in *Something of Value*, however, Ruark raises doubts about the purpose and value of torture in the war against the Mau Mau. In part three, the narrator highlights the racist logic of the emergency powers, and the scapegoating of the Kikuyu for Mau Mau atrocities: 'Merely to be black and at large was dangerous'.[54] The sadism of the settlers toward their prisoners in the detention camps is also hinted at in a comment that 'confession is good for the soles'.[55] This homophonic metonym evokes an image of casual and systematic torture in the detention camps. Such a sadistic attitude demonstrates how the settlers' acts of violence towards Kikuyu prisoners are 'as bad as the Mau Mau, maybe worse',[56] as Peter

51 Ruark, *Something of Value*, p. 452.
52 Elkins, *Britain's Gulag*, p. 100.
53 Elkins, *Britain's Gulag*, p. 391 n. 54.
54 Ruark, *Something of Value*, p. 472.
55 Ruark, *Something of Value*, p. 408.
56 Ruark, *Something of Value*, p. 458.

McKenzie puts it. As well as suggesting that McKenzie is aware of the moral implications of his violent actions, the narrator highlights the psychic effects of the anti-colonial insurgency on the mind of white settlers by describing McKenzie's obsessive hand-washing and restless nights following the cold-blooded execution of Kikuyu detainees. Such psychic maladies may be interpreted as a symptom of the mental disorders that Fanon associated with colonial wars in *The Wretched of the Earth*. Yet if McKenzie's 'Kenya nerves' are a symptom of the singular forms of pathology that Fanon attributed to the experience of European colonisation and anti-colonial resistance, this is not to suggest that *Something of Value* ever really questions the 'systematized negation of the other' that Fanon associates with European colonialism.[57] Instead, the novel perpetuates the predominant colonial myth that the violent anti-colonial resistance struggle was a sign of 'African savagery'.

Postcolonial Literary Narratives of Kenya's Colonial State of Exception

If ethno-psychiatric fictions of Kikuyu society and culture were used to justify the rehabilitation of Mau Mau detainees to an international public, they also worked to mask the use of detention and torture as a means of disciplining the civilian population and punishing the Mau Mau. In the special detention camp at Manyani reserved for prisoners labelled as 'hardcore', for instance, sadistic public spectacles of torture such as forced anal penetration and rolling detainees in barbed wire were used to punish Mau Mau detainees, and to terrorise and subdue other detainees in the camp.[58] Other forms of physical punishment and forced labour in the British colonial detention camps in Kenya may seem banal by comparison to such extreme forms of violence, but they were no less effective in controlling the population. In his account of life in the Manda Island detention camp, for instance, Gakaara describes how the camp provided an extra-legal space in which the camp officer forced the detainees to comply with the colonial government's demand that the detainees work. While the officer states that 'the law of Kenya had now made a provision for forced labour for detainees' and that 'all detainees would now work whether or not they volunteered for it', he also refuses to show the prisoners the confidential document containing the order.[59] In this respect, Gakaara suggests that the colonial detention camp is a space beyond the normal rule of law, a view that is confirmed by the camp officer's assertion that 'we had gone beyond the regard of the law courts of the British Government'.[60] The ambivalent legal space of the detention camp also allows the camp commanders and prison guards to control the bodily lives of the prison population. Gakaara details this biopolitical function of the

---

57 Elkins, *Britain's Gulag*, p. 182.
58 Elkins, *Britain's Gulag*, pp. 156–57.
59 Gakaara wa Wanjaū, *Mau Mau Author in Detention* (Nairobi: Heinemann Kenya, 1988), p. 64.
60 Gakaara, *Mau Mau Author in Detention*, p. 64.

detention camp by documenting the ways in which the prison guards torture some of the detainees, police their diet, regulate their access to prison education and sentence them to solitary confinement. On a superficial reading, the colonial detention camp in Kenya may seem to support Agamben's account of the state of exception – a space that relegates the detainee to a position beyond the law in which she or he can be tortured or killed with impunity. Indeed, the British colonial state's demand that Mau Mau detainees 'confess' to having taken an oath would seem to confirm Agamben's suggestion that sacred forms of power continue to underpin modern forms of sovereignty that are deemed to be secular. But what such a reading crucially overlooks is the agency and social organisation of detainees in prison camps such as that at Manda Island. For, as Gakaara repeatedly suggests, it was the prisoner's networks that allowed them to win small concessions within the detention camp.

Gakaara's prison diary offers a vivid first-hand testimony of the conditions within Manda Island detention camp during the state of emergency in Kenya, and for this reason can be seen to offer an insight into the shared historical experiences of the state of emergency from the standpoint of Kikuyu detainees. Like Gakaara, Ngũgĩ draws on his autobiographical experience of the state of emergency in colonial Kenya in novels such as *Weep Not, Child* and *A Grain of Wheat*. The specific details of Ngũgĩ's experiences of the emergency and his elder brother's involvement in the Land and Freedom struggle are detailed in his memoir *Dreams in a Time of War* (2010).[61] As a child during the emergency, Ngũgĩ did not have direct experience of the detention camps. Yet he weaves together family stories and memories of the emergency period in his postcolonial fiction to articulate the relationship between the state of emergency and the broader history of British colonialism in Kenya. In so doing, Ngũgĩ encourages us to read the state of emergency in Kenya as a continuation and intensification of violent colonial sovereignty and dispossession under the guise of the colonial rhetoric of the civilising mission. The 'civilising' process of rehabilitation in the detention camps that Gakaara unmasks as a brutal lesson in violent colonial subjection is reframed by Ngũgĩ as a critical engagement with the European *Bildungsroman* genre in his first novel, *Weep Not, Child*. By working with and against the resources of the European *Bildungsroman*, in other words, Ngũgĩ raises important questions about the ideological function of colonial education, and its relationship to colonial sovereignty.

The genesis of the *Bildungsroman* as novelistic form is associated with the rise of the bourgeois individual in the late eighteenth and early nineteenth centuries, and by an attempt to contain conflict between the two dominant economic classes of the epoch. In Franco Moretti's words, 'the classical *Bildungsroman* narrates "how the French Revolution could have been avoided"'.[62] Moretti's observation that the *Bildungsroman* has 'accustomed us to looking at

---

61 Ngũgĩ wa Thiong'o, *Dreams in a Time of War: A Childhood Memoir* (London: Harvill Secker, 2010).

62 Franco Moretti, *The Way of the World: The Bildungsroman in European Culture* (London: Verso, 1986), p. 64.

normality *from within* rather than from the stance of its exceptions' may seem to elude the violence and conflict associated with the French Revolution.[63] Yet, as Moretti goes on to suggest through a passing reference to Foucault, normality is an effect of power that is produced through social institutions. Significantly, Moretti adds that the 'literary expression' of normality is 'nineteenth-century mass narrative: the literature of states of exception, of extreme ills and extreme remedies'.[64] Moretti does not elaborate on what he means by 'the literature of states of exception'; instead, he proceeds to argue that the novel tries to elude 'the spatio-temporal confines of the given world'.[65] When the *Bildungsroman* is mapped onto the geopolitical imagination of western imperialism, however, it becomes possible to see how the aesthetic form of the *Bildungsroman* is marked by the imperialist determinants of European aesthetics, and by the civilising mission of English literature.[66] In a gloss on the meaning of the term *Bildung*, Marc Redfield identifies a 'profound homology between pedagogy and aesthetics, the education of a subject and the figuration of a text'.[67] In Redfield's account, the project of aesthetic education underpinning the *Bildungsroman* has 'enormous political utility and is in fact inseparable [...] from the rhetoric of class struggle and colonial administration'. Citing David Lloyd, Redfield argues that the 'individual narrative of self-formation is subsumed in the larger narrative of the civilizing process, the passage from savagery to civility, which is the master narrative of modernity'.[68]

It is precisely this connection between the 'individual narrative of self-formation' and the 'larger narrative of the civilizing process' that Ngũgĩ interrogates in his first published novel, *Weep Not, Child*. Through a critical engagement with the *Bildungsroman*, Ngũgĩ gradually reveals how the civilising mission of education serves to further alienate the colonised from their land and their culture. As Simon Gikandi puts it, 'the sight of the father's broken body is the son's best education in the ways of colonial violence'.[69] The novel begins with an account of the male protagonist's desire for an education. Although it is Njoroge's mother, Nyokabi, who facilitates Njoroge's education, Ngũgĩ frames his protagonist's education in relation to the nationalist rhetoric of Kenyatta. As his brother Kamau explains, 'Your learning is for all of us. Father says the same thing. He is anxious that you go on, so you might bring light to our home. Education is the light of Kenya. That's what Jomo says'.[70] In this passage, Njoroge and his family are interpellated by the belief that education will lead to their emancipation. Following the imprisonment of Kenyatta, the death of Ngotho (Njoroge's father), and Njoroge's own torture in the wake of the state of

63 Moretti, *The Way of the World*, p. 111.
64 Moretti, *The Way of the World*, p. 12.
65 Moretti, *The Way of the World*, p. 12.
66 Marc Redfield, *Phantom Formations: Aesthetic Ideology and the Bildungsroman* (Ithaca, NY: Cornell University Press, 1996), p. viii.
67 Redfield, *Phantom Formations*, pp. 38–39.
68 Redfield, *Phantom Formations*, p. 51.
69 Simon Gikandi, *Ngugi wa Thiong'o* (Cambridge: Cambridge University Press, 2000), p. 96.
70 Ngũgĩ wa Thiong'o, *Weep Not, Child* (London: Heinemann Educational, 1964), p. 38.

emergency, however, Ngũgĩ suggests that colonial education is a myth designed to preserve colonial sovereignty.

Ngũgĩ's critique of colonial education in *Weep Not, Child* is a powerful example of what Lazarus – following Theodor Adorno – has called hating tradition properly. To hate tradition properly, as we saw in the introduction, means to hate the modern tradition of western bourgeois humanism properly, and to do so in such a way that opposes the false universality of western bourgeois humanism in favour of 'a true universality, with the idea of a radically transformed social order'.[71] In this respect, the task of hating tradition properly may also help to elucidate the critical relationship between the oppressed and tradition that Benjamin outlines in his Eighth Thesis on the Concept of History. More importantly though, Lazarus's re-reading of Adorno is apposite for reading *Weep Not, Child* because it provides a critical vocabulary through which to understand Ngũgĩ's critique of the European *Bildungsroman* and its aesthetic ideology. By reframing the *Bildungsroman* in the context of Kenya's colonial state of emergency, Ngũgĩ demonstrates how the civilising mission of colonial education alienates the colonised from their land and their culture.

If *Weep Not, Child* exemplifies what Franco Moretti calls the literature of states of exception, it is a literary text that also reveals how the colonial state of emergency is a continuation and intensification of the violence of colonial sovereignty. The paradox of the narrative process of self-formation in *Weep Not, Child* is that it leads the male protagonist to lose 'faith in all the things he had earlier believed in, like wealth, power, education, religion'.[72] This is not to suggest, however, that the novel simply reinforces the subordination of Ngũgĩ's Kikuyu characters to the wretched condition of bare life. Certainly Njoroge considers taking his own life at the end of *Weep Not, Child* following the death of his father, the imminent execution of his brother, Boro, and the uncertain fate of Kori, whose detention prompts Njoroge to ask whether 'He might be killed like those who had been beaten to death at Hola Camp'.[73] Yet it is Njoroge's mothers Nyokabi and Njeri who persuade him against suicide. Njoroge regards his failure to take his own life as a sign of his cowardice. But this is to overlook the important role of women in Ngũgĩ's fictional depiction of the emergent postcolonial nation. Such a role may be limited by the narrow, patriarchal view of women presented in some of Ngũgĩ's fiction. But what Njeri and Nyokabi's transgression of the curfew imposed during the colonial state of emergency at the end of the novel also gestures towards is a form of agency and collectivity that circumvents the violence of colonial sovereignty. By circumventing the spatial and temporal restrictions imposed by the emergency, Njeri and Nyokabi's transgression of the curfew offers a counterpoint to the necropolitical form of resistance which Njoroge imagines as the only available means of effective resistance to the colonial state.

71 Lazarus, *Nationalism and Cultural Practice in the Postcolonial World*, p. 3.
72 Ngũgĩ, *Weep Not, Child*, p. 134.
73 Ngũgĩ, *Weep Not, Child*, p. 134.

A Grain of Wheat, *Matigari* and the Emergency Powers
of the Postcolonial State

If the narrative time of *Weep Not, Child* ends in the middle of the state of emergency, much of Ngũgĩ's subsequent fiction reflects on the traumatic aftermath of the colonial state of emergency. In *A Grain of Wheat* (1967), for example, the formal end of the colonial state of emergency and the emancipatory promises of Kenyan independence are haunted by the events of the emergency, which are gradually revealed through the use of analepsis and multiple focalisation. Just as *Weep Not, Child* uses the conventions of the European *Bildungsroman* in order to foreground the contradictions of the civilising mission, so Ngũgĩ's use of multiple focalisation and a betrayal plot structure in *A Grain of Wheat* are techniques adapted from European fiction. Yet such formal techniques do not simply mark Ngũgĩ's failure to develop a postcolonial literary form that is appropriate to articulate the 'organised popular resistance, or principled collective solidarity' of the Land and Freedom movement, as the critic David Maughan-Brown has suggested.[74] Rather, Ngũgĩ's use of European fictional techniques to represent the limitations of national independence formally mirrors the way in which the violence of the colonial state of emergency fragmented the Kenyan social body, as we will see.

A Grain of Wheat is set on the eve of Kenya's independence, and the narrative is structured as a series of separate analeptic sequences that document the emergency period in Kenya from the multiple perspectives of different characters. This use of analepsis is significant because it formally registers the process of deferred action through which the traumatic experiences of torture, violence and betrayal are gradually known and articulated by many of the novel's protagonists. In this sense the novel formally registers the discontinuous structure that Benjamin associates with the tradition of the oppressed. From the start of the novel, for instance, the character Mugo is described as an enigmatic and reclusive figure who appears to be in a state of psychological distress:

> Mugo felt nervous. He was lying on his back and looking at the roof [...] A clear drop of water was delicately suspended above him. The drop fattened and grew dirtier as it absorbed grains of soot. Then it started drawing towards him. He tried to shut his eyes. They would not close. He tried to move his head: it was firmly chained to the bed-frame. The drop grew larger and larger as it drew closer to his eyes. He wanted to cover his eyes with his palms; but his hands, his feet, everything refused to obey his will.[75]

In this quotation the use of simple sentence construction immediately establishes a sense of tension. Mugo's fixation on the drop of water and his apparent state of physical paralysis evokes a subject who appears to lack agency. Through the use of multiple focalisation, the narrator goes on to suggest that Mugo is

---

74 Maughan-Brown, *Land, Freedom and Fiction*, p. 250.
75 Ngũgĩ wa Thiong'o, *A Grain of Wheat* (London: Penguin, 2002 [1967]), p. 1.

a hero who supported the national independence struggle against the British colonial administration and the Kenyan loyalists. This is particularly apparent in a subsequent conversation between Gikonyo and Wambui:

> 'He is a strange man,' Wambui commented.
> 'Who?' Warui asked.
> 'Mugo.'
> 'It is the suffering,' Gikonyo said. Do you know what it was to live in deten-tion? It was easier, perhaps, with those of us not labelled hard-core. But Mugo was. So he was beaten, and yet would not confess the oath'.[76]

The Thabai villagers' construction of Mugo as a hero of the national liberation struggle, who fought alongside the revolutionary leader, Kihika, and refused to confess the Kikuyu nationalist oath of unity in the detention camp, is under-mined by the revelation at the end of the novel that Mugo voluntarily betrayed Kihika to District Officer John Thompson during the early period of the nation-alist insurgency.

That Mugo informs on Kihika in order to distance himself from the violent, nationalist insurgency movement and is subsequently mistaken for a hero of the same revolutionary movement is significant because it seems to undermine the emancipatory claims of national independence in Kenya. Indeed, many critics have argued that Mugo's betrayal of Kihika not only undermines the narrative of national independence that the novel seems to establish, but also cautions against the transition from a period of European colonialism to neocolonialism, in which an elite, educated bourgeoisie rules over the Kenyan working class.[77] For Gikandi, Ngũgĩ's use of analepsis to raise doubts about the messianic promises of the national independence celebrations exemplifies what he calls Ngũgĩ's ironic temporality. Such an ironic temporal mode 'allows the author to provide his readers with a trenchant critique of a stillborn decolonization, while his overall ideological commitment is to the ideals of the anticolonial movement'.[78] This 'ironic temporal mode' does not merely signal 'Ngũgĩ's mastery of the great tradition of the bourgeois novel and his break with it',[79] it also raises questions about the future of the postcolony after the formal end of the emergency, and about whether the new political elite will recognise the material and political demands of the Kenya Land and Freedom Army. After Kenya's independence, Kenyatta's return to politics may have sought to promote reconciliation and national unity between loyalist and former Kikuyu detainees. But what this national reconciliation effectively involved was the erasure of the history of the Mau Mau, the experiences in the detention camps, as well as the massa-cres, punishments and dispossession from Kenya's official national narrative, as

---

76 Ngũgĩ, *A Grain of Wheat*, p. 27.
77 See Maughan-Brown, *Land, Freedom and Fiction*, pp. 247–58; and Byron Caminero-Santan-gelo, 'Neocolonialism and the Betrayal Plot in *A Grain of Wheat*: Ngũgĩ wa Thiong'o's Re-Vision of *Under Western Eyes*', *Research in African Literatures*, 29/1 (1998), pp. 139–52.
78 Gikandi, *Ngugi wa Thiong'o*, pp. 112–13.
79 Gikandi, *Ngugi wa Thiong'o*, p. 113.

David Anderson has argued.[80] Indeed, Kenyatta's silencing of the political cause of the Mau Mau parallels Fanon's prescient reflections on the limitations of the political elite in the postcolony in *The Wretched of the Earth*:

> Before independence, the leader, as a rule, personified the aspirations of the people – independence, political liberty and national dignity. But in the aftermath of independence, far from actually embodying the needs of the people [...] the leader will unmask his inner purpose: to become the CEO of the company of profiteers composed of a national bourgeoisie intent only on getting the most out of the situation.[81]

Fanon's concern with the failures of the political elite after independence to translate the promises of independence into a social democratic nation-building project is developed further in Ngũgĩ's satire of the postcolonial dictator his Excellency ole Excellence in his 1986 novel *Matigari*, as we will see.

By reassessing the history of the state of emergency in Kenya after the formal end of the emergency has been declared, *A Grain of Wheat* suggests that there is a danger that the violent and divisive legacy of the colonial state of emergency will continue in the aftermath of decolonisation, and that the political cause of Land and Freedom will be betrayed by the narrow self-interests of the neocolonial bourgeois elite. In this sense the ironic temporality of *A Grain of Wheat* sheds light on the temporality of a colonial state of emergency, which is presented as if it were an exceptional and temporary measure precipitated by political unrest rather than an intensification and consolidation of the 'normal' colonial rule of law. In the situation of postcolonial Kenya, however, the formal suspension of emergency legislation did not lead to what Benjamin calls a *real* state of emergency, or to the decolonisation that Fanon had in mind in *The Wretched of the Earth*. The passing of the Preservation of Public Security Act by Kenyatta's government in 1966 retained the main provisions of the British Emergency Powers Order of 1939, and permitted detention without trial, censorship, prohibition of public meetings, declaration of state of emergency and other draconian measures.[82] The deletion of the word 'emergency' from the Preservation of Public Security Act might appear to reinforce the Kenyatta government's claim to have repealed the Emergency (Powers) Orders in Council that were in place during British colonial rule. But as Ngũgĩ explains in the memoir of his arrest and imprisonment by the Kenyatta government, *Detained* (1981), the differences between the colonial emergency legislation and the Kenyatta government's Preservation of Public Security Act were 'Sweet semantics': 'the 1939 order in council, itself an enlargement of the 1897 Native Courts Regulations, was in substance adopted in granting emergency powers to the new independent government'.[83]

80 Anderson, *Histories of the Hanged*, p. 336.
81 Fanon, *The Wretched of the Earth*, p. 112.
82 See Carol Sicherman, *Ngugi wa Thiong'o: The Making of a Rebel: A Source Book in Kenyan Literature and Resistance* (London: Zell, 1990), p. 88; and Ngũgĩ wa Thiong'o, *Detained: A Writer's Prison Diary* (London: Heinemann, 1981), p. 51.
83 Ngũgĩ, *Detained*, p. 51.

This return of repressive laws after the colonial state of emergency casts a shadow over the emancipatory claims of independence, which are also figured in the spectres haunting Ngũgĩ's fiction. During his *Uhuru* speech to mark Kenya's independence General R. recalls Koina's talk 'of seeing the ghosts of the colonial past still haunting independent Kenya'.[84] If the fictionalised event of national independence in *A Grain of Wheat* is haunted by the ghosts of freedom fighters such as Kihika or Dedan Kimathi, whose demands for land and freedom have not been recognised, in Ngũgĩ's 1986 novel *Matigari*, this revolutionary *revenant* takes the form of a forest fighter, who returns to an unnamed African country to discover that the social divisions between the nationalist bourgeoisie and the peasantry are even more pronounced than they were before independence. Named after the 'patriots who survived the bullets' Matigari ma Njirũũngi buries his AK47 and his sword in the forest, puts on the belt of peace, and seeks to return home. In so doing, Matigari suggests that his defeat of Settler Williams in the forest – and the colonial order that Williams symbolises – will lead to the social and economic transformation of the unnamed African country to which he returns. Matigari's political optimism for the postcolonial future of his country after independence is undermined by the realisation that the children of the new nation are forced to subsist on a rubbish dump and to live in a scrap yard, and that the home he had fought for is now occupied by the son of Settler Williams and John Boy Junior, the British-educated son of Williams's cook, John Boy. Pheng Cheah has suggested that the dispossessed children in *Matigari* are a synecdoche for the people and that the home to which Matigari invites the children to return with him is a symbol of the nation:

> An allegory for the unfinished nationalist project, Matigari's homecoming is an attempt to find habitation in one's land when it has become so alien that it is no longer a home, a place to which one belongs [...] Ngũgĩ figures the people's reappropriation of the country's economic infrastructure and polit-ical superstructure as Matigari's attempt to repossess and rebuild his house.[85]

Such a reading of *Matigari* as national allegory is compelling, but it elides the significance of Matigari's moral challenge to the quasi-legal commandments of the dictator, his Excellency ole Excellence.

Ngũgĩ's suggestion in *Matigari* that the fictional decrees of the authoritarian postcolonial leader carry the force of law mirrors the continuities between the colonial state of emergency in Kenya and the public security legislation in postco-lonial Kenya. These continuities are exemplified in the public speech delivered by the minister for truth and justice to a group of villagers in chapter 17:

> I am the soul of this government. I am the soul of this nation. I am the light in the dark tunnel. I am the torch of development. Why do I say this? Because, without the rule of law – truth and justice – there is no government, no

---

84 Ngũgĩ, *A Grain of Wheat*, p. 216.
85 Pheng Cheah, *Spectral Nationality: Passages of Freedom from Kant to Postcolonial Literatures of Liberation* (New York: Columbia University Press, 2003), pp. 371–72.

nation, no civilisation. The rule of law is the true measure of *civilisation*. I should know. I was brought up in the law. I abide by the law, and the law abides in me. I have been taught by the law, and I staunchly believe in it. I am the guardian of the law today. I make the law, and I ensure that it is kept. My father was the first person in this country to advocate loyalism to the Crown at the beginning of the century. Some might wonder: Loyalty to whose law? The colonial law? Law is law. Those who realised this from the beginning are the only people of any worth in this country today. Yes, we loyalists are the ones in power today. Long live loyalism![86]

In this speech, the minister's repetition of the verbal phrase 'I am' identifies the subject of the law that the first-person pronoun denotes with the 'rule of law' that the minister claims to embody. In so doing, the minister demystifies the origins of legal authority by highlighting his role as a sovereign figure who defines legal rights and freedoms for himself while denying them to his subjects. This performance corresponds with Mbembe's claim that the postcolonial commandment transforms the autocratic leader of the postcolony into a fetishistic form of domination that is accountable only to itself.[87] What Mbembe means by commandment is the absolute sovereignty of the ruler to determine and limit the rights of his or her subjects. Crucially, Mbembe emphasises that this form of postcolonial sovereignty is inherited from the colonial state.[88] Mbembe's reflections on the formation and colonial genealogy of commandment in the postcolony are apposite for reading Ngũgĩ's satire of postcolonial sovereignty in *Matigari*. Indeed, by suggesting that the origins of legal authority in this fictional postcolonial African state can be traced to the 'colonial law' and the history of 'loyalism to the Crown', the minister contradicts his tautological and ahistorical claim that 'Law is law'. In this fictionalised postcolonial Kenya, the rule of law is not timeless; rather, it is coeval with the political and economic interests of the dominant political party, embodied in his Excellency ole Excellence.

The minister's use of colonial law to maintain political power over the masses is further borne out in his framing of the trade union leader Ngarũru wa Kĩrĩro's public call for strike action as an act of sedition and treason.[89] Here, the minister's recourse to the laws of sedition and treason offer a metacommentary on the novel's public critique of political power in the postcolony. As Ngũgĩ explains in a prefatory note to the English language edition of the novel, after the first publication of the novel in Kikuyu in 1986, rumours started to circulate

---

86 Ngũgĩ wa Thiong'o, *Matigari*, trans. Waugui wa Goro (Oxford: Heinemann, 1989 [1986]), p. 102.
87 Achille Mbembe, *On the Postcolony* (Berkeley, CA: University of California Press, 2001), p. 111. For a further discussion of Mbembe's account of the postcolony and *Matigari*, see Gitahi Gititi, 'Ferocious Comedies: Henri Lopes's *The Laughing Cry* and Ngũgĩ wa Thiong'o's *Matigari* as "Dictator" Novels', in Charles Cantalupo (ed.), *Ngũgĩ wa Thiong'o: Texts and Contexts* (Trenton, NJ: Africa World Press, 1996), pp. 211–26.
88 See Mbembe, *On the Postcolony*, pp. 25–26.
89 Ngũgĩ, *Matigari*, p. 110.

among the peasants 'about a man called Matigari who was roaming the whole country making demands about truth and justice'. Ngũgĩ then proceeds to describe how the state responded to these rumours: 'There were orders for his immediate arrest, but the police discovered that Matigari was only a fictional character in a book of the same name. In February 1987, the police raided all the bookshops and seized every copy of the novel'.[90] This statement does not only comment on the banality of power in a postcolonial dictatorship, it also highlights the subversive potentiality of orature within Kikuyu public culture. By circulating a rumour about a freedom fighter who returns from the forest to continue the struggle for land and freedom, Ngũgĩ rearticulates the histories of subaltern insurgency which have been buried by the neocolonial state. If British colonial historiography attempted to 'bury the living soul of Kenya's history of struggle and resistance, and the attempt to normalise the tradition of loyalism to imperialism has continued into neocolonial Kenya',[91] Matigari threatens the authority of this systematic historical repression by asking discomfiting questions about truth, justice and the limitations of postcolonial freedom after the act of national liberation.

What is particularly threatening about Matigari's return from the forest is that he seems to herald the end of the neocolonial state. The minister of truth and justice tries to discredit Matigari's public demands and questions by comparing him to Rip van Winkle, the protagonist in Washington Irvine's eponymous short story who sleeps through the American Revolution and wakes up to find that everything has changed.[92] Against this charge of belatedness, the popularity of Matigari's public speeches suggests that his untimely meditations on the redistribution of wealth and land prefigure a postcolonial future after neocolonialism for the fictional African country depicted in the novel. Matigari's prescience has prompted some readers to speculate on his messianic status as a Christ-like figure or a Marxist prophet.[93] For other readers such as Gikandi, Matigari's spectral presence in the text is indeterminate, and it is precisely because of this indeterminacy that Matigari 'can function as a sign of resistance and identity'. As Gikandi explains, 'Without a thorough knowledge of who he is and the forces he represents, the state cannot imprison him; and because he has no knowable or fixed character, the populace can transform him, in their imagination, into an agent of social change'.[94]

If Matigari functions as a rhetorical figure in the text, the circulation of his proper name in the Kikuyu public sphere both contributes to and helps to

90 Ngũgĩ, *Matigari*, p. viii.
91 Ngũgĩ wa Thiong'o, *Moving the Centre: The Struggle for Cultural Freedoms* (Oxford: James Currey/Heinemann, 1993), p. 98.
92 Ngũgĩ, *Matigari*, p. 118.
93 See David Maughan-Brown, 'Matigari and the Rehabilitation of Religion', *Research in African Literatures*, 22/4 (1991), pp. 161–67; and Ann Bierseker, '*Matigari ma Nirũũngi*: What Grows from Leftover Seeds of "Chat" Trees?', in Cantalupo (ed.), *The World of Ngũgĩ wa Thiong'o*, pp. 141–58.
94 Gikandi, *Ngugi wa Thiong'o*, pp. 245–46.

organise the emergence of the tradition of the oppressed. The temporality of this emergence may threaten predominant historical narratives of the nation by invoking the ghosts of freedom fighters who remain disillusioned with the contemporary political claims of the neocolonial state after independence. And in this respect, the temporal structure of *Matigari* may appear to parallel the concept of messianic time which underpins Benjamin's materialist thought. In a thesis that was posthumously discovered in his notes for the 'Thesis on the Concept of History', Benjamin wrote that 'in his conception of the class-less society, Marx secularized the conception of messianic time'.[95] The cultural origins of Matigari in Kikuyu political songs and euphemisms of the emergency period, and his magical powers of resistance – such as his miraculous escape from prison – may raise questions about the extent to which Matigari's return from the forest can be understood as secular. Yet by revealing how Matigari's escape from imprisonment is made possible by Guthera's sleeping with a policeman, Ngũgĩ suggests that Matigari's worldly struggle against the betrayal of Kenya's national independence by the neocolonial government is made possible by what Brendon Nicholls has aptly called 'female sexwork-in-insurgency' rather than by some magical, messianic powers.[96] Like Mumbi's support for the anti-colonial insurgency in *A Grain of Wheat*, and Njeri and Nyokabi's support for Njoroge following his torture and the death of his father in *Weep Not, Child*, Guthera's support for Matigari's struggle stretches Marx's 'conception of the classless society' by foregrounding the crucial role of women in the future transformation of Kenyan society and politics. Such a role may be limited by Ngũgĩ's subordination of gender politics to a national struggle against neocolonialism led by a masculine figure such as Matigari, as Boehmer and Abdulrazak Gurnah have suggested.[97] Yet it is precisely figures such as Guthera who emphasise how a challenge to the repressive laws of the neocolonial state also involves a challenge to the patriarchal structures of Kenyan society.

Conclusion

The forms of political agency and collectivity that Ngũgĩ articulates in his writing may seem to illuminate the limitations of Agamben's reflections on the state of exception to account for the formation of sovereign power in the European colony, and the forms of resistance to it. As we have seen, Agamben's account of the state of exception does not offer a sustained account of the particular

---

95 Walter Benjamin, 'Paralipomena to "On the Concept of History"', in Howard Eiland and Michael W. Jennings (eds), *Selected Writings, Volume IV 1938–1940* (Cambridge, MA: Belknap Press of Harvard University Press, 2003), p. 401.

96 See Brendon Nicholls, *Ngugi wa Thiong'o, Gender, and the Ethics of Postcolonial Reading* (Farnham: Ashgate, 2010), p. 176.

97 Elleke Boehmer, *Stories of Women: Gender and Narrative in the Postcolonial Nation* (Manchester: Manchester University Press, 2005), pp. 42–53; and Abdulrazak Gurnah, '*Matigari*: A Tract of Resistance', *Research in African Literatures*, 22/4 (1991), pp. 169–72.

ways in which the state of exception has become normalised in formations of colonial sovereignty through cultural stereotypes that have been mobilised by the colonial state to justify the use of coercive techniques of governmentality. Yet, as the challenge that the Mau Mau Veterans' Association presented to the British government in April 2011 indicates, there are also ways in which Agamben's reflections on sovereignty and the state of exception can be recalibrated to account for the spatial and temporal 'dis-application' between the colonial laws of emergency that granted executive powers to a colonial governor or administrator and the techniques of violent colonial governmentality that such laws enabled. In their attempt to bring the British government to justice for the historical legacy of colonisation and violent forms of counter-insurgency during the emergency period, the Mau Mau Veterans' Association prompted the British Foreign Office to disclose 2,000 boxes of documents that may implicate the British Government in the violent practices of the colonial administration during the emergency period in Kenya.[98] In so doing, the Mau Mau veterans used the legal space of the British high court to highlight and contest the ways in which the violence of the colonial power of exception is buried in the archives of colonialism. Such tactics offer a powerful example of the way in which the subjects of colonial violence have used the juridical techniques associated with colonial power against the institutions of colonial sovereignty in order to demand justice and recognition for past wrongs committed. Just as Ngũgĩ uses the codes and conventions of literary fiction to foreground the process by which the rhetoric of the civilising mission worked to normalise the violence of colonial sovereignty, so the Mau Mau Veterans' Association use the juridical codes of the British legal system to disclose the systematic violence of colonial governmentality. In this respect, both Ngũgĩ and the Mau Mau Veterans' Association offer an important supplement to Agamben's gesture towards another more radical use of the law, which seeks both to study and play with the law in order to deactivate it.[99]

We have also seen how Ngũgĩ challenges the normalisation of emergency powers by the postcolonial state, and contests the historical erasure of the Land and Freedom movement from the postcolonial state's nationalist narrative in *Matigari*. *Matigari*'s contribution to the public commemoration of the Land and Freedom struggle after the disappointments of decolonisation is clearly exemplified by the circulating rumours confirming the existence of a freedom fighter who had returned from the forest to fight against the depredations of neocolonialism. And in so doing, *Matigari* clearly demonstrates how literary texts can do justice to the history and historiography of the oppressed. Yet if literary texts such as *Matigari* are to play a role in challenging the use of the law as a technique for postcolonial dictators to shore up their power and wealth, such texts also need to address the ways in which women have disturbed the

98 B. MacIntyre, 'Secret Colonial Files may show more blood on British hands', *The Times*, 7 April 2011, p. 14.
99 Agamben, *State of Exception*, p. 64.

patriarchal law of sovereign power both during and after Kenya's colonial state of emergency. The figure of Guthera, the sex worker as insurgent in *Matigari*, offers an illuminating example of such a strategy, as we have seen. For in sacrificing her body to the political cause of a renewed struggle against imperialism, Guthera not only disturbs the postcolonial sovereign's power over the bodies of the population, she also raises a crucial question about whether a subversive use of the law will make any significant difference to the patriarchal foundations of the postcolony. Such a question marks the limits of Ngũgĩ's vision of decolonisation and emphasises the need for a more detailed assessment of gendered forms of anti-colonial insurgency.

CHAPTER 5

Narratives of Torture and Trauma in Algeria's Colonial State of Exception

In the opening sequence of Gillo Pontecorvo's 1965 film *The Battle of Algiers*, a group of French paratroopers feed a half-naked Algerian man a cup of coffee. Shivering and visibly terrified, this prisoner's non-verbal physical gestures clearly suggest that he has been tortured. These non-verbal signs of a body in pain are further confirmed by the appearance of the French military colonel in the cinematic frame, who inquires whether the man has talked, and by the threat that they will start all over again if the man refuses to comply with their demand that he help them locate one of the leading figures in the FLN, Ali la Point. In the subsequent scene, which follows the opening credits, the French paratroopers' discovery of Ali la Point's hiding place at an apartment in the Casbah implies that the torture of the unnamed Algerian man in the previous scene has been successful.

This cinematic sequence is significant for a number of reasons. First, it suggests that the use of torture as a tactic of counter-insurgency is justified if it leads to the apprehension of 'violent insurgents', and to the prevention of a 'terrorist attack'. Second, the sequence privileges the point of view of the French paratrooper in the counter-insurgency campaign against the FLN insurgents – a perspective that is prevalent in many literary and cultural representations of the Algerian war of independence, as we will see. Third, this opening sequence and the subsequent flashback to the beginning of the 'Battle of Algiers' in 1954 draw attention to the wide powers that the French emergency legislation granted to the French colonial *départements* in Algeria to torture its colonial subjects. Related to this, the temporality of the sequence raises questions about the relationship between the supposedly finite temporality of the emergency legislation passed between 1955 and 1960 and the supposedly immutable duration of French colonial sovereignty in Algeria. The discrepancy between these different temporalities draws attention to the systematic violence of colonial sovereignty identified by thinkers such as Fanon and Mbembe. Finally,

146

by privileging the torture of a masculine Algerian subject, the sequence seems to marginalise the contribution and sacrifice that women made to the Algerian liberation struggle. In so doing, the sequence raises questions about the historical experiences and agency of Algerian women both before and after national independence in Algeria. Such experiences mark the limitations of Pontecorvo's vision of the tradition of the oppressed in an emergent postcolonial Algeria. If we take the tradition of the oppressed to mean the intellectual tradition of Third World political thought in the revolutionary context of decolonisation, it is important that this tradition addresses the structures of both colonial and patriarchal oppression, and the legacies of these structures in the foundations of the postcolonial state.

By beginning with this opening sequence from *The Battle of Algiers*, I want to consider how literary and cultural texts contribute to our understanding of the ways in which emergency legislation and the techniques of counter-insurgency they enabled were understood and experienced by the Algerian population that was subjected to such emergency laws. After an analysis of the rhetoric of necessity that was used to justify the recourse to emergency powers and the transfer of legal power to the military in the French emergency decrees of 1955 and 1956, this chapter proceeds to analyse how the French colonial state of emergency is figured in French colonial fictions of the Algerian war, specifically Leulliette's memoir *Saint Michel et le dragon* (1961) and Larteguy's fictional representation of the Algerian war, *Les centurions* (1962). If these narratives try to create a heroic mythology around the figure of the French paratrooper that justifies the recourse to emergency powers, memoirs of the Algerian war such as Henri Alleg's *La question* (1958) and Ighilahriz's *Algérienne* (2001) disclose the ways in which the emergency decrees empowered the French colonial state to detain, torture and kill the bodies of the Algerian population with impunity. Such narratives are significant not only because they illuminate the relationship between colonial sovereignty, law and violence, but also because they raise important questions about the political implications of representing the tortured body in pain. How, for instance, is it possible to represent the bodies of victims of torture without falling prey to a grotesque voyeurism that unwittingly reinforces the authority of the colonial state by participating in its spectacular logic of violence? And to what extent have such representations of torture and violence during Algeria's colonial state of emergency inadvertently contributed to the justification of postcolonial state violence against the Algerian population? As the final section of the chapter suggests, Assia Djebar's novels of the Algerian war and Guémar's poetry have attempted to think through and beyond the violent legacies of Algeria's colonial state of emergency. Whereas Djebar uses the literary conventions of autobiography and historical fiction to draw attention to the challenges of recovering women's lives from the colonial archive and from popular narratives of Algeria's national liberation struggle, Guémar uses images of torture and bodies in pain to foreground the continuities between the colonial state of exception and the violence of civil war in Algeria. In so doing, Djebar and Guémar give voice to the traumatic and fragmentary history of the oppressed that has been silenced by both the postcolonial Algerian state and the French colonial state before it.

Writing the Colonial Law of Emergency in Algeria

Like the states of emergency in Ireland, India and Kenya, the colonial state of emergency in Algeria needs to be understood in relation to a longer history of violent colonial sovereignty. In the case of Algeria, this colonial history stretches back to the French invasion of Algeria in 1830. As Marnia Lazreg puts it, 'Algeria in the mid 1950s resembled Algeria in the first half of the nineteenth century, when the military was a major actor in the colony'.[1] In a similar vein, the historian Alistair Horne juxtaposes the French military's massacre of between 6000 and 45,000 Algerian demonstrators at Sétif in 1945 with the history of French colonial occupation. In Horne's account,

> Laws specifically related to Algeria were adapted or initiated by a 'regime of decrees' established in 1834, controlled by the administration and thus escaping any parliamentary control. The nearest semblance to any Algerian legislative assembly was the Délégations Financières, composed of mixed European and Muslim members, but the competence of this body was limited to budgetary matters; and, in practice, for one reason or another it tended to reflect the interests of the *grands colons*.[2]

This lack of legal and political representation is further borne out by the fact that Algerian Muslims were French subjects, but they were denied the rights associated with French citizenship.[3] Such a contradiction relates to the structural disjunctions of the French imperial nation state, as Gary Wilder explains:

> Constitutionally, the Third Republic was simultaneously a parliamentary state whose authority derived from popular consent and a colonial state whose authority derived from political conquest. It had somehow to reconcile the precept of national-popular sovereignty with a legalized racial distinction between ruler and ruled. It is therefore appropriate to characterize France by World War I as an imperial nation-state. The term indicates the dual character of France as a single political formation in which parliamentary republican and authoritarian colonial elements were structurally interrelated and not simply added to one another.[4]

This structural interrelation of 'parliamentary republican and authoritarian colonial elements' placed the colonial subject in a double bind that subjected them to French colonial rule while denying them the political rights afforded to 'native' French citizens.

1 Lazreg, *Torture and the Twilight of Empire*, p. 38.
2 Alistair Horne, *A Savage War of Peace* (London: Macmillan, 1977), p. 33.
3 Horne, *A Savage War of Peace*, p. 35.
4 Gary Wilder, *The French Imperial Nation-State: Negritude and Colonial Humanism between the Two Wars* (Chicago: University of Chicago Press, 2006), p. 25.

The disjunctions of the French imperial nation state vis-à-vis its colonial subjects reveal how the logic of inclusive exclusion that Agamben associates with the state of exception operated within the specific historical context of colonial Algeria. While the political status of Algerians as French subjects subordinates them to the sovereign power of the French imperial nation state, the fact that they were also denied the rights associated with French itizenship suggests that they were relegated to a space outside the 'normal' rule of law in metropolitan France. As Raphaëlle Branche puts it, 'Colonial law was skilled at creating distinctions among "Frenchmen"'.[5] In this respect, the authoritarian system of rule by decree that was prevalent in the *départements* of colonial Algeria is structurally similar to the paradoxical relationship of inclusive exclusion between the state of exception and the normal rule of law described by Agamben.

Agamben's account of the state of exception may help to elucidate what Wilder calls the structural relationship between the parliamentary rule of law in metropolitan France and the rule by decree in the colonial territories of Greater France. Such a focus on the quasi-legal foundations of sovereignty may also help to explain why the state of emergency that was declared in 1955 was a continuation of French policy in colonial Algeria rather than an exceptional break with the colonial past. The French government's passing of a law declaring a state of emergency in 1955 was originally framed in order to preserve the semblance of peace within the French imperial order. Branche explains how 'for eight years, the French armed interventions in Algeria were officially referred to as "police operations" aimed at "maintaining order" on French territory'. Consequently, these military interventions 'were depicted [...] as an internal matter'.[6] What is more, the state of emergency licensed the increasing militarisation of the colonial state. Lazreg traces the aetiology of this military ascendancy to the emergency laws passed between 1955 and 1956. On 3 April 1955, a law was passed to decree a state of emergency in Algeria for six months. 'Article 12 of the law', Lazreg explains, 'set the stage for a transfer of power from civil to military court'.[7] This article declared that

> Lorsque l'état d'urgence est institué, dans tout ou partie d'un département, un décret pris sur le rapport du garde des sceaux, ministre de la justice, et du ministre de la défense nationale peut autoriser la juridiction militaire à se saisir de crimes, ainsi que des délits qui leur sont connexes, relevant de la cour d'assises de ce département.
>
> [When the state of emergency is established in part or all of a *département*, a decree issued by the minister of justice and the defence minister can authorise a military court to judge crimes, as well as related crimes that [normally] fall under the [jurisdiction of the] assize court of the *département*.][8]

---

5 Raphaëlle Branche, 'Torture and Other Violations of the Law by the French Army during the Algerian War', in Adam Jones (ed.), *Genocide, War Crimes and the West: History and Complicity* (London and New York: Zed Books, 2004), p. 134.

6 Branche, 'Torture and Other Violations of the Law', p. 135.

7 Lazreg, *Torture and the Twilight of Empire*, p. 36.

8 Michael Hardy, Hervé Lemoine and Thierry Sarmany (eds), *Pouvoir politique et autorité*

By granting authority to the military to hear crimes that were normally tried under the jurisdiction of a civil court, in other words, the colonial state sought to consolidate its sovereignty over Algeria and the native population. As the French historian Sylvie Thénault puts it, 'le pouvoir politique et l'armée font de la justice un instrument de lutte contre les indépendantistes algériens' ['the political authorities and the army made the law into a weapon of war which they used against the Algerian freedom fighters'].[9] Such a use of emergency law as a technique of power is further borne out by General Paul Aussaresses's suggestion, in his notorious account of torture during the Algerian war, that the French parliament's declaration of a state of emergency in 1955 gave the military license to torture and liquidate FLN leaders.[10]

In contrast to the colonial state of emergency in Kenya, the emergency regulations of April 1955 explicitly prohibited the establishment of detention camps, as article six made plain: 'En aucun cas, l'assignation à résidence ne pourra avoir pour effet la création de camps où seraient détenues les personnes' ['Under no circumstances will the powers to place under house arrest involve the establishment of detention camps'].[11] Despite the limits that the colonial state appeared to impose on the emergency powers granted to the French military by articles such as these – a legal fiction that was designed to preserve the façade of civil society in Algeria – the French colonial state's recourse to earlier colonial laws from 1834 and 1845 concerning 'terrorist attacks' and the possession of arms or ammunition clearly highlighted the constitutive role of the military and state violence in the maintenance of colonial sovereignty in Algeria.[12]

It is perhaps unsurprising that the military character of the French colonial state reinforces Fanon's suggestion that the colony is a divided space in which 'the language of pure violence' constitutes its political foundation, given that much of Fanon's reflections on the violence of colonialism focused specifically on French colonial sovereignty in Algeria.[13] What Fanon implies but does explicitly say here is that colonial sovereignty in Algeria, in the words of Mbembe, 'is not subject to legal and institutional rules'[14] – a point that seems particularly apposite to describe the use of emergency law in colonial Algeria. Of course, it is not generally true to say that all forms of colonial sovereignty were not subject to the law. During the Algerian war, however, emergency law seemed to license practices that blurred the distinction between legality and illegality. We have

militaire en Algérie. Hommes, textes, institutions, 1945–62 (Paris: Service Historique de l'Armée de Terre, L'Harmattan, 2002), p. 150. Cited in Lazreg, *Torture and the Twilight of Empire*, p. 36.

9 Sylvie Thénault, *Une drôle de justice: les magistrats dans la guerre d'Algérie* (Paris: Découverte, 2001), p. 9.

10 Paul Aussaresses, *The Battle of the Casbah*, trans. Robert L. Miller (New York: Engima, 2002), p. 27.

11 Hardy et al. (eds), *Pouvoir politique et autorité militaire en Algérie*, p. 149. Cited in Lazreg, *Torture and the Twilight of Empire*, p. 36..

12 See Lazreg, *Torture and the Twilight of Empire*, p. 37.

13 Frantz Fanon, 'On Violence', in idem, *The Wretched of the Earth*, trans. Richard Philcox (New York: Grove Press, 2004), p. 86.

14 Achille Mbembe, 'Necropolitics', *Public Culture*, 15/1 (2003), p. 25.

already seen how clause six of the emergency regulations of April 1955 prohibited the establishment of detention camps. Despite such a clause, the military
used the special powers that it was granted to confine suspects in internment
camps and re-education centres in a way that appeared to breach the terms of
this clause.[15] What is more, Lazreg's focus on the 'time period invoked by the
[emergency] laws' raises interesting questions about the distinction between
the 'exceptional' character of the emergency laws and the 'normal' rule of
colonial law in Algeria. To what extent does the French colonial state's use of
laws associated with an earlier period of military rule in Algeria suggest that
military rule is a continuation of the normal political order of violent colonial
rule in Algeria rather than an exceptional departure from that normal juridical-
political order? And what light can literary and cultural narratives of counter-
insurgency in Algeria shed on the techniques of violent colonial sovereignty that
were mobilised in Algeria before and during the war of independence?

To address questions such as these, it is helpful to consider some of the
prevalent images in literary and cultural narratives of counter-insurgency during
the Algerian war. As mentioned above, the figure of the French paratrooper is a
predominant trope in literary and cultural representations of the Algerian war.
Philip Dine describes how literary and media narratives of counter-insurgency
construct the French paratrooper as a mythic archetype. On Dine's account,
the paratrooper is a figure who defends the French Republic from the threat
of 'violent Muslim insurgents'. More specifically, the paratroopers' 'removal of
the threat of bomb attacks from the streets, cafés, cinemas, and dance-halls of
the territory's capital [...] marked a crucial stage in the paratroopers' identification with the cause of *Algérie française*'.[16] In literary narratives such as the war
journalist and former paratrooper Lartéguy's popular novel *Les centurions* and
Leulliette's memoir *Saint Michel et le dragon*, the paratrooper is depicted as an
agent of state violence whose heroic function is to protect the French Republic
from the barbaric violence of the Algerian 'rebels'.

Leulliette's *Saint Michel et le dragon* offers a first-hand account of the French
military's counter-insurgency tactics against the Algerian rebels. Written from
the first-person perspective of a French paratrooper during a tour of military
duty in Algeria, the narrator repeatedly describes his battalion's relentless
pursuit of a seemingly elusive enemy through harsh physical conditions. If Leulliette's account of the physical demands of marching, reconnaissance and surveillance evokes the challenges of fighting a counter-revolutionary war against
FLN freedom fighters who had to be caught 'avant qu'ils ne se diluent dans
le paysage' ['before they could vanish into the countryside'],[17] it also conveys
the violent measures that the French paratroopers used to assert colonial

15 See Lazreg, *Torture and the Twilight of Empire*, pp. 40–42.
16 Philip Dine, *Images of the Algerian War: French Fiction and Film, 1954–1992* (Oxford:
    Clarendon Press, 1994), p. 27.
17 Pierre Leulliette, *Saint Michel et le dragon: souvenirs d'un parachutiste* (Paris: Les Éditions de
    Minuit, 1961), p. 190. Pierre Leulliette, *Saint Michael and the Dragon: A Paratrooper in the
    Algerian War*, trans. Tony White (London: Heinemann, 1964), p. 132. Translation modified.

sovereignty. As the narrator puts it during a gun battle with FLN rebels, 'la guerre est surtout un jeu psychologique où le plus important est de faire peur' ['the war is above all a psychological game in which the most important thing is to terrify'].[18] In consequence, the narrator details how the paratroopers' military orders empower them to torture, rape and execute the Algerian population with impunity. While the writerly self of Leulliette's memoir of the Algerian war tries to distance himself from monstrous acts of physical and sexual violence such as the torture of Algerian prisoners and the rape of an Algerian woman by a company corporal, he is nevertheless implicated in the violent 'pacification' of the Algerian population that the French colonial state of emergency enables. During the 'battle of Algiers', the narrator describes how the French colonial parachute regiment were entrusted to survey the Algerian population, and how the soldiers were in effect given 'tout license d'appréhender n'importe qui sans explication, sans même un simple mandat d'arrêt en poche, par la seule grace de nos mitraillettes' ['license to apprehend anyone without explanation, without even a simple arrest warrant in our pockets, by the mere grace of [their] machine guns'].[19] In so doing, Leulliette foregrounds the way in which the emergency decrees of 1955 and 1956 gave the French military carte blanche to arrest, imprison, torture and kill without reference to the normal rule of law.

Lartéguy's novel *Les centurions* traces the French paratroopers' attempt to defend the political sovereignty of the French Republic in Algeria after their defeat in the Indochinese war. In this respect, the novel attempts to historicise the techniques of French counter-revolutionary warfare for a French-reading public.[20] During one episode in *Les centurions*, the narrator describes a military briefing between a French military general and Lieutenant Colonel Raspéguy of the parachute regiment, during which the general gives Raspéguy orders to recover arms that have been stolen by a gang of freedom fighters led by Si Lahcen in the unnamed Algerian town of 'P'. Significantly, the general gives Raspéguy a free hand in this counter-insurgency operation and explicitly states, 'les méthodes que vous emploierez m'importent peu' ['the methods you use are of little importance to me'].[21] This licence to use any means necessary to recover the stolen weapons from the Algerian insurgents exemplifies the ways in which the paratroopers were empowered by the French colonial state to transgress the 'normal' rule of colonial law, and to adopt the tactics of revolutionary war in order to defeat the Algerian rebels. The subsequent murder of two paratroopers by Si Lahcen's gang prompts a counter-insurgency campaign that

---

18 Leulliette, *Saint Michel et le dragon*, p. 224. Leulliette, *Saint Michael and the Dragon*, p. 165. Translation modified.

19 Leulliette, *Saint Michel et le dragon*, p. 302. Leulliette, *Saint Michael and the Dragon*, p. 227. Translation modified.

20 See David Connell, 'Jean Lartéguy: Student of Revolutionary Warfare', *Research Studies*, 40/1 (1972), pp. 1–9.

21 Jean Lartéguy, *Les centurions* (Paris: Presses de la cité, 1960), p. 280. Jean Lartéguy, *The Centurions*, trans. Xan Fielding (London: Hutchinson & Co., 1961), p. 329. Translation modified.

mimes the gruesome spectacle of the paratroopers' mutilated bodies: 'Nous racontons que nous venons défendre les Algériens contre la barbarie du F.L.N. et mes hommes et moi nous nous conduisons comme les tueurs d'Ahmed et de Si Lahcen' ['We say that we come to protect Algerians against the barbarism of the F.L.N., and my men and I behave in the same way as Ahmed or Si Lahcen's killers'].[22] The paratroopers' violent tactics of counter-revolutionary war not only give the lie to the civilising mission of French colonialism in Algeria, they also suggest that violence is central to the civilising mission of colonialism.

On discovering the dead soldiers, the narrator describes how the paratroopers 'découvirent les deux corps allongés sur la butte, devant les mechtas, la gorge tranchée, le ventre ouvert, les parties enfoncées dans la bouche' ['discovered two bodies lying on the mound, in front of the *mechtas*, their throats cut, their guts ripped open, and their genitals stuffed into their mouths'].[23] What is more, 'Le sous-lieutenant de réserve Azmanian fit remarquer que les deux corps étaient tournés vers La Mecque, comme des bêtes sacrifiées en holocauste. On lui avait raconté que jadis les Turcs faisaient la même chose en Arménie. Il se détourna pour vomir' ['Second lieutenant Azmanian observed that the two bodies were turned towards Mecca, like beasts that had been sacrificed in a ritual killing. He had been told that at one time the Turks did the same thing in Armenia'].[24] Such a grotesque spectacle of violence, combined with the reference to the Armenian genocide, may seem to rehearse colonial stereotypes of Muslims and Islam as a culture of violence and death. Yet the fact that the soldiers avenge this act of violence through a grotesque parody also raises questions about the heroic myth of the paratrooper, and about the system of colonial sovereignty that they defend:

> Leur fureur, le besoin du sang et de vengeance qui leur montait du ventre étaient si violents qu'ils en devenaient calmes et détaches […] Vingt-sept corps de musulmans étaient alignés les uns à côté des autres, la gorge tranchée, tournés vers l'Occident, là où se trouvait Rome. Des mouches déjà tournoyaient et pompaient le sang.

> [Their anger, the thirst for blood and vengeance was so overwhelming that they became calm and detached […] Twenty-seven Muslim bodies were lined up together, their throats cut, turned towards the West, pointing in the direction of Rome. Flies were already buzzing around them, sucking the blood.][25]

In this elliptical description of the soldiers' summary execution of Algerian civilians, the narrator evokes a scene of violent counter-insurgency that not only mimes the violence of the FLN through a grotesque inversion, but also calls the civilising mission of French colonialism in Algeria into question through

22 Lartéguy, *Les centurions*, p. 316. Lartéguy, *The Centurions*, p. 372. Translation modified.
23 Lartéguy, *Les centurions*, p. 294. Lartéguy, *The Centurions*, p. 346. Translation modified.
24 Lartéguy, *Les centurions,* p. 294. Lartéguy, *The Centurions*, p. 346. Translation modified.
25 Lartéguy, *Les centurions*, p. 295. Lartéguy, *The Centurions*, p. 347. Translation modified.

its evocation of a violent military masculinity. Indeed, the subsequent rumours that circulate among the Algerian population about the French paratroopers in response to this spectacle of violence call into question the dichotomy between good and evil:

> Et c'est ainsi que naquit la cruelle légende des «lézards en laquettes», des guerriers au poignard plus redoutable que les «mouseblines» du F.L.N. Dans le fond des douars on commença à parler d'eux comme les démons à l'épreuve des balles, fils d'Alek et Azraël, l'ange de la Mort.

> ['And this is how the notorious legend of the lizards in caps, of the warriors with daggers, who were more terrifying than the FLN irregulars was first conceived. In the depths of the *douars*, they were referred to as bulletproof demons, sons of Alek and Azrael, the angel of death.][26]

Here, Lartéguy's representation of the paratroops as demons in the imaginary mindset of the FLN and the Algerian population corresponds with Philip Dine's account of the ambivalent literary myth of the French paratrooper as both *para angelique* and *para demonique*. This ambivalent image of the paratrooper as both angel and devil mirrors the ambivalent meaning of the emergency laws that granted increasing power to the military over the life and death of the Algerian population. That is to say, the emergency legislation empowers the paratroopers to act in a way that transgresses the normal rule of colonial law in order to defend the sovereignty of the French Republic. From the standpoint of *Algérie française*, the emergency legislation empowers the French military to protect the security, sovereignty and ideology of the French colonial state: a role that is in keeping with the image of the *para angélique*.[27] Yet from the standpoint of the Algerian population and the French left intelligentsia, the violent means used to defend the sovereignty of the French colonial state in Algeria during the state of emergency also seem to foreground the systematic violence of the French colonial project from its inception. Such a reading is further borne out in Lartéguy's fictional staging of a debate about whether the use of military force against the Muslim population of Algiers is legal: 'la légalité ne sert plus qu'à protéger une bande de terroristes et d'assassins [...] La légalité n'est intéressante que lorsqu'elle nous sert et joue en notre faveur' ['the law serves only to protect a gang of terrorists and murderers [...] the law is only interesting when it is useful to us and plays in our favour'].[28] In the fictional world of Lartéguy's Algeria, law is presented as one technique of colonial governmentality among others, which can be invoked or suspended according to the exigencies of the situation.

Indeed, what is significant about Lartéguy's framing of the paratroopers in *Les centurions* is not only that 'ils sont au-delà des notions conventionnelles du bien et du mal' ['they are beyond conventional notions of good and evil'],[29] but

---

26 Lartéguy, *Les centurions*, p. 256. Lartéguy, *The Centurions*, p. 349. Translation modified.
27 See Dine, *Images of the Algerian War*, p. 28.
28 Lartéguy, *Les centurions*, p. 363. Lartéguy, *The Centurions*, p. 429.
29 Lartéguy, *Les centurions*, p. 369. Lartéguy, *The Centurions*, p. 436.

also that the violent techniques that the paratroopers employ to counter the armed struggle of the Algerian 'rebels' in both the mountains and the country-side serve to reassert colonial sovereignty in Algeria irrespective of the rule of law. The supposedly exceptional measures of counter-insurgency employed by the military to protect the French Republic can be understood in terms of a political logic of autoimmunity, in which the violent means used to defend colonial sovereignty against the nationalist demands of the FLN threaten the supposedly democratic values of the French Republic. Such a heroic function accords with Raphaëlle Branche's account of the French colonial state's system-atic use of torture during the Algerian war: 'avec la torture, on est au centre d'une réalité explosive où l'État accepte de se mettre lui-même en danger, pour tenter de se protéger' ['with torture, one is at the centre of an explosive reality where the state agrees to put itself at risk in order to protect itself'].[30] It is this political logic of autoimmunity – of the state putting itself in danger in order to protect itself – that Lartéguy's fictional officer Marindelle calls 'la loi atroce de la nouvelle guerre' ['the dreadful law of the new type of war'].[31]

Rather than offering a critique of the de facto condition of martial law that the emergency decrees of 1955 enabled, *Les centurions* seems to implicitly endorse the use of emergency law, and the transfer of power to the military. This is particularly exemplified in Lartéguy's representation of a ticking-time-bomb scenario, in which Captain Esclavier tries to persuade Arouche, an FLN bomb-maker and dentist, to divulge the location of 15 bombs that have been planted in European shops in Algiers. At the start of the interrogation, Esclavier is presented as an intellectual soldier, who 'cherchant dans sa tête tous les arguments de raison, d'humanité que l'on pouvait débiter à ce bloc immobile et sans fissure qui était assis sur le fauteuil à housse blanche' ['rack[ed] his brains to find some argument based on reason and humanity which might appeal to this motionless, unshakeable body sitting in the white-upholstered arm-chair'].[32] This technique of interrogation prompts Arouche to regard Esclavier as 'un faible' ['a weakling'] who is 'rempli de contradictions' ['full of contradictions'].[33] By emphasising Esclavier's reluctance to torture Arouche, Lartéguy raises doubts about his military masculinity, and 'feeds on a long-felt, common anxiety that democracy has made us weak and [that] there are no real men anymore'.[34] It is only after Esclavier learns that the grandfather of his lover, Isabelle Pélissier, has been brutally murdered on his farm by Algerian national-ists that Esclavier sees red and forces Arouche to confess. By suggesting that the safety and security of the family and private property are under threat, Lartéguy thus invents a fictional state of necessity which simultaneously attempts to

---

30 Raphaëlle Branche, *La torture et l'armée pendant la guerre d'Algérie: 1954–1962* (Paris: Galli-mard, 2001), p. 15.

31 Lartéguy, *Les centurions*, p. 389. Lartéguy, *The Centurions*, p. 460. Translation modified.

32 Lartéguy, *Les centurions*, p. 404. Lartéguy, *The Centurions*, p. 477.

33 Lartéguy, *Les centurions*, p. 403. Lartéguy, *The Centurions*, p. 477.

34 Darius Rejali, *Torture and Democracy* (Princeton, NJ: Princeton University Press, 2008), p. 548.

justify the suspension of the normal rule of law and the use of torture while also effacing the history of French settler colonialism in Algeria that precipitated the violent, anti-colonial struggle.

The literary prose of counter-insurgency in *Les centurions* may seem to correspond with Agamben's reflections on the state of necessity, sovereignty and the state of exception as a paradigm of government. Yet this correspondence does not simply confirm the explanatory power of Agamben's arguments; on the contrary, it also raises questions about whether Agamben's political thought provides the conceptual tools to think beyond the French colonial state's use of emergency law as a technique of power. We have already seen how *Les centurions* justifies the techniques of violent counter-revolutionary war, in which the French paratrooper *qua para demonique* transgresses the normal rule of law by presenting the FLN as a violent and subhuman other who is threatening to the moral and political order of the French Republic and its settler colony. In this respect, *Les centurions* could be seen to fetishise the violence, authority and power of the French colonial state. Given the narrative's unequivocal political commitment to the cause of the French military campaign of counter-revolutionary warfare, this is perhaps unsurprising. Agamben's reflections on the relationship between law and violence under a state of exception can certainly help to demystify the fetishisation of the French colonial state in Lartéguy's narrative of counter-insurgency. By asking what the suspension of the normal rule of law associated with the colonial state of exception can tell us about the violence of state sovereignty, a critical reading of *Les centurions* informed by Agamben's reflections on the state of exception can help to elucidate the way in which narratives of counter-insurgency are founded on a metalepsis, where acts of violent anti-colonial resistance are presented as the cause of violent colonial insurgency rather than a meaningful political response to the depredations of colonial rule. The problem, however, with such a critical approach to the prose of counter-insurgency and the violent formation of colonial sovereignty of which it is a part is that it does not account for the agency and history of the subjects of colonial violence. It is this problem that the next section of the chapter attempts to address.

Testimonies of Torture: Henri Alleg's *La question* and Louisette Ighilahriz's *Algérienne*

If literary narratives of counter-insurgency such as Lartéguy's *Les centurions* present the torture and summary execution of Algerian 'rebels' as exceptional and necessary measures that were employed to prevent the deaths of French settlers and paratroopers, testimonial narratives such as Alleg's *La question* (1958) and Ighilahriz's *Algérienne* (2001) convey the different ways in which state violence was employed as a systematic technique of French colonial sovereignty. Fanon's suggestion that violence and torture are constitutive of the political techniques of colonial governmentality in Algeria is given further support by Alleg's testimonial narrative of his torture by the French paratroopers, *La question*. Alleg was a French communist and writer living in Algiers, where he edited the independent leftist newspaper, *Alger républicain*.[35] By offering a testimony of his own account of torture as a Frenchman to the French-reading public, Alleg could be seen to encourage readers to reflect on the experience of colonial violence and its relationship to the democratic values of French society and culture. In the eyes of Jean Paul Sartre, 'Henri Alleg was the best illustration of the decentred "European"/colonial Frenchman who *experienced* what it meant to be a (or like a) native in the hands of Frenchmen defending the colonial system'.[36] In his preface to Alleg's narrative, Sartre suggested that torture in colonial Algeria 'était devenue routine avant même qu'on s'en fût avisé' ['had become routine even before we knew about it']. 'Mais la haine de l'homme qui s'y manifeste', Sartre adds, 'c'est le racisme qu'elle exprime' ['But the hatred of man that manifests itself [in the practice of torture] is an expression of racism'] – a racism that is expressed primarily but not exclusively towards the Algerian population.[37] In a similar vein, Alleg describes in his prefatory remarks on his experiences in a French military interrogation centre in the El-Biar district of Algiers how torture 'est la pratique courante dans cette guerre atroce et sanglante' [is common practice in this savage and bloody war],[38] and proceeds to catalogue the numerous tactics used by the French paratroopers to interrogate him, including the rituals of communication. Such practices included electrocution, drowning, burning the victim's naked body with a blow torch or a match, suspending the victim's body upside down from a rope, putting barbed wire inside the victim's mattress in a prison cell and experimenting on the victim's body with 'truth drugs' such as sodium pentothal. In presenting such a detailed account of his ordeal, Alleg is not suggesting that his experience is unique or exceptional. On the contrary, Alleg's reference to several other Algerian victims of torture whom he knew, and his account of the spatial organisation of the torture factory at an unfinished apartment building in which 15 or 20 prisoners were kept in rooms that had been converted to dungeons, suggests that the practice of torture had become an industrialised and almost banal technique of counter-insurgency.

If, as Kristin Ross has suggested, the 'legitimacy of Alleg's testimony was later ascertained by the military authorities because of his ability to describe by memory several of the rooms in the torture building of El-Biar',[39] Alleg's autobiographical account of his ability to withstand pain, and his refusal to

---

35 James Le Sueur, 'Introduction', in Henri Alleg, *The Question*, trans. John Calder (Lincoln, NE, and London: University of Nebraska Press, 2006), p. xvi.

36 Lazreg, *Torture and the Twilight of Empire*, p. 228

37 Jean Paul Sartre, 'Une victoire', in Henri Alleg, *La question suivi de Une victoire par Jean Paul Sartre* (Paris: Les Editions de Minuit, 1965 [1958]), pp. 119–20. Jean-Paul Sartre, 'A Victory', in Alleg, *The Question*, p. xlii. Translation modified.

38 Alleg, *La question*, p. 18. Alleg, *The Question*, p. 34.

39 Kristin Ross, *Fast Cars, Clean Bodies: Decolonization and the Reordering of French Culture* (Cambridge, MA: MIT Press, 1995), p. 111.

crack under torture constructs a French masculine subject of colonial violence who demonstrates his political commitment to the cause of Algerian independence. As a French citizen who 'a choisi les «ratons» contre nous' ['sided with the rats against us'],[40] as one of his torturers puts it, Alleg attempts to challenge the lawful violence of the French colonial state by appealing to the rule of law: 'Si vous avez de quoi m'inculper, transférez-moi à la justice: vous avez vingt-quatre heures pour cela' ['If you have any charge to bring against me, hand me over to the appropriate authorities: you have 24 hours in which to do it'].[41] Just as the magistrate in Coetzee's *Waiting for the Barbarians* starts to lose faith in the principle of justice after his tormentors subject his body to extreme physical pain (see Chapter 3), so Alleg's appeal to the language of justice seems to be undermined by his experience of electrocution and beating, and by his observation that Ali Boumendjel, barrister at the Court of Appeal of Algiers, had supposedly committed suicide by throwing himself from a balcony. The death of a figure that represents justice may seem to reinforce the absolute power and authority of the French military during the Algerian war, and the denial of rights and justice to the Algerian population. Yet this would be to overlook the power of Alleg's writing and testimony to contest and challenge the French military's use of torture as a technique of counter-revolutionary warfare.

By recounting in meticulous detail how the practice of torture attempted to reduce the human subject to a body in pain, Alleg encourages readers to question the myths that have been invoked by military figures to justify torture in novels such as *Les centurions*. While much of *La question* presents a descriptive testimony of Alleg's ordeal during his detention, and the psychological techniques he used to resist the will of his torturers, the conclusion offers some insights into the political significance of the book. In an account of his incarceration in cell 72 of the civil prison of Algiers, Alleg describes the execution of three Algerians, how one of the condemned men cries out 'Tahia El Djezair! Vive l'Algérie!' before he is gagged and how this man's cry provokes a collective recitation of the anthem of free Algeria from the women's section of the prison.[42] Alleg does not elaborate on the significance of this anecdote, but it does suggest parallels to and affinities with his own ordeal. Just as the execution of the three condemned Algerians are framed as a sacrifice to the political cause of national independence for Algeria, so Alleg implies that his own suffering at the hands of the French military can also be understood as a form of sacrifice – both to the cause of Algeria's national independence and to the democratic principles of the French Republic. Like Sartre, who wrote an afterword to the second edition of *La question*, Alleg's anti-colonialism 'professed a deep humanism and commitment to democracy'.[43] By emphasising that the French-reading public 'faut qu'ils sachent pourtant ce qui se fait ici EN

40 Alleg, *La question*, p. 26. Alleg, *The Question*, p. 41
41 Alleg, *La question*, pp. 28–29. Alleg, *The Question*, p. 43.
42 Alleg, *La question*, p. 95. Alleg, *The Question*, p. 96.
43 Paige Arthur, *Unfinished Projects: Decolonization and the Philosophy of Jean Paul Sartre* (London: Verso, 2010), p. 73.

LEUR NOM' ['must know what is done IN THEIR NAME'],[44] Alleg also encourages contemporary readers to reflect on the relationship between torture and the French colonial state. In this respect, Alleg's tortured body is not simply a proxy for the routine violence perpetrated against the Algerian population, but a trope through which the dehumanisation of French colonial sovereignty in Algeria can be understood.

One of the striking things about *La question* is the way in which the masculine subject of testimony is constructed as a hero who can both withstand immense physical pain and recall in specific detail the chain of events surrounding his detention. Although the narrator tells us in the conclusion that he wrote this testimony with great difficulty,[45] the narrative is presented as a syntactically coherent account of Alleg's ordeal *after the event*. In this respect, the linguistic style and narrative form of *La question* does little to register why the composition of this testimony was difficult, or how torture works to undermine the subject's capacity to use language as a referential system. If, as Elaine Scarry has suggested, one of the goals of the torturer is to make the voice emphatically absent by destroying the body,[46] Alleg's testimony can be seen as an attempt to assert sovereignty over his voice and his story after his body has been subjected to extreme physical pain. One of the problems with Alleg's testimonial account of his ordeal, in other words, is that it tries to represent the body in pain rather than evoking how the experience of torture destroys the very ground of representation. It is this complex relationship between torture and representation that preoccupies the writing of the Francophone Algerian writer Djebar, as we will see.

If Alleg's narrative of his treatment at the 'torture factory' at El Biar foregrounds the way in which torture is a technique of power by which the French colonial state attempted to reassert its authority over the Algerian body politic, Ighilahriz's testimonial narrative *Algérienne* (2000) discloses the sexualised dimension of torture as a technique of French colonial sovereignty. Ighilahriz was a former FLN militant who was severely wounded during an ambush in 1957, before being captured, tortured and raped by a French paratrooper at the Paradou Hydra barracks of the 10th Parachute Regiment. Specifically, the first-person narrator offers a harrowing account of how her torturer, Captain Graziani, would exert physical pressure on her bandaged and wounded leg: 'il fourrageait à l'intérieur de mes pansements à l'aide d'un objet contondant, ravivait et envenimait mes plaies. Un jour, ivre de rage, il a même utilisé une baïonnette pour tenter de lacérer les pansements' ['he rifled through my dressings with a blunt object in order to inflame and aggravate my wounds. One day, drunk with rage, he even used a bayonet to try to rip the dressings'].[47] Left to

---

44 Alleg, *La question*, p. 95. Alleg, *The Question*, p. 96.
45 Alleg, *La question*, p. 94. Alleg, *The Question*, p. 95.
46 Elaine Scarry, *The Body in Pain: The Making and Unmaking of the World* (New York and Oxford: Oxford University Press, 1985), p. 49.
47 Louisette Ighilahriz, *Algérienne*, récit recuelli par Anne Nivat (Paris: Fayard/Calmann-Lévy, 2001), p. 111.

languish in her own urine and faeces,[48] the narrator further asserts that Captain Graziani regarded her as 'disgusting' and implies that Graziani did not rape her during her imprisonment because of her physical condition.[49] And yet, the narrator also details how Graziani forced 'toutes sortes d'accessoires dans le vagin' ['all kinds of objects into my vagina'].[50]

The first-person narrator's testimony of Ighilahriz's torture at the hands of the French military during her imprisonment clearly draws attention to the sexualised dimension of the violence of the colonial state that was made possible by the state of emergency. And in this respect, her testimony accords with the work of cultural historians such as Lazreg and political theorists such as Butler who have emphasised the ways in which the relationship between the torturer and the body of the tortured victim is often profoundly sexualised. Writing on the practice of torture during the Algerian war, Lazreg recounts how prisoners were rendered vulnerable by being stripped naked, and how male and female prisoners were subjected to different forms of sexualised violence. Whereas male prisoners were threatened with castration, forced to sit on bottles and had electrodes applied to their genitals, female prisoners were subjected to sexual abuse and rape as a part of the French army's counter-insurgency strategy.[51] In a similar vein, Butler has described how a debased form of homosexuality informed US military practices of torture during the war in Iraq, 'in which the torturer acts as the "top" who only penetrates and who coercively requires that penetrability be located in the body of the tortured'.[52] Such theories of torture may shed significant light on the use of torture as a technique of sovereign power from the standpoint of the colonial state, but they tell us less about the complex and vulnerable process of articulation through which subjects of torture reassert their sovereignty and agency after the traumatic experience of torture and sexual violence. It is for this reason that we need to assess the contribution that testimonies of torture and postcolonial narratives of the Algerian war have made to our understanding of the colonial state of emergency in Algeria.

Two years after the book version of her testimony was published as *Algérienne* in 2001, Louisette Ighilahriz revised her testimony at a court hearing against the French military General Schmitt in 2003, and described how Captain Graziani had raped her with his penis.[53] It might be argued that the ellipses and inconsistencies in these different versions of Ighilahriz's testimony point to her unreliability as an honest witness, but this would be to overlook the ways in which traumatic experiences of sexual violence can often defy the standards of consistent and coherent self-representation that historical research demands of witnesses of trauma. Sylvia Durmelat has suggested that Ighilahriz's

48 Ighilahriz, *Algérienne*, p. 112.
49 Ighilahriz, *Algérienne*, p. 113.
50 Ighilahriz, *Algérienne*, p. 113.
51 See Lazreg, *Torture and the Twilight of Empire*, pp. 123–30, 154–69.
52 Butler, *Frames of War*, p. 90.
53 Sylvia Durmelat, 'Revisiting Ghosts: Louisette Ighilahriz and the Remembering of Torture', in Alec G. Hargreaves (ed.), *Memory, Empire, and Postcolonialism: Legacies of French Colonialism* (Lanham, MD: Lexington Books, 2005), pp. 153–54.

testimonies about her rape form a complex text, characterized by inconsistencies, semi-truths, and partial statements. They give a conflicting and conflicted depiction of her painful experience, while making visible for us how such trauma is locked and unlocked, repressed and expressed, and how it can only come out as fragments and only later reassembled as a cogent, presentable whole.[54]

The inconsistencies in Ighilahriz's multiple testimonies may be accounted for in part by the shame she felt about her sexual violation during her imprisonment, and by her desire to keep the truth from her mother. For her mother died after the publication of the book *Algérienne* in 2001, when Ighilahriz suggested that Captain Graziani had not attempted to rape her,[55] and before Ighilahriz testified to the contrary at a court hearing in 2003 that Graziani had in fact raped her.[56] Yet it is important to emphasise that this feeling of shame is inextricably connected with the wider difficulties of recalling and narrating experiences of sexual and physical violence that are too painful to speak of. In her phenomenological analysis of the body in pain, Scarry has argued that 'World, self, and voice are lost, or nearly lost, through the intense pain of torture'.[57] Scarry's observations help to illuminate the inconsistencies in Ighilahriz's testimonies of torture, for by repressing some of the details of her torture in the testimonial narrative that forms *Algerienne*, the writerly self of Louisette Ighilahriz discloses the ways in which the experience of torture alienated her body from the social world that she associates with her family and, more specifically, with her mother. As Joshua Cole puts it, 'Torture and rape were about establishing a particular relationship between French soldiers and Algerian Muslims, one in which the most essential part of the victim's personality – the integrity of their bodies, their relations with their families, their connection to a religion, a cause – were annihilated'.[58]

Moreover, as a testimony to the systemic violence of the French colonial state, Louisette Ighilahriz's *Algerienne* could be seen to give voice to what Benjamin has called the tradition of the oppressed, and its challenge to the sovereign violence of the colonial state that the legal fiction of the state of exception tries to efface. This is not to suggest, however, that the traumatic experience of torture or sexual violence can be narrated or represented in a straightforward way, or that a coherent subject of trauma can be recovered through narrative. Indeed, if we take the tradition of the oppressed to denote the traumatic historical narratives of oppression which have also been repressed by the very formations of state violence that have precipitated those very traumatic historical narratives of oppression, then the challenges of representing the tradition of the oppressed

54 Durmelat, 'Revisiting Ghosts', p. 153.
55 Durmelat, 'Revisiting Ghosts', p. 153.
56 Durmelat, 'Revisiting Ghosts', p. 154.
57 Scarry, *The Body in Pain*, p. 35.
58 Joshua Cole, 'Intimate Acts and Unspeakable Relations: Remembering Torture and the War for Algerian Independence', in Hargreaves (ed.), *Memory, Empire, and Postcolonialism*, p. 133.

are doubled. For not only are the traumatic historical experiences of torture and state violence unrepresentable in straightforward terms, but the repression of that traumatic historical experience works to further silence and foreclose the history of the oppressed. Against this silencing and foreclosure, Felman has suggested that Benjamin's term 'the expressionless' (*das Andrückslose*) provides 'a mute yet powerful' concept for understanding the ways in which the 'tradition of the oppressed' can be articulated. For Felman, 'the expressionless' (*das Andrückslose*) are 'those whom violence has deprived of expression; those who, on the one hand, have been historically reduced to silence, and who, on the other hand, have been historically made faceless'.[59] As a concept that defies the conventions of representation, the expressionless also guards against the risks of transforming the repressed history of pain and trauma associated with the tradition of the oppressed into a spectacle for consumption or a dominant nationalist narrative of victimisation that appropriates the memories of colonial violence to justify policies and practices of state repression in the postcolonial present.

We have already seen how Ighilahriz's historical experiences of her torture by the French military during the Algerian war defy the temporal conventions of linear narrative. It is worth noting too that Ighilahriz's voice was mediated by *Le monde* journalist Florence Beaugé in the first version of her testimony, which appeared as a published interview in *Le monde* in 2000, before the longer version of her testimony, published as the book *Algérienne* (2001) was transcribed by the French war journalist Anne Nivat.[60] The precise details of how Ighilahriz's testimony are mediated are significant for at least two reasons. First, the transmission of Ighilahriz's writerly self draws attention to the ways in which Ighilahriz's testimony was packaged and commodified for a French-reading public by the national press and the publishing industry. In so doing, the representation of Ighilahriz's torture runs the risk of falling prey to what Joanna Bourke, in an article on the photographs of American soldiers humiliating Iraqi detainees at the Abu Ghraib detention camp in Iraq, has called 'a pornographic spectacle of pain' that is 'fundamentally voyeuristic in nature'.[61] Ighilahriz's testimony also foregrounds the way in which her published testimonial narratives are not an unmediated reflection of her voice and historical experience, even though the testimony is presented in the first-person narrative voice. By doing so, the testimony raises questions about the politics of representation. In a critique of the French philosophers Deleuze and Foucault, Gayatri Spivak has cautioned against the dangers of a radical politics that effaces the position of the intellectual as a proxy who speaks for the oppressed.[62] Although Spivak's critique of Deleuze and Guattari is not the main focus of her essay, it does help to illuminate

59 Felman, *The Juridical Unconscious*, p. 13.
60 Durmelat, 'Revisiting Ghosts', pp. 143–44.
61 Joanna Bourke, 'Torture as Pornography', *The Guardian* (7 May 2004).
62 Gayatri Chakravorty Spivak, 'Can the Subaltern Speak?', in Cary Nelson and Lawrence Grossberg (eds), *Marxism and the Interpretation of Culture* (Urbana and Chicago: University of Illinois Press, 1988), pp. 271–80.

the dangers of speaking for the disempowered or the subaltern – a topic that Spivak addresses in her critical reflections on the liberal ideology of nineteenth-century British colonialism and its attempt to speak for the gendered subaltern by prohibiting the practice of *sati*-suicide, and in Spivak's anecdote about the circumstances of Bhubaneswari Bhaduri's death, following Bhaduri's inability to carry out a political assassination for an armed nationalist group. Spivak's critique of the politics of representation from the perspective of the gendered subaltern has important implications for reading Anne Nivat's transcription of Ighilahriz's story in *Algérienne* because it raises questions about whether Nivat's use of the first-person narrative voice is an appropriate means of expressing the trauma of Ighilahriz's historical experiences during the Algerian war. Such questions about the politics of representation also inform and inflect the fiction of Assia Djebar, as we will see.

The Postcolonial Tradition of the Oppressed and the Gendered Body in Pain: The Fiction of Assia Djebar

If the mediation of Ighilahriz's story suggests that the self, voice and agency of the gendered subaltern subject of trauma and sexual violence can be recovered, the literary fiction and experimental filmmaking of the Algerian writer and filmmaker Assia Djebar examines the ethical and political limitations of representing the traumatic historical experiences of the oppressed. Indeed, the difficulties of recovering and representing the historical experiences of women freedom fighters who fought in the Algerian war of independence is a recurrent concern in many of Djebar's novels and films, as I will now suggest. In Djebar's third novel, *Les enfants du nouveau monde* (1962), the narrator describes a scene in which Salima, a schoolteacher at a local girl's school, who is arrested and imprisoned, overhears a man being tortured by the French police in another prison cell. The screams of this man strike Salima with panic at first, and she tries to drown out the terrifying screams of the man by covering her ears and reciting Qur'anic verses. But in a move that echoes and transforms the Homeric story of Ulysses and the sirens, Salima gradually begins to listen to the man's screams, and identifies how 'ces hurlements qui font un long chant, un thrène' ['the screams make a long chant, a threnody']. By listening closely to the screams of the tortured man – as 'un nouveau signe de vie et d'horreur à la fois' ['a new sign of life and horror at the same time'] – Salima interprets the man's screams as a song of national resistance and struggle:

> Elle tremble comme si elle a froid, mais serre les dents encore, tend sa volonté à rester ainsi debout, mains maintenant collées au hanches, à écouter. Pourquoi s'échapper? Il faut écouter! Une exaltation sauvage la saisit. «Voici le chant du mon pays, voici le chant de l'avenir» murmure-t-elle à mi-voix, silhouette jaillie au centre de ce cachot vide, frémissante d'ardeur et pourquoi pas […]

['She trembles as if cold, but then grits her teeth again, stretches her willpower to remain standing, hands now glued to her thighs as she listens. One must listen. A wild exaltation seizes her. 'This is the song of my country, this is the song of the future,' she whispers, an empty silhouette in the middle of an empty cell, trembling with passion and why not [...]][63]

Salima's interpretation of the tortured man's screams as a nationalist song may offer her some temporary relief from the fear and anxiety that she too may be tortured by the French police. Yet the danger of such a reading is that it runs the risk of transforming the body in pain into an aesthetic object that abstracts the screams of the tortured man from the traumatic experience of violence.

Rather than simply giving voice to the history of the oppressed, Djebar has increasingly sought to foreground the traumatic historical conditions that have deprived the oppressed of the means of expressing their historical experiences. Such an ethical approach to the history of the oppressed has also involved an increasingly self-conscious approach to aesthetic form. Djebar's film *La nouba des femmes du mont Chenoua* (1978), for example, is constructed 'as a "musical suite" that is itself made up of heterogeneous fragments'.[64] The film juxtaposes the stories of Algerian women who participated in the revolution with an account of the martyrdom of Zouleikha, and Lila's concern with her own subjectivity, without privileging any of these narrative perspectives. The ethical dimension of Djebar's use of the fragment as an aesthetic form is developed further in *L'amour, la fantasia* (1985), a novel which juxtaposes the first-person narrator's autobiographical reflections on her childhood and education in colonial Algeria with historiographic reflections on the archives of the French colonial occupation of Algeria during the 1830s and 1840s, nineteenth-century French Orientalist representations of the colonial harem, such as those of Eugène Delacroix and Eugène Fromentin, as well as accounts of Algerian women who fought in the national liberation struggle. By staging the process of interviewing women veterans of the national liberation struggle, the narrator draws attention to the difficult process of articulating the painful memories of trauma and violence associated with the war. More specifically, in a chapter with the heading 'Conciliabules' ['Secret Meetings'], the narrator as interviewer/ historian describes how 'la seule question vivante s'arrête dans ma gorge' ['one vital question stick[s] in [her] throat'], a question that she 'ne peux la formuler...sinon par un mot de passé, un mot doux, neutre, ruisselant' ['cannot formulate...except by some coded word, some soft, neutral, whispering word'].[65] As the narrator goes on to explain, the subject that she is trying to broach concerns the very sensitive question of whether the women were tortured or raped by French soldiers

63 Assia Djebar, *Les enfants du nouveau monde* (Paris: René Julliard, 1983 [1962]), pp. 181–82. Assia Djebar, *The Children of the New World*, trans. Marjolijn De Jager (New York: Feminist Press, 2005), pp. 112–13.

64 Réda Bensmaïa, *Experimental Nations, or, the Invention of the Maghreb* (Princeton, NJ and Oxford: Princeton University Press, 2003), p. 84.

65 Assia Djebar, *L'amour, la fantasia: roman* (Paris: Albin Michel, 1995), p. 282. Assia Djebar, *Fantasia: An Algerian Calvacade*, trans. Dorothy Blair (London: Quartet, 1989), p. 201.

during the Algerian war of independence: 'Ma sœur, y-a-t-il eu, une fois, pour toi «dommage»?' ['Sister, did you at any time, suffer "damage"?'].[66] For the narrator, the difficulty in posing this question marks both an ethical anxiety about representing the pain of others, and a recognition that there is no rhetorical space in the postcolonial public sphere for Algerian women to speak of their shared experiences of pain and violence. By comparing her own silenced position to a reflection both of her own barrenness and of her own aphasia,[67] Djebar's narrator-historian foregrounds the condition of being expressionless in order to encourage readers to reflect on the repressed, subaltern histories of the Algerian women freedom fighters whom she interviews.

Djebar's commitment to convey what Felman calls the condition of being expressionless in an experimental aesthetic form is developed further in her novel *La femme sans sépulture* (2002). Focusing on the life and death of Zoulikha Oudai, an Algerian freedom fighter who disappeared after being arrested and tortured by the French army, the narrator, an Algerian filmmaker, attempts to recover Zoulikha's history by interviewing her daughters, Hania and Mina, and her female comrades, Lla Lbia (Dame Lionne) and Zohra Oudai (Zoulikha's sister-in-law). In this respect, much of the narrative is a self-conscious polylogue of multiple voices rather than a conventional biography or historical novel. Significantly, the novel contains a frame narrative that draws attention to the narrator's position as a filmmaker: '«L'histoire de Zoulikha» est esquissée en ouverture. Deux heures du film s'écoulent ensuite en fleuve lent: fiction et documentaire, son direct souvent, quelques dialogues entre femmes; des flots de musique, traditionnelle aussi bien que contemporaine' ['The history of Zoulikha is outlined in the opening sequence. This is followed by two hours of slow-moving film: fiction and documentary, with some conversations between women, and a soundtrack combining traditional and contemporary music'].[68] This frame narrative is significant not only because it contains an intertextual allusion to the experimental form of Djebar's filmmaking practice, and to her interest in the history of Zoulikha in *La nouba des femmes du mont Chenoua*, but also because it draws our attention to the aesthetic status of the narrative as a fictional representation of Zoulikha's life. Indeed, this metafictional narrative technique is announced in the very first line of the novel: 'Histoire de Zoulika: l'inscrire enfin, ou plutôt la réinscrire' ['The History of Zoulika is inscribed at last, or rather it is re-inscribed'].[69] By foregrounding the history of the novel's composition between 1976 and 2001, the narrator suggests that the history of Zoulikha's life and the circumstances of her death cannot be recovered.

As a woman whose history disappeared along with her body during the Algerian war in 1956, Zoulikha can be read as a spectral figure that is resistant to narrative representation – and it is this resistance to representation that

---

66 Djebar, *L'amour, la fantasia*, p. 202. Djebar, *Fantasia*, p. 202.

67 Djebar, *L'amour, la fantasia*, p. 283. Djebar, *Fantasia*, p. 202.

68 Assia Djebar, *La femme sans sépulture: roman* (Paris: Albin Michel, 2002), p. 16.

69 Djebar, *La femme sans sépulture: roman*, p. 13.

Djebar's narrator discloses. As Anne Donadey puts it, 'The constant use and staging of mediation underscores the fact that fiction is being used to supplement history, all the while highlighting that no voice may fix Zoulikha or pin her down for good'.[70] It may seem surprising, then, that the novel also inserts four chapter-length 'monologues' that are attributed to Zoulikha between the pages of the other chapters. If we read these fictional 'monologues' as a speculative, subaltern history of Zoulikha's imprisonment and torture at the hands of the French military, it is possible to interpret Zoulikha's mediated voice as an embodied history of French colonial violence that traces the way in which the Algerian freedom fighter tried to contest the sovereignty of French colonial violence by attempting to assert sovereignty over her own body. In a central passage from the final monologue, the fictional voice of Zoulikha describes her disorientation and loss of consciousness at the hands of her torturers.[71] In so doing, Djebar foregrounds the 'annihilating negation' that Scarry associates with the body of the tortured subject, a negation that separates the body and the voice of the tortured subject.[72] This 'annihilating negation' is registered in Zoulikha's confusion of pain with memories of sexual desire, and her suggestion that 'la torture sur mon corps aurait le même effet que presque vingt ans de nuits d'amour avec trois époux successifs' ['the torture of my body was to have the same effect as twenty years of nights of love with three successive husbands'].[73] By asking whether her confusion between torture and sexual intimacy is sacrilegious, the fictional voice of Zoulikha certainly foregrounds the radical implications of this confused association, with its suggestion that her torturers are also lovers – an association that recalls Wicomb's representation of torture in *David's Story* (discussed in Chapter 3). More importantly, though, this confusion raises crucial questions about Zoulikha's sovereignty over her body and voice. Against the cold fury and determination of the French soldiers to reduce her body to a mechanical object of colonial sovereignty,[74] the narrator's rewriting of Zoulikha's body in pain could be read as a sign of her 'annihilating negation' from the world of her social, linguistic and cultural values as well as from her commitment to the political cause of Algerian independence. Indeed, Djebar's subsequent account of the way in which Zoulikha's voice escaped her evokes a disturbing image of the sexualised dimension of torture during the Algerian war, and of Zoulikha's attempt to hold on to the names of her daughters and of her 'disappeared' husband:

> Ma voix qui n'émettait aucun mot, ni arabe, ni berbère, ni français. Peut-être, il me semble, «ô Dieu, ô Prophète chéri», ou le dessin en creux de ces mots familiers; peu à peu, ensuite, je déroulai, en lent chapelet, chacun de vos prénoms, y compris celui d'El Habib disparu, ton doux nom en dernier, modulé

70 Anne Donadey, 'Introjection and Incorporation in Assia Djebar's *La Femme sans sépulture*', *L'Esprit Créateur*, 48/4 (2008), p. 85.
71 Djebar, *La femme sans sépulture*, p. 197.
72 Scarry, *The Body in Pain*, pp. 27–59.
73 Djebar, *La femme sans sépulture*, p. 198.
74 Djebar, *La femme sans sépulture*, p. 200.

sans cesse tandis que mon vagin électrifié vrillait entièrement comme un puits sans fond … Dans cet antre autrefois de jouissance, ton prénom, tel un fil de soie pour s'enrouler infiniment jusqu'au fond de moi, pour m'assourdir et m'adoucir […] «Ô Dieu, ô doux prophète» et l'arabe ancestral me revenait, eau de tendresse dans cette traversée.

[My voice did not utter a word, neither Arab, nor Berber, nor French. Perhaps, it seemed to me, 'o God, o Dear Prophet', or the engraved pattern of these familiar words; I then gradually recited, in slow incantation, each of your names, including that of the disappeared El Habib, your sweet last name, modulated constantly while my vagina fully electrified whirling like a bottomless pit … In this den of pleasure past, your name, like a silken thread to wrap up infinitely deep inside me, softens and deafens me […] 'o God, o Dear Prophet' and the Arab ancestry returns to me, comforting water on this journey.][75]

In what appears to be the most excruciating point of Zoulikha's torture, the narrator highlights the fragmented and barely intelligible thoughts of a tortured body in pain that struggles to assert sovereignty over her body by recalling memories of her family and of her lovers. Yet such confusion also raises questions about whether the narrator's expressions of desire under conditions of intense physical pain and sexual humiliation might instead be a sign of the narrator's subjection to colonial violence. In this way, the narrator's ambivalence about Zoulikha's agency over her body and voice encourages readers to reflect on the difficulty of recovering the agency, voice and embodied history of the gendered Algerian freedom fighter as subaltern.

Felman has suggested that literary narratives can do justice to trauma in a way that the law cannot.[76] If *La femme sans sépulture* is a literary narrative that attempts to do justice to the systematic violence that was perpetrated by the French colonial military against the Algerian population under the aegis of the colonial state's emergency legislation, it also raises questions about how such traumatic narratives are commemorated by the postcolonial state. Throughout the novel, the narrator stages the way in which Zoulikha is a spectral figure that haunts the collective memory of postcolonial Algeria.[77] More specifically, the narrator underscores the way in which the contemporary monumentalisation of Zoulikha's body runs the risk of incorporating the violence of the colonial past into the postcolonial body politic. As the narrator puts it, 'Ils dissent : mon «cadavre» ; l'indépendance venue, peut-être, diront-ils, ma «statue», comme si on statufiat un corps de femme, n'importe lequel, comme si, simplement, pour le dresser dehors, contre un horizon plat, il ne fallait pas de siècles de silence bâillonné' ['They say, my "corpse"; come independence, perhaps they will say, my "statue", as if one could monumentalise any woman's body, as if by

---

75 Djebar, *La femme sans sépulture*, pp. 200–1.

76 Felman, *The Juridical Unconscious*, p. 8.

77 See Michael O'Riley, *Postcolonial Haunting and Victimization: Assia Djebar's New Novels* (New York: Peter Lang, 2007), pp. 57–81.

simply placing her against a flat horizon, centuries of gagged silence were not needed'].[78] Here, the narrator's anticipation of how her own dead body will be transformed into a statue draws attention to the gap between dominant forms of public commemoration and the silencing of Zoulikha's singular historical experiences as a female freedom fighter. Moreover, if, as Michael O'Riley has suggested, Zoulikha's fictional narrative of torture at the hands of the French military 'evokes those contemporary figures tortured in the post-independence period by Algeria's repressive military regime and retributive violence',[79] the incorporation of Zoulikha's dead body into the national narrative of the Algerian postcolony threatens to destabilise rather than reinforce that narrative by highlighting the way in which militarised state violence has become normalised in the Algerian postcolony.

Conclusion

In his poetry collection, *State of Emergency/État d'urgence* (2007), Guémar evokes an image of postcolonial Algeria 'commandée à la gégène' ['ruled by the electrodes'].[80] In poems such as 'Gégène' and 'État d'urgence', Guémar's poetic speaker draws attention to the ways in which the techniques of colonial sovereignty have been adopted by the military regime in postcolonial Algeria. The metonymic representation of a tortured body in 'Gégène', for instance, raises questions about the context and perpetrators of the violence, both of which are entirely absent from the poem:

> ces yeux perdus
> ce crane rasé
> ces dents rasé
> ces nez qui saigne
>
> ce corps nu
> est assis
> sur le goulot d'une bouteille
>
> [these lost eyes
> this shaven skull
> these broken teeth
> this nose that bleeds
>
> this naked body
> is sitting
> on the neck of a bottle].[81]

78 Djebar, *La femme sans sépulture*, p. 207.
79 O'Riley, *Postcolonial Haunting and Victimization*, p. 61.
80 Soleïman Adel Guémar, *État d'urgence/State of Emergency*, trans. by Tom Cheeseman and John Goodby (Todmorden: Arc, 2007), p. 142–43.
81 Guémar, *État d'urgence/State of Emergency*, p. 86.

The title of the poem, 'Gégène', clearly refers to the portable electrical genera-tors, which were widely used by French colonial forces during the Algerian war as an instrument of torture.[82] Like the brutal practice of forcing prisoners to sit on the neck of glass bottles, such a specific reference to techniques of torture employed by the French colonial military may seem to situate the poem in the historical context of the Algerian war of independence. Yet the absence of any other significant spatio-temporal referents from the poem also allows for the possibility that such repressive techniques persisted after independence. Indeed, if we read this poem in the light of other poems included in the collec-tion, it becomes clear that the poems which form *État d'urgence* are crucially concerned with the ways in which the repressive measures employed to protect French Algeria during the colonial state of emergency became normalised after independence.[83] In the poem 'État d'urgence', for example, the speaker conveys an image of contemporary Algeria that is terrorised by 'l'œil passif des généraux' ['the blank gaze of generals'].[84] Following a litany of violent acts perpetrated by the military state against the body of Guémar's poetic personae, the speaker emphasises how 'je suis toujours colonisé' ['I am still colonised'].[85] Here, the word 'toujours' signifies the indefinite temporality of the violent techniques of governmentality which the poetic speaker associates with the violence of French colonial rule. In so doing, Guémar marks the limitations of Algeria's national sovereignty by calling attention to the way in which postcolonial freedom is experienced as a routine practice of state violence and terror from the standpoint of its citizens.

In response to the 'systematic disposability of bodies in struggles for sover-eignty' during the Algerian war of independence, Ranjana Khanna has raised a crucial question about the limitations of sovereignty in postcolonial states such as Algeria:

> if the revolutionary desire for national sovereignty ends with exceptional violence as the norm, how is it possible to think of the postcolonial project as anything other than a lost cause in which a military-backed state of excep-tion can be declared at any time and without much need for rationalization?[86]

Against the necropolitical pessimism of a postcolonial state that conflates the protection of sovereignty and democracy with the disposability of its citizens, Khanna suggests that critical melancholia offers a conceptual resource in which to 'find demands for justice, and therefore hope for the future'.[87] It is precisely such a form of critical melancholia that underpins Djebar's commitment to

---

82 See Darius Rejali, *Torture and Democracy* (Princeton, NJ: Princeton University Press, 2007), pp. 161–66.

83 See Ranjana Khanna, *Algeria Cuts: Women and Representation, 1830 to the Present* (Stanford, CA: Stanford University Press, 2008), p. 26.

84 Guémar, *État d'urgence/State of Emergency*, p. 142.

85 Guémar, *État d'urgence/State of Emergency*, p. 140.

86 Khanna, *Algeria Cuts*, p. 26.

87 Khanna, *Algeria Cuts*, p. 27.

articulate the history of the gendered subaltern in her fiction and filmmaking. If Guémar's *État d'urgence* traces the fault lines in the contemporary Algerian body politic, and the way in which the permanent state of emergency in the postcolony has betrayed the political ideals of national liberation, the fiction and filmmaking of Djebar interrogates the uses of narratives of mourning in the postcolony through a form of ghost writing. In so doing, Djebar raises crucial questions about the emancipatory potential of anti-colonial violence and its impact on the Algerian population, both during the period of French colonial rule and its aftermath. Against the claims of thinkers such as Benjamin and Fanon that revolutionary violence offers a means of achieving justice for the oppressed, Djebar encourages readers to think through the persistence of the colonial state of emergency in the Algerian postcolony, and 'la mécanique de la violence et du carnage' ['the mechanics of violence and bloodshed'] to which it gives rise.[88]

---

88 Assia Djebar, *Le blanc de l'Algérie* (Paris: Albin Michel, 1995), p. 134. Assia Djebar, *Algerian White*, trans. David Kelley and Marjolijn de Jager (New York: Seven Stories Press, 2000), p. 115.

Part III

The Palestinian Tradition of the Oppressed and the Colonial Genealogy of Israel's State of Exception

It was in part the colonial state of emergency in British Mandatory Palestine that provided a legal and political framework for the formation of the state of Israel and its legislative order. For the Emergency Defence Regulations, as Said explains in a passing reference to the uses of British colonial law in Israel-Palestine, 'were originally devised and implemented in Palestine by the British to be used against the Jews and Arabs' during the mandate period, and especially during the Arab revolt of 1936–39. But after 1948, Israel retained the emergency regulations 'for use in controlling the Arab minority', and 'forbade Arabs the right of movement, the right of purchase of land [and] the right of settlement'.[1] In this context, the declaration of a state of emergency was used as the legal pretext for a large-scale land grab: 'the Emergency Defense Regulations were used to expropriate thousands of acres of Arab lands, either by declaring Arab property to be in a security zone or by ruling lands to be absentee property'.[2] The contradiction between Jewish opposition to the emergency regulations during the British mandate period on the grounds that the regulations were colonial and racist, and Israel's subsequent adoption of these regulations after 1948 may seem to be self-evident. Yet what this contradiction also points to is a broader tension within the discourse of Zionism between a movement of national liberation from British rule and European anti-Semitism on the one hand, and a movement of settler-colonialism on the other.[3]

This is not to say that the British Emergency Defence Regulations provided

---

1 Edward Said, *The Question of Palestine* (London: Vintage, 1992), p. 36.
2 Said, *The Question of Palestine*, 105. See also Hanna Dib Nakkara, 'Israeli Land Seizure under Various Defense and Emergency Regulations', *Journal of Palestine Studies*, 14/2 (1985), pp. 13–34.
3 See Joseph Massad, 'The Post-colonial Colony: Time, Space, and Bodies in Palestine/ Israel', in Fawzia Afzal-Khan and Kalpana Seshadri-Crooks (eds), *The Pre-occupation of Postcolonial Studies* (Durham, NC: Duke University Press, 2000), pp. 311–46.

the exclusive means by which the state of Israel was established and the Palestinians were displaced from their land. Such a claim would be to ignore the role of the different Zionist organisations, the British mandatory government, the United Nations partition plan and the various military plans that the Haganah implemented during 1948. Yet the Defence Regulations provided the British colonial state and the Israeli state with a technique of governmentality – a technique that has worked in mutually reinforcing ways with other techniques of rule such as partition, forced expropriation, house demolitions, curfews, permit regimes, torture and extra-judicial executions. In this respect, Israel's adoption of the Emergency Defence Regulations may help to shed light on the logic of inclusive exclusion that underpins Zionism's settler colonial ideology.

Compared to recent scholarship on the political and legal techniques that Israel has used to control the Occupied Palestinian Territories since 1967, Said's reflections on Israel's use of the British emergency regulations in *The Question of Palestine* may seem rather perfunctory, and perhaps even a little dated. Theorists such as Adi Ophir, Yehouda Shenhav and Yael Berda have traced the spatial, visual and legal technologies of power that constitute the occupation of the West Bank and Gaza. These scholars offer an important and nuanced account of Israel's state of exception in the Occupied Palestinian Territories and its political logic of exclusive inclusion – the logic by which the occupied territories are excluded from the state of Israel in order that Israel can include Palestine under its system of control. As Ophir, Givoni and Hanafi put it in the introduction to *The Power of Inclusive Exclusion*, 'colonization and separation both presuppose the exclusion of the Occupied Palestinian Territories and their inhabitants from the pale of law and the normalisation of a state of exception in which the Palestinian population as a whole and individuals within it are exposed to arbitrary violence and coercive regulation of daily life'.[4] Yet in focusing almost exclusively on the topology of power that constitutes the occupation they also separate the occupation as an object of inquiry from the contested colonial genealogy of Zionism, and the disputed 'ethnic cleansing of Palestine' in 1948.[5] They mention, for example, how the Palestinian population

> have been ruled for more than four decades by a power that denies their political rights and that too often violates their basic human rights under the pretext of an indefinite state of exception justified by Israel's 'belligerent occupation' that has become part of the framing and justification of the annual renewal of a formal state of emergency.[6]

Yet they do not address the specific colonial history of these emergency regulations. Rereading Said's brief, scattered, but nonetheless urgent remarks on the colonial genealogy of Israel's emergency regulations in light of such recent

4 Adi Ophir, Michael Givoni and Sari Hanafi, 'Introduction', in idem (eds), *The Power of Inclusive Exclusion: Anatomy of Israeli Rule in the Occupied Palestinian Territories* (New York: Zone, 2009), p. 23.
5 See Ilan Pappé, *The Ethnic Cleansing of Palestine* (Oxford: Oneworld, 2006).
6 Ophir, Givoni and Hanafi, 'Introduction', p. 18.

scholarship on the technologies of power that form the occupation, then, it becomes possible to relate the regime of Israel's emergency legislation in the Occupied Palestinian Territories to the specific history of Zionism as a settler colonial ideology that developed in the shadow of European anti-Semitism. Indeed, to the extent that his comments on Israel's use of emergency legislation form part of a broader series of reflections on Zionism from the standpoint of its victims, Said's words may seem to echo Benjamin's account of the permanent state of exception in his Eighth Thesis on the Concept of History. For just as Benjamin's thesis is marked by his own failed attempt to escape from Nazi-occupied Europe as a German Jew, so Said's account of the emergency regulations that Israel implemented after 1948 is marked by his exile from Palestine, and by a profound understanding of what exile meant for the Palestinian refugees displaced during the *nakba* or catastrophe of 1948. Reading Said after Benjamin, can, in other words, help to re-imagine the tradition of the oppressed as a critical position from which to challenge and contest violent and exclusionary forms of state sovereignty.[7]

The permanent state of emergency, which, in the words of Yvonne Schmidt, 'became a fundamental and effective part of Israel's legal order' after 1948, is often justified in terms of the axiom of state security, the rejection of the legitimacy of the state of Israel by much of the Arab world and the ongoing conflict between the state of Israel and the Palestinian people living in Israel and the Occupied Territories in the West Bank and in Gaza.[8] In a certain sense, then, Israel's territorial sovereignty is bound up with the indefinite extension of the British Defence (Emergency) Regulations of 1936–39 and 1945. As the anthropologist and activist Uri Davis explains,

> The vast properties of the Palestinian Arab people inside the State of Israel remain vested with the Custodian of Absentee Property under the Absentees' Property Law of 1950 so long as 'the state of emergency declared by the Provisional Council of State in 1948' has not been declared to have ceased to exist. Presumably, when the said 'state of emergency' is declared to have ceased to exist, all 1948 Palestinian refugees' property vested with the Israeli Custodian of Absentees' Property could be claimed back by its 'absentee' owners.[9]

The inference that Davis draws from Israel's use of the British Defence (Emergency) Regulations raises questions about why these supposedly temporary regulations have not been repealed over 60 years after they first became

---

7 For a further discussion of the relationship between exile and the tradition of the oppressed in the thought of Walter Benjamin, see Gabriel Piterberg, *The Returns of Zionism: Myth, Politics and Scholarship in Israel* (London: Verso, 2008), pp. 114–26.

8 Yvonne Schmidt, 'Foundations of Civil and Political Rights in Israel and the Occupied Territories', p. 288. Available at <www.flwi.ugent.be/cie/yschmidt/index.htm>. Accessed 11 August 2011. See also Ariella Azoulay and Adi Ophir, *The One-State Condition: Occupation and Democracy in Israel/Palestine*, trans. Tal Haran (Stanford, CA: Stanford University Press, 2013).

9 Uri Davis, *Apartheid Israel* (London: Zed, 2003), p. 126.

law, and why a state of emergency has become normalised in a modern nation state that claims to be a liberal democracy. The specific connections between the emergency regulations of the British mandatory government in Palestine and Israel's use of those emergency powers to assert sovereignty over Palestinian land and to control the Palestinian population point to a specifically colonial regime of power, law and sovereignty, which is immanent to the political foundations of Israel. In this respect, Ariella Azoulay's use of Walter Benjamin's term constituent violence – a term denoting the connection between state violence and the law – to describe the legal foundations of the state of Israel seems rather appropriate if one considers that the Defence (Emergency) Regulations of 1945 were used to appropriate territory from the Palestinian population and to defend Israeli sovereignty over that territory against the very refugee population that had been dispossessed.[10] In the context of the Occupied Palestinian Territories, the circular logic between what Benjamin called law-making violence and law-preserving violence is palpable.

The use of the law as a technique of preserving sovereignty in Israel-Palestine is mediated through a series of mutually reinforcing institutions and practices, such as the military court system in the West Bank and Gaza, and the proliferation of military checkpoints in the West Bank. The sociologist Lisa Hajjar explains how the military court system in the Occupied Palestinian Territories is 'part of a broader array of governing institutions and practices in which Palestinians are enmeshed and tracked in grids of surveillance, subjected to restrictive codes of conduct and interaction, physically immobilized through the use of permits, closures, curfews, checkpoints, and walls, and incarcerated in huge numbers'.[11] Yet this permanent state of emergency would also appear to be incommensurate with Israel's claim to be a modern liberal democracy because it denies basic human rights to the Palestinian population.[12] The characterisation of the British emergency regulations as colonialist and fascist by Jewish lawyers such as Yacob Shimshon Shapira may appear to reinforce Said's insistence in *The Politics of Dispossession* that Israel's treatment of Palestinians needs to be understood in terms of a 'long-standing and equally unfaltering anti-Semitism that in [the twentieth] century produced the Holocaust of the European Jews'.[13] At the same time, however, it is important that we take seriously Said's argument that support for the expansionist policies of the Jewish state of Israel under the guise of state security also involves 'support for the exile and dispossession of the Palestinian people'.[14] For not only does such an argument call the necessity

10 Ariella Azoulay, 'Declaring the State of Israel: Declaring a State of War', *Critical Inquiry*, 37/2 (2011), pp. 265–85.
11 Lisa Hajjar, *Courting Conflict: The Israeli Military Court System in the West Bank and Gaza* (Berkeley: University of California Press, 2005), p. 186.
12 Schmidt, 'Foundations of Civil and Political Rights in Israel and the Occupied Territories', p. 290.
13 Nakkara, 'Israeli Land Seizure under Various Defense and Emergency Regulations', p. 13; Edward Said, *The Politics of Dispossession* (London: Chatto and Windus, 1994), p. 167.
14 Said, *The Politics of Dispossession*, p. 167.

for emergency legislation into question, it also highlights the way in which the finite temporality of the state of emergency in Israel-Palestine is a legal fiction that is invoked to justify the militarised occupation of Palestinian territory. As Rose puts it in a statement that recalls the terms of Benjamin's Eighth Thesis on the Concept of History, the 'Occupation can no longer be seen as a state of exception, a temporary and regrettable episode; it has become the reality of the nation'.[15]

To understand this political 'reality', we need to take account of the specific historical framework within which Israel's emergency legislation was formulated. In a critique of Agamben's theory of the state of exception, Ilan Pappé has suggested that Israel's emergency legislation is not a sign of a collapsing republic or democracy, but is rather integrated into the ideology of its colonising regime.[16] Significantly, the normalisation of the 'abuses of power, law and sovereignty' in the occupied Palestinian territories that have become integrated into the ideology of Israel's colonising regime have their origins in the complex relationship between Zionism and European colonialism.[17] As Shenhav and Yael Berda have argued, the racial logic of the permit regime between Israel and the West Bank can be traced back to the British colonial bureaucracies of India and Egypt.[18] Shenhav and Berda's attempt to track the colonial genealogy of Israel's bureaucratic system of control in the West Bank is compelling in many respects, but it is surprising that they do not mention the British mandatory government's use of emergency powers in Palestine. For the specific historical connections between the emergency regulations of the British mandatory government in Palestine and Israel's use of emergency powers to control the Palestinian population point to a more complex and contested genealogy of colonial power, law and sovereignty. As David Lloyd puts it, 'what is announced in the settler colony, in Israel/Palestine, is itself a state of exception, determined in large part by Israel's urgent desire to normalise the exceptional status of its regime of occupation in accord with law'.[19] It is partly for this reason, I suggest, that a consideration of literary representations of British counter-insurgency in Mandatory Palestine and of the Israeli war of 1948 helps to make sense of the violent forms of sovereignty that such colonial laws and emergency powers have enabled.

If writers such as Arthur Conan Doyle, E.M. Forster and Robert Louis Stevenson have found histories of anti-colonial struggle, such as the Indian Rebellion of

15 Jacqueline Rose, *The Last Resistance* (London: Verso, 2007), p. 13.
16 Ilan Pappé, 'The *Mukhabarat* State of Israel: A State of Oppression Is Not a State of Exception', in Ronit Lentin (ed.), *Thinking Palestine* (London: Zed Books, 2008), p. 159.
17 Pappé, 'The *Mukhabarat* State of Israel', p. 159.
18 Yehouda Shenhav and Yael Berda, 'The Colonial Foundations of the State of Exception: Juxtaposing the Israeli Occupation of the Palestinian Territories with Colonial Bureaucratic History', in Ophir, Givoni and Hanafi (eds), *The Power of Inclusive Exclusion*, pp. 337–74.
19 David Lloyd, 'Settler Colonialism and the State of Exception: The Example of Palestine/Israel', *Settler Colonial Studies*, 2/1 (2012), p. 75. Available at <http://ojs.lib.swin.edu.au/index.php/settlercolonialstudies>. Accessed 3 April 2012.

1857 or the Fenian Uprising of the late nineteenth century in Ireland, to be a rich resource for literary narratives of counter-insurgency, it is striking how comparatively few novels seem to have been written about the Palestinian anti-colonial rebellion of the 1930s, or the armed Jewish struggles against the British mandatory government of the 1940s. Certainly, British imperial fiction for children, or so-called 'boy's own' adventure narratives such as Alan Western's *Desert Hawk* (1937) and Douglas Valder Duff's *Harding of the Palestine Police* (1937) worked to contain the crisis in colonial authority that the Palestinian rebellion represented by highlighting the heroic efforts of the British colonial police force and the military to preserve British colonial sovereignty in Palestine.[20] Yet it is in Maurice Callard's popular romantic narrative about 'Zionist terrorism' and British counter-insurgency in Mandatory Palestine, *The City Called Holy* (1954), that the relationship between the colonial rule of law and the violence of British colonial sovereignty are explicitly foregrounded, as we will see. If *The City Called Holy* raises questions about the measures employed by the British colonial authorities to maintain colonial sovereignty, Yizhar's novella about the 1948 war, *Khirbet Khizeh* (1949), outlines the founding violence of the Israeli state. By moving from Callard's late imperial British novel about the waning sovereignty of the British mandate in Palestine to Yizhar's Hebrew modernist novella about the 1948 war, the chapter considers how these literary texts can help to elucidate the complex and contested genealogy of colonial power, sovereignty and legality that underpins the formation of the state of Israel.

We have already seen how the state of Israel adopted its Emergency Legislation from British colonial law after 1948, and how there may seem to be a structural resemblance between the British colonial government's repression of the Arab rebellion in the 1930s, armed Zionist freedom fighters in the 1940s and the national security measures adopted by Israel in 1948. Yet, this is not to say that Zionism can be simply explained away as a monolithic colonial ideology or that it conformed to a single coherent narrative.[21] Zionism was partly founded on a singular articulation of Jewish socialism and nationalism in which the equal rights of Jewish workers were privileged to the exclusion of Arab workers.[22] Zionism has also included dissident forms that sought to challenge the maltreatment of Palestinians.[23] The predominant nationalist narrative of the formation of the state of Israel was also founded on a powerful myth of anti-colonial nationalism, in which the Zionists managed to kick the British foreign invader out of the motherland.[24] At the same time, as Ronen Shamir has argued, leading

20 Alan Western, *Desert Hawk* (London and New York: F. Warne & Co., 1937); Douglas Valder Duff, *Harding of the Palestine Police* (London and Glasgow: Blackie & Son, 1941).
21 Ronen Shamir, *The Colonies of Law: Colonialism, Zionism, and Law in Early Mandate Palestine* (Cambridge: Cambridge University Press, 2000), p. 8.
22 Zeev Sternhell, *The Founding Myths of Israel: Nationalism, Socialism, and the Making of the Jewish state* (Princeton, NJ: Princeton University Press, 1998), p. 8.
23 See Ronit Lentin, *Co-memory and Melancholia: Israelis Memorialising the Palestinian Nakba* (Manchester: Manchester University Press, 2010); and R. Carey and J. Shainin (eds), *The Other Israel: Voices of Refusal and Dissent* (New York: New Press, 2000).
24 Shamir, *The Colonies of Law*, p. 9.

figures within the Zionist national movement such as Chaim Weizman 'always sought the protection of one imperialist power or another, well aware that the Jewish community, being a minority in Palestine, could not have realized its goals without the internationally legitimate physical and material authoritative presence of an imperial power'.[25] In this respect, Gabriel Piterberg is right to suggest that 'Zionism was both a Central-Eastern European national movement and a movement of European settlers which sought to carve out for itself a national patrimony to the east'.[26]

The territorial ambitions of Zionism were of course inextricably linked to the nationalist imperative to establish a state of Israel, which was partly a response to anti-Semitism in Europe. Yet even if colonisation was not the *raison d'être* of Zionism, there is no disputing the basic fact that Zionism involved the 'conquest of land and the creation of an independent state through work and settlement, if possible, or by force, if necessary'.[27] It is perhaps for this reason that commentators such as Ran Aaronsohn argue that 'Zionism had been a colonizing movement but not a colonialist one'.[28] Such an analytic distinction between a geographical process of immigration and a political process of imperialist domination might enable some Zionist historians to distinguish between a just project of Zionism and a morally bankrupt project of European colonialism. Yet this does not alter the fact that for many Palestinians the national security policies of the Israeli state are experienced as a permanent form of colonial occupation. As Said puts it, 'Zionism and European imperialism are epistemologically, hence historically and politically, coterminous in their view of resident natives'.[29]

The insights of this historical knowledge may seem to correspond with Derrida's concern that Israel's policy towards Palestine and the Palestinians threatens to undermine rather than to secure the sovereignty and safety of Israel, and with Rose's psychoanalytic reflections on Zionism. As we saw in the introduction, Derrida has criticised Israel's repressive policies towards the Palestinian population in the Occupied Palestinian Territories on the grounds that these policies perpetuate an aporetic logic of autoimmunity, in which the state of Israel works to destroy its sovereign power through the repressive political and military techniques it employs to secure that very sovereignty. In a similar vein, Rose's psychoanalytic reflections on the parallels between the defence mechanisms of the ego and the nationalist faith of Zionism highlight the importance of violence to both the formation and security of the Israeli state, as we will see. At the same time, it is important to note that both Derrida and Rose are silent on the question of what the cultural memories and narratives of the Palestinians reveal about the settler–colonial framework of Israel's sovereign power over the Occupied Palestinian Territories. As a consequence, their critique of Israel's policies is somewhat limited in terms of what it can

25 Shamir, *The Colonies of Law*, p. 10.
26 Piterberg, *Returns of Zionism*, p. xii.
27 Shamir, *The Colonies of Law*, p. 15.
28 Shamir, *The Colonies of Law*, p. 17.
29 Said, *The Question of Palestine*, p. 83.

tell us about the collective voice, will and agency of the stateless Palestinian population. In view of such limitations, I suggest that a consideration of how Palestinian writing has represented the *nakba* and the occupation is crucial, not only because of the light it sheds on how Zionism was regarded as synonymous with European colonialism from the standpoint of its victims, but also because of the ways in which it both contributes to and criticises the invention of a Palestinian national narrative.

This chapter begins by examining the ways in which the permanent state of emergency in Israel-Palestine is registered in British narratives of counter-insurgency, as well as Zionist and Palestinian writing. Referring to the thought of Said, Arendt and Rose, the first part of the chapter considers the extent to which the literary prose of counter-insurgency in Israel-Palestine serves to reinforce the sovereignty of colonial occupation under a permanent state of emergency by foreclosing the voice and agency of the Palestinian. By moving from Callard's popular fictional representation of 'Jewish terrorism' in *The City Called Holy* to Yizhar's modernist representation of the 1948 war in *Khirbet Khizeh*, the chapter considers how the prose of counter-insurgency in Mandatory Palestine is recoded as a narrative of sovereignty in Zionist settler–colonial discourse: a narrative that, in the words of Rose, 'folds catastrophe into identity, an identity which then closes on the Palestinians and then on itself'.[30] As a counterpoint to this narrative of sovereignty, the second part of the chapter considers how the emergence of a Palestinian national consciousness is framed in relation to the *nakba*, or catastrophe. If the *nakba* can be understood as a means of both naming and mourning the violent legacy of Israel's policies from the standpoint of the Palestinians who were forced into exile in 1948, this chapter asks how an emergent Palestinian literature of the oppressed has negotiated with that legacy of violence, trauma and mourning. We have already seen in the introduction how Felman has interpreted Benjamin's 'tradition of the oppressed' as a 'theory of history as trauma'.[31] In light of Felman's argument, I suggest that Palestinian writers have developed narrative techniques and rhetorical strategies that not only address the collective trauma of the *nakba* and the subsequent military occupation of the West Bank and Gaza in 1967, but also raise important questions about the limitations of a Palestinian national narrative. With reference to the fiction of Kanafani and Khoury, the final section of the chapter considers how contemporary Palestinian writing attempts to think through and beyond the necropolitical double bind of military occupation and violent anti-colonial insurgency in Israel-Palestine. In so doing, I suggest that Kanafani and Khoury contribute to the invention of a Palestinian tradition of the oppressed – a tradition which recognises and acknowledges the trauma of European anti-Semitism, even as it rejects the violent and exclusionary grounds of sovereignty associated with the ethno-nationalist legacy of Zionist settler colonialism that constantly places the lives of the Palestinian population in jeopardy.

30 Jacqueline Rose, 'The Political Edge of Fiction', in Müge Gürsoy Sökmen and Basak Ertür (eds), *Waiting for the Barbarians: A Tribute to Edward Said* (London: Verso, 2008), p. 18.
31 Felman, *The Juridical Unconscious*, p. 33.

'In Palestine, you have to be prepared – just like Boy Scouts': Romance and Counter-insurgency in Maurice Callard's *The City Called Holy*

The genealogy of Israel's emergency regime can be traced to the British colonial government's introduction of emergency regulations during the Palestinian anti-colonial rebellion of 1936–39 and in response to the armed insurgency of militant Jewish organisations such as the Irgun Zvai Leumi and the Stern group after the Second World War. Significantly, these militant groups borrowed the language of anti-colonial resistance struggles to justify the use of violence against the British government in Palestine. Yet this language worked to obscure the settler colonial ambitions of the Zionist project, as we will see. The emergence of a militant, anti-colonial Zionism was prompted in part by 'the 1939 British-issued White Paper restricting Jewish immigration to Palestine', a statute which was drafted 'in response to the anti-colonial Palestinian Revolt of 1936–1939'.[32] For the leader of the Irgun Zvai Leumi, Menachem Begin, it was the British mandatory government's restrictions on Jewish immigration to Palestine and the Nazi campaign of extermination of the Jews of Europe which were regarded as the immediate causes of the armed Jewish revolt in 'Eretz Israel' during the 1940s.[33] Indeed, for Begin, the British mandatory government in Palestine was 'a colonial regime that lives by the legend of its omnipotence'.[34] And it was precisely this legend of colonial sovereignty that underground organisations such as the Irgun Zvai Leumi and the Stern group sought to challenge through actions such as the bombing of the King David Hotel in July 1946. While the British government sought to label Begin and the Irgun as 'terrorists', Begin objected to the label on the grounds that instilling fear or terror was not the goal of the armed Jewish revolt; on the contrary, 'The underground fighters of the Irgun arose to overthrow and replace a regime. We used physical force because we were faced by physical force'.[35]

Callard's fictionalisation of the armed Jewish insurgency against the British government in Mandatory Palestine in his 1954 novel *The City Called Holy* mirrors the crisis in colonial authority that armed Jewish organisations worked to bring about. The romantic narrative of Callard's novel takes place against the backdrop of a 'terrorist plot' by the Irgun Zvai Leumi to destroy the British police headquarters in Jerusalem. The narrative is written from the first-person perspective of Dendry, a disaffected colonial police officer stationed in Jerusalem who is deeply pessimistic about the future of the British mandate in Palestine in the aftermath of the Arab rebellion, the Holocaust and the rise of violent Jewish organisations such as the Irgun. The novel's romantic plot details his relationship with Leah, a Jewish woman who is suspected by the police of having links to the Irgun. Dendry's position as a colonial police officer assigned

32 Joseph Massad, *The Persistence of the Palestinian Question: Essays on Zionism and the Palestinians* (London: Routledge, 2006), p. 18.

33 Menachem Begin, *The Revolt*, trans. Samuel Katz (London: W.H. Allen, 1951), p. 38.

34 Begin, *The Revolt*, p. 52.

35 Begin, *The Revolt*, p. 60.

to prevent 'terrorist outrages' in Mandatory Palestine is clearly compromised by his relationship with Leah, and it is the tension between the romantic plot and the counter-terrorist plot of *The City Called Holy* that animates the narrative.

Significantly, the novel also highlights the contradictions between the legal fiction of the British mandate and the use of violence to maintain colonial sovereignty in Palestine. During a raid on a Jewish apartment block in Jerusalem, for instance, Dendry informs his subordinates that 'We're not exactly in the position of a conquering army', and at the same time grants the soldiers permission to use force where necessary.[36] It is precisely this use of force which gives the lie to Dendry's subsequent defence of his position as a colonial policeman in a rather heated conversation with Leah about the British mandate in Palestine:

> The British are the legal government of Palestine, answerable, once to the League of Nations, nowadays to the United Nations for the way they run the country. We did not come as conquerors as the Germans did in Norway, opposed by the people who were living here. We are not an opposition force in time of war, but the appointed government.[37]

Dendry is certainly critical of the British colonial government's security policies, especially its recourse to emergency powers. He says at one point during a conversation with Frank, 'Everything to-day is security. It's security this, security that. Security officers, security forces, security handbook. And, I ask you, exactly how secure do we feel?'[38] As a colonial policeman, Dendry is scandalised by the way in which the District Court of Jerusalem allowed an Arab villager to be sentenced 'to only six months' imprisonment' for knocking 'the brains out of his unmarried sister with a bludgeon when he had found her in bed with a lover',[39] while 'Arabs who had been found with barely serviceable revolvers and Jews carrying in their pockets bits of metal from which a hand-grenade could be fashioned were sent to prison by the Military courts for years'.[40] The justification of the British colonial government's Defence Regulations is also called into question by Dendry's account of a 'terrorist attack' on a government building in chapter 15:

> The tension was mounting fast in Jerusalem and in the country. Every morning news came of a fresh act of violence. Sometimes it was the railway lines that were blown up and a train ambushed; sometimes a police station had been attacked by night. Early one morning the terrorists invested [*sic*] the Railway station and held it for three hours. They broke into the Government Printing Press building and destroyed the presses which were producing copies of the new Emergency Regulations. Unsuccessfully they attempted to blow up the Police Headquarters in Haifa, and without success, also, they tried to free two hundred Jewish internees detained at Latrun on the plain between Jerusalem

36 Maurice Callard, *The City Called Holy* (London: Jonathan Cape, 1954), p. 24.
37 Callard, *The City Called Holy*, p. 83.
38 Callard, *The City Called Holy*, p 122.
39 Callard, *The City Called Holy*, pp. 47–48.
40 Callard, *The City Called Holy*, p. 48.

and the sea. Seditious pamphlets were almost daily collected from the streets and the cafés, and during the nights posters of a like nature appeared on hoardings throughout the Jewish quarters of the town.[41]

As well as establishing the unpredictable character of the 'terrorist attacks' on the British mandatory state, Dendry's account of these attacks offers an illuminating if fictional mediation of the relationship between writing, colonial sovereignty and the law: for it is the printing presses that the Jewish militants destroy in an attempt to undermine the public declaration of the British mandatory government's recourse to emergency measures.

Yet if Callard's fictionalised Irgun attack the government printing presses in order to prevent the British colonial government from disseminating repressive emergency measures, Dendry's criticism of the government's use of emergency powers has more to do with the efficacy of the government's security policies than with the human rights implications of this legislation per se. Indeed, Dendry's defence of 'the iron fist without the velvet glove' against militant Jewish groups serves to undermine further the liberal colonial rhetoric of the British mandate which is epitomised in his colleague Frank's observation that 'officially we are here until we have brought the Arabs and the Jews of the country to a point in their education where they can be trusted to run their own affairs'.[42] What Dendry means by the iron fist – a metaphor that is often used to describe totalitarian forms of governmentality – is revealed in his later suggestion to Frank that the British air force should launch a bomb attack on Tel Aviv to counter the violence between Arabs and Jews. Such a view clearly undermines the colonial rhetoric of the civilising mission in Palestine that is rehearsed in this conversation. But the metaphor of the iron fist within the velvet glove also reveals how the liberal rhetoric of British colonialism in Palestine constantly wrestled with the demand for emergency measures to maintain law and order. As Townshend explains, the British colonial government were uneasy with officially declaring a state of martial law in Palestine, for to do so would be tantamount to acknowledging the failure of Britain's civil administration.[43]

It is precisely this failure that *The City Called Holy* seems to announce. The novel's romantic denouement sees Dendry relinquishing his position as a colonial policeman in British Palestine for a marriage with Leah, and a life in Palestine. Yet this romantic ending is also overshadowed by Dendry's account of Leah's trial as a traitor by a paramilitary court that is established by the fictional members of the Irgun in the novel. When Dendry protests the paramilitary court's decision to remove all of Leah's hair, he does so on the grounds of the court's illegality: 'You pretend you are a military organisation. You set yourself up as a court. But you are not a legal court and you have no right to carry out this sentence'.[44] Dendry's account of the military court here can be

---

41 Callard, *The City Called Holy*, p. 133.
42 Callard, *The City Called Holy*, p. 138.
43 Charles Townshend, *Britain's Civil Wars: Counterinsurgency in the Twentieth Century* (London: Faber, 1986), p. 118.
44 Callard, *The City Called Holy*, p. 219.

read as a form of chiasmus in that it is an inverted mirror image of British colonial rule in Palestine which uses the law to exercise its political authority over the Jewish and Arab population. Such a statement is significant not only for its irony, in that Dendry is presumably perceived as a figure who represents an illegal occupying force by the very Jewish group he condemns for acting illegally, but also for its prescience. For in highlighting the parallels between British colonial law and that of the emergent Jewish state, Callard anticipates the importance of emergency legislation in the legal and political formation of the Jewish state of Israel. As Sabri Jiryis has argued, the military government in Israel 'owes its legal existence to the British Mandate Government's Defence Laws (State of Emergency) 1945, and the Israeli Defence Laws (Security Areas) 1949'.[45] A detailed consideration of the continuities between British colonial law and Israel's use of emergency law as a technique of governing the Palestinian population is beyond the scope of Callard's novel. Yet the paramilitary court in *The City Called Holy* can be seen to foreshadow both the continuities and the differences between British colonial law and the emergent Israeli rule of law. Specifically, Dendry's exchange with the paramilitary court foregrounds the relationship between violence, sovereignty and legality that is common to both the British colonial government and the legal foundations of the state of Israel.

The British emergency regulations in Palestine were first 'enacted in order to subdue the Arab population after the 1936 Arab Revolt in Palestine', and were subsequently re-enacted at 'the end of World War II' in order to counter the insurgency of militant Jewish organisations.[46] We have already seen how after the formation of the state of Israel in 1948, the Israeli government adopted the very emergency laws that the Jewish settlers had opposed during the last years of the British mandate in Palestine on the grounds that they were repressive and imperialist. Yet such a comparison can also overlook crucial differences between the ideology of the British colonial government in Palestine and the Israeli state. Whereas the British emergency regulations aimed to criminalise and control both the Arab and the Jewish populations in order to consolidate the civil authority of the British mandatory government, Israel's emergency regulations provided a legal framework to justify the expropriation of Palestinian land and the forced migration of the Palestinian population in order to consolidate its sovereignty – as we will see in the following section.

Some Zionist intellectuals, writers and political leaders have been very careful to distinguish the nation-building project in Israel from the settler project of European colonisation in South Africa, Australia or Zimbabwe. F.H. Kisch, the chairman of the Zionist commission, for example, argued in his diary that the word 'colonization' is not appropriate to describe Jewish settlement in Palestine as 'one does not set up colonies in a homeland, but abroad'. Significantly, Kisch also recognised that 'from the point of view of Arab opinion the verb "to

45 Sabri Jiryis, *The Arabs in Israel, 1948–1966*, trans. Meric Dobson (Beirut: Institute for Palestine Studies, 1969), p. 2.
46 Jiryis, *The Arabs in Israel*, p. 2.

colonize" is associated with imperialism and aggressiveness'.[47] More recently, the historian Yoav Gelber has argued that the identification of Zionism with colonialism is not only historically inaccurate, but it also serves 'primarily as a propagandist and ideological weapon in the persisting Arab–Jewish conflict'.[48] Gelber emphasises that unlike European colonial powers, 'Jewish immigrants to Eretz Israel did not come armed to the teeth and made no attempt to take the country from the native population by force'; that Jewish settlers also imported private and national capital into 'Eretz Israel' rather than exploiting colonies for the benefit of the imperial centre; and finally that Jewish settlers did not conquer but rather purchased land in Palestine.[49] In doing so, Gelber not only downplays the role of the British Empire and its legal institutions in the estab-lishment of a state of Israel, he also ignores the way in which Zionism was experienced as a form of colonisation from the standpoint of its victims. Indeed, as several writers and intellectuals including Arendt, Ian Lustick, Said, Rashid Khalidi, Ilan Pappé, Rose, Joseph Massad and Gabriel Piterberg have suggested, this distinction between the Zionist project in Palestine and European settler colonialism rests on a disavowal of the dispossession and expropriation of Palestinian villages in 1948, the subsequent exile of Palestinian refugees and the occupation of the West Bank and Gaza in 1967. It is precisely this disavowal that the Israeli writer S. Yizhar (the pen name of Yizhar Smilansky) explores in his novella, *Khirbet Khizeh* (1949), the story of a fictional Palestinian village that is occupied by the Israeli army in 1948. The publication of this novella in 1949 and its subsequent adaptation for Israeli national television in 1978 has provoked widespread debate in the Israeli public sphere for desecrating the 'honor of the IDF' by exposing the young Israeli soldiers as sadists, and for distorting the image of the war of independence.[50] By drawing attention to the soldiers' attempt to disavow the forced expulsion of Palestinian villagers, however, *Khirbet Khizeh* offers an already articulated response to the state of Israel's attempt to repress the memory of the Palestinian disaster, as we will see in the following section.

'The land itself couldn't bear me': Exile, Dispossession and the Return of the Repressed in S. Yizhar's Khirbet Khizeh

Khirbet Khizeh is the Arabic name of a fictional Palestinian village that was conquered without much resistance by an Israeli military force in 1948. In this respect, the village can be understood as a 'lieu de mémoire for unearthing Yizhar's experience of the erasing of rural Arab Palestine', as Gabriel Piterberg

47 F.H. Kisch, *Palestine Diary* (London: Victor Gollancz, 1938), p. 420.
48 Yoav Gelber, 'The History of Zionist Historiography: From Apologetics to Denial', in Benny Morris (ed.), *Making Israel* (Ann Arbor: University of Michigan Press, 2008), p. 67.
49 Gelber, 'The History of Zionist Historiography', p. 67.
50 Anita Shapira, 'Hirbet Hizar: Between Remembrance and Forgetting', *Jewish Social Studies*, 7/1 (2000), pp. 1–62.

puts it.[51] The novella is written from the first-person narrative point of view of an Israeli soldier who tries to account for his complicity in the erasure of rural Arab Palestine and the creation of a Palestinian refugee population. The story begins with a moment of self-reflection in which the homodiegetic narrator describes how there are two different approaches to telling the story. The first option, the narrator continues, is to frame the story in terms of the formal conventions of literary realism:

> One option is to tell the story in order, beginning with one clear day, one clear winter's day, and describing in detail the departure and the journey, when the dirt paths were moistened by the earlier rain, and the cactus hedges surrounding the citrus groves were burned by the sun and moist, their feet, as of cold, licked by flocks of dense damp dark-green nettles, as the noonday gradually advanced, a pleasant unhurried noonday, which moved on as usual and turned into a darkening twilight chill, when it was all over, finished, done.[52]

The second option, which the narrator suggests might be 'better', is to relay the story in terms of the military orders that the soldiers received, and to account for the way in which the soldiers interpreted these euphemistic military orders in order to justify the use of force to remove the Palestinian population from their homes and from their land:

> Another and possibly better option, however, would be to begin differently, and to mention straightaway what had been the purpose of the entire mission from the start, 'operational order' number such and such, on such and such a day of the month, in the margin of which, in the final section that was simply entitled 'miscellaneous,' it said, in a short line and a half, that although the mission must be executed decisively and precisely, whatever happened, 'no violent outbursts or disorderly conduct' – it said – 'would be permitted,' which only indicated straightaway that there was something amiss, that anything was possible (and even planned and foreseen), and that one couldn't evaluate this straightaway final clause before returning to the opening and also scanning the noteworthy clause entitled 'information,' which immediately warned of the mounting danger of 'infiltrators,' 'terrorist cells,' and (in a wonderful turn of phrase) 'operatives dispatched on hostile missions,' but also the subsequent and even more noteworthy clause, which explicitly stated, 'assemble the inhabitants of the area extending from point X (see attached map) to point Y (see same map) – load them onto transports, and convey them across our lines; blow up the stone houses, and burn the huts; detain the youths and the suspects, and clear the area of 'hostile forces,' and so on and so forth – so that it was now obvious how many good and honest hopes were being invested in those who were being sent out to implement all this 'burn-blow-up-imprison-load-convey,' who would burn blow up imprison load and convey with such courtesy and with a restraint born of true culture,

51 Piterberg, *Returns of Zionism*, p. 207.
52 S. Yizhar, *Khirbet Khizeh*, trans. Nicholas de Lange and Yaacob Dweck (Jerusalem: Ibis Editions, 2008), pp. 7–8.

and this would be a sign of a wind of change, of decent upbringing, and perhaps, even of the Jewish soul, the great Jewish soul.[53]

By noting the inconsistencies and ellipses in the military orders, the narrator foregrounds the tension between the military imperative to employ restraint and the violent practice of expropriation signalled in the complex verb phrase 'burn-blow-up-imprison-load-convey'. According to the Israeli historian Anita Shapira, such a violent ideology was anathema to Yizhar, who 'was revolted' by the Israeli state's use of violence during the war of 1948.[54] Yet by suggesting that this violent process of destruction and expropriation is 'born of true culture' and is the sign of 'the great Jewish soul', the narrator suggests that the military commandments are themselves a part of a Zionist *mission civilisatrice*, an idea which is epitomised in Theodor Herzl's argument that a state for the Jews would be 'a rampart of Europe against Asia, an outpost of civilisation as opposed to barbarism'.[55]

The linear temporality of the story and the frequent descriptions of the landscape that follow from this initial narrative frame might suggest that the narrator chooses to compose the story according to the formal conventions of literary realism. Yet this linear narrative is constantly interrupted by the narrator's account of the empty villages and the soldier's excessive use of military force against unarmed targets, whether human or animal. At one point, the narrator describes how some of the soldiers would kick an old Arab and shoot dozens of bullets at a terrified dog until it fell; at another, two soldiers discuss the 'incredible vitality'[56] of donkeys after one soldier pumps three bullets into a donkey at close range, and it doesn't die; and at another, the soldiers refuse to allow an Arab farmer to leave his village with his camel and his donkey.[57] Such passages might appear to recall the lawless violence of colonial sovereignty depicted in novels such as Conrad's *Heart of Darkness*, but they also raise important ethical questions about the human–animal distinction in the minds of the Israeli soldiers. The mindless shooting of animals, in other words, can be seen to exemplify the way in which the Arab population more generally are regarded by the Israeli military as animals, or more precisely as *homines sacri*, or a form of bare life that the military has the sovereign right to kill with impunity.[58] As the wireless operator puts it, 'Forget these Ayrabs—they're not even human'.[59] It is passages such as these that prompted Israeli critics such as Mordechai Shalev to argue that Yizhar failed to explain the psychological changes in his heroes: '"Pure souls trying to conceal that purity", who suddenly turned into "sadists worse than the Nazis. Because the Nazis at least had a theory of race, while

53 Yizhar, *Khirbet Khizeh*, p. 9.
54 Shapira, 'Hirbet Hizar', p. 10.
55 Theodor Herzl, *The Jewish State* (London: Central Office of the Zionist Organization, 1934 [1896]), p. 29.
56 Yizhar, *Khirbet Khizeh*, p. 19.
57 Yizhar, *Khirbet Khizeh*, p. 49.
58 See Agamben, *Homo Sacer*.
59 Yizhar, *Khirbet Khizeh*, p. 25.

Yizhar's characters murder from boredom'".[60] What this criticism of the Israeli soldiers' brutality in *Khirbet Khizeh* overlooks is the soldiers' adherence to the military orders that were put in place in March 1948 to expel systematically the Palestinians from their villages.[61] More than this, Shalev's criticism ignores the way in which the Zionist narrative had displaced the traumatic history of anti-Semitism and the displacement of the European Jewish population onto a nationalist narrative, which prevented identification with the displaced Palestinian population.

The narrator's account of the landscape, like the Israeli soldiers' brutalisation of animals, also registers the violence of colonial dispossession. The fields surrounding the village are described as 'a putrid patch of disgusting dirt, spat upon by generations that had cast their water and excrement and the dung of their cattle and camels upon it'.[62] And yet at the same time, the narrator describes the 'abundant water, good soil, and celebrated husbandry' that surrounds the village.[63] This antithesis between the image of the land as 'putrid' and 'disgusting' because it is uncultivated on the one hand and ripe for plantation on the other clearly intimates that the objective of the military campaign is not simply the security of the state of Israel, but also the occupation of Arab land in the interests of expanding settlements. By framing the Palestinian's land as uninscribed earth, in other words, the narrator seems to justify the appropriation of territory.[64]

Yet the narrator's persistent suggestion that the land the Israeli soldiers are depopulating is also haunted offers a crucial ethical counterpoint to the dominant narrative of military occupation. The novella opens with the narrator's confession that the expulsion of Palestinian villagers from Khirbet Khizeh 'happened a long time ago, but it has haunted me ever since'.[65] This spectral undertone continues to inflect the narrator's account of the empty spaces of occupation he describes in the text. The Palestinian villages, he explains, were 'nothing but gaping emptiness screaming out with a silence that was at once evil and sad'.[66] By suggesting that these 'bare villages [...] would begin to cry out',[67] the narrator articulates the absent presence of the Palestinian voice in the empty spaces of occupation. In so doing, the narrator highlights a tension between the nationalist rhetoric of Zionism and the history of violence associated with the exercise of military dispossession.

In a reading of the Zionist thought of Herzl, Martin Buber, Hans Kohn and Arendt, Rose has suggested that the utopian aspirations of Zionism make it 'the

60 Shapira, 'Hirbet Hizar', p. 16.
61 See Pappé, *The Ethnic Cleansing of Palestine*.
62 Yizhar, *Khirbet Khizeh*, p. 12.
63 Yizhar, *Khirbet Khizeh*, p. 10.
64 For further discussion of the significance of uninscribed earth in the rhetoric of colonialism, see Gayatri Chakravorty Spivak, 'The Rani of Sirmur: An Essay on Reading the Archives', *History and Theory*, 24/3 (1985), pp. 253–54.
65 Yizhar, *Khirbet Khizeh*, p. 7.
66 Yizhar, *Khirbet Khizeh*, p. 26.
67 Yizhar, *Khirbet Khizeh*, p. 26.

most wonderful exemplar of the work of the psyche in the constitution of the modern nation state'.[68] This is not to say that the constitution of the psyche is either equivalent or homologous to that of the nation state. On the contrary, Rose's point ise that the defensive mechanisms of the ego can tell us something about the security policies of the state. For Rose, what the Jewish state of Israel most fears is the self-critical introspection associated with psychoanalysis, and more specifically, analysis of the ways in which Zionism has inscribed violence into the very foundations of the Jewish nation. One of the ways in which the Jewish state of Israel has done this is through the law, as we will see. The originary inscription of violence that Rose identifies in the foundations of the Jewish nation is partly exemplified in Hans Kohn's critique of nationalism as a faith that 'permits and excuses everything'.[69] Yet if Zionism is a nationalist faith that 'permits and excuses everything'[70] – a phrase which itself links the idea of the nation to the extra-legal violence associated with a state of emergency – it is precisely this belief in the nationalist myth of Zionism and the non-existence of Palestinian political sovereignty that the narrator of *Khirbet Khizeh* begins to question. The empty spaces that continue to haunt the narrator's memory from the very start of the novella highlight the way in which the violent military depopulation of Khirbet Khizeh is repressed in the Zionist national narrative. And it is the persistent return of this repressed event that haunts the narrator in his return to the history of the 1948 war.

It is significant also that the narrator attempts to comprehend the soldiers' violence against the village and the villagers of Khirbet Khizeh in terms of an attempt to rid themselves of guilt:

> These bare villages, the day was coming when they would begin to cry out. As you went through them, all of a sudden, without knowing where from, you found yourself silently followed by invisible eyes of walls, courtyards, and alleyways [...] These bare villages ... As though you were actually to blame for anything that happened here?[71]

In a reading of Arendt's *Eichmann in Jerusalem*, Rose has suggested that the 'strength of Arendt's analysis' of the Eichmann trial 'is that she recognises that there is something deadly in the law'. In Rose's account, what Arendt calls the 'reason of state' takes the place of the moral law or superego, and instructs 'the most terrifying components of your own unconscious to go stalking'.[72] Rose's observation on the connection between the violence that the law can permit in the name of state security and the terrifying potential of the unconscious sheds significant light on the relationship between emergency law and the practices of

---

68 Jacqueline Rose, *The Question of Zion* (Princeton, NJ: Princeton University Press, 2005), p. 68.
69 Hans Kohn, 'Nationalism', in Arthur A. Cohen (ed.), *The Jew: Essays from Martin Buber's Journal 'Der Jude' 1916–1928* (Tuscaloosa, AL: University of Alabama Press, 1980), p. 30.
70 Kohn, 'Nationalism', p. 30.
71 Yizhar, *Khirbet Khizeh*, p. 27.
72 Rose, *The Last Resistance*, p. 146.

state violence that such a law enables. It is this legalised violence that troubles the narrator in *Khirbet Khizeh*. The 'bare villages' seem to confront the soldiers with their complicity in the ethnic cleansing of Palestine, and yet the soldiers are unable to acknowledge that they were 'to blame for anything', precisely because the military actions they are carrying out are part of the 'reason of state'. In the face of these empty villages, the narrator describes how 'some kind of question [...] posed itself of its own accord'. The narrator does not seem able to specify exactly what 'kind of question' poses itself in this encounter, but attempts instead to define this question through recourse to simile: 'like pity for a beggar or a revolting cripple'. This 'pity', he continues, 'left an unpleasant sourness [...] which merely irritated and pestered the soul'. And the only way to 'rid oneself' of this 'unpleasant sourness', the narrator adds, was to 'assume a furious glance and translate the glance into an out-and-out curse'.[73]

This 'furious' response to the empty Palestinian villages at *Khirbet Khizeh* may be interpreted as an example of what the French psychoanalyst Jacques Lacan called foreclosure. In the language of psychoanalysis, the term foreclosure denotes a form of psychic defence, one which involves the rejection of affect. In this respect, the term foreclosure bears a conceptual resemblance to the Freudian concept of repudiation – a term that refers to a psychic defence mechanism that Freud studied in patients suffering from psychosis, in which the 'ego rejects (*virwift*) the incompatible idea together with its affect and behaves as if the idea had never occurred to the ego at all'.[74] Jacques Lacan's use of the term foreclosure in his *Seminar I* expands and develops Freud's discussion of repression in his case study on the wolf-man, 'From the History of an Infantile Neurosis'.[75] Invoking the Hegelian concept of *Aufhebung*, Lacan emphasises that repression cannot 'purely and simply disappear, it can only be gone beyond'.[76] In Lacan's reading, foreclosure refers to the 'Something [that] has not yet been got over – which is precisely beyond discourse, and which necessitates a jump in discourse'.[77] In Yizhar's rendering of the Israeli soldier's response to the empty Palestinian villages, it is precisely the soldiers' complicity in the depopulation of Palestinian villages such as Khirbet Khizeh that they cannot accept, and so the feeling of 'pity' for the villages and their former inhabitants that 'left an unpleasant sourness [...] which merely irritated and pestered the soul' is rejected.[78]

Yet in spite of this attempt to reject the affect of pity and complicity associated with the depopulation of Palestinian villages in 1948 by cursing, this

---

73 Yizhar, *Khirbet Khizeh*, p. 27.
74 Sigmund Freud, *The Standard Edition of the Complete Psychological Works of Sigmund Freud*, vol. 3, ed. James Strachey (London: Hogarth Press and the Institute of Psycho-Analysis, 1953–74), p. 58.
75 Jacques Lacan, *The Seminar of Jacques Lacan Book 1: Freud's Papers on Technique*, trans. John Forrester (New York and London: Norton, 1988), p. 67.
76 Lacan, *The Seminar of Jacques Lacan Book 1*, p. 67.
77 Lacan, *The Seminar of Jacques Lacan Book 1*, p. 67.
78 Yizhar, *Khirbet Khizeh*, p. 27.

repressed event and the affect it produces cannot be 'got over'; instead, it returns to confront the narrator towards the end of the novella. In the following passage, the narrator reflects on the condition of exile that the formation of the state of Israel has brought about:

> Exalted in their pain and sorrow above our – wicked – existence they went on their way and we could also see how something was happening in the heart of the boy, something that, when he grew up, could only become a viper inside him, that same thing that was now the weeping of a helpless child.
>
> Something struck me like lightening. All at once everything seemed to mean something different, more precisely: exile. This was exile. This was what exile was like. This was what exile looked like.
>
> I couldn't stay where I was. The place itself couldn't bear me.[79]

The epiphany that marks the narrator's encounter with the Palestinian refugees here prompts the narrator to reflect on his 'wicked existence', and his complicity in the militarised occupation of Palestinian territory. More than this, the word 'exile' itself – *galut* in Hebrew – names the elusive question prompted by the empty Palestinian villages, and condenses the confused feelings that the narrator and the soldiers try to foreclose with a curse. Exile is also the condition subtending the 'reason of state' that empowered the Israeli soldiers to expel the Arabs from their villages: 'Our nation's protest to the world: exile! It had entered me, apparently, with my mother's milk. What, in fact, had we perpetrated here today?'[80] In the novel's denouement, the narrator thus calls into question the violent foundations of the state of Israel, the nationalist myth of Zionism and the non-existence of Palestinian political sovereignty.

If the narrator of *Khirbet Khizeh* articulated the ethical and existential crisis of the Zionist settler colonial subject at the precise moment of occupation during the 1948 war in a way that questions the ideological foundations of the Jewish state of Israel, such a narrative also forecloses the voice of the Palestinian refugee. For although the narrator recognises the devastating impact of the occupation in the faces of the Palestinian refugees he meets in the village of Khirbet Khizeh, and is able to draw a parallel between the Jewish and Palestinian experiences of exile, he is unable to engage in a dialogue with the Palestinian refugees he encounters. This failure not only marks the limits of the text's representation of Palestinian people, it also marks the limitations of psychoanalytic readings of Zionism and Zionist literature. For just as the novel reduces the Palestinian characters to symbols of guilt and exile, so psycho-analytic readings of Zionism can tend to reduce the Palestinian to a symptom of the repressed violence associated with the foundation of the state of Israel. As Ronit Lentin put it, 'Yizhar did not accord the Palestinians a voice or the right of resistance, turning them instead into "an uncontrollable symptom, clouding the Israeli consciousness"'.[81] *Khirbet Khizeh* certainly explores the way in which

79 Yizhar, *Khirbet Khizeh*, p. 104.
80 Yizhar, *Khirbet Khizeh*, p. 105.
81 Lentin, *Co-memory and Melancholia*, p. 118.

military orders empowered Jewish soldiers to expel the Palestinian population of Khirbet Khizeh from their land, but in denying the Palestinian characters in the novella a voice, it also overlooks the history, will and agency of the Palestinians. The writing of Kanafani and Khoury offers an important counterpoint to the foreclosure of the Palestinian refugee in Zionist narratives by examining the ways in which the agency and resistance of Palestinian refugees as well as the traumatic history of the Palestinians' dispossession and forced migration have been commemorated and narrativised, as we will see. In so doing, Kanafani and Khoury have made a significant critical contribution to a Palestinian tradition of the oppressed.

From the standpoint of the Palestinian refugees who were forced to leave their villages in 1948 by Zionist forces,[82] the condition of being stateless was framed as the *nakba*, or catastrophe. For Ahmad H. Sa'di and Lila Abu-Lughod the *nakba* is a watershed in Palestinian history because it marks the emergence of a Palestinian national and historical consciousness. As they explain,

> The Nakba is often reckoned as the beginning of contemporary Palestinian history, a history of catastrophic changes, violent suppression, and refusal to disappear. It is the focal point for what might be called Palestinian time. The Nakba is the focal point of reference for other events, past and future. The Balfour declaration of 1917 gains its significance from being followed by the Nakba. Landmark events in Palestinian history such as Black September, the massacre at Sabra and Shatila, Land Day, and the first and second intifadas would not have occurred if they had not been preceded by the Nakba, to which they refer back. The Nakba has become a key event in the Palestinian calendar – the baseline for personal histories and the sorting of generations. Moreover, it is the creator of an unsettled inner time. It deflects Palestinians from the flow of social time into their own specific history and often into a melancholic existence [...] or a ghostly nostalgia.[83]

In Sa'adi and Abu-Lughod's account, the Palestinians' collective public memory of the *nakba* provides a powerful counter-memory to the predominant myth of the birth of Israel as a struggle against European racism and anti-Semitism.[84] But the *nakba* also marks the 'melancholic existence' of a stateless nation, which is epitomised in Said's assertion that 'Palestine does not exist, except as a memory or, more importantly, as an idea, a political and human experience, and an act of sustained popular will'.[85] If, as Benjamin suggested, the history of the oppressed is a discontinuum in a dominant historical narrative,[86] the writing of Kanafani and Khoury can be seen to articulate the discontinuous structure

---

82 For a discussion of the exact number of Palestinians required to leave their home in 1948, see Benny Morris, *The Birth of the Palestinian Refugee Problem Revisited* (Cambridge: Cambridge University Press, 2004), pp. 602–4.

83 Ahmad H. Sa'di and Lila Abu-Lughod (eds), *Nakba: Palestine, 1948 and the Claims of Memory* (New York: Columbia University Press, 2007), p. 6.

84 Sa'di and Abu-Lughod (eds), *Nakba*, p. 6.

85 Said, *The Question of Palestine*, p. 5.

86 Benjamin, cited in McCole, *Walter Benjamin*, p. 295.

of dispossession and displacement associated with Palestine's history through the use of literary techniques such as analepsis and historiographic metafiction. Whereas Kanafani's use of analepsis in *Men in the Sun* obliquely evokes the traumatic experience of statelessness instantiated by the *nakba* through a temporally disjointed narrative, Khoury's use of historiographic metafiction in *Gate of the Sun* encourages readers to question the rhetoric of melancholia and martyrdom that has pervaded Palestine's national narrative since 1948. It is significant also that both narratives are preoccupied with the way in which gender inflects the emergent discourse of Palestinian nationalism. If Kanafani uses metaphors of castration to articulate the experience of statelessness and dispossession associated with the *nakba* and figures the body of the Palestinian woman as a trope of the land/nation, Khoury in *Gate of the Sun* examines the way in which the histories and experiences of Palestinian women refugees are often occluded in narratives of the Palestinian nation. In so doing, Khoury raises important questions about the constituency of the oppressed, and about women's contribution to the writing of Palestinian history.

The *Nakba* and the Refugee in Ghassan Kanafani's *Men in the Sun*

It is the singular historical experience of statelessness and the trauma of the *nakba* that marks Ghassan Kanafani's 1963 novella *Men in the Sun*.[87] Located on the border between Iraq and Kuwait, the novella depicts the plight of three male Palestinian refugees who have left their home in search of employment and a better life in Kuwait. Yet in a failed attempt to cross the border illegally in the tank of a water truck, the three protagonists perish while the border guards detain their driver at the checkpoint. On discovering the bodies of the deceased men in the empty water tanker, the Palestinian driver and smuggler, Abul Khaizuran, asks the question, 'Why didn't you knock on the sides of the tank? Why didn't you say anything? Why?'[88] Abul Khaizuran's questions can be read as highlighting the legal and political constraints preventing the three Palestinian refugees from acting or participating in public discourse. The three men cannot 'knock' or 'say anything' because they are stateless and illegal immigrants in Iraq who are not empowered to speak as sovereign subjects before the law that the border guards symbolise. And yet by highlighting the abject conditions of the Palestinian refugees' disenfranchisement and dispossession, Kanafani also enjoins readers to recognise Palestinians as a distinctive people with a shared culture and history.

In an extensive and illuminating reading of *Men in the Sun*, Joe Cleary has suggested that one of the aporias at the heart of *Men in the Sun* is 'that the novel demands a kind of strategic resistance it is unable to name'.[89] For Cleary,

---

87 Ghassan Kanafani, *Men in the Sun, and other Palestinian Stories*, trans. Hilary Fitzpatrick (London: Heinemann Educational, 1978).
88 Kanafani, *Men in the Sun*, p. 74.
89 Cleary, *Literature, Partition and the Nation State*, p. 219.

Kanafani's inability to name this 'strategic resistance' is partly a sign of the historical context in which the story is set. Since the novella takes place in 1958, at a time when 'the Palestinians seemed to have disappeared from the political map as an independent actor, and indeed as a people', *Men in the Sun* can be seen to reflect a 'hiatus in manifestations of Palestinian identity', which Rashid Khalidi has called the '"lost years" between 1948 and the emergence of the Palestinian Liberation Organization in 1964'.[90] Yet this constitutive aporia in the novella also relates to the challenge of writing a story about a place that does not officially exist: 'On the one hand, *Men in the Sun* attempts to give expression to the national longing for form but, at the same time, it sternly insists on the intractable obstacles that must be overcome if that dream is ever to be realised'.[91] In so far as the novella documents the traumatic affect of the *nakba* on the Palestinian population dwelling in exile, *Men in the Sun* can certainly be read as an example of what the literary critic Harlow has called 'resistance literature'. In Harlow's definition, resistance literature is a term that denotes writing that is situated in relation to Third World national liberation struggles and revolutionary movements. It is significant indeed that Harlow draws on Kanafani's 1966 study, *Literature of Resistance in Occupied Palestine*, to clarify her definition of resistance literature:

> Kanafani's critical essay was, significantly, written in 1966, before the June War of 1967 whose culmination in the defeat of the Egyptian and Jordan River and the Gaza Strip and the opening of the border between these territories, now referred to as the 'Occupied Territories', and Israel. As such, it proposes an important distinction between literature which has been written 'under occupation' and 'exile' literature. Such a distinction presupposes a people's collective relationship to a common land, a common identity, or a common cause on the basis of which it becomes possible to articulate the difference between the two modes of historical and political existence, between, that is, 'occupation' and 'exile'. The distinction presupposes furthermore an 'occupying power' which has either exiled or subjugated, in this case both exiled and subjugated, a given population and has in addition significantly intervened in the literary and cultural development of the people it has dispossessed and whose land it has occupied. Literature, in other words, is presented by the critic as an arena of *struggle*.[92]

Kanafani's essay was subsequently submitted as a document of the Third Afro-Asian People's Solidarity Conference, Beirut in 1967, and published in English translation in the summer 1968 issue of *Afro-Asian Writings*. In this essay, Kanafani details the impact of the disaster on the social composition of the population living in occupied Palestine: 'A whole generation, or more accurately, generations of intellectuals had left Palestine for exile, leaving only a predominantly

---

90 Rashid Khalidi, *Palestinian Identity: The Construction of Modern National Consciousness* (New York: Columbia University Press, 1997), p. 178.

91 Khalidi, *Palestinian Identity*, p. 220.

92 Harlow, *Resistance Literature*, p. 2.

rural Arab community subject to a cultural, social and political siege seldom known throughout the world'.[93] In Kanafani's argument, this experience of living and writing under a state of cultural siege produced a form of resistance literature known as 'siege poetry' that was 'spread by word of mouth, without being printed'.[94] Kanafani also describes how the Israeli state regulated Arab education and publishing, and suggests that this control of education and print culture limited the formation of a Palestinian national literature, and a Palestinian reading public. Against these constraints, Kanafani contends that love poetry provided a literary form that was able to articulate the loss of the homeland and the 'desertion' of those who left Palestine.

Kanafani's distinction between literature which has been written 'under occupation' and 'exile' literature may seem to clarify the differences between the condition of living as well as writing under occupation as compared to the condition of life in the Palestinian diaspora. In *The Secret Life of Saeed: The Ill-fated Pessoptimist* (1974), for example, the Palestinian writer Habiby depicts the conditions of life for Palestinians living in Israel using the generic conventions of Menippean satire. By behaving in an obsequious manner towards the Israeli authorities, Saeed not only mocks the 'oppressive system' of the Israeli occupation, but also foregrounds the 'passivity and complicity of its victims'.[95] In a conversation with an Israeli military leader called 'the big man', Saeed, the first-person narrator, recounts the 'lessons' that the 'big man' teaches him about following orders inside Shatta prison:

> While he was going through these lessons, I became ever more certain that what is required of us inside prison is no different from what is required of us on the outside [...] He went on, 'If a jailer should call you, your first response must be: "Yes sir!" And if he should tell you off, you must reply: "At your command, sir!" And if you should hear your fellow inmates engaging in any conversation that threatens the security of the prison, even by implication, you must inform the warden. Now if he should give you a beating, then say –'
> I interrupted him with the proper response, 'That's your right, sir!'
> How did you know that? Were you ever imprisoned before?
> 'Oh, no. God forbid, sir, that anyone should have beaten you to this favor! I have merely noticed according to your account of prison rules of etiquette and behavior that your prisons treat inmates with great humanitarianism and compassion – just as you treat us on the outside. And we behave the same, too.[96]

Here, Saeed performs the subservient verbal responses that the Israeli state requires of Palestinian prisoners, and in so doing mimics the power structures

---

93 Ghassan Kanafany [sic], 'Resistance Literature in Occupied Palestine', *Afro-Asian Writings: Quarterly of the Permanent Bureau of Afro-Asian Writers*, 1/2–3 (1968), p. 66.

94 Kanafany, 'Resistance Literature in Occupied Palestine', p. 66.

95 Stefan Meyer, *The Experimental Arabic Novel: Postcolonial Literary Modernism in the Levant* (Albany, NY: State University of New York Press, 2001), p. 60.

96 Emile Habiby, *The Secret Life of Saeed: The Ill-fated Pessoptimist*, trans. Salma Khedra Jayyusi and Trevor LeGassick (Northampton, MA: Interlink, 2003), p. 124.

that deny civil rights to Israel's Palestinian population. In the terms of the emergency regulations that existed in Israel between 1948 and 1966 to control the Palestinian population, the state's powers of administrative arrest and its severe restrictions on the movements of the Palestinian population inside and outside a designated area can be seen to blur the boundaries between prison and a democratic civil society.[97] Indeed, by suggesting that conditions for Palestinian prisoners inside Shatta prison are similar to those conditions outside the prison, Saeed implies that Israel's Palestinian population are treated with anything but 'humanitarianism and compassion'. In this way, Habiby can be seen to question Kanafani's distinction between Palestinian literature written from the standpoint of exile and Palestinian literature written under conditions of occupation. For whether they dwell under conditions of exile or occupation, the Palestinian population are stripped of their sovereignty and legal rights, and treated as an historically specific form of bare life – a concept to which I will return later on.

In formal terms, Habiby's satirical account of the conditions of life for Palestinians in Israel after 1948 in *The Secret Life of Saeed: The Ill-fated Pessoptimist* may appear to contrast strikingly with Kanafani's tragic account of the *nakba* in *Men in the Sun*. Yet like *The Secret Life of Saeed*, *Men in the Sun* does not offer a direct, transparent representation of the *nakba*. For, although the four main characters in *Men in the Sun* are Palestinian, the action of the novella 'takes place thousands of miles away on the border between Iraq and Kuwait'.[98] This apparent disjunction between the novella's national preoccupation (the loss of Palestine) and its geographical location is bridged by Kanafani's use of analepsis to register both the deferred action and the spatial displacement associated with the traumatic experience of the *nakba*.

One of the clearest examples of Kanafani's use of analepsis is the opening passage of the novella, in which Abu Qais, an old Palestinian peasant, recalls the loss of his homeland as he rests in the scorching heat of Basra. In this passage, Abu Qais links the scent and feeling of the 'damp ground' on the bank of the river Shatt to 'his wife's hair when she had just walked out of the bathroom, after washing with cold water'.[99] This detail is significant for two reasons. First, it illustrates the way in which the Palestinian nation is figured as feminine, and 'the national story becomes the story of the possession of the land/woman by a man'.[100] In the patriarchal logic of Kanafani's national narrative, the dispossessed masculine Palestinian subject in exile is by implication emasculated. This motif of the emasculated Palestinian refugee is an organising metaphor in *Men in the Sun*, as we will see. Second, this opening passage exemplifies the way in which Palestinian refugees such as Abu Qais are trapped in a condition of

---

97 Ilan Pappé, *The Forgotten Palestinians: A History of the Palestinians in Israel* (New Haven: Yale University Press, 2011), pp. 46–93.
98 Cleary, *Literature, Partition and the Nation State*, p. 198.
99 Kanafani, *Men in the Sun*, p. 21.
100 Amal Amireh, 'Between Complicity and Subversion: Body Politics in Palestinian National Narrative', *South Atlantic Quarterly*, 102/4 (2003), p. 751.

melancholia for the lost homeland. It is telling in this respect that Abu Qais interrupts his nostalgia for Palestine with the following admonition: 'Have you forgotten where you are? Have you forgotten?'[101] By forgetting where he is, Abu Qais begins to comprehend what it means to have lost his land, and what it is to live as a refugee. In so doing, Abu Qais contributes to the process of mourning the loss of the homeland, which can also be understood as part of a broader struggle for national self-determination. 'Perhaps the greatest battle Palestinians have waged as a people' Said contends, 'has been over the right to a remembered presence and, with that presence, the right to possess and reclaim a collective historical reality, at least since the Zionist movement began its encroachments on the land'.[102] By drawing attention to Abu Qais's nostalgia for his imaginary homeland, Kanafani encourages readers to recognise the constitutive role of memory in Palestine's national narrative.

At the precise moment Abu Qais recognises that he is on the banks of the Shatt, he recalls overhearing a geography lesson in Palestine ten years earlier, in which the village schoolteacher Ustaz Salim explains the physical geography of Iraq, and the source of the river Shatt in Basra. What is particularly noteworthy about this analeptic sequence is Abu Qais's commemoration of Ustaz Salim's death. In his account of how Ustaz Salim died fighting against the Israeli army during the *nakba*, Abu Qais asserts that 'God was certainly good to you when he made you die one night before the wretched village fell into the hands of the Jews'.[103] Such an act of commemoration is significant not only because it discloses a sacrificial logic in the construction of Palestine's national narrative, but also because it draws attention to the difference between a life (and death) lived under occupation and a life lived in exile. Ustaz Salim's death can be read as a desperate act of resistance to the condition of being occupied.[104] Indeed, for Abu Qais, Ustaz Salim's death is a sign of his political agency, sovereignty and resistance to colonial occupation; his act of heroism is that he 'stayed there'.[105] It is the memory of this heroic act that marks Abu Qais's own feelings of 'humiliation and wretchedness' as he fled 'across the desert to Kuwait to find a crust of bread'.[106]

What the dichotomy between occupation and exile overlooks, however, is the significance of the refugee as a political figure, and the insights that such refugee narratives contribute to understanding the trauma of dispossession associated with the *nakba*. In the patriarchal world of *Men in the Sun*, the experience of dispossession and displacement is figured in terms of emasculation and castra-

---

101 Kanafani, *Men in the Sun*, p. 21.
102 Edward W. Said 'Invention, Memory and Place', *Critical Inquiry*, 26/2 (2000), pp. 175–92.
103 Kanafani, *Men in the Sun*, p. 23.
104 For further discussion of the relationship between the colonial occupation of Palestine and biopolitics, see Diane Enns, 'Bare Life and the Occupied Body', *Theory and Event*, 7/3 (2004). Available at <http://muse.jhu.edu/journals/theory_and_event>. Accessed 25 August 2011. See also Mbembe, 'Necropolitics', pp. 36–40.
105 Kanafani, *Men in the Sun*, p. 23.
106 Kanafani, *Men in the Sun*, p. 24.

tion; it is a sign, in other words, of weakness and political passivity. In another central analeptic sequence, the narrator reveals how Abul Khaizuran, the 'excellent' Palestinian driver who tries to smuggle the three Palestinian refugees in his water tanker, was physically castrated after being wounded by a Zionist bomb during the 1948 war.[107] As the men are driving across the desert towards the border with Kuwait, Abul Khaizuran is blinded by 'the sunlight that had suddenly struck the windscreen',[108] and recalls a scene in a field hospital ten years earlier, which is evoked by the image of a 'circular light above his head'.[109] Following this metonymic chain of association, the third-person narrator proceeds to evoke the painful experience of Abul Khaizuran's castration during the 1948 war, and his inability to accept this loss ten years after the event:

> Now … ten years had passed since that horrible scene. Ten years had passed since they took his manhood from him, and he had lived that humiliation day after day and hour after hour. He had swallowed it with his pride, and examined it every moment of those ten years. And still he hadn't got used to it, he hadn't accepted it. For ten long years he had been trying to accept the situation? But what situation? To confess quite simply that he had lost his manhood while fighting for his country? And what good had it done? He had lost his manhood and his country, and damn everything in this bloody world.[110]

The explicit connection that Kanafani draws here between Abul Khaizuran's castration and the *nakba* suggests that the disfiguration of Abul Khaizuran's body is a symbol for the occupation of Palestine in 1948. To the extent that Abul Khaizuran's castration mirrors the emasculation of Abu Quais, Assad and Marwan, the three Palestinian refugees, the novella could be read as a national allegory, a concept that the cultural critic Fredric Jameson first introduced in his essay, 'Third-World Literature in the Era of Multinational Capitalism'. In Jameson's 'sweeping hypothesis', what distinguishes 'third-world texts' from their 'first-world counterparts' is that 'third-world texts' 'are to be read [...] as national allegories'.[111] What Jameson suggests, in other words, is that literary texts produced in the Third World necessarily reflect the history and socio-economic conditions of life in Third World nation states. Jameson's hypothesis has since provided a literary critical paradigm through which to interpret the metaphorical connection between the private world of familial relationships and sexual desire and the public world of politics, economics and communal violence in much postcolonial writing. Such a hypothesis might account for the destabilisation of the patriarchal family structure that is precipitated by the *nakba* in *Men in the Sun*. For just as Abu Qais is forced to leave his wife and children in search of a living wage in Kuwait, so the young teenager Marwan

---

107 Kanafani, *Men in the Sun*, p. 47.
108 Kanafani, *Men in the Sun*, p. 52.
109 Kanafani, *Men in the Sun*, p. 53.
110 Kanafani, *Men in the Sun*, p. 53.
111 Fredric Jameson, 'Third World Literature in the Era of Multinational Capitalism', *Social Text*, 15 (1986), p. 69.

leaves his family in Palestine in search of work after his father deserts his family for another woman, and he is forced to assume the paternal role as head of the household. That Marwan patently fails to live up to this masculine role in his confrontation with an Iraqi smuggler who humiliates him further underscores the parallel between masculine impotency and the significance of the Palestinian disaster. Yet if, as Jameson suggests, the literary form of the national allegory is overdetermined by the forces of 'indirect economic penetration and control' of Third World nation states[112] – forces which are exemplified by the increasing influence of the United States in Israel-Palestine[113] – Kanafani's narrative of Palestine in *Men in the Sun* would seem to stage the impossibility of a national allegory for Palestine.

One of the reasons for this impossibility is that the three protagonists are stripped of the political and human rights associated with national belonging, and would as a consequence appear to exemplify the condition of bare life that Agamben attributes to the refugee. In a commentary on Arendt's chapter 'The Decline of the Nation-State and the End of the Rights of Man' in her book *The Origins of Totalitarianism*, Agamben argues that 'the refugee is the sole category in which it is possible today to perceive the forms and limits of a political community to come'.[114] For Agamben, the figure of the refugee calls into question the universal claims of human rights declarations by 'breaking up' the assumption that the 1789 Declaration of the Rights of Man and the Citizen includes human subjects who are not citizens. What is more, the refugee highlights the fiction that national belonging is guaranteed by nativity or birth, and thereby 'throws into crisis the original fiction of sovereignty'.[115] For Agamben as for Arendt, it is the Nazi Holocaust of the European Jews that clearly exemplifies the failure of universal human rights declarations to protect the rights of human populations. Yet Agamben's argument also has important implications for understanding the condition of the Palestinian refugee. For just as Arendt argued in *The Origins of Totalitarianism* that the formation of the state of Israel had created a new population of Palestinian refugees and a new regime of violent political sovereignty, so Agamben suggests that the 'four hundred and twenty-five Palestinians who were expelled by the State of Israel' in the early 1990s and 'dwell in a sort of no-man's-land between Lebanon and Israel' constitute what Arendt termed 'the avant-garde of their people'.[116] Crucially for Agamben, Arendt's term 'does not necessarily or only mean' that these Palestinian refugees 'might form the original nucleus of a future national state'. For such a political solution 'would probably resolve the Palestinian problem just as inadequately as Israel has resolved the Jewish question'. Instead, Agamben argues that the 'no-man's-land' where the Palestinians have found refuge offers a means of altering the

---

112 Jameson, 'Third World Literature in the Era of Multinational Capitalism', p. 69.
113 See Bashir Abu Manneh, 'Israel in US Empire', *New Formations*, 59 (2006), pp. 34–51.
114 Giorgio Agamben, 'We Refugees', trans. Michael Rocke. Available at <www.egs.edu/faculty/agamben/agamben-we-refugees.html>. Accessed 8 April 2009.
115 Agamben, 'We Refugees'.
116 Agamben, 'We Refugees'.

political territory in such a way that 'the citizen will have learned to acknowledge the refugee that he himself [*sic*] is'.[117]

There is an important parallel to be drawn here between the expelled Palestinian refugees that Agamben describes in 'Beyond Human Rights' and the three refugees in *Men in the Sun* who inhabit a 'juridical "no-man's land" between states that defies representation'.[118] For the three male protagonists in *Men in the Sun*, the experience of exile is not only an ideological sign of a 'panicky or peremptory political strategy not firmly grounded in an objective and dispassionate appraisal of the political disabilities incurred by Palestinians after 1948'.[119] More than this, the historical experience of exile and statelessness provides an opportunity to question and challenge the dominant meaning of political sovereignty, citizenship and national belonging as defined by the state of Israel. The four protagonists of *Men in the Sun* may be unable to recognise or name the violence of political sovereignty and the limitations of national belonging. Yet such a reading is implicit in the novel's inability to imagine a form of collective political resistance to the traumatic experience of colonial dispossession and displacement that it documents.

If the tragic ending of *Men in the Sun* demands a form of collective political action that it is unable to name,[120] for the Lebanese novelist Khoury in his epic metafictional novel *Gate of the Sun* (1998), the relationship between the public commemoration of armed struggle and the promise of national liberation is a source of significant ethical concern and critical scrutiny. In aesthetic terms, this critical scrutiny is articulated as a radical literary experimentation with the form of the novel – a technique that not only builds on Khoury's earlier experiments with narrative form in novels such as *Little Mountain* or *The Journey of Little Gandhi*,[121] but may also appear to resemble the fragmentary narrative structure of *Men in the Sun*. Yet, such a formal comparison overlooks a crucial difference between the historical and political formations in which the two fictional narratives were produced. Kanafani's experiments with literary form in *Men in the Sun* were written in a context of tricontinental socialism when the role of the radical Palestinian writer and intellectual could be articulated to an emergent anticolonial struggle for self-determination. In Khoury's *Gate of the Sun*, by contrast, the idea of resistance literature proposed by Kanafani seems somewhat belated in the aftermath of over twenty years of armed struggle, violence and death in Lebanon and the Occupied Palestinian Territories; and following the widespread view among many Palestinians that the 1993 Oslo Accords were a betrayal of the national struggle for Palestinian self-determination. This is not to suggest that the critical reflections on the history of revolutionary nationalism

---

117 Agamben, 'We Refugees'.
118 Cleary, *Literature, Partition and the Nation State*, p. 198.
119 Cleary, *Literature, Partition and the Nation State*, p. 217.
120 Cleary, *Literature, Partition and the Nation State*, p. 219.
121 Elias Khoury, *Little Mountain*, trans. Maia Tabet (Manchester: Carcanet, 1989); idem, *The Journey of Little Gandhi*, trans. Paula Haydar (Minneapolis, MN: University of Minnesota Press, 1994). See also Meyer, *The Experimental Arabic Novel*, pp. 117–74.

expressed in *Gate of the Sun* are opposed to the idea of a Palestinian history of the oppressed that takes issue with Israel's colonial sovereignty over Palestine, and the methods it uses to secure that sovereignty. On the contrary, *Gate of the Sun* uses the techniques of historiographic metafiction and embedded story-telling to find a literary form that is appropriate to convey the fragmented and discontinuous structure of Palestine's history of the oppressed. In so doing, *Gate of the Sun* raises important questions about who 'the oppressed' are, and whether narratives of mourning, sacrifice and martyrdom are appropriate to articulate their history and struggle.

Historiographic Metafiction and the Palestinian History
of the Oppressed in Elias Khoury's *Gate of the Sun*

The disappointments and limitations of violent anti-colonial resistance to the occupation are clearly expressed in a central passage in *Gate of the Sun* where Khaleel, the first-person narrator, confesses to his father figure, mentor and comrade-in arms, Yunis, a coma patient in a Galilee field hospital, that

> I'm scared of a history that has only one version. History has dozens of versions, and for it to ossify into one leads only to death.
> We mustn't see ourselves only in their mirror, for they're prisoners of one story, as though the story had abbreviated and ossified them.
> Please, father – we mustn't become just one story. Even you, even Naheeleh – please let me liberate you from your love story, for I see you as a man who betrays and repents and loves and dies. Believe me, this is the only way if we're not to become ossified and die.[122]

It is significant first of all that Khaleel links his fear of monolithic versions of history to Yunis's 'love story', or the story of his relationship with his wife, Naheeleh. In Khaleel's account, Yunis did not fight 'for the land or for history' but 'for the sake of a woman [he] loved'.[123] Yet, as Khaleel suggests, this 'love story' may nonetheless be interpreted as an allegory of Palestine's national narrative if Naheeleh is understood as a gendered symbol of the nation. We have already seen how Kanafani frames the body of the Palestinian woman as a trope of the land/nation in *Men in the Sun*. Such metaphors may offer a powerful rhetorical technique for evoking the loss of sovereignty associated with the *nakba*, and the violent and exclusionary techniques of colonial sovereignty that Israel has mobilised against the Palestinian population since 1948.[124] Yet such a trope of the gendered nation does little to recognise the particular ways in which women have been treated as a gendered form of bare life in Palestinian

---

122 Elias Khoury, *Gate of the Sun*, trans. Humphrey Davies (London: Harvill Secker, 2005 [1998]), p. 275.
123 Khoury, *Gate of the Sun*, p. 275.
124 See Ophir, Givoni and Hanafi (eds), *The Power of Inclusive Exclusion*.

refugee camps – a form of life that Ronit Lentin has aptly called *femina sacre* in a powerful rereading of Agamben's theory of sovereign power and bare life.[125] And neither for that matter do such tropes help to recognise the contribution that Palestinian women have made to the struggle for Palestinian national self-determination.[126] By interrogating such metaphors, and the monolithic patri-archal national narrative they support, *Gate of the Sun* parallels the efforts of historians and sociologists such as Rosemary Sayigh and Ronit Lentin to articu-late the experiences of Palestinian women's lives in the refugee camps of South Lebanon and the occupied territories of the West Bank, as we will see.

It is this concern with the lives and deaths of Palestinians who are margin-alised and silenced by history that underpins Khaleel's refusal to reduce the historiography of Palestine to 'one version'. We have already seen in Chapter 5 how Felman equates Benjamin's concept of the tradition of the oppressed with the condition of being silenced or rendered expressionless. By foregrounding the danger of allowing a Palestinian history of the oppressed to become 'ossified' into a monolithic narrative of mourning for the dead heroes and martyrs of Palestine, *Gate of the Sun* offers an important critical supplement to Palestinian historiography.

Khaleel's critique of monolithic versions of history can also be read as a critique of the nationalist narratives of revolutionary violence, evidenced in the pamphlets and memoranda of revolutionary groups such as Fateh. In Fateh's rhetoric of the 1960s, for instance, military action and revolutionary violence were regarded as essential strategies in the mobilisation of the Pales-tinian people.[127] Such a causal link between revolutionary violence and political mobilisation is clearly evidenced in a Fateh memorandum of 1965, which boldly declared that

> We, the people of Palestine, are in need of a revolutionary upheaval in our daily lives after having been afflicted by the Catastrophe [of 1948] with the worst diseases of dependency, division and defeatism. This upheaval in [our] lives will not occur except through our practise of the armed struggle and our assumption of responsibility for it and leadership of it.[128]

The founding leaders of Fateh appropriated Fanon's writings on the Algerian revolution in *The Wretched of the Earth*, in which 'he stressed the "cleansing" or "purifying" effect of violence in the psyche of the oppressed', and compared

---

125 Ronit Lentin, 'Femina Sacra: Gendered Memory and Political Violence', *Women's Studies International Forum*, 29/5 (2006), pp. 463–73, and idem, 'Palestinian Women from Femina Sacra to Agents of Active Resistance', *Women's Studies International Forum*, 34 (2011), pp. 165–70.

126 See Rosemary Sayigh, 'Gendering the "Nationalist Subject": Palestinian Camp Women's Stories', in Gautam Bhadra, Gyan Prakash and Susie Tharu (eds), *Subaltern Studies*, vol. 10 (New Delhi: Oxford University Press, 1999), pp. 234–52.

127 Yazid Yusuf Ṣayigh, *Armed Struggle and the Search for State: The Palestinian National Movement, 1949–1993* (Oxford: Oxford University Press, 1997), p. 91.

128 Ṣayigh, *Armed Struggle and the Search for State*, p. 91.

the struggle of the Palestinians to 'the struggle waged by US blacks, the Mau Mau movement in Kenya, and the Algerians'.[129] For Khaleel in *Gate of the Sun*, however, violence is not purifying or redemptive, but rather a strategy without a clear political goal, as he asserts in a conversation with a group of Israelis who were involved in the massacre in the refugee camps of Shatila:

> We too killed and destroyed, but at that moment, I felt just how banal evil is. Evil has no meaning, and we were just its tools. We're nothing. We make war and kill and die, and we're nothing – just fuel for a huge machine whose name is War. I said to myself it's impossible. Especially with this Nasri, I felt as though I was standing in front of a mirror, as though he resembled me! If I'd been able to talk, I'd have talked more than he did, but a big stone stopped up my mouth.[130]

Khaleel's understanding of the banality of evil here is significant for two reasons. First, it is an obvious allusion to Arendt's thesis on the banality of evil in her report on the Eichmann trial of 1963, *Eichmann in Jerusalem*. As Khoury explains in an interview published in the journal *Banipal*,

> Hannah Arendt, when writing about Eichmann, tried to explain how the power structure dominating a whole society can lead to the 'banality of evil'. In the Lebanese context it is more complicated because everybody who lived through the Lebanese civil war experienced the feeling of becoming and reacting like an animal and worse.[131]

By invoking Arendt's study, Khoury clearly highlights the relationship between European anti-Semitism, the military occupation of Palestine and the wars in Lebanon. But Khoury's claim also gestures towards another reading of his use of Arendt, which questions the logic of revolutionary violence. In this reading, Khoury's allusion to Arendt in the context of the Palestinian liberation struggle recalls her cautionary remarks on the practice of revolutionary violence in anti-colonial liberation struggles. We have already seen in the Introduction and in Chapter 1 how Arendt cautioned against revolutionary violence 'even if it moves consciously within a nonextremist framework of short-term goals' on the grounds that the means of political violence will overwhelm the goal of political freedom, and violence will be introduced 'in the whole body politic'.[132] Here, Arendt seems to echo and amplify Fanon's own concern, hinted at in his criticism of spontaneity, that the tactic of revolutionary violence will become an end in itself.[133] In her critique of Fanon, Arendt is not simply disputing Fanon's suggestion that the use of violence in the context of national liberation from far more violent and systematic forms of colonial oppression is justified. On the

129 Ṣayigh, *Armed Struggle and the Search for State*, p. 91.
130 Khoury, *Gate of the Sun*, p. 256.
131 Elias Khoury and Sonja Mejcher, 'Elias Khoury: The Necessity to Forget – and Remember', *Banipal*, 12 (2001), pp. 8–14.
132 Arendt, *On Violence*, p. 80.
133 See Fanon, *The Wretched of the Earth*, pp. 83–86.

contrary, she is concerned that in this subordination of the political end or goal of national liberation to the means of violent struggle, the postcolonial state will itself perpetuate the very violent political formation of colonial power that the national liberation struggle was attempting to oppose.

It is partly this concern that violence has been introduced into 'the whole body politic' by the armed resistance struggle that seems to underpin Khaleel's critical reflections on the history and historiography of the Palestinian liberation struggle in *Gate of the Sun*. In an interview with Sonja Mejcher, Khoury insisted on a clear distinction between historical narrative and literary narrative, and yet at the same time, he suggested that the novel can also 'fill gaps': 'When asked about *Bab al-Shams*, I said that the victorious write history and the defeated stories. But actually I think that the novel can only fill gaps. It does not replace writing history, and it is not its role to do so'.[134] Khoury's contention that 'the novel can only fill gaps' resonates with the supplementary logic of the South Asian subaltern studies historians who have sought to rethink dominant historical records and archives from the perspective of those who are excluded from or marginalised by dominant nationalist narratives. For historians such as Ranajit Guha and Dipesh Chakrabarty, and for the literary critic Gayatri Chakravorty Spivak, the critical task of subaltern history is to imagine a historical narrative for which no official record or historical archive exists. In a similar vein, Khaleel in *Gate of the Sun* seeks to question and complicate the Orientalist view of Palestinian history as a history based on martyrdom and a politics of death. Khaleel confesses to Yunis that he had had a 'psychological reaction' to a conversation with the Israelis about the Lebanese civil wars, and that the 'stone that stopped in [Khaleel's] mouth' is the word 'intifada',[135] the Arabic word for resistance or shaking off. What Khaleel's momentary experience of inarticulacy seems to reinforce here is his earlier self-diagnosis as a 'tool' of evil and 'fuel for a huge machine whose name is War'. For if the stone that 'stopped up' his mouth is the word 'intifada', this word is part of a narrative of war of which Khaleel, like many Palestinians and Israelis, is a prisoner.

A crucial intertextual paradigm for Khaleel/Khoury's rewriting of Palestine's fragmented national narrative is *The Arabian Nights*. Like Shahrazad in *The Arabian Nights*, Khaleel 'employs the healing words of the act of narrating and their power to trigger memory and delay death'.[136] By telling stories to Yunis, in other words, Khaleel tries to prevent his friend and mentor's death – just as Shahrazad, the female narrator in *The Arabian Nights*, tells stories to her husband, the sovereign figure of Shahrayar, in order to prevent him from executing her. What is more, the *mise en abîme* narrative structure of *The Arabian Nights* provides Khoury with an apposite literary form to question the possibility of a single, unified Palestinian national narrative. Like Shahrazad, Khaleel

---

134 Khoury and Mejcher, 'Elias Khoury: The Necessity to Forget – and Remember', p. 11.
135 Khoury, *Gate of the Sun*, p. 257.
136 Maher Jarrar, '*The Arabian Nights* and the Contemporary Arabic Novel', in Saree Makdisi and Felicity Nussbaum (eds), *The Arabian Nights in Historical Context: Between East and West* (Oxford: Oxford University Press, 2008), p. 308.

weaves together the stories of a number of different characters whose lives have been marginalised and dislocated by the history of dispossession and conflict in the Occupied Palestinian Territories and the refugee camps of South Lebanon.

In his account of the story of Adnan, for instance, Yunis describes how this Palestinian refugee challenged the authority of an Israeli judge who attempted to charge him with infiltration and sabotage. In a riposte to the judge's sentence, Adnan boldly declares,

> This is the land of my fathers and my forefathers. I am neither a saboteur nor an infiltrator. I have returned to my land.
>
> When the judge announced the sentence, Adnan burst out laughing and slapped his hands together as though he'd just heard a good joke. The judge asked him what he thought he was doing.
>
> 'Nothing. But do you really think your state is going to last another thirty years?'
>
> The judge listened to the translation of the defendant's words, and as they were leaving, Adnan began yelling, 'Thirty years! Your state won't last, and I'll put you all on trial as war criminals'.[137]

By embedding Adnan's story within his narrative of Yunis's life, Khaleel foregrounds the injustice of the military occupation and questions the Israeli state's use of the law as a technique of colonial governmentality to justify the dispossession of the Palestinian people. Just as Shahrazad uses embedded stories to question and postpone King Shahrayar's use of violence to assert his sovereign power in *The Arabian Nights*, so Khaleel in recounting the story of Adnan appears to question the legality and justice of the military occupation. And yet, by revealing how Adnan subsequently goes mad after his imprisonment in an Israeli prison, Khaleel also questions heroic narratives of the Palestinian national liberation struggle: an idea that is epitomised in Khaleel's suggestion that revolutions – like people – go senile and ramble and wet themselves.[138] Just as Emile Habiby uses the figure of the madman in the asylum in *The Secret Life of Saeed: The Ill-fated Pessoptimist* to evoke and criticise the powerlessness of the Palestinian population dwelling in Israel, so Khoury uses the figure of a demented revolutionary to raise questions about the political efficacy of revolutionary violence.

Such critical reflections on the violent means used to counter the violence of colonial occupation are interwoven with Khaleel's elegies to Umm Hasan, the midwife exiled from Galilee who helped to deliver many of the children born in the Shatila refugee camp after 1948; Naheeleh, Yunis's long-suffering wife; and Shams, Khaleel's lover who led an armed detachment of PLO fighters known as 'Shams's group', who are caught up in the war of the camps in South Lebanon. Khoury's attempt to narrativise these women's lives draws attention to women's role in the Palestinian national liberation struggle – a role that parallels attempts by feminist historians such as Rosemary Sayigh to find an

137 Khoury, *Gate of the Sun*, p. 128.
138 Khoury, *Gate of the Sun*, p. 133.

appropriate methodology for reading women's agency and experience in the Palestinian liberation struggle and the civil wars in Lebanon. Khaleel's account of Shams recounts her abusive relationship with her first husband, and Khaleel's own infatuation with Shams as a lover and as a freedom fighter: 'The woman was amazing. After we'd made love and screamed and moaned, she'd light a cigarette and sit on the end of the bed and tell me about her adventures and her journeys. Sometimes she'd tell me she'd been in Amman, or Algiers, or Tunis'.[139] In Khaleel's monologue, Shams is presented as both a powerful agent of her own sexuality and as an important revolutionary figure in the PLO who is subsequently executed by a rival political group. Khaleel's fragmented history of Shams's life and death functions as a counterpoint to the patriarchal narrative of the masculine revolutionary hero that Yunis cautions against.

The stories of Umm Hassan and Naheeleh may seem to be less exceptional than the story of Shams in their contribution to the discourse of Palestinian revolutionary nationalism. Yet, as Khaleel suggests, their stories are no less significant than that of Shams. Ronit Lentin has emphasised the ways in which the Israeli state has targeted Palestinian women as boundary markers, as symbols of the Palestinian national struggle and as the producers of future generations.[140] Against this targeting of Palestinian women as ethnic subjects, Lentin traces the ways in which Palestinian women have attempted to resist the sovereign power of the Israeli state through 'participation in protests and vigils [...] membership in NGOs [...] political parties, rapping, participation in education [...] personal narratives as sites of empowerment [... as well as] armed resistance'.[141] In a similar vein, Rosemary Sayigh has argued that women's contribution to the resistance movement in the refugee camps of Lebanon was 'essential': 'in addition to "giving sons", they mothered *fedayy'een* from other parts of the diaspora, visited prisoners and the wounded, carried food and water to the battle front, mourned the dead, tended graves, sustained camp solidarity, and cleaned up after battles'.[142]

By beginning his narrative with the death of the midwife, Umm Hassan, Khaleel not only emphasises the important work that Umm Hasan did to support the lives of Palestinians living in the refugee camps, he also suggests that Umm Hassan memorised and disseminated the history of the Palestinians dwelling in the camps: 'Umm Hassan told me everything about Palestine',[143] as Khaleel puts it. Like Umm Hasan, Naheeleh played a crucial role in supporting the Palestinian struggle for national self-determination. This support is particularly exemplified in Naheeleh's refusal to divulge the location of Yunis's hiding place in a cave known as *Bab al-Shams* during her interrogation by the Israeli military, and the subsequent performance of a grief-stricken widow who mourns the loss of her martyred husband. As Khaleel explains,

139 Khoury, *Gate of the Sun*, p. 39.
140 Lentin, 'Palestinian Women from Femina Sacra to Agents of Active Resistance', p. 169.
141 Lentin, 'Palestinian Women from Femina Sacra to Agents of Active Resistance', p. 168.
142 Ṣayigh, 'Gendering the "Nationalist Subject"', p. 238.
143 Khoury, *Gate of the Sun*, p. 22.

Naheeleh woke to their [the Israeli military's] violent knocking, and when they failed to find you [Yunis] they took her in for a week-long interrogation. When she left the prison, she found the village surrounded and realised they'd let her out as bait to lure you with. She acted out her celebrated play and buried you, praying for your absent corpse and receiving condolences while she wept and wailed and smeared ashes on her face. Naheeleh's excessive carrying-on drove your mother crazy – the old woman couldn't see why she was behaving that way. She understood the play had to be staged to save you, but Naheeleh turned the play-acting into something serious. She wept as women weep. She lamented and wailed and fainted. She let down her hair and tore her clothes in front of everybody.[144]

In Khaleel's account, Naheeleh's mimicry of a Palestinian widow's grief for her martyred husband while she is under Israeli military surveillance is such a perfect imitation that it convinces Yunis's father that Yunis is really dead.[145] Yet the sacrifice Naheeleh makes to support her husband's involvement in the armed struggle also leads to the fragmentation of her subjectivity – a process of fragmentation that is exemplified in Khaleel's description of seven different Naheelehs.[146] Significantly, Khaleel implies that there is a parallel between the fragmentation of Naheeleh's subjectivity and Yunis's perception of his life 'as scattered fragments – from Palestine to Lebanon, from Lebanon to Syria, from one prison to another'.[147] This parallel is particularly significant because it foregrounds the ways in which the struggle for Palestinian national sovereignty is made possible by the tireless and often unacknowledged sacrifice of women's contribution to the Palestinian liberation struggle.

Conclusion

A consideration of the continuities between British colonial representations of Palestine during the mandate and Zionist representations of Palestine can help to illuminate the colonial genealogy of Israel's occupation of the Palestinian territories, and the techniques of governmentality it uses to maintain its sovereignty. As we have seen, literary narratives of the British mandate period in Palestine such as Callard's *The City Called Holy* not only highlight the role of colonial discourse in justifying the use of violent forms of sovereignty, they also tell us something about the use of the law as a technique of governmentality in Palestine. By reading Yizhar's *Khirbet Kizeh* after Callard's *The City Called Holy*, I have attempted to trace a mutually reinforcing relationship between the representation of Palestine as a lawless and uncivilised space ripe for settlement and the law-making violence of colonial sovereignty, which is exemplified in Israel's appropriation of the British mandatory government's emergency legislation. At

144 Khoury, *Gate of the Sun*, p. 122.
145 Khoury, *Gate of the Sun*, p. 123.
146 Khoury, *Gate of the Sun*, p. 372.
147 Khoury, *Gate of the Sun*, p. 373.

the same time, Yizhar's narrator's fictional account of the violent expropriation of the Palestinian population of Khirbet Khizeh that the Zionist military
orders enable raises important questions about the relationship between state
violence and the law in the formation of the Zionist settler project. This is not
to suggest, however, that Yizhar's critical reflections on the 1948 war and the
expropriation of Palestinian villages gives voice to the victims of the *nakba* or
to the collective will, agency and struggle of the Palestinians. Indeed, it is only
by reading Palestinian narratives with and against Zionist narratives such as
Yizhar's that one can begin to understand Zionism from the standpoint of its
victims. Certainly, the writing of Kanafani and Khoury provides a rich narrative
resource to think through and beyond the ideology of Zionism and its traumatic
impact on the lives and histories of the Palestinians. Yet far from offering a
coherent oppositional narrative to the nationalist narrative of Zionism, Kanafani's *Men in the Sun* and Khoury's *Gate of the Sun* trace the conditions of exile
and displacement that have rendered such a coherent oppositional narrative
impossible. It is partly for this reason that Kanafani and Khoury have adapted
experimental techniques of writing associated with modernism to evoke the
fragmentary and discontinuous narrative structure that Benjamin attributed to
the history of the oppressed. Such a fragmentary and discontinuous narrative
form does not merely reinforce the collective melancholia associated with the
nakba and the occupation of the West Bank and Gaza; on the contrary, both
Kanafani and Khoury have sought to trace the specific conditions and challenges
of writing a Palestinian history of the oppressed. Such a self-conscious approach
to historiography does not merely foreground the ways in which the sovereign
power of the Israeli state has relegated Palestinian women and men to a condition of bare life, it also valorises the historical experience of exile and statelessness as a radical position from which to pose important questions about the
exclusionary foundations of Israel's national narrative as it is defined by the
dominant discourse of Zionism.

Conclusion

This book has assessed the ways in which states of emergency operated as a technique of governmentality in former European colonial states and the postcolonial legacies of such laws and techniques. As a law that suspends the normal rule of law, colonial states of emergency cannot be understood with reference to the rule of law alone, but also demand an engagement with the technologies of power, discourse and representation that stabilise particular formations of colonial sovereignty. As we have seen, colonial stereotypes and narratives have played a significant role in framing anti-colonial insurgents as the cause of colonial states of emergency and the often violent and repressive practices of counter-insurgency they enable. In different ways, the representation of the Indian revolutionary in Candler's *Siri Ram Revolutionist*, of the Mau Mau in Ruark's *Something of Value*, and the FLN in Larteguy's *Les centurions*, can be seen to justify the law-preserving violence of the colonial state. Against such stereotypes and narratives, writers such as Wicomb, Ngũgĩ, Djebar and Khoury have not only contested the truth claims of colonial narratives of emergency, they have also articulated forms of agency and collective resistance to colonial sovereignty and its often violent postcolonial legacies. In so doing, they have tried to do justice to the fragmented and often traumatic history of the oppressed.

A consideration of the colonial genealogy of states of emergency can also shed light on contemporary formations of colonial power and counter-insurgency, which Gregory has aptly called the colonial present. In common with Gregory, this book has examined the legal and extra-legal techniques of power that have been used in a range of different colonial situations in order to suggest continuities between the colonial past and the colonial present. Yet whereas Gregory considers how colonial interventions in Palestine, Afghanistan and Iraq have been made possible by 'imaginative geographies' of those territories that have been produced by 'regimes in Washington, London, and

Tel Aviv', this book has focused more specifically on the various ways in which literary texts have either contributed to or contested the use of emergency law as a technique of colonial power and sovereignty. To assess the value of such a critical approach for understanding the colonial present, this concluding chapter aims to consider first how the readings of the literary prose of counter-insurgency and legal narratives of emergency presented in the main body of this book shed light on contemporary formations of counter-insurgency and stereo-typical representations of Muslims in the 'post-9/11' novel; and second, how contemporary writers of Muslim background have attempted to challenge and contest the framing of Muslims as violent extremists. In so doing, this chapter suggests that contemporary fiction by writers of Muslim background not only highlights the imperialist provenance of contemporary British and American foreign policy and the stereotypical representations that stabilise that policy, it also offers a narrative form through which to re-imagine the historical legacies of anti-colonialism as a countervailing narrative to the 'war on terror' and its aftermath.

One of the aims of this book has been to examine how particular colonial regimes have used the law as a technique of power to produce states of exception, and how the literary prose of counter-insurgency has produced narratives and stereotypes that often reinforce those laws and states of exception. A critical analysis of the law's historical implication in colonial states of emergency also suggests strong parallels with contemporary formations of colonial sovereignty, as the legal theorist Nasser Hussain has argued. In an article on the United States detention camps at Guantánamo Bay, Hussain contends that 'Guantánamo points to a long history of imperial powers carving out spaces on the globe not only for their military and geopolitical needs but also as depositories for their "dangerous classes"'.[1] In Hussain's argument, this colonial origin 'should not lead us to conclude' that 'Guantánamo is and always has been a space beyond regular law'.[2] 'What is typically colonial about' the United States government's claim over Guantánamo Bay, Hussain adds,

> is not that they claim a space is beyond law but rather that a space is between laws, in the interstices of multiple legal orders. What is claimed is a mixture of laws and legal orders that both ties the space to the metropole and yet demands that it be free of some legal constraints.[3]

Hussain's suggestion that the colony is defined in juridical terms by its position at 'the interstices of multiple legal orders' is certainly borne out in the militarisation of the Royal Irish Constabulary during the nineteenth and early twentieth centuries; in the formulation of the sedition law in the British Indian Penal Code, and in the drafting of Kenya's emergency legislation during the last decade of British colonial rule, as we have seen. It is also worth noting that the

1 Nasser Hussain, 'Beyond Norm and Exception: Guantánamo', *Critical Inquiry*, 33/4 (2007), p. 737.
2 Hussain, 'Beyond Norm and Exception: Guantánamo', p. 737.
3 Hussain, 'Beyond Norm and Exception: Guantánamo', p. 738.

relationship between the law of the metropolis and that of the colony outlined by Hussain was reversed during the riots in the Parisian *banlieu* of 2005: in this example, the emergency decrees passed during the Algerian liberation struggle in the 1950s provided a legal framework for the French state to contain the Parisian riots of 2005.[4]

A consideration of statutes and legal reports may reveal the scope of the repressive measures which emergency regulations empowered institutions such as the police and the military to use in particular colonial situations in order to maintain sovereignty. Yet it is often what such legal texts do not say – the ellipses, tacit assumptions and contradictions – that help us to comprehend the relationship between emergency laws and the violent forms of colonial govern-mentality that such laws permit. It is these grey areas between the legal and the extra-legal that this book has sought to unpack through close readings of the literary prose of counter-insurgency and emergency law from the era of European colonialism and its aftermath. In the colonial present, such a critical task continues to be important, especially in the face of the production of new legal terms, categories and subjects that work to codify and even mask the law-making violence of the state. During the 'war on terror', the production of the new category of the 'unlawful' or 'enemy combatant' has allowed the Bush administration's legal team to argue that the Geneva Convention and the laws of armed conflict '"do not protect" members of al Qaeda and the Taliban militia'.[5] This quasi-legal category of the 'enemy combatant' has worked in mutually reinforcing ways with media and cultural representations to frame, detain and criminalise Muslims. Developments in the 'post-9/11 novel' have tended to contribute to these pernicious stereotypes of Muslims by suggesting that Islam is the cause of political violence, rather than examining the ways in which different Muslim populations have been the victims of a violent western foreign policy in Palestine, Afghanistan and Iraq. In this respect, the writing of Martin Amis and Ian McEwan bears a certain resemblance to the literary prose of counter-insurgency in India, Kenya, Algeria and Israel-Palestine, as we will see.

Representations of Muslims in the Post-9/11 Novel

Over the last decade, the western media has been replete with Islamophobic stereotypes that associate Muslims with terrorism, Sharia law, the practice of veiling and the preaching of global jihad. From the notorious cartoon illus-trations depicting the Prophet Muhammad in the Danish newspaper *Jyllands-Posten* and the representation of the Muslim cleric Abu Hamza al-Masri as a synecdoche for the British Muslim population to the television images of Pales-

4 See Sylvie Thénault, 'L'état d'urgence (1955–2005). De l'Algérie coloniale à la France contemporaine: destin d'une loi', *Le Mouvement social*, 218 (janvier–mars 2007), pp. 63–78.
5 Karen J. Greenberg, 'Caught in the War on Terror', in Karen J. Greenberg, Joshua Dratel and Jeffrey Grossman (eds), *The Enemy Combatant Papers: American Justice, the Courts, and the War on Terror* (Cambridge: Cambridge University Press, 2008), p. x.

tinians cheering in response to the attacks of 11 September 2001, the representation of Muslims in the western media reconfigures an orientalist conceit. As Said emphasised in *Covering Islam* (1981), the dominant, western-based global media and government experts tend to reproduce damaging verbal and visual images of the Muslim world in order to justify western economic and foreign policies towards Iran, Iraq, Palestine, Pakistan or Afghanistan.[6]

The prevalent image that Said refers to describes certain verbal and visual stereotypes that are reproduced by the western media and foreign policy to stand in for the Muslim world.[7] In the aftermath of the global 'war on terror', Said's reflections seem strikingly apposite. For Peter Morey and Amina Yaqin,

> Said succinctly captures what we would call the frame governing representations of Muslims and the resulting attenuation of real knowledge about what is in fact a heterogeneous set of cultural systems, when he suggests that there is an 'incitement to discourse' about Islam, which 'canonizes certain notions, texts and authorities' confirming its 'medieval', 'dangerous' and 'hostile' nature.[8]

Following Maxwell McCombs's analysis of the media frame, Morey and Yaqin further claim that in the global discourse of terrorism, Muslims are framed in the terms of 'belonging, "Otherness" and threat'.[9] In mainstream popular cultural narratives such as Fox's US thriller series, *24*, for instance, the figure of the 'Muslim terrorist' is framed as a dangerous enemy within: a westernised Muslim who is marked as a threatening 'Other' even though that figure also performs the rituals associated with the Protestant work ethic and the heteronormative nuclear family.[10]

The framing of Muslims in the dominant discourse of terrorism has also provided the justification for political techniques such as the suspension of human rights for Muslims in the diaspora, the 'rendition' of Muslims suspected of terrorism to locations beyond the jurisdictions that guarantee the rights of such prisoners and the indefinite detention of so-called 'enemy combatants' at global war prisons such as Camp Delta, Guantánamo Bay. Judith Butler has shown how the 'racial and ethnic frames by which the human is currently constituted' are also crucial to the techniques of US imperial sovereignty employed during the 'war on terror'.[11] Citing the Bush administration's argument that 'the involuntary hospitalization of mentally ill people who pose a danger to themselves and others' provides a 'legal precedent' for the detention of 'suspected terrorists' without criminal charge, Butler argues that such

---

6 Edward W. Said, *Covering Islam: How the Media and the Experts Determine How We See the Rest of the World* (London: Vintage, 1997), p. 144.
7 Said, *Covering Islam*, p. 147.
8 Peter Morey and Amina Yaqin, 'Muslims in the Frame', *Interventions*, 12/2 (2010), pp. 145–56 (146).
9 Morey and Yaqin, 'Muslims in the Frame', p. 147.
10 See Peter Morey, 'Terrorvision', *Interventions*, 12/2 (2010), pp. 251–64.
11 Judith Butler, *Precarious Life: The Powers of Mourning and Violence* (London: Verso, 2006), p. 90.

an analogy has broad and significant implications.[12] Specifically, the imagery and rhetoric framing the stereotype of the 'Muslim terrorist' as an irrational and dangerous Other is as important to the techniques of 'extraordinary rendition', indefinite detention, and torture employed during the 'war on terror' as those techniques of counter-insurgency themselves. For this reason, it is crucial that we consider the extent to which literary and cultural representations of Muslims have participated – either directly or indirectly – in the techniques of US imperial sovereignty, which Priyamvada Gopal has aptly called the 'war on terror'.[13]

One might assume that developments in the so-called 'post-9/11 novel' would offer a more nuanced representation of Muslims than that which is offered in American popular cultural narratives such as *24*. It may thus strike some readers as surprising to find that the very analogy between the 'Muslim terrorist' and the mentally ill, which Butler critiques in *Precarious Life*, is reiterated in McEwan's novel *Saturday* (2005). Focalised through the consciousness of Henry Perowne, a neurosurgeon living in a large house on London's Fitzrovia Square, the novel details Perowne's ambivalence about the demonstration in London against the Iraq war in March 2003 and documents his encounter with Baxter, a criminal figure suffering with Huntingdon's disease who forcibly enters Perowne's home and attempts to sexually assault his daughter, Daisy, after Perowne and Baxter collide in a car accident. In this novel, it is McEwan's use of Mathew Arnold's poem 'Dover Beach' that provides the cultural frame of reference for the novel's codified representation of Muslims. As a staunch advocate of the ideological role of culture at a time of religious crisis, the allusion to Arnold functions as a metonym for a timeless view of the literary artwork that can counter the anarchy associated with the Iraq war. As some critics have noted, it is precisely Daisy's performance of Matthew Arnold's poem 'Dover Beach' that prevents her from being sexually assaulted by the deranged and degenerate working-class figure of Baxter in front of her family at their London home in Fitzrovia. Elaine Hadley, for example, states that 'at the climactic crisis in Ian McEwan's recent novel, *Saturday* (2005), set in the days before the United States declares war on Iraq, Matthew Arnold's "Dover Beach" (1867) saves the day'.[14] It is by reciting part of Arnold's poem, argues Hadley, that Daisy manages to magically 'tranquilize the savage pathology of a home intruder'.[15] It is moments such as these which lead Arthur Bradley and Andrew Tate to suggest that '*Saturday* is a fragile profession of faith in the supernatural power of literature itself'.[16] McEwan's use of

---

12 Butler, *Precarious Life*, p. 72.
13 Priyamvada Gopal, 'Of Capitalism and Critique: Trajectories of Anglophone Pakistani Fiction after September 11th 2001', Paper presented at 'South Asian Fiction: Contemporary Transformations' Conference, 3 November 2012.
14 Elaine Hadley, 'On a Darkling Plain: Victorian Liberalism and the Fantasy of Agency', *Victorian Studies*, 48/1 (2005), p. 92.
15 Hadley, 'On a Darkling Plain', p. 92.
16 Arthur Bradley and Andrew Tate, *The New Atheist Novel: Fiction, Philosophy and Polemic after 9/11* (London: Continuum, 2010), p. 34.

Matthew Arnold in the novel thus raises broader questions about the novel's relationship to the ideology of liberal humanism (with which Arnold's writing and criticism are associated) prior to the start of the war in Iraq in March 2003. Such questions are played out in the third-person narrator's reflections on the war, which are focalised through the eyes of Perowne. In a heated exchange with his daughter about the war and the anti-war demonstration in London, Perowne accuses Daisy of being a member of the iPod generation which ignores Saddam's military dictatorship: 'The genocide and torture, the mass graves, the security apparatus, the criminal totalitarian state'.[17] He also points out that the Bali bombings were an attack on western liberal lifestyles: 'What do you think the Bali bombing was about? The clubbers clubbed. Radical Islam hates your freedom'.[18] Perowne's supposedly liberal defence of the war and his critique of Islam may seem to reinforce the Blair government's case for the war in Iraq, and it is this political stance – however ambivalent or plural it might be – that has prompted one reviewer to suggest that the novel might have been the product of a Tony Blair appointed committee.[19] Such a reading may overlook those moments in the novel wherein the third-person narrator encourages us to think critically about Perowne's liberal beliefs and values. For the narrator says at one point in the novel that Perowne recognises that he has become a 'docile citizen' who has 'lost the habits of scepticism [... and] isn't thinking independently'.[20] Yet McEwan's narrator not only foregrounds the contradictions and problems with Perowne's liberal view of contemporary geopolitics and Islam, he also draws attention to his attempt to discipline and control Baxter's very body and life. For after Perowne and his son successfully overpower Baxter by knocking him down the staircase and rendering him unconscious, Perowne proceeds to surgically remove a blood clot from Baxter's brain in a local hospital. This act of care towards a violent criminal suffering from mental illness may seem to be unusual, but I would suggest that it is consistent with the novel's critical engagement with the ideology of liberalism. For Perowne's clinical treatment of Baxter mirrors the liberal British state's regime of biopolitical control: the attempt to control and regulate the life of the population, and those individuals and groups who transgress its norms and values. What I am suggesting, in short, is that the novel's representation of Perowne's clinical treatment of Baxter as a dangerous individual parallels the British state's attempt to control its Muslim population.

Baxter's act of terror could be understood as an attempt to assert his sovereignty over his own life in response to Perowne's attempt to control the life and death of subjects who are deemed to threaten the values of the liberal state. And by framing Baxter in this way, McEwan encourages readers to think about the parallels between Baxter's degeneracy and what Perowne calls 'Radical Islam'.[21]

17 Ian McEwan, *Saturday* (London: Vintage, 2006), p. 191.
18 McEwan, *Saturday*, p. 191.
19 John Banville, 'A Day in the Life', *New York Review of Books*, 26 May 2005, p. 14.
20 McEwan, *Saturday*, p. 181.
21 McEwan, *Saturday*, p. 191

For if Perowne's attempt to diagnose Baxter's violent actions against his family are understood as an attempt to reform and civilise Baxter, this narrative could be read as an allegory for the British state's attempt to define and produce a 'good British Muslim' subject in the aftermath of 9/11 and 7/7.

Yet for all the self-consciousness of *Saturday*, there are clearly limitations to McEwan's critical engagement with British liberalism. In an interview published in the *Telegraph* magazine, McEwan has spoken against the charge that criticising Islam is racist. As he puts it, 'Chunks of left-of-centre opinion have tried to close down the debate by saying that if you were to criticise Islam as a thought system you are a de facto racist. That is a poisonous argument'.[22] In making this claim, McEwan seems to ignore how the criticism of Islam has been linked to the framing of Muslims in the current 'global war on terror'. Such an Islamophobic discourse has allowed western nation states to define Muslims as a threat to the secular, democratic values of liberal societies. Yet in contemporary fiction, this Islamophobic discourse is often codified. In his short story 'The Last Days of Muhammad Atta', Amis attempts to forensically reconstruct the thoughts and bodily ablutions of Atta on 10 September 2001. Drawing on *The 9/11 Commission Report* and the instruction manual given to each of the men involved in the attacks on America of 11 September, the story proceeds to suggest that Muhammad Atta was a misogynist and a cold-blooded killer. At one point in the story, the narrator describes how Atta had been given 'a four page booklet in Arabic, put together by the Information Office in Kandahar (and bound by a grimy tassel)',[23] but he had chosen not to read this until the day before their deadly mission. By fictionalising Atta's last day, Amis recounts how Atta is unable to separate his mind and his body, or to achieve 'sublimation by means of jihadi ardour'.[24] Instead, Amis suggests that Atta was motivated by what he calls the 'core reason':

> The core reason was of course all the killing – all the putting to death. Not the crew, not the passengers, not the office workers in the Twin Towers, not the cleaners and the caterers, not the men of the NYPD and FDNY. He was thinking of the war, the wars, the war cycles that would flow from this day.[25]

Amis's suggestion that Atta's reasons for participating in this attack were to provoke more death might seem to question the religious rhetoric that was invoked in the instruction manual to frame the attack. In this respect, Amis's fictionalisation of Atta could be seen to interrogate the causal relationship that has been drawn between religion and violence. The anthropologist Talal Asad, for instance, has suggested that what has been described in the western media as 'the Islamic roots of violence' is very misleading because it assumes

---

22 Stephen Adams, 'Ian McEwan: Criticising Islam is not racist', *The Telegraph Magazine*, 13 March 2010.

23 Martin Amis, 'The Last Days of Muhammad Atta', in idem, *The Second Plane: September 11: 2001–2007* (London: Vintage, 2008), p. 100.

24 Amis, 'The Last Days of Muhammad Atta', p. 101.

25 Amis, 'The Last Days of Muhammad Atta', p. 122.

a necessary correlation between religion and violence, where there is no such correlation. The crucial point for Asad is that religion is supplementary to an 'act of terrorism': it can under certain circumstances provide a transcendental structure that justifies acts of violence in retrospect, but a scriptural precedent is not in itself essential for a violent act to be carried out.[26] Yet in 'The Last Days of Muhammad Atta' there are clear limits to Amis's interrogation of the equation of violence and religion. Specifically, Amis's attempt to evoke the interior consciousness of Muhammad Atta can be read as a criminal psychological profile that encourages readers to equate Muslims with terrorism, even if the protagonist of Amis's story is an apostate who seems to be more motivated by nihilism and a fear of endless existence than a commitment to religious extremism.[27] In doing so, Amis provides further justification for the criminalisation of Muslims in the 'war on terror'. Such a view is reinforced by Amis's notorious argument in an interview published in *The Times Magazine* that

> The Muslim community will have to suffer until it gets its house in order. What sort of suffering? Not letting them travel. Deportation – further down the road. Curtailing of freedoms. Strip-searching people who look like they're from the Middle East or from Pakistan [...] Discriminatory stuff, until it hurts the whole community and they start getting tough with their children.[28]

Amis's literary and non-literary representations may not have the same authority as the law, but his framing of Muslims and of Islam as a threat to western liberal values aids and abets the argument for emergency legislation that empowers western liberal states to discipline and punish individuals it deems to be dangerous. And in this respect, Amis's writing on Muslims can be seen to parallel the causal logic that underpins colonial narratives of counter-insurgency.

Writing against the Prose of Counter-insurgency in the Colonial Present

It is precisely this mutually reinforcing relationship between cultural representations of Muslims and the techniques of law and sovereign power used to frame and detain Muslims that former prisoners who were arrested and detained at Guantánamo Bay have sought to question and challenge through the conventions of life-writing. In his prison memoir *Enemy Combatant* (2006), Moazzam Begg details the circumstances that led to his arrest and imprisonment and the lived experience of detention. Following his abduction by American and Pakistani intelligence services from his family home in Islamabad, Begg describes how the British secret service appears to be indifferent to his treatment, and complicit with the American intelligence service in his detention and framing. The stony-faced response of one MI5 agent to Begg's request for access to the

---

26 See Talal Asad, *Formations of the Secular: Christianity, Islam, Modernity* (Stanford: Stanford University Press, 2003), and idem, *On Suicide Bombing* (Stanford: Stanford University Press, 2007).

27 See Bradley and Tate, *The New Atheist*, pp. 53–55.

28 Martin Amis interviewed by Ginny Dougary, *The Times Magazine*, 9 September 2006.

British Consulate after his arrest, and the feeling that the British secret service abandons him, prompts Begg to surmise that the agent regards him as 'a Paki' rather than a British citizen.[29] In so doing, Begg implies that the production of subjects as enemy combatants in the 'global war on terror' is bound up with a racist discourse that excludes certain groups of people from the category of (British) citizen – a form of exclusion that enables enemy combatants to be detained indefinitely and tortured with impunity. Indeed, Begg's lived experience of state kidnapping and detention works to destabilise the legal rights that he takes for granted as a British citizen:

> I didn't know what the parameters of the law were anymore: everyone had said that after 9/11, new laws had taken immediate effect in the US, and that was frightening. How could American laws apply, in retrospect, to a British citizen, who had never travelled west of Dublin, for crimes that never existed in the first place?[30]

After his journey in a US military aircraft from Islamabad to Afghanistan, Begg evokes the experience of being 'under military jurisdiction', of being verbally and physically abused by US troops, being forcibly strip searched, and having his beard removed. For Begg, what was 'most humiliating […] was witnessing the abuse of others, and knowing how utterly dishonoured they felt'. 'These were men', he says referring to the other prisoners,

> who would never have appeared naked in front of anyone, except their wives; who had never removed their facial hair, except to clip their moustache or beard; who never used vulgarity, nor were likely to have had it used against them. I felt that everything I held sacred was being violated, and they must have felt the same.[31]

Against the sovereign power of the Bush administration and the US military, which sought to define him as an enemy combatant who should be stripped of the legal rights defined by the terms of the Geneva Convention and International law, Begg uses the techniques of life-writing to construct a writerly self that persistently questions the authority of his captors and the suspension of his political rights, and affirms his cultural identity as a British Muslim. In a letter addressed to the military administration in Guantánamo, for example, Begg presses his captors for 'an explanation of all [his] rights'; 'access to a telephone that is able to call [his] family in the UK'; 'a full inventoried list, detailing all items seized from his residence in Islamabad, Pakistan on January 31st 2002'; and 'a full and legitimate explanation as to why [he has] been held in solitary confinement since [his] arrival in Cuba on February 8, 2003'.[32] By demanding his rights as a British citizen 'under US and international law pertaining to deten-

---

29 Moazzam Begg, *Enemy Combatant: A British Muslim's Journey to Guantanamo and Back* (London: Free Press, 2006), p. 10
30 Begg, *Enemy Combatant*, p. 200
31 Begg, *Enemy Combatant*, p. 112
32 Begg, *Enemy Combatant*, pp. 60–61

tion' when it is precisely those rights to have rights that have been withdrawn by the US military in redefining his body as enemy combatant 'number 00558',[33] Begg draws attention to the performative contradiction of making a formal legal demand as a British citizen who has been stripped of the very rights associated with citizenship. Despite this contradiction, Begg uses the conventions of life-writing to construct a narrative of his own embodied life during his detention that circumvents the constraints of the military regime in the camp. Begg's account of his daily exercise regime and his confession that this made him 'very fit',[34] his outspoken refusal to recognise the military terminology that is used to describe him and to justify his detention[35] and his fearless defiance of his interrogators exemplify the ways in which he attempted to construct a self that refuses the sovereignty of the US military over his bodily life.

Moazzam Begg also describes his experience of negotiating with the official military language and procedures that were used by his interrogators to justify his detention as Kafkaesque.[36] Such a parallel seems particularly apposite when one considers that Begg's detention without trial was founded in part on a signed confession that was obtained under the threat of torture. In a reading of Kafka's *The Trial* and 'In the Penal Colony', Giorgio Agamben has argued that confession and torture are bound together. For Agamben, Josef K.'s self-slandering exemplifies the way in which the law depends on the baseless self-accusation of the human subject, which Agamben distinguishes from a confession.[37] Whereas the baseless self-accusation is a 'strategy that seeks to deactivate and render inoperative the accusation, the indictment that the law addresses toward Being', the 'one who has confessed is already judged'.[38] Yet if a confession is obtained under torture, how is this different from a baseless self-accusation? By emphasising the falsity of his signed confession, and the use of torture to obtain this confession, Moazzam Begg suggests that his confession to interrogators is nothing more than a baseless self-accusation obtained through the use of force. In so doing, Begg also questions the demonisation and dehumanisation of detainees at Guantánamo Bay.

If Begg's *Enemy Combatant* uses the conventions of life-writing to contest the extra-legal grounds of his detention, Hamid's novel *The Reluctant Fundamentalist* (2007) foregrounds the mutually reinforcing relationship between cultural stereotypes of Muslims and the law-preserving violence of the United States government during the 'war on terror'. By framing the narrative as a monologue between Changez, a recently returned Pakistani immigrant from the United States, and an unnamed American visitor to Lahore, whom Changez suspects of being an undercover intelligence agent, Hamid places the reader in the

---

33 Begg, *Enemy Combatant*, p. 260.
34 Begg, *Enemy Combatant*, p. 319.
35 Begg, *Enemy Combatant*, p. 324
36 Begg, *Enemy Combatant*, p. 155.
37 Giorgio Agamben, 'K.', in idem, *Nudities*, trans. David Kishik and Stefan Pedatella (Stanford, CA: Stanford University Press, 2011), pp. 20–36.
38 Agamben, 'K.', pp. 24–25.

position of the unnamed American, who is encouraged to pass judgement on Changez' story and character. In doing so, the narrative foregrounds how the legal violence of the US-led 'war on terror' works in mutually reinforcing ways with cultural stereotypes of Muslims, such as Changez. Bhabha has suggested that the cultural stereotype is a particular kind of fetish, or a sign of cultural difference, which conceals a lack of difference between the subject and object of the cultural stereotype. Put differently, the stereotype is grounded in nothing except the repetition of its own construction. In this respect, the cultural stereotype parallels the fetish character of the law, which is predicated on the repetition of judgements and speech acts, which – through their repetition – have the force and authority of law.

In *The Reluctant Fundamentalist*, Changez' frank account of how he smiled on first seeing the media spectacle of the World Trade Center in New York collapsing on 9/11, and his decision to grow a beard as a sign of protest against US foreign policy in South Asia during the 'war on terror' may encourage readers such as his unnamed American interlocutor to interpret his behaviour and appearance in the terms of an Islamophobic stereotype of Muslims as violent, anti-western, religious fundamentalists.[39] If we read the unnamed American in the Lahore café as a US intelligence agent, it is also possible to read this scene of interpretation as a staging of legal authority, in which Hamid draws readers' attention to the possibility that the unnamed American as a representative of US sovereignty may form a judgement about Changez' character according to the way in which his version of events corresponds with an Islamophobic stereotype of Muslims.

What complicates this reading, however, is the way in which the novel also foregrounds the colonial genealogy of the 'war on terror', and questions the Orientalist representation of the west as more civilised and developed than countries such as Pakistan. As a highly educated, cosmopolitan figure, Changez performs the role of a native informant who advises the unnamed and silent American visitor about different aspects of Pakistani culture, including the food and drink on the menu in the Lahore café where they share a meal, the informal practice of drinking alcohol, the young women from the National College of Arts wearing paint-speckled jeans and the city planning of Lahore. This representation of Pakistani culture seeks to contest the ahistorical representation of Pakistan in the dominant western media as an uncivilised, rogue state of terrorists and Islamic fundamentalists. As Changez puts it,

> Four thousand years ago, we, the people of the Indus River basin, had cities that were laid out on grids and boasted underground sewers, while the ancestors of those who would invade and colonize America were illiterate barbarians. Now our cities were largely unplanned, unsanitary affairs, and America had universities with individual endowments greater than our national budget for education. To be reminded of this vast disparity was, for me, to be ashamed.[40]

39 Mohsin Hamid, *The Reluctant Fundamentalist* (London: Hamish Hamilton, 2007), pp. 72, 128–31.
40 Hamid, *The Reluctant Fundamentalist*, p. 34.

What makes Changez 'ashamed' is not simply the social and economic decline of Pakistan, but his own self-confessed complicity in the economic process of neoliberal globalisation that aids and abets the 'vast disparity' in wealth and resources between Pakistan and the United States. After working for the American multinational, Underwood Samson, for a few months, Changez begins to see the rest of the world in terms of the capitalist values of corporate America. During an assignment in Chile, for instance, where he is required to value a book-publishing company that is not profit making, the owner of the publishing company, Juan-Bautista, compares him to the Christian boys who were captured by the Ottoman Empire and trained to be Muslim soldiers. These boys, who were known as 'janissaries', 'were ferocious and utterly loyal: they had fought to erase their civilizations, so they had nothing else to turn to'.[41] Juan-Bautista's comparison prompts Changez to reflect on how he had become 'a modern-day janissary, a servant of the American empire at a time when it was invading a country with a kinship similar to mine and was perhaps even colluding to ensure that my own country faced the threat of war'.[42] Changez' reflections on his own complicity in the US-led 'war on terror', and his slow realisation that 'finance was a primary means by which the American empire exercised its power', can be seen to parallel Ugo Mattei's contention that a 'state of emergency is a stabilizing political category, a true foundation for predatory capitalism'.[43] During the war in Iraq in 2003, for example, a narrative of emergency was constructed around the possibility that Saddam Hussein's regime was in possession of weapons of mass destruction in order to justify a military intervention that prepared the ground for the 'full privatization of public enterprises [and the] full ownership rights of Iraqi businesses by foreign firms'.[44] By refusing to play the role of modern janissary to the west, Changez brings this economic agenda of the US-led 'war on terror' to the fore. In this respect, Changez can be read as a cosmopolitan critic of globalisation during the war in Afghanistan.[45] As someone who has enjoyed the benefits of working for an American corporation, but who also witnessed the violence and depredation that is wreaked in 'Vietnam, Korea, the straits of Taiwan, the Middle East, and now Afghanistan' to maintain the economic dominance of US multinational corporations,[46] Changez allows us to understand how neoliberal globalisation operates as a form of imperialism.

This criticism of globalisation is continued toward the end of the novel,

41 Hamid, *The Reluctant Fundamentalist*, p. 151.
42 Hamid, *The Reluctant Fundamentalist*, p. 152.
43 Ugo Mattei, 'Emergency-Based Predatory Capitalism: The Rule of Law, Alternative Dispute Resolution and Development', in Didier Fassin and Mariella Pandolfi (eds), *Contemporary States of Emergency* (New York: Zone Books, 2010), p. 89.
44 David Harvey, *A Brief History of Neoliberalism* (Oxford: Oxford University Press, 2007), p. 6.
45 For a discussion of cosmopolitan criticism as a materialist critique of imperialism, see Robert Spencer, *Cosmopolitan Criticism and Postcolonial Literature* (Basingstoke: Palgrave Macmillan, 2011).
46 Hamid, *The Reluctant Fundamentalist*, p. 156

where Changez offers a series of reflections on the justification for the wars in Iraq and Afghanistan. He observes how

> a common strand seemed to unite these conflicts, and that was the advancement of a small coterie's concept of American interests in the guise of a fight against terrorism, which was defined to refer only to the organized and politically motivated killing of civilians by *killers* not wearing the uniforms of killers.[47]

Here, Changez offers an insightful criticism of the way in which the meaning of 'terrorism' is defined by narratives of counter-terrorism to justify the state's use of military force. The slipperiness of this definition may seem to allow for the possibility that the unnamed American could also be a 'terrorist'; for if the unnamed American is an undercover intelligence agent, he too could be defined in the terms of a killer not wearing the uniform of a killer. Yet this would be to ignore how 'terrorism' and 'American interests' are defined by a 'small coterie' that possesses the military and economic power to make words mean whatever they say. As a counterpoint to this dominant discourse of terrorism, Changez demonstrates that the word 'terrorism' itself masks the ways in which the 'war on terror' serves American economic and geopolitical interests at the expense of human lives in Iraq, Pakistan and Afghanistan. He observes that 'the lives of those of us who lived in lands in which such killers also lived had no meaning except as collateral damage'.[48] The precarious lives of civilians in Pakistan during the US war in Afghanistan is further borne out by Changez' story of a boy who was allegedly involved in a plot to assassinate an American development worker. This boy, as Changez explains, 'had disappeared – whisked away to a secret detention facility, no doubt, in some lawless limbo between' America and Pakistan.[49] The framing of this boy may seem to mirror Changez' own experiences of Islamophobia, which are manifested in the responses of other people to the beard he grew as a sign of solidarity with Muslims in Pakistan and Afghanistan after the attacks of 9/11. More than this, however, the story of the young boy exemplifies how the novel is concerned with the way in which the discourse of counter-terrorism is itself a product of an imperialist policy that uses stereotypes to frame, detain and kill individuals and groups who are seen to oppose that policy.

This is not to suggest, however, that *The Reluctant Fundamentalist* is exclusively concerned to deconstruct the discourse of counter-insurgency that underpins the 'war on terror' and the imperialist genealogy of that discourse. The novel also encourages its readers to recognise and to mourn the precarious lives and deaths of the civilian population in Afghanistan and Pakistan. And in this respect the novel exemplifies a broader commitment to justice for the oppressed that is evident in other postcolonial texts written in the wake of the 'war on terror',

47 Hamid, *The Reluctant Fundamentalist*, p. 178.
48 Hamid, *The Reluctant Fundamentalist*, p. 178.
49 Hamid, *The Reluctant Fundamentalist*, p. 182.

such as Kamila Shamsie's *Burnt Shadows* and Salman Rushdie's *Shalimar the Clown*. Throughout this book, we have seen how colonial sovereignty operates according to a necropolitical logic, in which colonised populations are often subjected to the lawful violence of the state. It is against this relegation of the colonised to a condition of expendable life that the postcolonial tradition of the oppressed needs to be understood. In the colonial present, the tradition of the oppressed does not only teach us that the colony is a political space in which the state of exception is normalised as a technique of governmentality, it also emphasises the political importance of the work of mourning.

Political theorists such as Butler have asked important questions about why some forms of human life are deemed to be more valuable than others. Against President George W. Bush's assertion on 21 September 2001 that 'we have finished grieving and that *now* it is time for resolute action to take the place of grief',[50] Butler argues that grief can be a 'resource for politics' if it leads to 'a consideration of the vulnerability of others' and a questioning of the political norms that determine why the lives of Americans are grievable and the lives of Iraqis, Palestinians and Afghanis are not.[51] Furthermore, by arguing that 'the world itself as a sovereign entitlement of the United States must be given up, lost and mourned',[52] Butler offers a radical democratic vision of global power relations in the twenty-first century. If, as Danilo Zolo has suggested, the predominant system of international law and the liberal discourse of humanitarian intervention aid and abet the violence of contemporary forms of imperialism,[53] Butler contends that narratives of mourning can help us to inter-rogate contemporary forms of imperialist violence that are committed in the name of human rights.

An exemplary case of such a narrative of mourning can be found in Shamsie's novel *Burnt Shadows* (2009). Much of the novel is focalised through the consciousness of Hiroko Tanaka, a Japanese survivor of the US atomic bombing of Nagasaki in 1945, and chronicles her transnational movements from Nagasaki to Delhi, Karachi and New York over a period of fifty years. This narra-tive is juxtaposed with an account of how her son, Raza, came to be framed as a 'suspected terrorist' in the aftermath of the attacks on America of 9/11. By decentring the attacks and situating them in relation to a broader history of western imperialism that includes the nuclear bombing of Nagasaki, the parti-tion of India after independence, the Soviet invasion of Afghanistan and the US war in Afghanistan, *Burnt Shadows* uses Hiroko's narrative of mourning and trauma to offer a counter-history of the colonial present from the standpoint of people excluded from the benefits of capitalist imperialism.

It is Hiroko's own experience of mourning and violence during the bombing of Nagasaki that leads her to question the framing of Muslims in the so-called

---

50 Butler, *Precarious Life*, p. 29.
51 Butler, *Precarious Life*, pp. 30, 34.
52 Butler, *Precarious Life*, p. 40.
53 Danilo Zolo, *Victor's Justice: From Nuremburg to Baghdad*, trans. Gregory Elliott (London: Verso, 2009).

'war on terror'. Hiroko's painful memories of Nagasaki are not only inscribed in the scars on her back, but also shape and determine her fears about whether she will be able to have children following a miscarriage. As well as being marked by the discourse of the bomb, Hiroko's narrative is haunted by the image of her dead fiancée, Konrad Weiss. As she explains to her husband Sajjad,

> Those nearest the blast were eradicated completely, only the fat from their bodies sticking to the walls and rocks around them like shadows [...] I looked for Konrad's shadow. I found it. Or I found something that I believed was it. On a rock. Such a lanky shadow. I sent a message to Yoshi Watanabe and together we rolled the rock to the International Cemetery [...] And buried it.[54]

By commemorating the death and injury caused by the atomic bombing of Nagasaki, Shamsie encourages readers to question predominant American histories of the Second World War, which frame the atomic massacres in Hiroshima and Nagasaki as a necessity, and imply that the deaths of those killed in the massacres are not worth grieving. The parallel here with the violent response to the attacks on America of 9/11 is striking. Just as Hiroko's post-Nagasaki narrative of mourning and trauma raises questions about the framing of the Japanese population as dispensable, racialised bodies in the necropolitical logic of America's atomic war machine, so the novel implies that the Bush administration rehearses this necropolitical logic by framing Muslims as dispensable, racialised bodies in its 'war on terror'.

How, though, can such narratives of mourning help to make sense of the colonial present? The analeptic narrative structure of *Burnt Shadows* demands a recursive reading that can address the question posed in the novel's prologue by an as-yet-unnamed protagonist as he waits to be clothed in an orange jumpsuit: '*How did it come to this?*'[55] If we take this masculine figure to be Raza, and the orange jumpsuit to be an iconic metonym of contemporary global war prisons such as those at Guantánamo Bay, then the question and the context in which it is posed can be read as a rhetorical statement about the way in which Muslims have been framed in the 'war on terror'. But if we reread the prologue in light of the multiple narratives that follow, the question can also be read as a reflection on the way in which the colonial present and the 'war on terror' are overdetermined by the violent legacies of western imperialism in the twentieth century, such as the atomic bombing of Nagasaki and Hiroshima, India's partition, the CIA's covert war against the Soviet military in Afghanistan and the proliferation of nuclear weapons in India and Pakistan. In this way, *Burnt Shadows* can be seen to engage readers in a collective work of mourning that offers an important historical counterpoint to dominant narratives of the 'war on terror' – narratives which have ignored the historical role of the United States in the training of groups such as the *mujahideen* in the

54 Kamila Shamsie, *Burnt Shadows* (London: Bloomsbury, 2009), pp. 76–77.
55 Shamsie, *Burnt Shadows*, p. 1.

war against communism.[56] Butler has suggested that the political dimension of mourning resides in its capacity to foster a shared recognition of vulnerability and dependency across cultures.[57] Butler's rethinking of mourning and the recognition of a common corporeal vulnerability as a political and critical form of memory work is presented in part as a challenge to the Bush administration's cynical transformation of 'the liberation of women into a rationale for its military actions against Afghanistan'.[58] Mourning work can also help to make sense of other genealogies of colonial violence that are eclipsed by the narratives surrounding the 'war on terror'.

If the spatial stories and legal narratives of emergency in Guantánamo Bay, Afghanistan and Iraq help to make sense of the relationship between violence, law and sovereignty in the colonial present, literary and cultural texts can help to shed light on the condition of possibility for justice in these contexts. As this concluding chapter has suggested, literary narratives such as *The Reluctant Fundamentalist* and *Burnt Shadows*, and autobiographical narratives such as *Enemy Combatant*, offer valuable narrative resources for imagining an alternative to a colonial present in which exceptional violence has become the norm. This is not to suggest that such narratives offer a blueprint for effective political intervention. And neither do they always directly address the political economy of imperialism and its material effects as they are experienced in contemporary Afghanistan, Iraq and Pakistan.[59] Yet insofar as they convey the fragmented and often traumatic experiences of violent colonial sovereignty, these narratives allow us to mourn the lives and deaths of the oppressed, and to imagine a form of justice beyond the liberal fictions of human rights, democracy and the normal rule of law.

56 For a further critique of such dominant narratives, see Jacques Derrida and Jürgen Habermas, *Philosophy in a Time of Terror: Dialogues with Jürgen Habermas and Jacques Derrida* (Chicago and London: University of Chicago Press, 2003); John Cooley, *Unholy Wars: Afghanistan, America and International Terrorism* (London: Pluto, 2003); Steve Coll, *Ghost Wars: The Secret History of the CIA, Afghanistan, and bin Laden, from the Soviet Invasion to September 10, 2001* (London: Penguin, 2004); Jason Burke, *Al-Qaeda: The True Story of Radical Islam* (London: Penguin, 2004); idem, *The 9/11 Wars* (London: Allen Lane, 2011).
57 Butler, *Precarious Life*, p. 41.
58 Butler, *Precarious Life*, p. 41.
59 See Priyamvada Gopal, 'Of Capitalism and Critique'.

Bibliography

Adams, Stephen, 'Ian McEwan: Criticising Islam is not racist', *The Telegraph Magazine*, 13 March 2010. Available at <www.telegraph.co.uk/culture/books/booknews/7428769>. Accessed 30 August 2011.

Agamben, Giorgio, *Language and Death: The Place of Negativity*, trans. Karen E. Pinkus and Michael Hardt (Minneapolis, MN: University of Minnesota Press, 1991).

—, *Homo Sacer: Sovereign Power and Bare Life*, trans. Daniel Heller-Roazen (Stanford, CA: Stanford University Press, 1998).

—, 'We Refugees', trans. Michael Rocke. Available at <www.egs.edu/faculty/agamben/agamben-we-refugees.html>. Accessed 8 April 2009.

—, *State of Exception*, trans. Kevin Attell (Chicago and London: University of Chicago Press, 2005).

—, 'K.', in idem, *Nudities*, trans. David Kishik and Stefan Pedatella (Stanford, CA: Stanford University Press, 2011), pp. 20–36.

—, *The Sacrament of Language: An Archaeology of the Oath*, trans. Adam Kotsko (Cambridge: Polity, 2011).

Alleg, Henri, *La question suivi de Une victoire par Jean Paul Sartre* (Paris: Les editions de minuit, 1965).

—, *The Question*, trans. John Calder (Lincoln, NE, and London: University of Nebraska Press, 2006).

Amireh, Amal, 'Between Complicity and Subversion: Body Politics in Palestinian National Narrative', *South Atlantic Quarterly*, 102/4 (2003), pp. 747–72.

Amis, Martin, interviewed by Ginny Dougary, *The Times Magazine*, 9 September 2006. Available at <www.martinamisweb.com/documents/voice_of_experience.pdf>. Accessed 30 August 2011.

—, *The Second Plane: September 11: 2001–2007* (London: Vintage, 2008).

Anderson, David, *Histories of the Hanged: Britain's Dirty War in Kenya and the End of Empire* (London: Weidenfeld & Nicolson, 2005).

Anidjar, Gil, *The Jew, the Arab: A History of the Enemy* (Stanford, CA: Stanford University Press: 2003).

Arendt, Hannah, *The Origins of Totalitarianism* (New York: Meridian Books, 1958).

—, *On Violence* (London: Allen Lane, 1970).

—, *Eichmann in Jerusalem: A Report on the Banality of Evil* (London: Penguin Books, 1994).

The Amritsar Massacre: General Dyer in the Punjab 1919 (The Stationery Office, 2000).

Aretxaga, Begoña, *States of Terror: Begoña Aretxaga's Essays* (Reno, NV: Center for Basque Studies, University of Nevada, 2005).

—, *Shattering Silence: Women, Nationalism, and Political Subjectivity in Northern Ireland* (Princeton, NJ: Princeton University Press, 1997).

Arnold, David, *Police Power and Colonial Rule: Madras 1859–1947* (Delhi: Oxford University Press, 1986).

Arthur, Paige, *Unfinished Projects: Decolonization and the Philosophy of Jean Paul Sartre* (London: Verso, 2010).

Asad, Talal, *Formations of the Secular: Christianity, Islam, Modernity* (Stanford, CA: Stanford University Press, 2003).

—, *On Suicide Bombing* (New York: Columbia University Press, 2007).

Attridge, Derek, *J.M. Coetzee and the Ethics of Reading: Literature in the Event* (Chicago: University of Chicago Press, 2004).

Aussaresses, Paul, *The Battle of the Casbah*, trans. Robert L. Miller (New York: Engima, 2002).

Azoulay, Ariella, *The Civil Contract of Photography* (New York: Zone, 2008).

—, 'Declaring the State of Israel: Declaring a State of War', *Critical Inquiry*, 37/2 (2011), pp. 265–85.

Azoulay, Ariella and Adi Ophir, *The One-State Condition: Occupation and Democracy in Israel/Palestine*, trans. Tal Haran (Stanford, CA: Stanford University Press, 2013).

Bahri, Deepika, *Native Intelligence: Aesthetics, Politics and Postcolonial Literature* (Minneapolis, MN: University of Minnesota Press, 2003).

Banville, John, 'A Day in the Life', *New York Review of Books*, 26 May 2005, pp. 11–14.

Barrell, Howard, 'Conscripts to Their Age: African National Congress Operational Strategy, 1976–1986', doctoral dissertation (University of Oxford, 1993).

Barrier, N. Gerald, *Banned: Controversial Literature and Political Control in British India, 1907–1947* (Columbia, MO: University of Missouri Press, 1974).

Baudrillard, Jean, 'L'esprit du terrorisme', *South Atlantic Quarterly*, 101/2 (2002), pp. 403–15.

Bayly, C.A., *Empire and Information: Intelligence Gathering and Social Communication in India, 1780–1870* (Cambridge: Cambridge University Press, 1996).

Begg, Moazzam, *Enemy Combatant: A British Muslim's Journey to Guantanamo and Back* (London: Free Press, 2006).

Begin, Menachem, *The Revolt*, trans. Samuel Katz (London: W.H. Allen, 1951).

Benjamin, Walter, 'Critique of Violence', in Marcus Bullock and Michael W. Jennings (eds), *Selected Writings, Volume 1: 1913–1926* (Cambridge, MA: Harvard University Press, 1996), pp. 236–52.

—, 'On the Concept of History', in Howard Eiland and Michael W. Jennings (eds), *Selected Writings, Volume IV: 1938–1940* (Cambridge, MA: Harvard University Press, 2003), pp. 389–400.

—, 'Paralipomena to "On the Concept of History"', in Howard Eiland and Michael W. Jennings (eds), *Selected Writings, Volume IV 1938–1940* (Cambridge, MA: Belknap Press of Harvard University Press, 2003), pp. 401–11.

Bensmaïa, Réda, *Experimental Nations, or, the Invention of the Maghreb* (Princeton, NJ and Oxford: Princeton University Press, 2003).

Benton, Lauren, *Law and Colonial Cultures: Legal Regimes in World History, 1400–1900* (Cambridge: Cambridge University Press, 2002).

Bernstein, Hilda, *Death Is Part of the Process* (London: Sinclair Browne, 1983).

Bhabha, Homi, 'Foreword: Framing Fanon', in Frantz Fanon, *The Wretched of the Earth*, trans. Richard Philcox (New York: Grove Press, 2004), pp. xxviii–xxxii.

—, *The Location of Culture* (London: Routledge, 2004).

Birmingham, Peg, *Hannah Arendt and Human Rights* (Bloomington and Indianapolis: Indiana University Press, 2006).

Bierseker, Ann, '*Matigari ma Nirũũngi*: What Grows from Leftover Seeds of "Chat" Trees?', in Charles Cantalupo (ed.), *The World of Ngũgĩ wa Thiong'o* (Trenton, NJ: Africa World Press, 1996), pp. 141–58.

Boehmer, Elleke. *Empire, the National, and the Postcolonial, 1890–1920: Resistance in Interaction* (Oxford: Oxford University Press, 2002).

—, *Stories of Women: Gender and Narrative in the Postcolonial Nation* (Manchester: Manchester University Press, 2005).

—, 'Postcolonial Writing and Terror', *Wasafiri*, 22/2 (2007), pp. 4–7.

—, *Nelson Mandela: A Very Short Introduction* (Oxford: Oxford University Press, 2008).

Boehmer, Elleke, and Stephen Morton, 'Introduction', in idem (eds), *Terror and the Postcolonial* (Oxford: Blackwell, 2009), pp. 1–24.

Boland, Eavan, *In Her Own Image* (Dublin: Arlen House, 1980).

—, *The Journey* (Manchester: Carcanet, 1987).

—, *Object Lessons: The Life of the Woman and the Poet in Our Time* (Manchester: Carcanet, 1995).

Bose, Purnima, and Laura Lyons, 'Dyer Consequences: The Trope of Amritsar, Ireland, and the Lessons of the "Minimum" Force Debate', *boundary 2*, 26/2 (1999), pp. 199–229.

Bourke, Joanna, 'Torture as Pornography', *The Guardian*, 7 May 2004. Available at <www.guardian.co.uk/world/2004/may/07/gender.uk>. Accessed 30 August 2011.

Bradley, Arthur, and Andrew Tate, *The New Atheist Novel: Fiction, Philosophy and Polemic after 9/11* (London: Continuum, 2010).

Branche, Raphaëlle, *La torture et l'armée pendant la guerre d'Algérie: 1954–1962* (Paris: Gallimard, 2001).

—, 'Torture and Other Violations of the Law by the French Army during the Algerian War', in Adam Jones (ed.), *Genocide, War Crimes and the West: History and Complicity* (London and New York: Zed Books, 2004), pp. 134–45.

Breckenridge, Keith, 'Verwoerd's Bureau of Proof: Total Information in the Making of Apartheid', *History Workshop Journal*, 59 (2005), pp. 85–108.

Bredekamp, Horst, 'Walter Benjamin to Carl Schmitt, via Thomas Hobbes', *Critical Inquiry*, 25/2 (1999), pp. 247–66.

Brown, Wendy, *Walled States, Waning Sovereignty* (New York: Zone, 2010).

Bull, Malcolm, 'States don't really mind their citizens dying (provided they don't all do it at once): they just don't like anyone else to kill them', *London Review of Books*, 26/24, 16 December 2004, pp. 3–6.

Bunting, Brian, *The Rise of the South African Reich* (Harmondsworth: Penguin, 1969).

Burke, Jason, *Al-Qaeda: The True Story of Radical Islam* (London: Penguin, 2004).

—, *The 9/11 Wars* (London: Allen Lane, 2011).

Burnaby, Fred, *Our Radicals: A Tale of Love and Politics*, 2 vols (London: Richard Bentley & Son, 1886).

Butler, Judith, *Precarious Life: The Powers of Mourning and Violence* (London: Verso, 2004).

—, *Frames of War: When Is Life Grievable?* (London: Verso, 2009).

Cahm, Caroline, *Kropotkin and the Rise of Revolutionary Anarchism* (Cambridge: Cambridge University Press, 1989).

Callard, Maurice, *The City Called Holy* (London: Jonathan Cape, 1954).

227

Caminero-Santangelo, Byron, 'Neocolonialism and the Betrayal Plot in *A Grain of Wheat*: Ngũgĩ wa Thiong'o's Re-Vision of *Under Western Eyes*', *Research in African Literatures*, 29/1 (1998), pp. 139–52.

Campbell, Colm, *Emergency Law in Ireland 1918–1925* (Oxford: Oxford University Press, 1994).

Candler, Edmund, 'Siri Ram Revolutionist: A Transcript from Life', in Saros Cowasjee (ed.), *A Raj Collection* (Delhi: Oxford University Press, 2005).

Carey, R., and J. Shainin (eds), *The Other Israel: Voices of Refusal and Dissent* (New York: New Press, 2000).

Chakravarti, Aruna, *Sarat Chandra: Rebel and Humanist* (New Delhi: National Book Trust, 1985).

Chatterjee, Sarat Chandra, *Pather Dabi*, trans. Prasenjit Mukherjee (New Delhi: Rupa, 1993).

Chatterji, Agnana P., 'The Militarized Zone', in Tariq Ali et al. (eds), *Kashmir: The Case for Freedom* (London: Verso, 2011), pp. 93–124.

Cheah, Pheng, *Spectral Nationality: Passages of Freedom from Kant to Postcolonial Literatures of Liberation* (New York: Columbia University Press, 2003).

Chirol, Valentine, *Indian Unrest* (London: Macmillan & Co., 1910).

Chowdhury, Indira, *The Frail Hero and Virile History* (Delhi: Oxford University Press, 1998).

Churchill, Winston, 'Address to the House of Commons', *Parliamentary Debates: House of Commons*, 131 (8 July 1920), p. 1725.

Cleary, Joe, *Literature, Partition and the Nation State* (Cambridge: Cambridge University Press, 2002).

Clemens, Justin, 'The Role of the Shifter and the Problem of Reference in the Thought of Giorgio Agamben', in Justin Clemens, Nicholas Heron and Alex Murray (eds), *The Work of Giorgio Agamben: Law, Literature, Life* (Edinburgh: Edinburgh University Press, 2008), pp. 43–65.

Cleveland, Todd, '"We Still Want the Truth": The ANC's Angolan Detention Camps and Post-Apartheid Memory', *Comparative Studies of South Asia, Africa and the Middle East*, 25/1 (2005), pp. 63–78.

Coetzee, J. M., *Waiting for the Barbarians* (London: Minerva, 1997 [1980]).

—, 'The Novel Today', *Upstream*, 6 (1988), pp. 2–5.

—, 'Into the Dark Chamber', in David Atwell (ed.), *Doubling the Point* (Cambridge, MA: Harvard University Press, 1992), pp. 361–68.

Cohn, Bernard S., 'The Census, Social Structure, and Objectification in South Asia', in idem, *An Anthropologist among the Historians* (Delhi: Oxford University Press, 1987), pp. 224–54.

—, *Colonialism and Its Forms of Knowledge: The British in India* (Princeton, NJ: Princeton University Press, 1996).

Cole, Joshua, 'Intimate Acts and Unspeakable Relations: Remembering Torture and the War for Algerian Independence', in Alec G. Hargreaves (ed.), *Memory, Empire, and Postcolonialism: Legacies of French Colonialism* (Lanham, MD: Lexington Books, 2005), pp. 125–41.

Coll, Steve, *Ghost Wars: The Secret History of the CIA, Afghanistan, and bin Laden, from the Soviet Invasion to September 10, 2001* (London: Penguin, 2004).

Collett, Nigel, *The Butcher of Amritsar: General Reginald Dyer* (London: Hambledon and London, 2005).

Connell, David, 'Jean Lartéguy: Student of Revolutionary Warfare', *Research Studies*, 40/1 (1972), pp. 1–9.

Conrad, Joseph, 'Letter to Edmund Candler', 12 November 1918, in Laurence Davies, Frederick R Karl and Owen Knowles (eds), *The Collected Letters of Joseph Conrad Volume VI* (Cambridge: Cambridge University Press, 2002), pp. 303–4.

Cooley, John, *Unholy Wars: Afghanistan, America and International Terrorism* (London: Pluto, 2003).

Corkill, Rachael, 'Preface to Siri Ram Revolutionist: A Transcript from Life', in Saros Cowasjee (ed.), *A Raj Collection: On the Face of the Waters, Flora Annie Steel; Siri Ram-Revolutionist, Edmund Candler; Indigo, Christine Weston; The Wild Sweet Witch, Philip Mason* (Delhi: Oxford University Press, 2005), pp. 397–98.

Cullingford, Elizabeth, *Gender and History in Yeats's Love Poetry* (Cambridge: Cambridge University Press, 1993).

Curtis, Robert, *Curiosities of Detection; or, the Seacoast Station, and Other Tales* (London: Ward & Lock, 1862).

Darnton, Robert, 'Literary Surveillance in the British Raj: The Contradictions of Liberal Imperialism', *Book History*, 4 (2001), pp. 133–76.

Davenport, Rodney, and Christopher Saunders, *South Africa: A Modern History* (Basingstoke: Macmillan, 2000 [1977]).

Davis, Uri, *Apartheid Israel* (London: Zed, 2003).

Derrida, Jacques, *Aporias*, trans. Thomas Dutoit (Stanford, CA: Stanford University Press, 1993).

—, *The Beast and the Sovereign*, vol. 1, trans. Geoffrey Bennington (Chicago: University of Chicago Press, 2009).

Derrida, Jacques, and Hélène Cixous, 'The Language of Others', *Jewish Book Week*, 1 March 2004. Available at <http://jewishbookweek.com/archive/010304e/transcripts2.php>. Accessed 24 March 2009.

Derrida, Jacques, and Jürgen Habermas, *Philosophy in a Time of Terror: Dialogues with Jürgen Habermas and Jacques Derrida* (Chicago and London: University of Chicago Press, 2003).

Devereux Jones, William, 'A Plot to Kill the Queen', *New York Historical Quarterly*, 51/4 (1967), pp. 311–25.

Dicey, Albert Venn, *Introduction to the Study of the Law of the Constitution* (London: Macmillan, 1897).

Dickinson, Colby, *Agamben and Theology* (London: T&T Clark, 2011)

Dine, Philip, *Images of the Algerian War: French Fiction and Film, 1954–1992* (Oxford: Clarendon Press, 1994).

Dirks, Nicholas, *The Scandal of Empire: India and the Creation of Imperial Britain* (Cambridge, MA: Belknap Press of Harvard University Press, 2006).

Djebar, Assia, *Les enfants du nouveau monde* (Paris: René Julliard, 1983 [1962]); *The Children of the World*, trans. Marjolijn de Jager (New York: Feminist Press, 2005).

—, *L'amour, la fantasia: roman* (Paris: Albin Michel, 1995); *Fantasia: An Algerian Cavalcade*, trans. Dorothy Blair (London: Quartet, 1989).

—, *Le blanc de l'Algérie* (Paris: Albin Michel, 1995); *Algerian White*, trans. David Kelley and Marjolijn de Jager (New York: Seven Stories Press, 2000).

—, *Les alouettes naïves: roman* (Arles: Actes Sud, 1997).

—, *La femme sans sépulture: roman* (Paris: Albin Michel, 2002).

Doggett, Rob, 'Writing out (Of) Chaos: Constructions of History in Yeats's "Nineteen Hundred and Nineteen" and "Meditations in Time of Civil War"', *Twentieth Century Literature*, 47/2 (2001), pp. 137–68.

—, *Deep Rooted Things: Empire and Nation in the Poetry and Drama of William Butler Yeats* (Notre Dame, IN: University of Notre Dame Press, 2006).

Donadey, Anne, 'Introjection and Incorporation in Assia Djebar's *La femme sans sépulture*', *L'esprit créateur*, 48/4 (2008), pp. 81–91.

Donogh, Walter Russell, *The History and Law of Sedition and Cognate Offences in British India*, 3rd edn (Calcutta: Thacker, Spink & Co., 1917 [1911]).

Draper, Alfred, *Amritsar: The Massacre That Ended the Raj* (London: Cassell, 1981).

Driver, C.J., *Elegy for a Revolutionary* (London: Faber, 1969).

Duff, Douglas Valder, *Harding of the Palestine Police* (London and Glasgow: Blackie & Son, 1941).

Dugard, John, *Human Rights and the South African Legal Order* (Princeton, NJ: Princeton University Press, 1978).

Durantaye, Leland de la, *Giorgio Agamben: A Critical Introduction* (Stanford, CA: Stanford University Press, 2009).

Durmelat, Sylvia, 'Revisiting Ghosts: Louisette Ighilahriz and the Remembering of Torture', in Alec G. Hargreaves (ed.), *Memory, Empire, and Postcolonialism: Legacies of French Colonialism* (Lanham, MD: Lexington Books, 2005), pp. 142–59.

Dutt, Kalpana, *Chittagong Armoury Raiders Reminiscences* (New Delhi: People's Publishing House, 1979 [1945]).

'The Dynamite Conspiracy', *Illustrated London News*, 14 April 1883, pp. 356–58.

Eagleton, Terry, *Holy Terror* (Oxford: Oxford University Press, 2005).

Elkins, Caroline, *Britain's Gulag: The Brutal End of Empire in Kenya* (London: Jonathan Cape, 2005).

Ellmann, Maud, *The Hunger Artists: Starving, Writing, and Imprisonment* (Cambridge, MA: Harvard University Press, 1993).

Ellman, Stephen, *In a Time of Trouble: Law and Liberty in South Africa's State of Emergency* (Oxford: Clarendon Press, 1992).

Emery, Robert A., 'The Author of Tales of the *R.I.C.*', *Notes and Queries*, 57/2 (2010), pp. 226–28.

English, Richard, *Armed Struggle: A History of the IRA* (London: Macmillan, 2003).

Enns, Diane, 'Bare Life and the Occupied Body', *Theory and Event*, 7/3 (2004). Available at <http://muse.jhu.edu/journals/theory_and_event/v007/7.3enns.html>. Accessed 25 August 2011.

Evans, Ivan Thomas, *Bureaucracy and Race: Native Administration in South Africa* (Berkeley: University of California Press, 1997).

Fanon, Frantz, *Black Skins, White Masks*, trans. Charles Lam Markmann (London: Pluto, 1986 [1952]).

—, *The Wretched of the Earth*, trans. Richard Philcox (New York: Grove Press, 2004 [1961]).

—, 'Algeria Face to Face with the French Torturers', in idem, *Toward the African Revolution*, trans. Haakon Chevalier (Harmondsworth: Penguin Books, 1970 [1964]), pp. 74–82.

Farrell, Michael, *The Apparatus of Repression: Emergency Legislation* (Derry: Field Day Theatre, 1986).

Feldman, Allen, *Formations of Violence: The Narrative of the Body and Political Terror in Northern Ireland* (Chicago: University of Chicago Press, 1991).

Felman, Shoshana, *The Juridical Unconscious: Trials and Trauma in the Twentieth Century* (Cambridge, MA: Harvard University Press, 2004).

'The Fenian Murders in Dublin', *Illustrated London News*, 20 May 1882, pp. 489–93.

Foster, John Wilson, *Irish Novels, 1890–1940: New Bearings in Culture and Fiction* (Oxford: Oxford University Press, 2008).

Foucault, Michel, *Discipline and Punish: The Birth of the Prison*, trans. Alan Sheridan (New York: Vintage Books, 1995).

—, *The Will to Knowledge: The History of Sexuality, Volume One*, trans. Robert Hurley (Harmondsworth: Penguin, 1998).

—, *Society Must Be Defended: Lectures at the Collège de France, 1975–76*, trans. David Macey (London: Allen Lane, 2003).

Frankel, Philip, *An Ordinary Atrocity: Sharpeville and Its Massacre* (New Haven: Yale University Press, 2001).

Freud, Sigmund, *The Standard Edition of the Complete Psychological Works of Sigmund Freud*, vol. 3, ed. James Strachey (London: Hogarth Press and the Institute of Psycho-Analysis, 1953–74).

Furedi, Frank, 'Creating a Breathing Space: The Political Management of Colonial Emergencies', in Robert Holland (ed.), *Emergencies and Disorder in the European Empires after 1945* (London: Frank Cass, 1994), pp. 89–106.

Gakaara wa Wanjaũ, *Mau Mau Author in Detention* (Nairobi: Heinemann Kenya, 1988).

Gandhi, M.K., *Trial of Gandhiji* (Ahmedabad: V.R. Shah, 1965).

Ganguly, Keya, *States of Exception: Everyday Life and Postcolonial Identity* (Minneapolis and London: University of Minnesota Press, 2001).

Geertsema, Johan, 'Exceptions, Bare Life, and Colonialism', in Victor V. Ramraj (ed.), *Emergencies and the Limits of Legality* (Cambridge: Cambridge University Press, 2008), pp. 337–59.

Gelber, Yoav, 'The History of Zionist Historiography: From Apologetics to Denial', in Benny Morris (ed.), *Making Israel* (Ann Arbor: University of Michigan Press, 2008), pp. 47–80.

Ghose, Aurobindo (Sri Aurobindo), 'The Doctrine of Passive Resistance', in idem, *Sri Aurobindo Volume One: Bande Mataram: Early Political Writings* (Pondicherry: Sri Aurobindo Ashram, 1995), pp. 83–123.

Ghosh, Durba, 'Terrorism in Bengal: Political Violence in the Interwar Years', in Durba Ghosh and Dane Kennedy (eds), *Decentring Empire: Britain, India, and the Transcolonial World* (London: Sangam, 2006), pp. 270–92.

Gikandi, Simon, *Ngugi wa Thiong'o* (Cambridge: Cambridge University Press, 2000).

Gilley, S.W., 'Pearse's Sacrifice: Christ and Cuchulain Crucified and Risen in the Easter Rising, 1916', in S.W. Sykes (ed.), *Sacrifice and Redemption: Durham Essays in Theology* (Cambridge: Cambridge University Press, 1991), pp. 218–34.

Gitahi, Gititi, 'Ferocious Comedies: Henri Lopes's *The Laughing Cry* and Ngũgĩ wa Thiong'o's *Matigari* as "Dictator" Novels', in Charles Cantalupo (ed.), *Ngũgĩ wa Thiong'o: Texts and Contexts* (Trenton, NJ: Africa World Press, 1996), pp. 211–26.

Gopal, Priyamvarda, 'Of Capitalism and Critique: Trajectories of Anglophone Pakistani Fiction after September 11th 2001', Paper presented at 'South Asian Fiction: Contemporary Transformations' Conference, 3 November 2012.

—, and Neil Lazarus, 'Editorial', *New Formations*, 59 (Autumn 2006), pp. 7–9.

Greenberg, Karen J., 'Caught in the War on Terror', in Karen J. Greenberg, Joshua Dratel and Jeffrey Grossman (eds), *The Enemy Combatant Papers: American Justice, the Courts, and the War on Terror* (Cambridge: Cambridge University Press, 2008), pp. ix–xii.

Greer, Tom, *A Modern Dædalus* (London: Griffith & Co., 1885).

Gregory, Derek, *The Colonial Present* (Oxford: Blackwell, 2004).

Guémar, Soleïman Adel, *État d'urgence/State of Emergency*, trans. by Tom Cheeseman and John Goodby (Todmorden: Arc, 2007).

Guha, Ranajit, *Elementary Aspects of Peasant Insurgency in Colonial India* (Delhi: Oxford University Press, 1983).

—, 'The Prose of Counterinsurgency', in Ranajit Guha (ed.), *Subaltern Studies*, vol. 2 (Delhi: Oxford University Press, 1983), pp. 1–42.

La Guma, Alex, *In the Fog of the Season's End* (London: Heinemann, 1972).

—, 'State of Emergency', in Andre Odendaal and Roger Field (eds), *Liberation Chabalala: the World of Alex La Guma* (Belville, South Africa: Mayibuye Books, 1993), pp. 146–53.

Gurnah, Abdulrazak, '*Matigari*: A Tract of Resistance', *Research in African Literatures* 22/4 (1991), pp. 169–72.

Habiby, Emile, *The Secret Life of Saeed: The Ill-fated Pessoptimist*, trans. Salma Khedra Jayyusi and Trevor LeGassick (Northampton, MA: Interlink, 2003).

Hadley, Elaine, 'On a Darkling Plain: Victorian Liberalism and the Fantasy of Agency', *Victorian Studies*, 48/1 (2005), pp. 92–102.

Hajjar, Lisa, *Courting Conflict: The Israeli Military Court System in the West Bank and Gaza* (Berkeley: University of California Press, 2005).

Hamid, Mohsin, *The Reluctant Fundamentalist* (London: Hamish Hamilton, 2007).

Hansard House of Commons, vol. 190, col. 783 (14 February 1868).

Hardy, Michael, Hervé Lemoine and Thierry Sarmany (eds), *Pouvoir politique et autorité militaire en Algérie. Hommes, textes, institutions, 1945–62* (Paris: Service Historique de l'Armée de Terre. L'Harmattan, 2002).

Harlow, Barbara, *Resistance Literature* (London: Methuen, 1987).

—, *After Lives: Legacies of Revolutionary Writing* (London: Verso, 1996).

David Harvey, *A Brief History of Neoliberalism* (Oxford: Oxford University Press, 2007).

Heehs, Peter, *The Bomb in Bengal* (Delhi: Oxford University Press, 2004).

Herbert, Christopher, *War of No Pity: The Indian Mutiny and Victorian Trauma* (Princeton, NJ: Princeton University Press, 2008).

Herzl, Theodor, *The Jewish State* (London: Central Office of the Zionist Organization, 1934 [1896]).

Hiddleston, Jane, *Assia Djebar: Out of Algeria* (Liverpool: Liverpool University Press, 2006).

Hoffman, Bruce, *Inside Terrorism* (New York: Columbia University Press, 2006).

Horne, Alistair, *A Savage War of Peace* (London: Macmillan, 1977).

Howe, Stephen, *Ireland and Empire: Colonial Legacies in Irish History and Culture* (Oxford: Oxford University Press, 2000).

Howes, Marjorie, *Yeats's Nations: Gender, Class, and Irishness* (Cambridge: Cambridge University Press, 1996).

Houen, Alex, *Terrorism and Modern Literature from Joseph Conrad to Ciaran Carson* (Oxford: Oxford University Press, 2002).

—, 'Sovereignty, Biopolitics, and the Use of Literature', in Stephen Morton and Stephen Bygrave (eds), *Foucault in an Age of Terror: Essays on Biopolitics and the Defence of Society* (Basingstoke: Palgrave Macmillan, 2008), pp. 63–87.

House, Jim, and Neil MacMaster, *Paris 1961: Algerians, State Terror, and Memory* (Oxford: Oxford University Press, 2006).

Hussain, Nasser, *The Jurisprudence of Emergency: Colonialism and the Rule of Law* (Ann Arbor: University of Michigan Press, 2003).

—, 'Beyond Norm and Exception: Guantánamo', *Critical Inquiry*, 33/4 (2007), pp. 734–53.

Huxley, Elspeth, *A Thing to Love* (London: Chatto & Windus, 1954).

Ighilahriz, Louisette, *Algérienne*, récit recueilli par Anne Nivat (Paris: Fayard/Calmann-Lévy, 2001).

Innes, C.L., *Woman and Nation in Irish Literature and Society 1880–1935* (Hemel Hempstead: Harvester Wheatsheaf, 1993).

Jameson, Fredric, 'Third World Literature in the Era of Multinational Capitalism', *Social Text*, 15 (1986), pp. 65–88.

JanMohamed, Abdul R., *Manichean Aesthetics: The Politics of Literature in Colonial Africa* (Amherst, MA: University of Massachusetts Press, 1983).

Jarrar, Maher, '*The Arabian Nights* and the Contemporary Arabic Novel', in Saree Makdisi and Felicity Nussbaum (eds), *The Arabian Nights in Historical Context: Between East and West* (Oxford: Oxford University Press, 2008), pp. 297–316.

Jenkins, Brian, *The Fenian Problem: Insurgency and Terrorism in a Liberal State 1858–1874* (Montréal: McGill-Queen's University Press, 2008).

Jiryis, Sabri, *The Arabs in Israel, 1948–1966*, trans. Meric Dobson (Beirut: Institute for Palestine Studies, 1969).

Joffe, Joel, *The Rivonia story* (Bellville: Mayibuye, 1995).

Jolly, Rosemary, 'Territorial Metaphor in Coetzee's *Waiting for the Barbarians*', *Ariel*, 20 (1989), pp. 69–79.

Kanafani, Ghassan, *Men in the Sun, and Other Palestinian Stories*, trans. Hilary Fitzpatrick (London: Heinemann Educational, 1978).

Kanafany, Ghassan [*sic*], 'Resistance Literature in Occupied Palestine', *Afro-Asian Writings: Quarterly of the Permanent Bureau of Afro-Asian Writers*, 1/2–3 (1968), pp. 65–79.

Kearney, Richard, *Myth and Motherland* (Derry: Field Day, 1984).

—, *Transitions: Narratives in Modern Irish Culture* (Manchester: Manchester University Press, 1988).

Khalidi, Rashid, *Palestinian Identity: The Construction of Modern National Consciousness* (New York: Columbia University Press, 1997).

Khan, Yasmin, *The Great Partition: The Making of India and Pakistan* (Yale University Press, 2008).

Khanna, Ranjana, *Algeria Cuts: Women and Representation, 1830 to the Present* (Stanford: Stanford University Press, 2008).

Khoury, Elias, *Little Mountain*, trans. Maia Tabet (Manchester: Carcanet, 1989).

—, *The Journey of Little Gandhi*, trans. Paula Haydar (Minneapolis: University of Minnesota Press, 1994).

—, *Gate of the Sun*, trans. Humphrey Davies (London: Harvill Secker, 2005 [1998]).

Khoury, Elias, and Sonja Mejcher, 'Elias Khoury: The Necessity to Forget – and Remember', *Banipal*, 12 (Autumn 2001), pp. 8–14.

Kisch, F. H., *Palestine Diary* (London: Victor Gollancz, 1938).

Kohn, Hans, 'Nationalism', in Arthur A. Cohen (ed.), *The Jew: Essays from Martin Buber's Journal 'Der Jude' 1916–1928* (Alabama: University of Alabama Press, 1980), pp. 19–30.

Kohn, Margaret, 'Empire's Law: Alexis de Tocqueville on Colonialism and the State of Exception', *Canadian Journal of Political Science*, 41 (2008), pp. 255–78.

Kostal, R. W. *A Jurisprudence of Power: Victorian Empire and the Rule of Law* (Oxford: Oxford University Press, 2006).

Lacan, Jacques, *The Seminar of Jacques Lacan Book 1: Freud's Papers on Technique*, trans. John Forrester (New York and London: Norton, 1988).

Laclau, Ernesto, 'Bare Life or Social Indeterminacy?', in Matthew Calarco and Steven DeCaroli (eds), *Giorgio Agamben: Sovereignty and Life* (Stanford, CA: Stanford University Press, 2007), pp. 11–22.

Laine, James, *Shivaji: Hindu King in Islamic India* (Delhi: Oxford University Press, 2001).

—, 'The James Laine Affair: Terrorising Scholarship', *Economic and Political Weekly*, 19 May 2007, p. 1796.

Lartéguy, Jean, *Les centurions* (Paris: Presses de la Cité, 1960).

—, *The Centurions*, trans. Xan Fielding (London: Hutchinson & Co., 1961).

The Law of South Africa, 21, ed. W.A. Joubert (Durban Pretoria: Butterworths, 1984).

Lazarus, Neil, *Nationalism and Cultural Practice in the Postcolonial World* (Cambridge: Cambridge University Press, 1999).

—, *The Postcolonial Unconscious* (Cambridge: Cambridge University Press, 2011).

Lazreg, Marnia, *Torture and the Twilight of Empire: From Algiers to Baghdad* (Princeton, NJ: Princeton University Press, 2008).

Leadam, I.S., *Coercive Measures in Ireland 1830–1880* (London: National Press Agency, 1881).

Lee, Daryl Robert, 'A Rival Protest: The Life and Work of Richard Rive, a South African Writer', doctoral dissertation (University of Oxford, 1998).

Lenta, Patrick, '"Legal Illegality": *Waiting for the Barbarians* after September 11', *Journal of Postcolonial Writing*, 42/1 (2006), pp. 71–83.

Lentin, Ronit, 'Femina Sacra: Gendered Memory and Political Violence', *Women's Studies International Forum*, 29/5 (2006), pp. 463–73.

—, *Co-memory and Melancholia: Israelis Memorialising the Palestinian Nakba* (Manchester: Manchester University Press, 2010).

—, 'Palestinian Women from Femina Sacra to Agents of Active Resistance', *Women's Studies International Forum*, 34 (2011), pp. 165–70.

Lentin, Ronit (ed.), *Thinking Palestine* (London: Zed Books, 2008).

Leulliette, Pierre, *Saint Michel et le dragon : souvenirs d'un parachutiste* (Paris: Les Éditions de Minuit, 1961).

—, *St. Michael and the Dragon: A Paratrooper in the Algerian War*, trans. Tony White (London: Heinemann, 1964).

Lloyd, David, *Anomalous States: Irish Writing and the Postcolonial Moment* (Dublin: Lilliput, 1993).

—, 'Settler Colonialism and the State of Exception: The Example of Palestine/Israel', *Settler Colonial Studies*, 2/1 (2012), pp. 59–80. Available at: <http://ojs.lib.swin.edu.au/index.php/settlercolonialstudies>. Accessed April 2012.

Lodge, Tom, *Black Politics in South Africa since 1945* (London and New York: Longman, 1983).

Löwy, Michael, *Fire Alarm: Reading Walter Benjamin's 'On the Concept of History'*, trans. Chris Turner (London: Verso, 2005).

McClintock, Anne, 'The Angel of Progress: Pitfalls of the Term Postcolonial', *Social Text*, 31/2 (1992), pp. 84–98.

McCole, John, *Walter Benjamin and the Antinomies of Tradition* (Ithaca, NY and London: Cornell University Press, 1993).

McConville, Seán, *Irish Political Prisoners, 1848–1922: Theatres of War* (London: Routledge, 2002).

McDonald, Peter D., 'The Writer, the Critic, and the Censor: J.M. Coetzee and the Question of Literature', *Book History*, 7 (2004), pp. 285–302.

—, *The Literature Police: Apartheid Censorship and Its Cultural Consequences* (Oxford: Oxford University Press, 2009).

McEwan, Ian, *Saturday* (London: Vintage, 2006).

Macey, David, *Frantz Fanon* (London: Granta, 2000).

MacIntyre, B., 'Secret Colonial Files may show more blood on British hands', *The Times*, 7 April 2011, p. 14.

Maghraoui, Abdeslam E., *Liberalism without Democracy: Nationhood and Citizenship in Egypt, 1922–1939* (Durham, NC: Duke University Press, 2006).

Mamdani, Mahmood, *When Victims Become Killers: Colonialism, Nativism, and the Genocide in Rwanda* (Princeton: Princeton University Press, 2002).

Mandela, Nelson, *No Easy Walk to Freedom* (London: Heinemann, 1965).

—, *Nelson Mandela in His Own Words: From Freedom to the Future: Tributes and Speeches* (London: Little Brown, 2003).

Abu Manneh, Bashir, 'Israel in US Empire' *New Formations*, 59 (2006), pp. 34–51.

Maran, Rita, *Torture: The Role of Ideology in the French–Algerian War* (New York: Praeger, 1989).

Marx-Longuet, Jenny, 'Articles on the Irish Question'. Available at <www.marxists.org/archive/marx/bio/family/jenny/1870-ire.htm>. Accessed May 2011.

Massad, Joseph, 'The "Post-Colonial Colony": Time, Space, and Bodies in Palestine/Israel', in Fawzia Afzal-Khan and Kalpana Seshadri-Crooks (eds), *The Pre-occupation of Postcolonial Studies* (Durham, NC: Duke University Press, 2000), pp. 311–46.

—, *The Persistence of the Palestinian Question: Essays on Zionism and the Palestinians* (London: Routledge, 2006).

Mattei, Ugo, 'Emergency-Based Predatory Capitalism: The Rule of Law, Alternative Dispute Resolution and Development', in Didier Fassin and Mariella Pandolfi (eds), *Contemporary States of Emergency* (New York: Zone Books, 2010), pp. 89–107.

Maughan-Brown, David, *Land, Freedom and Fiction: History and Ideology in Kenya* (London: Zed, 1985).

—, 'Matigari and the Rehabilitation of Religion', *Research in African Literatures*, 22/4 (1991), pp. 161–67.

Mbeki, Govan, *Learning from Robben Island: The Prison Writings of Govan Mbeki* (London: James Currey in association with the UCW Historical & Cultural Centre Project, 1991).

Mbembe, Achille, *On the Postcolony* (Berkeley, CA: University of California Press, 2001).

—, 'Necropolitics', *Public Culture*, 15/1 (2003), pp. 11–40.

Mehta, Uday, *Liberalism and Empire: A Study in Nineteenth-century British Liberal Thought* (Chicago: University of Chicago Press, 1999).

Melas, Natalie, *All the Difference in the World: Postcoloniality and the Ends of Comparison* (Stanford, CA: Stanford University Press, 2007).

Meli, Francis, *South Africa Belongs to Us: A History of the ANC* (London: James Currey, 1988).

Metcalf, Barbara D., and Thomas R. Metcalf, *A Concise History of Modern India* (Cambridge: Cambridge University Press, 2006).

Meyer, Stefan, *The Experimental Arabic Novel: Postcolonial Literary Modernism in the Levant* (Albany, NY: State University of New York Press, 2001).

Moretti, Franco, *The Way of the World: The Bildungsroman in European Culture* (London: Verso, 1986).

Morey, Peter, 'Terrorvision', *Interventions*, 12/2 (2010), pp. 251–64.

Morey, Peter, and Amina Yaqin, 'Muslims in the Frame', *Interventions*, 12/2 (2010), pp. 145–56.

Morris, Benny, *The Birth of the Palestinian Refugee Problem Revisited* (Cambridge: Cambridge University Press, 2004).

Morton, Stephen, 'Terrorism, Orientalism and Imperialism', *Wasafiri*, 22/2 (2007), pp. 36–42.

—, 'Fictions of Sedition and the Framing of Indian Revolutionaries in Colonial India', *Journal of Commonwealth Literature* 47/2 (June, 2012), pp. 175–89.

Muddiman, A. P., 'British India', *Journal of Comparative Legislation and International Law*, 3rd series, 3/3 (1921), pp. 125–35.

Mzamane, Mbulelo Vizikhungo, 'Sharpeville and Its Aftermath: The Novels of Richard Rive, Peter Abrahams, Alex La Guma, and Lauretta Ngcobo', *Ariel*, 16/2 (1985), pp. 31–44.

Naas, Michael, '"One Nation … Indivisible": Jacques Derrida on the Autoimmunity of Democracy and the Sovereignty of God', *Research in Phenomenology*, 36/1 (2006), pp. 15–44.

Nakkara, Hanna Dib, 'Israeli Land Seizure under Various Defense and Emergency Regulations', *Journal of Palestine Studies*, 14/2 (1985), pp. 13–34.

Ndebele, Njabulo, *South African Literature and Culture: Rediscovery of the Ordinary* (Manchester: Manchester University Press, 1994).

Neocleous, Mark, *Critique of Security* (Edinburgh: Edinburgh University Press, 2008).

Nicholls, Brendon, *Ngugi wa Thiong'o, Gender, and the Ethics of Postcolonial Reading* (Farnham: Ashgate, 2010).

Ngũgĩ wa Thiong'o, *Weep Not, Child* (London: Heinemann Educational, 1964).

—, *A Grain of Wheat* (London: Penguin, 2002 [1967]).

—, *Homecoming: Essays on African and Caribbean Literature, Culture and Politics* (London: Heinemann Educational, 1972).

—, *Detained: A Writer's Prison Diary* (London: Heinemann, 1981).

—, *Matigari*, trans. Waugui wa Goro (Oxford: Heinemann, 1989 [1986]).

—, *Moving the Centre: The Struggle for Cultural Freedoms* (Oxford: James Currey/Heinemann, 1993).

—, *Dreams in a Time of War: A Childhood Memoir* (London: Harvill Secker, 2010).

Nkosi, Lewis, *Home and Exile* (London: Longmans, 1965).

Norval, Aletta J., *Deconstructing Apartheid Discourse* (London: Verso, 1996).

O'Brien, Conor Cruise, 'An Unhealthy Intersection', *New Review*, 2/16 (1975), pp. 3–8.

Ó Donghaile, Deaglán, *Blasted Literature: Victorian Political Fiction and the Shock of Modernism* (Edinburgh: Edinburgh University Press, 2011).

O'Donovan Rossa, Jeremiah, *Irish Rebels in English Prisons: A Record of Prison Life* (New York: P.J. Kennedy, Excelsior Catholic Publishing House, 1899 [1880]).

O'Malley, Ernie, *On Another Man's Wound* (Dublin: Anvil, 2002 [1936]).

—, *Raids and Rallies* (Dublin: Anvil, 1982).

Ophir, Adi, Michael Givoni and Sari Hanafi (eds), *The Power of Inclusive Exclusion: Anatomy of Israeli Rule in the Occupied Palestinian Territories* (New York: Zone, 2009).

Pappé, Ilan, *The Ethnic Cleansing of Palestine* (Oxford: Oneworld, 2006).

—, 'The *Mukhabarat* State of Israel: A State of Oppression Is Not a State of Exception', in Ronit Lentin (ed.), *Thinking Palestine* (London: Zed Books, 2008), pp. 148–70.

—, *The Forgotten Palestinians: A History of the Palestinians in Israel* (New Haven: Yale University Press, 2011).

Pearse, Padraic, *The Story of a Success, Being a Record of St. Enda's College September 1908 to Easter 1916*, ed. Desmond Ryan (Dublin and London: Mansuel, 1917).

Piterberg, Gabriel, *The Returns of Zionism: Myth, Politics and Scholarship in Israel* (London: Verso, 2008).

Pitts, Jennifer, *A Turn to Empire: The Rise of Imperial Liberalism in Britain and France* (Princeton, NJ: Princeton University Press, 2005).

Posel, Deborah, *The Making of Apartheid, 1948–1961: Conflict and Compromise* (Cape Town: Oxford University Press South Africa, 1997).

Redfield, Marc, *Phantom Formations: Aesthetic Ideology and the Bildungsroman* (Ithaca, NY: Cornell University Press, 1996).

Reid, Julian, *The Biopolitics of the War on Terror: Life Struggles, Liberal Modernity and the Defence of Logistical Societies* (Manchester: Manchester University Press, 2007).

Rejali, Darius, *Torture and Democracy* (Princeton, NJ: Princeton University Press, 2007).

O'Riley, Michael, *Postcolonial Haunting and Victimization: Assia Djebar's New Novels* (New York: Peter Lang, 2007).

Peterson, Derek R., 'The Intellectual Lives of Mau Mau Detainees', *Journal of African History*, 49/1 (2008), pp. 73–91.

Rive, Richard, *Emergency* (London: Faber & Faber, 1964).

—, *Writing Black* (Cape Town: David Phillip, 1981).

—, *Emergency Continued* (Claremont, South Africa: David Philip, 1990).

Rose, Jacqueline, *The Question of Zion* (Princeton: Princeton University Press, 2005).

—, *The Last Resistance* (London: Verso, 2007).

—, 'The Political Edge of Fiction', in Müge Gürsoy Sökmen and Basak Ertür (eds), *Waiting for the Barbarians: A Tribute to Edward Said* (London: Verso, 2008), pp. 15–32.

Rosenkranz, Susan A., 'Breathing Disaffection: The Impact of Irish Nationalist Journalism on India's Native Press', *South East Review of Asian Studies* (2005). Available at <www.uky.edu/Centers/Asia/SECAAS/Seras/2005/Rosenkrantz.htm>.

Roth, Philip, *The Plot against America* (London: Jonathan Cape, 2004).

Royal Irish Constabulary, *Tales of the R.I.C.* (Edinburgh & London: W. Blackwood & Sons, 1921).

Ruark, Robert Chester, *Something of Value* (London: Hamish Hamilton, 1955).

—, *Uhuru* (London: Hamish Hamilton, 1962).

Rushdie, Salman, *Shalimar the Clown* (London: Jonathon Cape, 2005).

Sachs, Albie, 'Preparing Ourselves for Freedom', in Ingrid de Kok and Karen Press (eds), *Spring Is Rebellious: Arguments about Cultural Freedom* (Cape Town: Buchu Books, 1990), pp. 19–30.

Sa'di, Ahmad H., and Lila Abu-Lughod (eds), *Nakba: Palestine, 1948 and the Claims of Memory* (New York: Columbia University Press).

Said, Edward W., *Orientalism: Western Conceptions of the Orient* (London: Routledge and Kegan Paul, 1978).

—, 'The Essential Terrorist', in Edward Said and Christopher Hitchens (eds), *Blaming the Victims: Spurious Scholarship and the Palestinian Question* (London: Verso, 1988), pp. 149–58.

—, *The Question of Palestine* (London: Vintage, 1992).

—, *Culture and Imperialism* (London: Vintage, 1994).

—, *The Politics of Dispossession* (London: Chatto and Windus, 1994).

—, *Covering Islam: How the Media and the Experts Determine How We See the Rest of the World* (London: Vintage, 1997).

—, 'Invention, Memory and Place', *Critical Inquiry*, 26/2 (2000), pp. 175–92.

Samuelson, Meg, 'The Disfigured Body of the Female Guerrilla: (De)Militarization, Sexual Violence and Re-Domestication in Zoë Wicomb's *David's Story*', *Signs: Journal of Women in Culture and Society*, 32/4 (2007), p. 833–56.

Sands, Bobby, *Skylark Sing Your Lonely Song: An Anthology of the Writings of Bobby Sands* (Dublin: Mercier, 1982).

Sarkar, Tanika, 'Bengali Middle-Class Nationalism and Literature: A Study of Saratchandra's "Pather Dabi" and Rabindranath's "Char Adhyay"', in D.N. Panigrahi (ed.), *Economy, Society and Politics in Modern India* (New Delhi: Vikas, 1985), pp. 449–62.

—, *Bengal 1928–1934: The Politics of Protest* (New Delhi: Oxford University Press, 1987).

Sayigh, Rosemary, 'Gendering the "Nationalist Subject": Palestinian Camp Women's Stories', in Gautam Bhadra, Gyan Prakash and Susie Tharu (eds), *Subaltern Studies*, vol. 10 (New Delhi: Oxford University Press, 1999), pp. 234–52.

Ṣayigh, Yezid, *Armed Struggle and the Search for State: The Palestinian National Movement, 1949–1993* (Oxford: Oxford University Press, 1999).

Scarry, Elaine, *The Body in Pain: The Making and Unmaking of the World* (New York and Oxford: Oxford University Press, 1985).

Schmidt, Yvonne, 'Foundations of Civil and Political Rights in Israel and the Occupied Territories'. Available at <www.flwi.ugent.be/cie/yschmidt/index.htm>. Accessed 11 August 2011.

Sedition Committee Report 1918 (Calcutta: Superintendent Government Printing India, 1918).

Shamsie, Kamila, *Burnt Shadows* (London: Bloomsbury, 2009).

Shamir, Ronen, *The Colonies of Law: Colonialism, Zionism, and Law in Early Mandate Palestine* (Cambridge: Cambridge University Press, 2000).

Shapira, Anita, 'Hirbet Hizar: Between Remembrance and Forgetting', *Jewish Social Studies*, 7/1 (2000), pp. 1–62.

Sharpe, Jenny, *Allegories of Empire: The Figure of Woman in the Colonial Text* (Minneapolis: University of Minnesota Press, 1993).

Shenhav, Yehouda, and Yael Berda, 'The Colonial Foundations of the State of Exception: Juxtaposing the Israeli Occupation of the Palestinian Territories with Colonial Bureaucratic History', in Adi Ophir, Michael Givoni and Sari Hanafi (eds), *The Power of Inclusive Exclusion* (New York: Zone, 2009), pp. 337–74.

Sicherman, Carol, *Ngugi wa Thiong'o: The Making of a Rebel: A Source Book in Kenyan Literature and Resistance* (London: Zell, 1990).

Siddiqi, Yumna, *Anxieties of Empire and the Fiction of Intrigue* (New York: Columbia University Press, 2008).

Silvestri, Michael, '"The Sinn Fein of India": Irish Nationalism and the Policing of Revolutionary Terrorism in Bengal', *Journal of British Studies*, 39 (2000), pp. 454–86.

Simpson, A.W. Brian, *In the Highest Degree Odious: Detention without Trial in Wartime Britain* (Oxford: Clarendon Press, 1992).

—, *Human Rights and the End of Empire: Britain and the Genesis of the European Convention* (Oxford: Oxford University Press, 2001).

Sitze, Adam, 'Emergency Continued', *Law and Humanities*, 2/1 (2008), pp. 49–74.

Sivanadan, A., 'Race, Terror and Civil Society', *Race and Class*, 47/3 (2006), pp. 1–8.

Sole, Kelwyn, 'The Role of the Writer in a Time of Transition', *Staffrider*, 11/1–4 (1993), pp. 90–98.

—, 'Democratising Culture in a "New South Africa": Organisation and Theory', *Current Writing*, 6/2 (1994), pp. 1–37.

Spencer, Robert, 'J.M. Coetzee and Colonial Violence', *Interventions*, 10/2 (2008), pp. 173–87.

—, *Cosmopolitan Criticism and Postcolonial Literature* (Basingstoke: Palgrave Macmillan, 2011).

Spivak, Gayatri Chakravorty, 'The Rani of Sirmur: An Essay on Reading the Archives', *History and Theory*, 24/3 (1985), pp. 247–72.

—, 'Deconstructing Historiography', in Ranajit Guha (ed.), *Subaltern Studies IV: Writings on South Asian History and Society* (Delhi: Oxford University Press, 1987), pp. 330–63.

—, *In Other Worlds: Essays in Cultural Politics* (New York: Methuen, 1987).

—, 'Can the Subaltern Speak?', in Cary Nelson and Lawrence Grossberg (eds), *Marxism and the Interpretation of Culture* (Urbana and Chicago: University of Illinois Press, 1988), pp. 271–80.

Sternhell, Zeev, *The Founding Myths of Israel: Nationalism, Socialism, and the Making of the Jewish State* (Princeton, NJ: Princeton University Press, 1998).

Stoler, Ann Laura, *Race and the Education of Desire: Foucault's History of Sexuality and the Colonial Order of Things* (Durham, NC: Duke University Press, 1995).

Swinhoe, Charles, *The Indian Penal Code* (Calcutta: Thacker, Spink and Co., 1909).

Tegart, Lady F., *Charles Tegart: Memoir of an Indian Policeman* (British Library, MSS EUR/ C235).

Terrorism Act 2006, Chapter 11 <www.legislation.gov.uk/ukpga/2006/11/pdfs/ukpga_ 20 060011_en.pdf>. Accessed 4 April 2012.

Thatcher, Margaret, 'Speech at Stormont Castle Lunch', 28 May 1981. Available at:

<www.margaretthatcher.org/document/104657>. Accessed July 2011.

Thénault, Sylvie, *Une drôle de justice : les magistrats dans la guerre d'Algérie* (Paris: Décou-verte, 2001).

—, 'L'état d'urgence (1955–2005). De l'Algérie coloniale à la France contemporaine: destin d'une loi', *Le mouvement social*, 218 (janvier–mars 2007), pp. 63–78.

Thurschwell, Pamela, *Literature, Technology and Magical Thinking, 1880–1920* (Cambridge: Cambridge University Press, 2001).

Tickell, Alex, 'Terrorism and the Information Romance: Two Early South Asian Novels in English', *Kunapipi*, 24/1 (2003), pp. 73–82.

—, *Terrorism, Insurgency and Indian-English Literature, 1830–1947* (London: Routledge, 2012).

Townshend, Charles, *The British Campaign in Ireland, 1919–1921: The Development of Polit-ical and Military Policies* (London: Oxford University Press, 1975).

—, *Political Violence in Ireland: Government and Resistance since 1848* (Oxford: Clarendon, 1983).

—, *Britain's Civil Wars: Counterinsurgency in the Twentieth Century* (London: Faber, 1986).

—, *Terrorism: A Very Short Introduction* (Oxford: Oxford University Press, 2002).

Valera, Eamon de, *India and Ireland* (New York: Friends of Freedom for India, 1920).

VanZanten Gallagher, Susan, *A Story of South Africa: J.M. Coetzee's Fiction in Context* (Cambridge, MA: Harvard University Press, 1990).

Vivekananda, Swami, *The Collected Works of Swami Vivekananda*, vol. 4 (Calcutta: Advaita Ashrama, 1968).

Ward, Margaret, *Unmanageable Revolutionaries: Women and Irish Nationalism* (London: Pluto Press, 1983).

Weber, Samuel, 'Taking Exception to Decision: Walter Benjamin and Carl Schmitt', *Diacritics*, 22/3–4 (1992), pp. 5–18.

Western, Alan, *Desert Hawk* (London and New York: F. Warne & Co., 1937).

Wicomb, Zoë, *David's Story* (New York: Feminist Press, 2000).

Wilder, Gary, *The French Imperial Nation-state: Negritude and Colonial Humanism Between the Two Wars* (Chicago: University of Chicago Press, 2006).

Wood, Michael, *Yeats and Violence* (Oxford: Oxford University Press, 2010).

Yeats, W.B., *The Variorum Edition of the Complete Poems of W.B. Yeats*, ed. Peter Allt and Russell K. Alspach (New York: Macmillan, 1957).

—, *The Variorum Edition of the Plays of W.B. Yeats*, ed. Russell K. Alspach (London: Macmillan, 1966).

—, *The King's Threshold, Manuscript Materials*, ed. Declan Kiely (Ithaca, NY and London: Cornell University Press, 2005).

Yizhar, S., *Khirbet Khizeh*, trans. Nicholas de Lange and Yaacob Dweck (Jerusalem: Ibis Editions, 2008).

Yoneyama, Lisa, *Hiroshima Traces: Time, Space, and the Dialectics of Memory* (Berkeley, CA: University of California Press, 1999).

Young, Robert J.C., *Postcolonialism: An Historical Introduction* (Oxford: Blackwell, 2001).

—, 'Terror Effects', in Elleke Boehmer and Stephen Morton (eds), *Terror and the Postcolo-nial* (Oxford: Wiley Blackwell, 2009), pp. 307–28.

Ziarek, Ewa Plonowska, 'Bare Life on Strike', *South Atlantic Quarterly*, 107/1 (2008), pp. 71–87.

Žižek, Slavoj, 'Welcome to the Desert of the Real!', *South Atlantic Quarterly*, 101/2 (2002), pp. 385–89.

Zolo, Danilo, *Victor's Justice: From Nuremburg to Baghdad*, trans. Gregory Elliott (London: Verso, 2009).

Index

Printed and bound by CPI Group (UK) Ltd, Croydon, CR0 4YY

09/06/2025

14685945-0002